# The Zen of C++

Adnan Zejnilovic

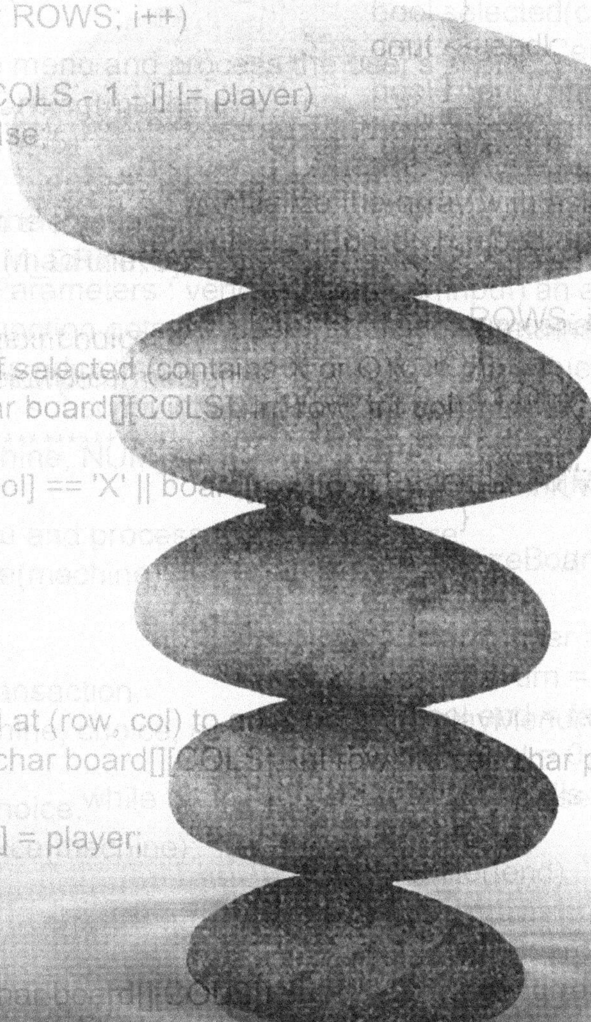

Kendall Hunt
publishing company

Cover design by Annette Delgado.

Pages 1-70 *From Introduction to Computer Information Systems*, 2nd Edition by Geoffrey Steinberg. Copyright © 2008 by Kendall Hunt Publishing Company. Reprinted by permission.

Kendall Hunt
publishing company

www.kendallhunt.com
*Send all inquiries to*:
4050 Westmark Drive
Dubuque, IA 52004-1840



ISBN 978-1-5249-2751-6



Printed in the United States of America

10 9 8 7 6 5 4 3 2 1

**This book is dedicated to my father,**

**Dr. Fehmija Zejnilovic,**

**and to my Toyo.**

# CONTENTS


| | | |
|---|---|---|
| *Acknowledgements* | | ix |
| **Chapter 1:** | **Introduction** | **1** |
| | Computer | 1 |
| | Input-Process-Output Model | 2 |
| | Computer History | 4 |
| | Modern Hardware | 12 |
| | Computer Styles | 45 |
| | Moore's Law | 46 |
| | Source Data Automation | 47 |
| | Recycling Hardware | 48 |
| | Chapter Review | 48 |
| | Mini Quiz | 49 |
| | Exercises | 51 |
| | Discussion Questions | 52 |
| | Activities | 53 |
| | Software | 54 |
| | The Operating System | 56 |
| | Computer Programming | 65 |
| | Programming Design, Paradigms, and Architecture | 67 |
| | Programming Languages | 69 |
| | History of C++ | 70 |
| | Algorithms | 71 |
| **Chapter 2:** | **Fundamental Data Types** | **73** |
| | C++ Programming Process | 73 |
| | Your 1st C++ Program | 76 |
| | Programming Style | 80 |
| | Fundamental Data Types | 81 |
| | Variable Assignments, Initializations, Scope | 93 |
| | End of Chapter Questions | 102 |
| **Chapter 3:** | **Interactive Input, Expressions, and Formatting** | **105** |
| | Interacting with the User | 105 |
| | Mathematical Library Functions | 112 |
| | Type Conversion | 113 |
| | Type Casting | 114 |
| | Expressions | 116 |
| | Operators | 117 |

| | | |
|---|---|---|
| | Conditional Statements | 120 |
| | Formatting Output | 139 |
| | End of Chapter Questions | 144 |
| **Chapter 4:** | **Loops** | **147** |
| | `While` Loop | 147 |
| | Do While Loop | 154 |
| | For Loop | 155 |
| | `Nested` Loops | 160 |
| | End of Chapter Questions | 164 |
| **Chapter 5:** | **Streams—Input, Output, and Customization** | **167** |
| | The Basics | 167 |
| | How to Read/Write from/to Files Programmatically | 168 |
| | Miscellaneous File Functions | 173 |
| **Chapter 6:** | **Functions** | **175** |
| | What Is a Function? | 175 |
| | Benefits of Using Functions | 177 |
| | Function Calls | 179 |
| | Function Definition | 179 |
| | Function Prototypes | 182 |
| | Passing by Value | 183 |
| | Functions with Multiple Parameters | 186 |
| | Pass by Reference | 188 |
| | Value Returning Functions | 191 |
| | void Functions and the return Statement | 195 |
| | Default Arguments | 197 |
| | Overloading Functions | 198 |
| | Scope | 199 |
| | Global Variables and Global Constants | 204 |
| | Local Variables | 206 |
| | Static Local Variables | 209 |
| | The exit(0) Function | 212 |
| | Stubs and Drivers | 212 |
| | End of Chapter Questions | 213 |
| **Chapter 7:** | **Arrays and Vectors** | **215** |
| | What Is an Array? | 215 |
| | Declaring an Array | 217 |
| | Array Initialization | 220 |
| | Bounds Checking | 224 |
| | Array Operations | 225 |
| | Arrays and Functions | 230 |

| | | |
|---|---|---|
| | Vectors | 243 |
| | End of Chapter Questions | 245 |
| **Chapter 8:** | **Pointers** | **247** |
| | Intro to Pointers | 247 |
| | Pointer Variables | 247 |
| | Dereferencing Pointers | 250 |
| | Pointers and Arrays | 251 |
| | Pointer Arithmetic | 253 |
| | Comparing Pointers | 255 |
| | Pointers and Functions | 256 |
| | Constant Pointers and Pointers to Constants | 261 |
| | Dynamic Memory Allocation | 262 |
| | Returning Pointers from Functions | 264 |
| | End of Chapter Questions | 267 |
| **Chapter 9:** | **Handling Text** | **269** |
| | Character Testing | 269 |
| | C-Style Strings | 272 |
| | Correctly Dimensioning Character Arrays | 272 |
| | Conversion Functions | 274 |
| | C++ string Class | 286 |
| | Assigning Strings | 287 |
| | Concatenating Strings | 287 |
| | String Comparisons | 288 |
| | Capacity Member Functions | 290 |
| | Accessing Elements | 291 |
| | Searching for a Substring | 292 |
| | Modifying a String | 293 |
| | Working with Legacy Code | 294 |
| | Conclusion | 295 |
| | End of Chapter Questions | 295 |
| **Chapter 10:** | **Abstract Data Types** | **297** |
| | Primitive Data Types vs. Abstract Data Types | 297 |
| | Structures | 297 |
| | Initialization | 298 |
| | Initialization List Initialization | 301 |
| | Member Access | 302 |
| | Math Operations on Structure Members | 303 |
| | Arrays as Structure Members | 304 |
| | Nested Structures | 306 |
| | Arrays of Structures | 308 |

Initializing an Array of Structures through an Initialization List 310
Passing Structures to Functions 310
Returning Structures from Functions 313
Design Strategies 316
Pointers to Structures 318
Pointers to Structures as Function Parameters 320
Returning Structure Pointers from Functions 323
Deleting Dynamically Allocated Memory 325
Enumerated Data Types 326
End of Chapter Questions 330

**Appendix A: Solutions** **331**
Chapter 2 331
Chapter 3 331
Chapter 4 332
Chapter 6 332
Chapter 7 333
Chapter 8 334
Chapter 9 335
Chapter 10 335

# ACKNOWLEDGEMENTS

I would like to thank my students, Sandro del Valle Arocha and Lazaro Alvarez, as well as my colleague Prof. Alicia Ibarra for providing their valuable input on end of chapter questions and exercises; Annette Delgado for designing the book cover; and Marla Swartz and Stefani DeMoss of Kendall Hunt Publishing Company.

# Chapter 1

# Introduction

***"Zen is a liberation from time. For if we open our eyes and see clearly, it becomes obvious that there is no other time than this instant, and that the past and the future are abstractions without any concrete reality."***

***—Alan Wilson Watts***

## Computer

A computer is a machine that can be programmed (it follows the commands in computer programs) to accept data (software—input) and process it into useful information (software—output). The computer may store data for future retrieval on storage devices and share data and messages over a network with other computers. Modern computers have a two hundred year legacy. Long before electronic computers there were mechanical devices.

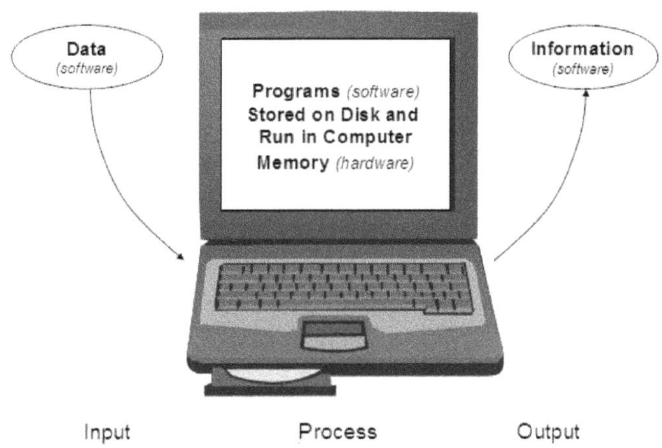


The Computer and Input-Process-Output

The computer plays a major role in the processing depicted in the **Input-Process-Output** model (**IPO**). This model is fundamental to data processing and to an information system. It is the basis for our discussion about data, information, and databases in another chapter, however, a brief introduction is beneficial here.

Data are facts that may or may not be relevant to decision making. Alone, facts mean nothing until they are combined with other data which provides a context for understanding—they then become the basis for information. The process of providing a **context** for data is known as **data processing** and that is the fundamental activity of an information system. The relationship between data, processing, and information is presented in the IPO model:

Input-Process-Output Model

The computer plays a pivotal role as it accepts input, runs programs that process the data, and generates output. In addition to data entered from a keyboard or received in an e-mail or spreadsheet, data processing often involves including data preserved in a storage device (disk, jump drive, CD, etc.) and the IPO model can be updated to reflect data storage this way:

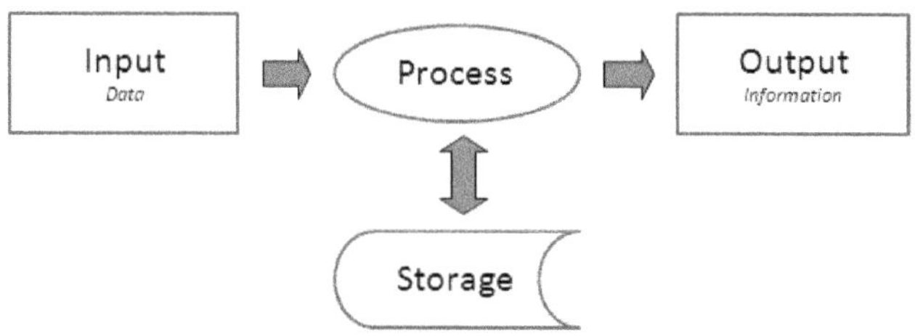


IPO Model with Data Storage

Before we delve into the particulars about what comprises a computer and how it works we consider the perspective of how and when computers came about.

## Input-Process-Output Model

**Data** are **facts** and can be thought of as raw material. Data alone is not particularly useful, but when data is associated with other facts information can be derived.

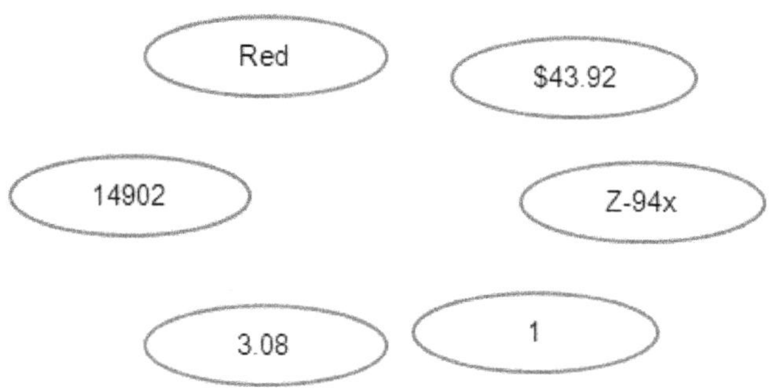


Data

The process of providing a **context for data** is known as **data processing,** which is the fundamental activity of an information system. Facts alone may or may not be relevant to **decision making.** Facts (numbers, characters, words, images) alone mean nothing until they are combined with other data and thus provide a **context** for understanding data—they then become the basis for information and decision making.

**Data in a Context**

Consider data to be raw material. Raw material is generally of little use by itself but when processed, useful results may be produced. When data is processed, information (known as output) may result. In essence, an information system processes raw material into something that is useful to people. This relationship between data and information is summarized in the Input-Process-Output (IPO) model:

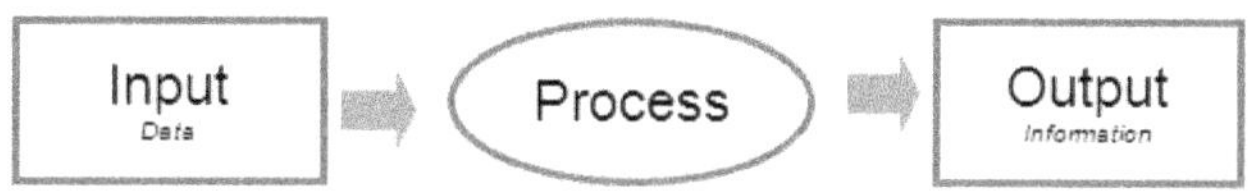


**Input-Process-Output Model**

## Storage

Processing data often requires including data that was stored earlier during collection or production. Storage is provided by hard disk, jump drive, CD and DVD, tape, and other storage devices. The IPO model is updated to reflect data storage this way:

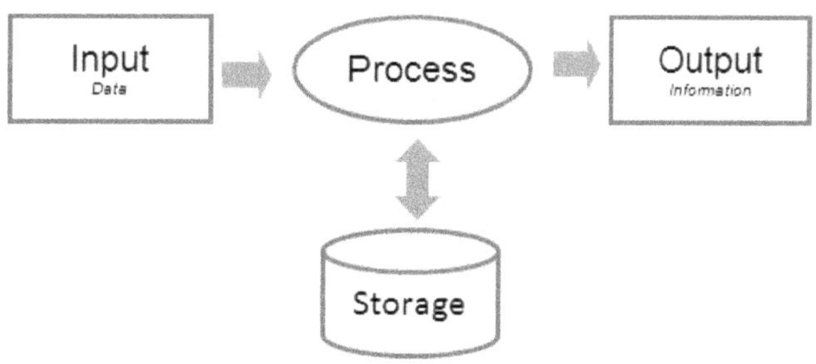


Input-Process-Output Model with Data Storage

## Feedback

Often the information received is not completely sufficient for a decision we are making. Sometimes the information we received is helpful but does not completely answer the question we are considering. So with our new knowledge we repeat the input-process-output sequence, this time asking a new question. The new question is refined by the knowledge we obtained in the first cycle of the model. This knowledge is known as **feedback** and is shown this way:

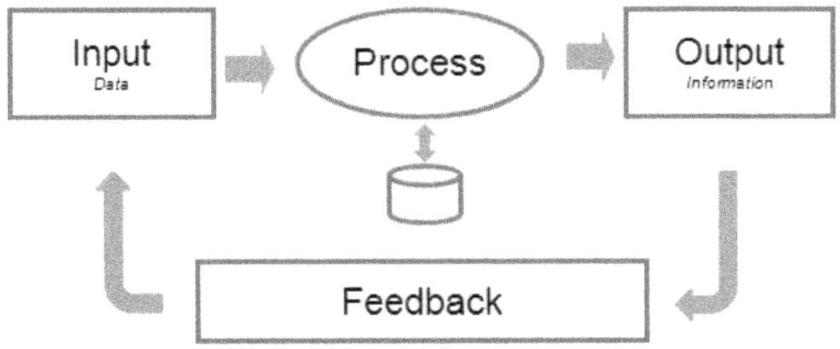


Input-Process-Output Model with Feedback

When information is used as input in a subsequent round of processing we describe the cyclical nature of data processing as **iterative.**

Here is an example of how feedback is used in decision making. When you want to withdraw money from your bank account at an ATM (automatic teller machine), you provide the computer with data (your account number) and instructions ("please report my balance") and the computer processes your request and gives you information (your balance). Then, based on your balance, you decide whether or not to make the withdrawal. This interchange illustrates the concept of feedback.

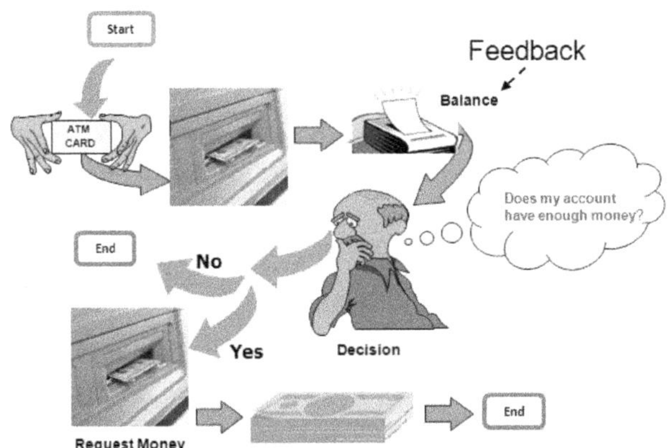


Feedback in Action

## Computer History

The electronic digital computer, that we use today, has its roots in machines invented in the 1800s. One of the most significant was the non-electrical machine, the **Analytical Engine,** designed by an English inventor, **Charles Babbage.** The Analytical Engine was too complex to be built with the technology of the early 1880s. However, in the 1980s, a model was produced from Babbage's original blueprints, and it worked! So Babbage is considered to be the father of the computer. But what is a computer if it cannot be programmed? The answer should be obvious: it does nothing. So who invented programming?

A friend of Babbage's, mathematician **Ada Lovelace,** wrote **procedures** that gave the Analytical Engine a set of instructions for processing data. Of course, Ada Lovelace's programs could not be tested until the Engine was built about 150 years later, but her programs worked! Ada Lovelace is often considered the first computer programmer. In 1979, the programming language, Ada, was named in her honor.

While many other inventors and inventions are historically important because they helped pave the way for computing as we know it today, several people and milestones are worth mentioning.

## Jacquard Loom

The Jacquard Loom, invented by **Joseph Jacquard** in 1801, used the holes punched in wooden cards to control the weaving of patterns in textiles. The loom enabled even unskilled weavers to produce complex designs. Each punched card corresponded to one row of the design and the cards were strung together in order of the pattern.

This loom was the first machine to use data stored as holes in punch cards to control a sequence of operations. While it performed no computations on the data, it is considered an important step in the history of computing hardware because it was the first example of a machine that used stored data to guide operations. This was important to the development of computer programming. Charles Babbage planned to use punch cards to store programs in his Analytical Engine. Although he did not live to see his ideas fulfilled, punch card data storage did prove to work reliably, as you will learn next.

Jacquard Loom

## Hollerith's Punch Card Data Storage

After graduating from college, **Herman Hollerith** took a job with the **U.S. Census Bureau** collecting and analyzing statistical information on the use of water and steam to power in the iron and steel industries. This assignment motivated his inspiration to devise a machine to automatically collect and store data for later analysis. He successfully found an outlet for his creativity when he developed equipment for recording census statistics.

The Census Bureau offered a substantial reward to the developer of devices that would streamline the collecting and counting of census data for the 1890 census. The rapid influx of immigrants to the United States in the 1880s caused the Census Bureau to believe that continued use of manual data collection practices would not permit a timely tabulation of the census.

Hollerith's Punch Card Data Storage System

Hollerith knew, from a relative who was involved in the textile industry, of the Jacquard Loom's use of punch cards for data storage. He was also inspired by the use of punch cards by railroad conductors when issuing railroad tickets. Holes punched in the tickets represented not only destinations and seat assignments but also provided an area in which passenger details (such as height and hair color) were recorded. He concluded that census takers could do the same, with the resulting cards being sorted and processed by machines. His device sensed holes electrically rather than mechanically and, unlike the loom, was sophisticated enough to accumulate data and calculate summaries.

With some of the award he received from the Census Bureau Hollerith founded the Tabulating Machine Company. In 1911 his firm merged with two others to form the Computing Tabulating Recording (CTR) Corporation and it was renamed International Business Machines (**IBM**) in 1924.

## Early Digital Computers

Modern computing began with accelerated development before and during World War II. During this period developments in electronics produced important inventions including electronic circuits, relays, vacuum tubes, and other devices replacing mechanical equivalents. The computers designed and constructed from these new devices have often been referred to as **first generation computers.** Computers such as the Atanasoff-Berry Computer, the Colossus and ENIAC, were built individually in research laboratories and typically used punched cards for input and as the primary data storage medium.

The **Atanasoff-Berry Computer** (ABC) was the first electronic digital computing device. The machine was developed in the late 1930s for the special purpose of solving simultaneous linear equations. The ABC lifted the curtain on modern computing, including binary arithmetic and electronic switching, but its special-purpose and lack of an alterable, stored program delineate it from modern general purpose computers. This machine was largely forgotten until the 1970s when a U.S. District Court invalidated the ENIAC patent and concluded that the ABC was the first "computer."

The **Colossus,** an early electronic digital computer, was used by British code breakers to read encrypted German messages during World War II. The encrypted message was read at high speed. The Colossus, a semi-special purpose computer, reduced the time to break German messages from weeks to hours. It was developed just in time for deciphering messages which gave significant information to the Allies prior to D-Day. The deciphered messages showed that Hitler had fallen for the deception campaigns designed to avert German opposition during the D-Day invasion.

**ENIAC,** the abbreviation for Electronic Numerical Integrator and Computer, is usually considered to be the first modern, general purpose computer. It was large (weighed thirty tons), power hungry (consumed two hundred kilowatts of power), all electronic, digital, and capable of being reprogrammed to solve general computing problems. ENIAC was designed and built originally to calculate artillery firing tables for the U.S. Army's Ballistics Research Laboratory. Due to war-time needs the first problems run on the ENIAC were related to the design of the atomic bomb.

A drawback on the machine was a side effect of its reliance on vacuum tubes, which tended to burn out often. This caused the machine to go through up and down periods.

All of the early electronic computers incorporated vacuum tubes for controlling the circuits that computers use while processing data. These tubes look and behave very much like light bulbs; they generate a lot of heat and have a tendency to burn out. The development of computing depended on a new breakthrough.

## The Impact of the Transistor

The next major step in the history of computing was the invention of the transistor in 1947. This device rapidly replaced the fragile and power hungry vacuum tube as an electronic switch. Transistorized computers are normally referred to as **second generation computers** and became available in the late 1950s and early 1960s. The use of transistors allowed a significant reduction in size and power requirements accompanied by an increase in reliability. Second generation computers were expensive and were primarily used by universities, governments, and large corporations.

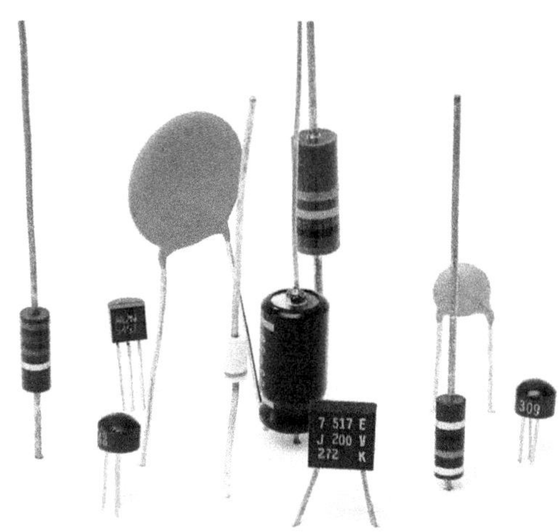



Transistors

Through the 1950s all computers manufactured were large scale and often referred to as **mainframe** computers. Several companies (most notably Digital Equipment Corporation) used the new second generation technology to design and market smaller computers known as mini computers but the technology was mostly no different from that of mainframes. The introduction of integrated circuits allowed the design and then rapid development of the next generation of computers.

## Integrated Circuits Promote Powerful Computing Expansion

When building a circuit, it is very important that all connections remain solid. If connections are loose the electrical current may be interrupted and the circuit fails. Before the integrated circuit, first and second generation computer circuits were assembled by hand, soldering each component in place and connecting them manually with wires. Engineers understood that manually assembling the substantial number of tiny components required in more powerful computers would be impossible without generating some faulty connections.

Another challenge was the complexity of the circuits and the distance between components. A complex computer circuit is dependent on speed for efficient operation. If the circuit's components were large, or the connections too distant, the electric signals could not travel rapidly enough, and the computer would not operate well, or at all. A new breakthrough was needed to advance beyond the second generation.

The **integrated circuit** combines numerous transistors and other electronic components and their connections in a single package thus eliminating the problems of distance between components. The circuits are machine manufactured therefore eliminating the tedious effort of hand soldering transistor based circuits and at the same time increasing the reliability of the circuits. Mass production coupled with enhanced reliability fueled the remarkable explosion in the use of computers known as the **third generation.**

The **microprocessor** (an integrated circuit that serves as a **central processing unit** or **CPU** in a computer system) made possible the development of the **microcomputer,** small, low-cost computers that could be owned by individuals and small businesses. Microcomputers which first appeared in the 1970s, became commonplace in the next two decades. Today such computers are known as **personal computers. Apple Computer** introduced the first mass-market personal computer.

By integrating the processor onto one integrated circuit (containing the equivalent of millions of transistors and other components), production and assembly cost was greatly reduced. Since the emergence of the integrated circuit the microprocessor has become the most common implementation of the central processing unit.

### Pause to Review #1

**What do you think?**

1. Why is hardware necessary for data to become visible?
2. From the standpoint of processing data, what was the significance of Hollerith's invention?
3. Why did Babbage's reliance on decimal-based architecture instead of binary-based architecture make his machine difficult to produce?
4. How did the development of the integrated circuit make possible the development of the microprocessor?

A Binary Digit

## Data Representation

Before we discuss modern hardware, we first consider data representation and why it is important. Computers only understand a very limited vocabulary comprised of 1 and 0. Certainly computers process business transactions, allow e-mail communication, stream video and audio from servers, and allow us to print pictures from our digital cameras. Yet ultimately all content that is processed or handled by a computer system is just 1s and 0s. Each 1 or 0 is known as a **bit.** This is called the **binary** system and is integral to what makes computers and data processing using computers plausible.

Binary means counting by twos. It is a numbering system that has two possible values: 0 and 1. As humans we count in the decimal system which has 10 values: 0, 1, 2, 3, 4, 5, 6, 7, 8, and 9. A decimal machine must have 10 possible states, one for each value that can be represented.

Binary works perfectly with the electrical nature of a digital computer system. Electrical currents can carry different voltages to represent a 1 or a 0. Early attempts at building computers were mechanical and so no inherent orientation toward binary existed. As a result the mechanics required to handle more complicated systems were too complicated to build. Babbage's Analytical Engine suffered from this problem.

So far so good, but we have a problem. What use would a computer be if it only could store and process 0s and 1s? We are interested in processing much more complex forms of data. What about the 26 letters of the alphabet? If a bit can have only two values how can we store and process all 26 letters?

If all data is represented as 1s or 0s (sometimes referred to as on or off) then the familiar letters of the alphabet, punctuation, numerals, and so on must be translated from key strokes with familiar symbols (A, B, . . . , Z, 0,1, . . . ,9) to numbers with just two values. Since a bit can only have two values (1 or 0) it would be impossible to represent every key on the keyboard as a single bit. The solution is to group bits together and assign the group to represent particular keys. Today a group of 8 bits is known as a **byte.**

To permit data transfer and sharing between computers and software of different manufactures it is necessary for vendors of participating equipment and programs to agree on the specific bit pattern (bytes) for each keystroke. An industry agreement in 1963 did just that by becoming the basis for data interchange. The American Standard Code for Information Interchange, **ASCII** for short, established standard bit pattern representations.

**ASCII** A document typed into a word processor would be of little interest if it were all 0s and 1s. While it is true that everything stored in a computer is stored as binary, when we use a keyboard we type letters of the alphabet, punctuation, numbers and so on. The computer must be able to accept what we type and yet still store it in binary.

The trick used is to group bits together so that more than two states (0 and 1) can be represented. Normally, 8 bits are combined to form a byte, and a byte can represent one character from the keyboard. The sequence of bits 01000001 represents the capital letter "A."

How in the world could the sequence of bits 01000001 represent the letter "A"? The answer is that most of the computer hardware and software manufacturers agreed on the ASCII convention that specifies what each sequence of bits is to represent. The figure shown here illustrates how the word "HELLO" is built from a sequence of five 8-bit bytes.

The chart that follows displays selected ASCII codes and the characters they represent. Notice that upper and lowercase require separate codes. The decimal equivalent of each binary code is also presented in this portion of the ASCII table:

| Binary | Dec. | Character | Binary | Dec. | Character | Binary | Dec. | Character |
|---|---|---|---|---|---|---|---|---|
| 010 0000 | 32 | Space | 011 0000 | 48 | 0 | 100 0001 | 65 | A |
| 010 0001 | 33 | ! | 011 0001 | 49 | 1 | 100 0010 | 66 | B |
| 010 0010 | 34 | " | 011 0010 | 50 | 2 | 100 0011 | 67 | C |
| 010 0011 | 35 | # | 011 0011 | 51 | 3 | 100 0100 | 68 | D |
| 010 0100 | 36 | $ | 011 0100 | 52 | 4 | 100 0101 | 69 | E |
| 010 0101 | 37 | % | 011 0101 | 53 | 5 | 100 0110 | 70 | F |
| 010 0110 | 38 | & | 011 0110 | 54 | 6 | 100 0001 | 97 | a |
| 010 0111 | 39 | ' | 011 0111 | 55 | 7 | 100 0010 | 98 | b |
| 010 1000 | 40 | ( | 011 1000 | 56 | 8 | 100 0011 | 99 | c |
| 010 1001 | 41 | ) | 011 1001 | 57 | 9 | 100 0100 | 100 | d |
| 010 1010 | 42 | * | | | | 100 0101 | 101 | e |
| 010 1011 | 43 | + | | | | 100 0110 | 102 | f |

**How Many Different Characters Can Be Represented?** The ASCII coding scheme actually uses 7 bits to represents characters (letters, numbers, and punctuation). Since each bit can be a 1 or 0 then the 7 bits can have $2^7$ or 128 possible arrangements. Bytes are formed of 8 bits and the eighth bit is used to form **Extended ASCII.** This is not part of the formal ASCII specification but rather a collection of an additional 128 combinations that are used by manufacturers for proprietary function. It is the first 128 characters that are defined as ASCII.

So how many different characters can 8 bits together represent? One bit can represent two things: 0 or 1. What about a byte with two bits? Since each bit can be a 0 or 1 then there are four possible sequences that 2 bits can represent. This can be determined algebraically as

$$2^{\text{number of bits}}$$

and is summarized here. The table on the left shows how many characters can be generated from bytes of different sizes and the chart on the right shows the four 2-bit sequences possible if the code set uses two bits per character. Most computers use eight bit bytes. From the table you can see that 256 characters are possible.

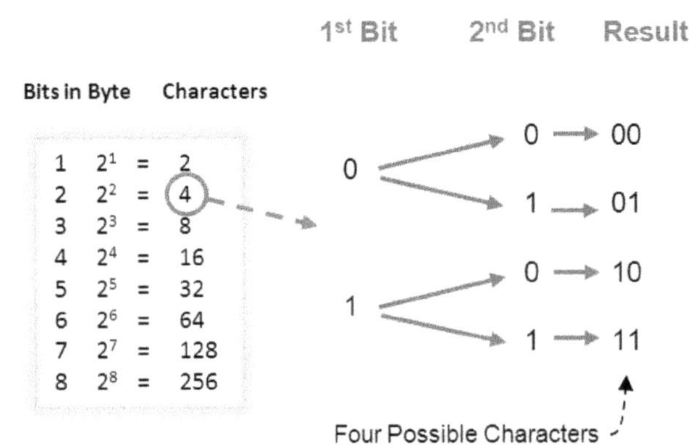


The Relationship Between Bits per Byte and Character Set Size

**Unicode** Unicode is an industry standard designed to allow text and symbols from all of the major writing systems of the world to be consistently represented and manipulated by computers. A **writing system** limited to 128 distinct representations is not sufficient for more than one alphabet, numbering system, and punctuation. The world has many such systems. Unicode handles multiple writing systems by using 2 bytes (16 bits) for each character's representation. This scheme provides about 65,536 distinct combinations of 16 bits and that is sufficient for human writing systems currently known. A few examples are shown here:

| Decimal | Unicode name | Display |
|---|---|---|
| 65 | Latin capital letter A | A |
| 223 | Latin small letter Sharp S | ß |
| 254 | Latin small letter Thorn | þ |
| 916 | Greek capital letter Delta | Δ |
| 1049 | Cyrillic capital letter Short I | Й |
| 1511 | Hebrew letter Qof | ק |
| 1605 | Arabic letter Meem | م |
| 3671 | Thai digit 7 | ๗ |
| 4688 | Ge'ez syllable Qha | ቐ |
| 12354 | Hiragana letter A (Japanese) | あ |
| 21494 | CJK Unified Ideograph-53F6 (Simplified Chinese "Leaf") | 叶 |
| 33865 | CJK Unified Ideograph-8449 (Traditional Chinese "Leaf") | 葉 |
| 46507 | Hangul syllable Tteolp (Korean "Ssangtikeut Eo Rieulpieup") | 떫 |

Unicode

**Other Data Encoding** Numerous other data encoding arrangements have been and are important. Here are a few that handle various types of data:

- **EBCDIC**—Extended Binary Coded Decimal Interchange Code is an 8-bit character encoding used on IBM mainframe operating systems. It originated in the 1950s.
- **BCD**—Binary-coded decimal is an encoding for decimal numbers in which each digit is represented by its own binary sequence. It allows easy conversion to decimal digits for printing or display and faster decimal calculations.

**Data Compression** Compression techniques are used to reduce the number of bytes required to store certain kinds of data. Compression is also used to permit faster transmission of data between computers.

- **MPEG**—A family of digital video compression standards. Storing sound or video requires encoding it into a sequence of binary 1s and 0s. A codec performs this task. It is a device or program capable of performing encoding and decoding on a digital data stream or signal. The word **codec** is derived from the two functions it performs: **coding** and **decoding**.
- **GIF**—The Graphics Interchange Format is an 8-bit-per-pixel bitmap image format that was introduced by CompuServe and is widely used on the Web.
- **WAV**—Standard digital audio file format for storing sound data; allows audio recordings to be captured and stored; often used to save CD-quality audio.

**Pause to Review #2**

**Try this:**

1. How many characters could a 9-bit byte represent?
2. What is the binary sequence for lower case h?
3. What does this binary sequence mean? Each byte has 8 bits.

   010101110100010101001100010000011010011110100110101000101

Type your answers in the window provided by Pamela.

**What do you think?**

1. Would the Internet have developed differently if data standardization had not occurred?
2. In early electronic computing, memory was quite expensive. To save cost, manufacturers might have agreed on a 5-bit byte rather than the 8-bit byte in use today. What impact might that have had on our use of computers?

## Modern Hardware

When we speak of hardware we are considering a collection of devices that allow us to enter, store, and process data, and display output. You are surely familiar with some of these devices. Today most computers are physically small (desktop and laptop) but mainframe computers are still quite important as they are used to process large volumes of data for governments, businesses, schools, the military, and research laboratories for example. Although physically large, mainframe computers share the same basic components of small computers. In this section the most common and important computer components are listed here and described afterward:

- **Motherboard**
  - Processor (CPU)
  - Bus (internal and external)
  - BIOS
- **Power Supply**
- **Input**
  - Keyboard
  - Mouse
  - Microphone
  - Camera
- **Output**
  - Monitor
  - Printer
  - Speaker
- **Storage**
  - Primary Memory: RAM
  - Secondary Memory

- Hard and Floppy Disks
- Flash Drives
- CD/DVD
- Zip Disk
- Magnetic Tape

❒ **Communication devices**

- Modem
- Network Interface Hardware

## Important Terms

Your understanding of computer hardware and software depends on understanding the following:

❒ **Bit**—A logical data value may be 0 or 1. Sometimes a bit is said to take on the values True or False.

❒ **Byte**—A unit of data storage consisting of 8 bits. It represents a single character, digit, or punctuation.

❒ **Kilobyte (KB)**—A unit of data storage consisting of about 1,000 bytes.

❒ **Megabyte (MB)**—A unit of data storage consisting of about one million bytes.

❒ **Gigabyte (GB)**—A unit of data storage consisting of about 1,000 megabytes or a billion bytes.

❒ **Terabyte (TB)**—A unit of data storage consisting of about 1,000 gigabytes.

❒ **Hertz**—A unit of frequency describing the number of electrical cycles that occur in a second. The speed of a computer's processor is measured in hertz. The larger the number, generally the faster the microprocessor.

❒ **Kilohertz (Khz)**—One thousand hertz.

❒ **Megahertz (Mhz)**—One million hertz.

❒ **Gigahertz (Ghz)**—One billion hertz.

❒ **RAM**—Random Access Memory. This memory holds programs as they execute and temporarily holds data as it is processed.

❒ **ROM**—Read-Only Memory. It cannot easily be written to and its main uses are the distribution of firmware (software that is very closely related to hardware).

❒ **bps**—Bits per second. The number of bits transmitted per second.

❒ **Kilobits per Second (Kbps)**—One thousand bits per second.

❒ **Megabits per Second (Mbps)**—One million bits per second.

❒ **Gigabits per Second (Gbps)**—One billion bits per second.

## Motherboard

This is the one component of a computer system that ties all other components together. This is where the core components of a computer reside. A computer is typically constructed with the processor (**CPU**), main memory (**RAM**), and other basic components on the motherboard.

The **system unit** is the main body of a computer. It provides an enclosure containing the motherboard, power supply, cooling fans, internal disk drives, and the memory modules and expansion cards that are plugged into the motherboard.

Components such as external storage, control circuits for video display and sound, and peripheral devices (printers, communication devices, etc.) are typically attached to the motherboard via cables plugged into connectors on the motherboard. The motherboard also supports expansion of the computer's functionality by providing a place for additional components to be added. Clearly the ability to expand is an important aspect of the computer.

A Computer's Motherboard

Several of the important components found on the motherboard are described next.

**Processor** The **central processing unit** (**CPU**), also called the processor, is the critical component in a digital computer that processes data by interpreting and executing instructions that are contained in computer programs. Generally a CPU that is manufactured using integrated circuits is known as a microprocessor.

This device responds to a program's commands and has a **clock** to keep all activities in the computer synchronized. Inside the CPU we find the **control unit** and the **arithmetic logic unit,** ALU. The control unit is like a **manager** who keeps things organized and synchronized and the ALU is where mathematical and logical operations are performed. The control unit fetches data and copies it into registers. The ALU performs operations on data in registers such as addition and subtraction. The ALU also performs logical tests on data which permits branching within programs.

Pentium: A Central Processing Unit

Several important terms that relate to the CPU or processor are:

- **System clock**—Time keeper that provides a synchronizing signal that the CPU follows.
- **Clock speed**—The rate in cycles per second (measured in hertz) at which a computer performs its most basic operations such as adding two numbers or transferring a value from one register to another.
- **Machine cycle**—The machine cycle is a four-phase cycle that includes reading and interpreting the machine language, executing the code, and then storing that code. The execution of program code (machine code) follows this cycle.
- **Machine instruction**—A small segment of code that contains steps that need to be executed by the computer processor. Normally an instruction performs one action like adding two numbers. Machine instruction speed is measured in the number of cycles an instruction requires for operation.
- **Machine language**—Sometimes referred to as machine code or object code, machine language is a collection of binary digits or bits that the computer reads and interprets. Machine language is the only language a computer is capable of understanding.
- **Instruction set**—This is the set of instructions that the processor knows how to perform. Instruction sets are built into the processor's circuitry, so different processors are not likely to be able to run the same version of the same program.
- **RISC**—A reduced instruction set computer is a processor designed for speed. It is a special purpose computer that requires only a subset of all operations to perform the processing it is assigned.
- **CISC**—Complex Instruction Set Computers preceded RISC. The primary goal of CISC architecture is to complete a task in as few lines of program code as possible.
- **Cache**—High speed memory that allows the processor to fetch data faster than from memory located elsewhere on the motherboard or on secondary storage like disk.
- **Serial processing**—The processor must execute all phases of the machine cycle before the next instruction is begun.
- **Pipelining**—A method for boosting performance in which the processor begins execution of the next instruction before the current instruction is complete.
- **Parallel processing**—Multiple instructions are processed simultaneously. This and pipelining improve system performance.
- **Multiprocessing**—The combination of several processors working together in a computer system. A multiprocessing system will allocate tasks among the several processors. This is not the same as parallel processing in which multiple instructions are simultaneously executed on the same processor.
- **Benchmarks**—Standard measures of performance used to allow comparison between processors.
- **Register**—A location within a processor used to store and process data. Registers are 16, 32, or 64 bits wide.
- **Word size**—The number of bits that can be manipulated by a single instruction. Registers hold one or more words but never parts of a word.
- **Data bus**—Part of the motherboard that allows transfer of data among the computer's components. A bus operates in parallel fashion so that all bits of each single byte travel together in unison. The data bus size (number of bits) will be the same as the word size.

A key feature of the processor is the amount of data that it can operate on simultaneously. Originally 4- or 8-bit architectures were available. Although it was possible to build a working computer with such chips it would not be particularly powerful. Advances have increased processor capability to 64-bit architectures allowing today's computers to process data quite efficiently.

Another measure of the processor's power is its speed. There are two measures that are relevant:

- The clock speed of the processor (measured in cycles per second or Hz)
- The number of instructions executed per clock cycle (IPC).

The clock speed is advertised when a computer is purchased, and numbers in the 3 Ghz+ range are common for desktop computers while laptop computers tend to run somewhat slower. The IPC is not advertised but the true horsepower of the processor is calculated by multiplying the IPC by the clock speed.

Another factor contributing to the computer's power is the amount of installed real memory (RAM).

Popular processors today include Intel's **Pentium** and **Core Duo** and Advanced Micro Devices (AMD) **Athalon** and **Opteron.**

**Dual Core Processor** A dual- or multi-core microprocessor is one that combines two or more independent processors into a single package, usually in a single integrated circuit. A multi-core device contains two or more independent microprocessors and permits multiprocessing without including multiple microprocessors in separate physical packages. This form of processing is often known as chip-level multiprocessing.

**Processor Speed** As processor and computer architecture have advanced, it has become more and more difficult to compare the performance of various computer systems simply by looking at their specifications. Here are some measures of performance:

- **Ghz**—One billion hertz—one billion cycles per second. Generally the faster that the processor cycles per second the faster the processor. As you will see in a moment, though, this is not always true. This is because no two processors are equally efficient per cycle.
- **MIPS**—Instructions per second (IPS) is a measure of a computer's processor speed and one MIP is one million instructions per second. MIPS is used to benchmark processors against others.
- **FLOPS**—Floating Point Operations per Second is the measure of a computer's performance. FLOPS is an especially useful measure in systems that perform scientific calculations and make heavy use of floating point (non-integer) operations.

As an example, an Intel Pentium 4 processor generally operates at a higher clock frequency than AMD Athlon XP processors, but this does not necessarily mean the Pentium has more computational power. In other words an AMD processor with slower clock frequency can perform as well on benchmark tests as an Intel processor operating at a higher frequency.

**Intel and AMD Announcements** Recent announcements by the premier processor manufacturers (Intel and American Micro Devices) indicate their intent to produce ultralow-power chips. In March 2007 Intel announced that it was on track in developing a new generation of chips that would achieve a significant increase in performance without consuming more power. The new processor families, named **Penryn** and **Nehalem**, may in some cases help Intel catch up technically with its archrival, AMD.

AMD announced plans to introduce an improved processor code named **Barcelona** based on technology that uses four processing cores rather than the two currently used in AMD processors. The company believes that Intel would not be able to catch up with AMD's existing designs until it introduces the Nehalem microprocessor in 2008.

**Bus** In a computer, a bus is a subsystem of the motherboard that transfers data or power between computer components inside a computer or between a computer and external components which are typically controlled by device driver software.

Computers usually have **internal** and **external** busses. The internal bus (or local bus) connects the internal components of a computer to the motherboard (and therefore to the CPU and primary memory—RAM). The internal bus connects to devices that are local to the computer and not to those in other machines or to those external to the computer. An external bus connects external devices (peripherals) to the motherboard.

The internal bus is really three busses that work in a coordinated fashion:

- The **control bus** is used by CPUs for sending commands to other devices within the computer.
- The **address bus** carries the information about which device the CPU is communicating with.
- The **data bus** carries the actual data being processed.

The external bus provides card slots which are used to hold device controller cards for devices such as video cards, sound cards, external storage units, or network cards. This is a mechanism by which external devices are connected to the computer. To gain access to the external bus the computer's case is opened and cards are plugged in to open slots in the bus. Some motherboards today include video and sound or even communication devices thus eliminating the need for the addition of extra cards.

**USB** Today the use of the **Universal Serial Bus (USB)** allows peripheral devices to be connected without the need to plug expansion cards into the computer's external bus. In effect the USB **port** is an extension of the external bus. Devices with a USB plug are connected to the computer by inserting the plug into the USB port. A major advantage of this arrangement (aside from eliminating the need to open the computer's case when attaching a new device) is that devices may be **hot-swapped** (connected or disconnected without powering down or rebooting the computer). When a device is connected the computer identifies it and loads the appropriate device driver.

Corbis.

A USB Plug

USB 2.0 (the current standard) has a raw theoretical data rate at 480Mbps, and it is rated about 40 times faster than the earlier USB 1.1, with top speed at 12Mbps.

**Plug and Play** Plug and play is not a component of the motherboard but describes the process for attaching a new device to the computer system. It is a feature that allows the addition of a new device, normally a peripheral, without requiring reconfiguration or manual installation of device drivers. It allows the device to be added without requiring rebooting of the computer. Normally the device is added by connecting with a USB plug. The processor senses this connection and assigns an internal bus address to the device. Plug and play is a significant advancement over the manual and arduous process that was required in earlier days when adding peripherals.

**BIOS** The **Basic Input/Output System** (BIOS) is a small program run by a computer when first powered on. Its primary function is to stabilize the machine and devices on the motherboard so that the **operating system** can be loaded and take control of the computer. This process is known as **booting up.**

The **BIOS** is software code (known as **firmware**) embedded in a chip that recognizes and controls various devices that make up the computer. It resides in read only memory (**ROM**) and therefore cannot be altered unless the chip is removed and replaced. Without the BIOS the computer cannot start.

At times it may be desirable to interrupt the boot process to reconfigure certain aspects of the computer's environment. How to enter setup mode differs on various computer systems but generally a specific key is pressed (Esc, Del, F1, F2, Ctrl-Esc, etc.) during the start sequence. Once in setup mode, numerous options are available, including these:

- **System Time/Date**—Set the system time and date.
- **Drive Configuration**—Configure hard drives, CD-ROM, and floppy drives.
- **Boot Sequence**—The order that storage devices will be searched for the operating system.
- **Mouse/Keyboard**—Enable Num Lock; Enable the Keyboard; Auto-Detect Mouse.
- **Security**—Set a password for accessing the computer's hardware.
- **Power Management**—Set various power management parameters.
- **Exit**—Save changes, discard changes, or restore default settings.

**Expansion Slots** Some peripherals require more than a USB port for installation. Certain devices, especially devices with substantial electronics (sound and graphics cards especially) that must be close to the motherboard's bus, are usually connected to the computer with a card placed into an extension slot. Cards that fit into expansion slots are known as **expansion cards** and they provide additional functionality for the computer.

Expansion Slots on Motherboard

Once the board is inserted into the expansion slot, data is transferred between the expansion board and the computer's devices including RAM, disk, and other peripheral devices. The data bus is the vehicle that transports the data. Expansion cards are engineered to be compatible with one of several types of expansion slots. The slots vary in size depending on the number of data bits (data bus size) that the card requires. The slot provides data, address, and control bus lines.

Today, the Peripheral Component Interconnect bus (**PCI**) is commonly used. This high speed slot provides a 32- or 64-bit data bus (the number of bits that are simultaneously transferred per operation). It has largely replaced the older **ISA** (Industry Standard Architecture) technology.

Another common expansion card conforms to the **AGP** (Accelerated Graphics Port) standard. It is a high-speed port for attaching a graphics card to a computer's motherboard and is used primarily to assist in the acceleration of computer graphics.

Accelerated Graphics Card

**Network Adapter Card** A network card, network adapter or NIC (network interface controller) is a piece of computer hardware designed to allow computers to communicate over a computer network. It allows users to connect to each other either by using cables or wirelessly and provides an addressing scheme through the use of MAC addresses. The networking chapter provides additional information about NICs.

**Disk Controller Card** The disk controller is the electronic circuit which allows the processor to communicate with a hard disk, floppy disk, or other kind of disk drive. A computer will usually have disk controller hardware built onto the motherboard. If additional disks are added to the computer it may be necessary to add additional controllers by installing expansion cards.

**Sound Card** A sound card is an expansion card that can output and input sound under control of computer programs. Typically sound cards provide the audio for multimedia applications such as music composition, editing video or audio, and games. Many computers have sound capabilities built in, while others require these expansion cards if higher quality audio is desired.

A Sound Card Connects Speakers and Microphones

**Video Card** A video card, also referred to as a **graphics accelerator card**, **display adapter**, and **graphics card**, is responsible for generating output images to a display. The term usually refers to a separate expansion card plugged into a slot on the computer's motherboard and not a graphics controller integrated into the motherboard chipset.

Some video cards offer added functionalities, such as **video capture** and **TV tuning.**

**Port** A communication port is a doorway between an external device and a computer system. The port may carry data, voice, video, or other types of transmission. A port is used to send computer signals to a printer and to receive data from a scanner. Ports are vital to a computer's functionality. Ports are defined by the function they perform and the physical number of connections they provide. Specific connectors (plugs) fit into ports and must be physically matched.

Today the **USB** port is the most common. Specialty port types (for printers and other devices) have largely been replaced by USB ports. A **FireWire** port is of a different size and allows a FireWire to be connected for fast data transfer. Similarly a **Bluetooth** port allows connection of short distance wireless devices. The most common ports allow connection of a **mouse** or **keyboard.**

**FireWire** FireWire is used for fast data transfer with peripheral devices. It is Apple Computer's brand name for the IEEE 1394 interface used for high-speed data transfer. It is often used for connecting video sources to a computer. It is also used for connection of external hard-drive storage devices. Most digital camcorders include this connection and many computers intended for home or professional audio/video use have built-in FireWire ports. FireWire connectors have a similar appearance to USB and other plugs.

FireWire Plugs

**Bays** A bay is a standard-sized area for adding hardware to a computer. Bays are most commonly used to store disk drives, although they can also be used for front-end USB ports, I/O bays, card readers, fans, and other uses. Most bays are fixed to the inside of a case, but some newer ones can be removed. Two types are commonly in use today:

- **Half height bay**—Approximately 5.75" wide by 1.75" high, they are the standard housing for CD and DVD drives.
- **3.5' bay**—Approximately 4" wide by 1" high, those with an opening in the front of the case are generally used for floppy or Zip drives. Hard drives in modern computers are typically mounted internally.

**Cooling** Computers generate heat while running. Processors especially get hottest because they consume the most electricity. Several techniques are used to dissipate the heat because otherwise the electronic components would cease to function.

- **Fan**—A fan moves air and is used in a computer to move cooler air over a hot area (like a processor) and to vent hot air to outside the computer's cabinet.
- **Heat sink**—A heat sink is an object that absorbs heat from a hot object and dissipates it—usually into the air.
- **Heat pipe**—A heat pipe is a mechanism that transports heat with a very small difference in temperature between the hot and cold interfaces. It is used to move heat from where it is generated to somewhere that is not sensitive to heat. Heat pipes are generally quite efficient.

Heat Sink for Cooling

## Power Supply

A computer power supply is designed to convert 110 volts AC (alternating current) power to the low power DC (direct current) used by the internal components of a computer. The power supply is a metal box usually found inside the computer's case. It is next to the wall of the case allowing the installation of a cooling fan that is vented to the outside air. The power-cord receptacle is usually found outside the case next to the cooling fan. The power supply in laptop computers is usually external to the case.

Computer Power Supply

Power supplies are rated for certain wattages based on their maximum power requirements of the computer. Wattages in the range of 200 W to 500 W are typical, although computers used as servers or by gamers (video and processor intensive) often require more power.

## Input

Data and commands are given the computer through input devices. The most common input devices are the keyboard and the mouse. Microphones and cameras are increasingly important as input devices too.

### *Keyboard*

A **keyboard's** primary function is to act as an input device. With a keyboard, you can type a document, use keystroke shortcuts, access menus, and perform a variety of other tasks. Keyboards can have different special purpose keys depending on the manufacturer, the operating system they're designed for, and whether they are attached to a desktop computer or part of a laptop. Most keyboards have between 80 and 110 keys, including:

- **Typing keys**—These keys (letters, numbers, and punctuation) most often follow the **QWERTY** arrangement that was devised in the 1870s when typewriters were introduced. The name QWERTY comes from the first six letters in the top alphabet row. Although the pattern of keys seems to make no sense, it was designed so that consecutive keystrokes were unlikely to cause a typewriter jam as it pressed letter and number patterns into the paper. While this is no longer a concern with paperless systems (computers and monitors) the QWERTY arrangement remains the most common in use today.
- **Function and Control keys**—These keys were introduced by IBM. Function keys and control keys, when pressed simultaneously with typing keys, allow specific commands to be issued by the typist. In effect, function and control keys act as additional shift keys.
- **Windows Key**—Pressing this key brings up the Windows Start Menu. It also causes the icons on the task bar to appear. The Windows key or Windows logo key was originally introduced for the Windows 95 operating system. The key is usually near the space bar and is identified by the Windows logo on it.

Modifications to the QWERTY design are an attempt to make them safer or easier to use. For example some people have associated keyboard use with **carpal tunnel**

**syndrome. Ergonomic** keyboard designs are intended to prevent injuries while keeping a person's hands in a more natural position while typing.

### *Mouse*

A pointing device is a computer hardware component (specifically a **human interface device**) that allows a user to input spatial movements to the computer. The mouse is the most common pointing device in use.

The **mouse** is a **point and click** interface for entering commands which works well in graphical environments. Apple Computer did not invent the mouse but was the first to introduce it commercially in 1984 with the Apple Macintosh. The main goal of any mouse is to translate the movements of your hand into signals that the computer can use. The hand motion is displayed and tracked on the monitor as a pointer known as the **cursor.** When the mouse is over an active word processing document or text file it becomes known as the **insertion point.**

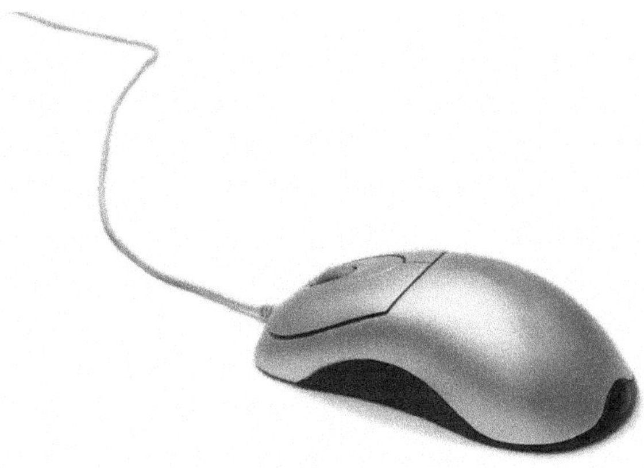



A Basic Two-Button Mouse

Today mice are available as mechanical (least expensive—a ball senses movement) or optical (a light signal senses movement). Mice may be connected to a computer with a wire or wireless transmitter. A mouse has one or more buttons that are pressed ("clicked") to indicate the initiation of an action. The two-button mouse has become the most commonly available design. The left button generally is used to select an object (**single click**) or act on the object (**double click**). The right button displays a menu of options relevant to an object—the menu is said to be **context sensitive.** Operating systems, like Windows, allow the use of the mouse buttons to be reversed for left-handed people. Window's Control Panel provides access to selecting left/right mouse preferences.

- **Mechanical mouse**—The original mouse was mechanical. A ball on the bottom of the mouse rolled over a surface and the ball's movement was converted into electrical signals that reflected the mouse's movement.
- **Optical mouse**—An optical mouse replaced the ball as a sensor of movement with light—most commonly, infrared light. The lack of movable parts makes the optical mouse more durable and allows it to be more accurate. The optical mouse comprises of a camera that takes pictures of the surface that it rests upon and compares the pictures to deduce its direction of travel.
- **Touchpad**—An input device commonly used in laptop computers. They are used to move the cursor by following motions of the user's finger. They are a substitute for a computer mouse.

- **Trackball**—A pointing device consisting of a ball housed in a socket containing sensors to detect rotation of the ball. It is like an upside-down mouse. The user rolls the ball with the thumb, fingers, or the palm of the hand to move a cursor.

**Tablet** The touch screen of a tablet PC allows the user to operate the computer with a stylus or digital pen, or a fingertip, instead of a keyboard or mouse. Since the tablet accepts movements of the **electronic pen** for input it is possible for the tablet PC to recognize human handwriting.

### *Microphone*

A microphone can be used for input when a computer is recording voice or live music. It is also needed when a computer is used for making Internet phone calls (known as **VoIP**). More sophisticated use of this input device involves speaking commands to the computer known as **speech recognition.**

### *Camera*

Digital cameras are easily connected to a computer, and since the images are in digital form a computer is an excellent device for storing and editing these images. When a computer is used for live communication a Web camera (or Webcam) may be used. Chat services like Yahoo! messenger permit users to speak and view each other in real time.

- **Digital camera**—A digital camera is an electronic device used to capture and store images electronically in a digital format, instead of using photographic film. It can be used as an input device for a computer. Images are stored in flash memory and transferred to the computer using a cable or by inserting the memory card into a special slot inside the computer's case. Digital cameras normally store images using the JPG image format.

Digital cameras record an image as a sequence of dots or **pixels.** The number of pixels per image is an indicator of the **resolution** or clarity of the image. Images with a larger number of pixels can be blown up to larger size without distortion.

- **Video camera**—Video cameras are digital photographic devices whose main purpose is to record moving images. Video recordings are mostly stored in **AVI** or **MPG** format. Once captured, video may be converted to other formats for streaming to clients or for compatibility with different systems. Codecs are devices or programs capable of performing encoding on a digital data stream or signal. More information about video formats and codecs is found in Chapter 2, Internet and World Wide Web.
- **Web camera**—A Web camera records a continuing sequence of digital images and transmits the images to the computer. Web cameras can also take single pictures, but most are for motion purposes. Generally, Web cameras offer lower resolution than digital or video cameras but at a much lower price. Popular uses for Webcams include instant messaging and video conferencing.

A Basic Web Camera for a Laptop Computer

### *Touch Screen*

A touch screen is an overlay that covers the computer's monitor and can receive movements of a user's finger in a fashion similar to the touchpad. The difference is that a user interacting with a touch screen views the monitor's image and moves or clicks a finger as if using a mouse over the same surface.

Touch screens are particularly useful in museums and retail settings where user input is required but a mouse and keyboard are undesirable because they require additional space and could easily be taken.

### *Scanner*

A scanner is a device that analyzes an image (most commonly a photograph) or document (printed text or handwriting) and converts it to a digital image. The most common are flatbed scanners.

- **Flatbed Scanner**—This type of scanner has a flat surface on which to place the item to be scanned and a top that closes holding the item securely during scanning.
- **Handheld Scanner**—Hand-held scanners are more portable but more difficult to use because of hand movements.

Scanner resolution is important because, just as with digital cameras, the resolution dictates the clarity and potential for enlargement of the scanned digital image.

Flatbed Scanner

### *Barcode Readers*

A barcode reader is a peripheral for reading printed barcodes. It is similar to a scanner because it consists of a light source, a lens, and a photo conductor translating optical impulses into electrical ones.

Barcode Reader

### *Speech Recognition*

Speech recognition is an input procedure that uses a microphone and other hardware to capture a speech signal and convert it into a sequence of words. The conversion is performed by an algorithm implemented as a computer program. The performance of a speech recognition system is often specified in terms of **accuracy** (word error rate—percent of words not understood) and **speed** (the lag behind spoken word that the conversion consumes).

Microsoft has included speech recognition capabilities in Windows for several versions. The implementation in **Windows Vista** is considerably better than earlier versions. It is, however, limited to being an alternative to giving commands from the mouse or keyboard. Other systems like **Dragon Naturally Speaking** have excellent algorithms and transcribe dictation rapidly with good accuracy. Systems of this type are commonly used for medical record keeping and court reporting.

## Output

The three most common computer output devices are monitors, printers, and speakers.

### *Monitor*

A monitor is the device that displays data on its screen—it displays signals generated by a computer as images on a screen. An image is made up of numerous dots, called **pixels,** so you want a monitor that can pack as many pixels onto the screen as possible! This device, which operates like a TV set, lets the user see how the computer is responding to their commands.

Older monitors (also known as **CRTs**) were based on cathode ray technology but most monitors today use **LCD** (Liquid Crystal Display) technology and are known as flat panel displays.

An Image Is Composed of Pixels

Monitors are used to view your data on a computer. The characteristics of a monitor are important for a system's performance since the quality of the video display will significantly affect the user's computing experience. Some of the more important specifications on the monitor are:

- **Screen size**—Expressed in inches, it is the size of the image measured diagonally from the lower left to the upper right corners.
- **Pixel spacing**—Expressed in **dot pitch** or known as **dots per inch.** This describes how close the pixels are spaced apart in the screen. Smaller is better.
- **Resolution**—It is the number of individual pixels contained on a display and it is expressed as the ratio of pixels on the horizontal axis to the number on the vertical axis. Currently, 1280 by 800 is the ratio supported by new monitors. If the past is a guide, that ratio will improve over the next years.
- **Refresh rate**—The frequency with which the monitor's display is refreshed or completely redrawn.
- **Color depth**—The array of colors that a monitor can display. A **24-bit** color monitor can display over 16 million distinct colors.

**Graphics Card** A graphics card takes data from the CPU and turns it into images displayed on the monitor. The CPU generates a binary stream of bits that are converted by the graphics card into a video signal that can be viewed on a monitor. The card accepts the CPU's bits and decides how to use the pixels on the screen to create the image. It then sends that information to the monitor through a cable.

The graphics card adapts the computer's signal for display in conjunction with the particular display hardware that is connected to the computer. The card must be compatible with the display type.

- **VGA**—Video Graphics Array is an analog computer display standard. It has been technologically outdated for some time due to its relatively low resolution (640 × 480 pixels).
- **SVGA**—Super Video Graphics Array was an extension to VGA. Originally it mandated 800 3 600 4-bit pixels allowing each pixel to be any of 16 different colors. It has been extended to 1024 3 768 8-bit pixels (256 colors) and beyond.
- **Widescreen**—Widescreen adapters allow a wider **aspect ratio** (width to height) than the standard monitor (4:3). Widescreen aspect ratios are in the range of about 16:9 allowing a wider display surface. Almost all new laptops sold today have widescreen displays. Apart from the aspect ratio, the technology for producing images

remains the same. Note: The concept of aspect ratio applies to images as well. As an image is resized the aspect ratio must be retained to ensure no distortion of the image.

### *Printer*

This is the device that puts data or information on paper. Printers are much less expensive than ever before. And that includes color printers, too. There are two fundamental styles of printers: **impact** and **non-impact.** An impact printer pushes pins into a ribbon and then the paper to create an image. Each pin displays a "dot" of ink on the paper. The arrangement of the dots (similar to pixels) creates the image that you see. These printers are louder than non-impact printers, but are required when you want to print on multi-part forms. A non-impact printer, like a **laser or ink-jet,** can produce a much finer image. Color lasers are more expensive, but color ink-jets can be purchased for less than $100.

Laser printers use technology virtually the same as that of copier machines. As ink is sprayed onto the page it is guided by an electro-magnetic force. Ink-jet printers use a series of nozzles to spray small droplets of ink onto the page.

Two measures of the printer's performance are important:

- **DPI**—Printed pages are produced in a way similar to images displayed on a monitor. The page is comprised of thousands of dots, and more is better. When you review printer advertising look for the number of dots per inch (DPI) the printer places on the paper.
- **PPM** (pages per minute)—this indicates how many pages a printer is able to produce each minute. Since not all pages are equally dense this is an average estimate.

Several types of printers are in common use. Other older types may still be found in use. Here several printer types are described:

- **Laser printer**—Laser printers are more common now than in the past since prices have dropped over the last several years. Originally black and white only, color laser printers are becoming more available. They produce high quality text and graphics on plain paper. Like photocopiers, laser printers employ a xerographic printing process in which the image is produced by the direct scanning of a laser beam across the printer's drum. The drum charge attracts ink that is directed to specific locations by the electrostatic charge of the latent image on the drum surface. Laser printers are fast and quiet.

  Color laser printers add colored toner (usually cyan, yellow, and magenta).

© Bettman/CORBIS.

Jacquard Loom

- **Ink-jet printer**—Ink-jet printers operate by propelling tiny droplets of liquid ink onto paper. They are the most common type of computer printer for the general consumer due to their low cost, high quality of output, capability of printing in vivid color, and ease of use.

When compared to earlier consumer-oriented printers, ink-jets have a number of advantages. They are quieter in operation than impact printers: dot matrix or daisy-wheel. They can print finer, smoother details through higher print head resolution, and many ink-jets with photorealistic-quality color printing are widely available. Ink-jet printers require two or more ink sources. One container always holds black ink, and the color ink is stored in one or several other containers.

The most common criticisms of ink-jet printers are:

- **Clogging of the print head**—This happens as a result of the printer not being used for a period.
- **High cost of the ink**—This is especially true when all color inks are contained in the same dispenser, so if blue is dry the other colors must be replaced anyway at additional expense.

© Wayne James, 2008, Shutterstock.

Ink-Jet Printer

- **Dot-Matrix printer**—A dot matrix printer or impact matrix printer refers to a type of printer with a print head that runs back and forth on the page and prints by impact. It operates much like a typewriter by striking an ink-soaked cloth ribbon against the

© Egidijus Mika, 2008, Shutterstock.

Dot-Matrix Printhead

paper. Letters are drawn out of a dot matrix, and thus, varied fonts and some graphics can be produced. Since printing involves mechanical pressure, dot-matrix printers can create carbon copies.

These machines are relatively noisy because of the mechanical movement and used mostly where multiple copies are required.

- **Photo printer**—A photo printer is a printer (usually an ink-jet printer) that is specifically designed to print high quality digital photos on special photographic quality paper. These printers usually have a very high number of nozzles and are capable of printing very small droplets. Good quality photo printers may have more than the standard three-color ink sources.

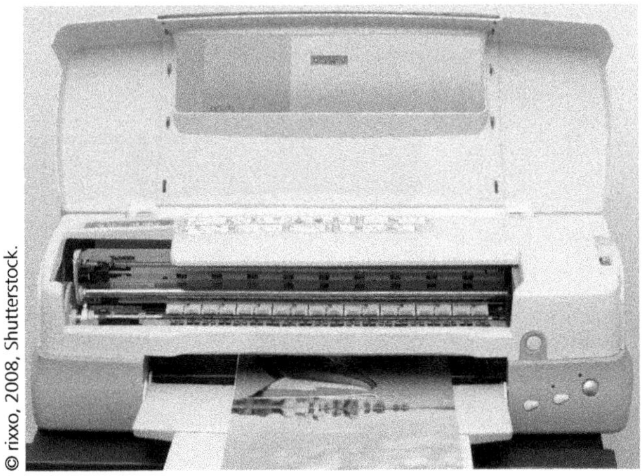



Photo Printer

- **Thermal printer**—A thermal printer produces a printed image by selectively heating coated heat-sensitive paper or thermal paper as the paper passes over the thermal print head. The coating turns black in the areas where it is heated, producing an image or characters. Two-color direct thermal printers are capable of printing both black and an additional color (most often red), by applying heat at two different temperatures.

  Thermal printers are in use where customer receipts are required for transactions based on automated machines like ATM and gasoline dispensers. Some FAX machines print using a thermal process.

**Printer Duty Cycle** The maximum usage level per month for a printer is considered to be the duty cycle. This rating takes into account printer specifics such as the paper-handling capacity and cartridge replacement. Running a printer at the top end of its duty cycle will require users to intervene with the printer to replace supplies more often. Choose a printer with a duty cycle that exceeds your production needs by a substantial margin to minimize interventions and maximize printer life expectancy.

**Printer Memory** Printers operate slower than a computer does as it sends documents and images to the printer. For this reason the actions of a printer can slow down a computer. To avoid this problem, many printers may have built-in memory that accepts the stream from the computer and holds it temporarily until the print mechanism catches up. This memory acts as a buffer between the computer and the printing process.

**Network Printer** A network printer is not a special type of printer but it is a printer attached to a network. One of the purposes of networking is to share resources, and printers are one of the most common resources shared.

**Plotter** Plotters print their output by moving a pen across the surface of a piece of paper. Because of using a pen, plotters are restricted to line art. They can draw complex line art, including text, but do it very slowly because of the mechanical movement of the pens. Plotters cannot create a solid region of color, but can draw close regular hatch lines to define an area.

Plotters may use paper supplied on long roles which allow very long images (measured in feet or yards) to be produced.

### *Speaker*

Originally an afterthought, the computer's speaker (or speaker system) has become an important output component. The first speakers made simple noises like squeaks, beeps, and squeals. Today computers come with stereo speaker systems that in some cases rival stand alone music boxes. Computers usually also have an output jack allowing users to attach headphones to the computer.

**All-in-One** An MFP (Multi-Function Peripheral) is an office machine which incorporates the functionality of several devices in one, allowing a smaller footprint in a home or office. The most common MFP combination includes these devices:

- Printer
- Scanner
- Photocopier

No multi-functional machine can be optimized for all functions that it performs. If high-quality printing or scanning is desired a dedicated machine should be considered.

**Pause to Review #3**

**Try this:**

1. If you have a desktop computer, open the case and determine how many expansion slots it provides.
2. If a microprocessor runs at 1.7 GHz, what is the speed in MHz?
3. How much RAM does your computer have?

Type your answers in the window provided by Pamela.

**What do you think?**

1. What is the role of a bus? Why does a computer have several?
2. Why is the motherboard considered a critical component of the computer?
3. Why are microphones and cameras input devices?
4. Today most printers are nonimpact. Can you think of a situation that would call for use of an impact printer?

## Storage

Computer storage, or computer memory, refers to computer components, devices, and recording media that retain data or programs for some interval of time (short or long term). Data and program retention is one of the key functions of the modern computer.

Computer memory refers to temporary (but fast) storage known as **primary memory** and permanent storage known as **secondary storage.** The former uses chip technology (integrated circuits) and is known as random access memory (RAM). Secondary storage is based on mechanical or electronic devices and is known as disk, flash memory, CDs, or DVDs, and other devices. Primary memory is faster than secondary memory.

### *Primary Memory*

A computer's RAM is considered main memory (or primary storage): the working area used for loading, displaying, and manipulating programs and data. This memory is usually in the form of integrated circuits. These are commonly called memory sticks because they are manufactured as small circuit boards with plastic. Most computers have slots for adding and replacing memory chips.

**RAM** This type of storage is within the computer, closely connected to the processor. This is where programs are held while running. Data that is being processed may be held here, too. The name for primary storage is **RAM**. RAM is **volatile**, which means that when the computer's power is shut off any program or data within it is lost. When you develop a spreadsheet, or other document, make sure to save your work periodically, because if the computer accidentally loses power you will lose your work. For that reason it is important for the user to save work in progress on a secondary storage device. Note: It is typical of some operating systems to periodically save files automatically so that in case a failure occurs, the file may be presented to the user as a recovered file.

Random Access Memory (RAM)

Primary storage in new computers is usually measured in **gigabytes.** This is especially true of computers running Windows Vista operating system.

Computers use RAM to hold programs and associated data during computation. An important characteristic of RAM is that all memory locations can be accessed at almost the same speed (hence "random access"). Most other secondary storage technologies have inherent delays for reading data because they have moving parts or because they are physically farther from the processor.

Computer capacity is a measure of how many programs can be run at once, and how big the programs can be. The computer's capacity will also impact how fast programs can run. The capacity, or amount of memory, is commonly measured in **bytes.** The computer's storage capacity relates to two types of storage: primary and secondary. This table presents the common measures of computer memory. Recall that one byte is the equivalent of one character, letter, or digit:

| Name | Amount of Bytes |
|---|---|
| Kilobyte (KB) | 1,000 |
| Megabyte (MB) | 1,000,000 |
| Gigabyte (GB) | 1,000,000,000 |
| Terabyte (TB) | 1,000,000,000,000 |

Storage Capacity in Bytes

The numbers above are approximations. 1KB is actually 1024 bytes.

**Memory Access Time** Memory **latency** is the time between the processor initiating a request for a byte (8 bits) or word (usually 16 bits) in memory until it is retrieved. Latency is a fundamental measure of the speed of memory: less latency defines faster reading operations.

If the requested data is in the processor's **cache** (special high-speed memory) it is not necessary for the processor to communicate with RAM.

**Memory Configuration** Several configurations of RAM are commonly available:

- **DRAM**—Random access memory that stores each bit of data in a separate capacitor within an integrated circuit. Since real capacitors leak charge, the information eventually fades unless the capacitor charge is refreshed periodically. Because of this refresh requirement, it is a **dynamic** memory as opposed to SRAM and other static memory. Its advantage over SRAM is its architectural simplicity.
- **SDRAM**—Synchronous dynamic random access memory has an asynchronous interface which means that it reacts as quickly as possible to changes in control bus inputs. SDRAM waits for a clock signal before responding to its control inputs. It is synchronized with the computer's system bus and with the processor. Because of the asynchronous nature, SDRAM can be used in pipelining architectures.
- **DDR SDRAM**—Effectively it nearly doubles the transfer rate of SDRAM by transferring data on the leading and trailing edges of the clock signal in a process known as double pumping. Basically DDR SDRAM transfers twice the data per machine cycle and it does it more frequently. It takes advantage of the chips electronic cycles to move data two times in the same period while SDRAM moves it only once.
- **SRAM**—Static random access memory retains its contents as long as power remains applied, unlike DRAM that needs to be periodically refreshed. SRAM should not be confused with read-only memory and flash memory since it is **volatile** memory and preserves data only while power is continuously applied.

**Memory Packaging** RAM is packaged in many configurations with names like: **DIP** (dual inline packages), **SIMM** (single inline memory module), and **DIMM** (dual inline memory module). These names relate to the physical configuration of the chip and its packaging.

The main difference between SIMMs and DIMMs is that DIMMs have double the **data path** (the **bus**) meaning that a DIMM can transfer twice the amount of data in a single operation. DIMMs come in two configurations: **SDRAM** (dynamic random access memory) and **DDR SDRAM** (double-data-rate synchronous dynamic random access memory).

- **SIMM**—A single in-line memory module is a type of memory module that differs from a DIMM (the most predominant form of memory module today) in that the contacts on a SIMM are redundant on both sides of the module.
- **DIMM**—The main difference between SIMMs and DIMMs is that SIMMs have a 32-bit data path, while DIMMs have a 64-bit data path. Since Intel's Pentium has (as do several other processors) a 64-bit bus width, it requires SIMMs.

Memory cards are added to the computer by inserting the card into a slot on the motherboard as shown here:

Adding RAM to the Motherboard

**Cache Memory** Cache memory is special memory that operates much faster than RAM memory. It is impractical to use this memory for the entire system because it is relatively expensive. Cache memory is often between the microprocessor and RAM. There are some levels of cache memory that also reside within the microprocessor. Cache is used as a buffer to reduce the time of data transfer between the processor and devices like the monitor and storage devices.

Cache is used to store a copy of frequently required data. The original copy is in RAM, but if the processor requests data that happens to be also found in cache it will retrieve it faster.

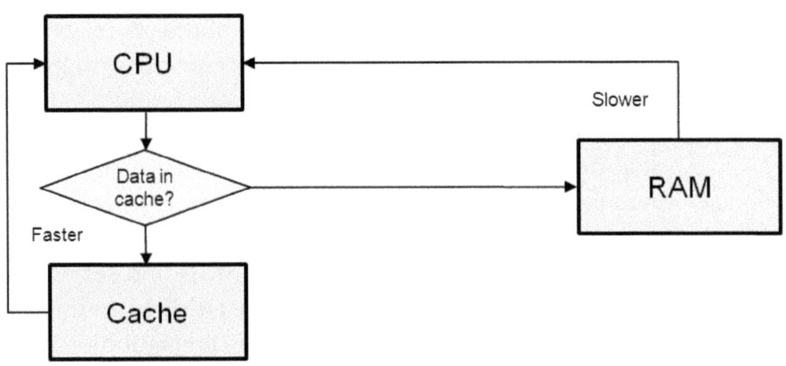


Cache Provides Data Faster than RAM

**ROM** Read-only memory cannot (easily) be written to, so its main uses lie in the distribution of firmware (software that is very closely related to hardware and not likely to need upgrading). Several variations of ROM are often found in computer systems.

- **PROM**—Programmable ROMs are used to store programs permanently. The key difference from a ROM is that the programming is applied after the device is constructed unlike a ROM in which programs are burned in during the manufacture process.
- **EEPROM**—Electrically Erasable Programmable ROM is a non-volatile storage used to store small amounts of data. Usually EEPROM is used to store system configuration data. When larger amounts of data are to be stored other memory types, like flash memory, are more economical.
- **BIOS**—The Basic Input/Output System is firmware code run by a computer when it is first powered on. The primary function of the BIOS is to prepare the machine so that the operating system can take over control of the hardware. This process is known as **booting** up.

**CMOS** Complementary metal–oxide–semiconductor is the technological base for many integrated circuits. It is used in RAM and processors. It has replaced earlier technologies including Transistor-Transistor Logic (TTL) because of these benefits:

- High immunity to circuit noise, thus high reliability.
- Low power consumption, thus easier on power supply.
- Less generation of heat.
- High density of logic functions per chip.

**Virtual Memory** Virtual memory is a memory management technique, used by multitasking computer operating systems like Windows. It is important because when several programs are running simultaneously (multitasking) they often require more RAM than is physically available in the computer. This technique allows the computer to pretend it has more real primary memory than it actually does. The computer's hard disk is used to swap running programs and their data in and out of RAM so fast the illusion of multitasking is maintained. Operating systems allow the user to control the amount of disk space allocated as virtual memory to support program swapping.

In this illustration when program 1 pauses the operating system moves it to disk and allows another program (in this case program 4) to have an opportunity to run for a little while. Later program 4 may be swapped with a program that is in virtual memory. Program 2 will eventually be swapped as well. This happens so frequently and so fast that computer users never know that it is occurring. A computer's processor can actually only run one program at any specific time so this technique really does create the illusion of multitasking.

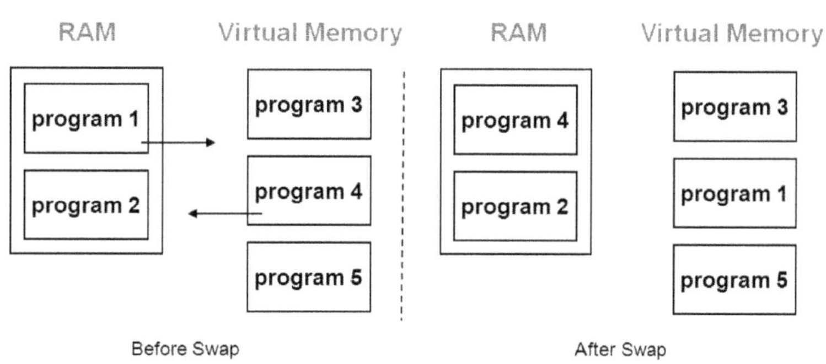


Virtual Memory

**Memory at the Speed of Light** Intel has experimented with the use of laser light to move data between devices inside the computer. Their experimentation has proven successful so far. Removing wires from inside chips would allow more components to be packaged in the same space. If their technology can be commercialized then extremely fast memory (and processors) could be expected in the future.

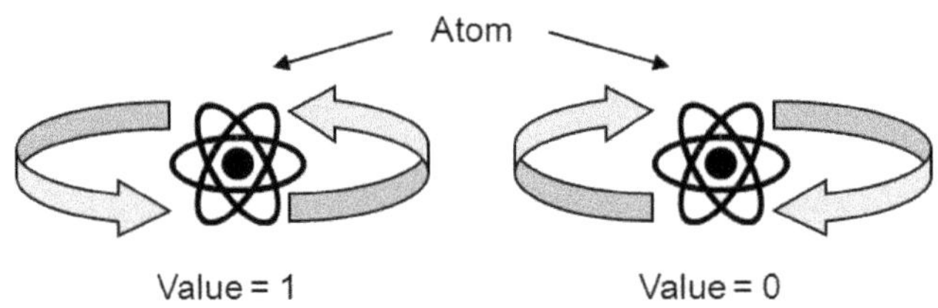


Quantum Computing

**Future Memory Architecture** The electronic switches that hold and manipulate the binary 1s and 0s are very small. Nevertheless they each contain billions of atoms. Scientists are experimenting with **quantum computing** which uses individual atoms to hold a value of one or zero. The obvious implication of such an achievement is the potential for extremely small computer processors or extremely powerful processors of current size. The binary value 1 or 0 is based on the atom's spin. A related variation on this concept is known as **nanotechnology**. Prospective hardware developments are explored in Chapter 14, Future of Computing.

- **Nanotechnology**—Engineering of functional systems at the molecular scale. This applies to memory and processors. Nanotechnology involves the manufacture of components at the nanometer scale, that is one billionth of a meter.
- **Quantum computing**—The basic principle is that the quantum properties (such as atomic spin) of particles can be used to represent and structure data.
- **Optical computing**—An optical computer uses light instead of electricity to manipulate, store, and transmit data.

**Secondary Storage** Secondary storage is **non-volatile**. This means that it holds data and programs even when there is no power in the computer. The most common kind of secondary storage is a hard disk. Other examples of **persistent** storage include floppy disks, CD-ROMs, DVDs, and flash memory (often known as jump drives).

**Hard Disk** Hard disks are built into the computer's cabinet or in external units, usually have a very large capacity, and are fast. These days, the storage capacity on hard disks is measured in **gigabytes** (one GB is 1,000 megabytes or one billion bytes). That's a lot of storage, but in a few years it will seem like next to nothing. In fact, the next size up, 1,000 gigabytes, is called a **terabyte**. Today a new desktop computer may have a hard disk of several hundred GB and a laptop computer would have somewhat less.

Hard drives consist of a series of round rotating metal plates called platters. They are coated with an electromagnetic material which can be electrically altered allowing the binary digits 1 and 0 to be recorded on the surface. Different areas of the surface move under the **read/write head** allowing data to be stored over all portions of the surface as the platter rotates. Data is written to the disk at high speed (a hard disk may spin at 7,200 rpm). The read/write head flies very close over the magnetic surface, often as close as the diameter of a single strand of cigarette smoke.

Hard Disk Rotating Under Read/Write Head

Each platter has data stored on it in a specific pattern for read and write access. The data is organized into concentric rings around the platter known as **tracks.** The distance the head moves into the platter will determine which track is read. A **sector** is a pie-shaped section of the platter. The intersection of a track and sector is a **block.**

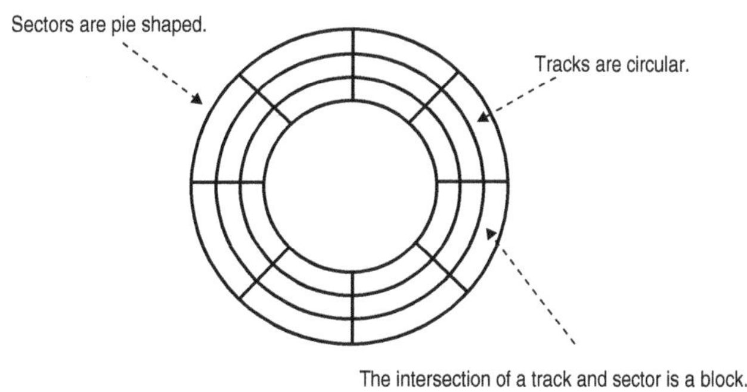


A Disk Surface

Hard disks provide **random access** to data. This means that any data (file, document, image, video) stored anywhere on the disk may be retrieved when requested by the processor. There are three ways to measure the performance of a hard disk:

- **Data transfer rate**—The number of bytes per second that the drive can deliver to the CPU.
- **Seek time**—The time is the amount of time between when the CPU requests a file and when the first byte of the file is sent to the CPU.
- **Latency time**—The average delay until a desired sector rotates to under the read/write head.

**Disk Organization** Content stored on a disk is arranged in a **hierarchical collection** of folders. The first folder encountered when a disk is examined is the **root** folder. Each folder may hold additional folders or files as shown here.

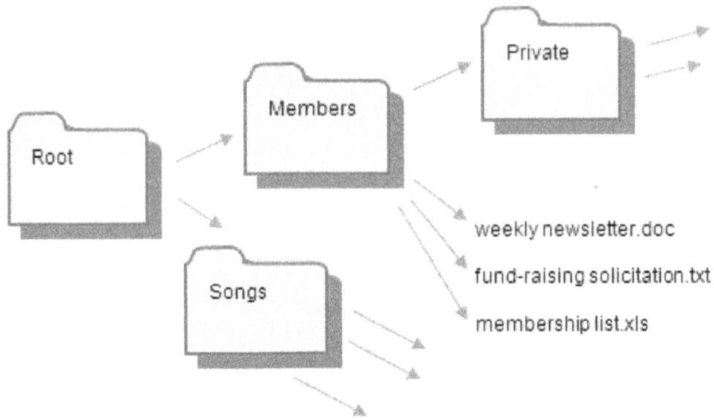


Disk Content Is Arranged Hierarchically in Folders

**Navigation** through a disk begins with the root folder and progresses until the desired content is located. Navigation is **logical** and not **physical.** This is because the actual (physical) location of a file on a disk is really of no concern to the user. The operating system stores files where it finds available space and not in a specific sequential order. To allow the user to navigate the operating system's file system maintains a directory that links logical content (folders) to the physical locations of files on the disk. This linkage is known as **mapping.**

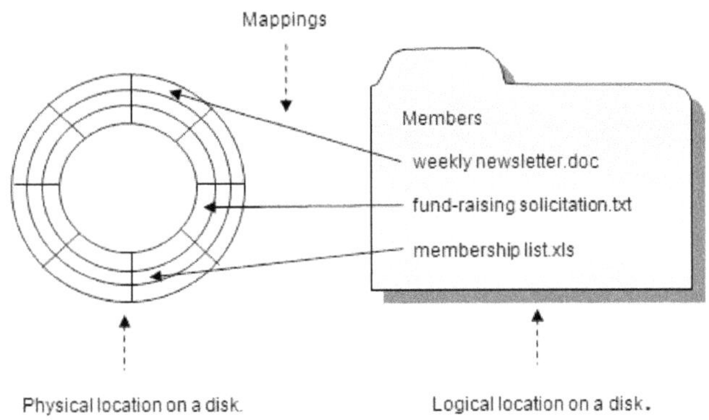


Disk Mapping

**Disk Fragmentation** As the disk fills with data, performance may suffer. When a file is saved to the hard drive, the operating system tries to keep everything in the same area (or cluster). Over time files will be deleted, leaving blank areas between files. When new programs are installed or large files saved, the hard drive tries to fill the holes thus breaking up the program or file into blocks. This situation is known as disk fragmentation and can cause serious performance degradation.

To understand how a disk gets fragmented and understand why it can harm your computer's performance you must understand how a disk is structured. Hard disks, CDs, and floppy disks are round and rotate. All rotating secondary storage defines sectors and tracks which intersect in blocks.

When a file (or document) is placed in secondary storage it fits in one block or, if it is too large for one block, it spreads over several blocks. No block ever contains parts of more than one file. It is desirable for files to be stored in **contiguous blocks** because the entire file can be accessed fastest that way. Suppose the first file stored on an otherwise empty disk requires four blocks of space. After that file is stored the disk would look as shown here:

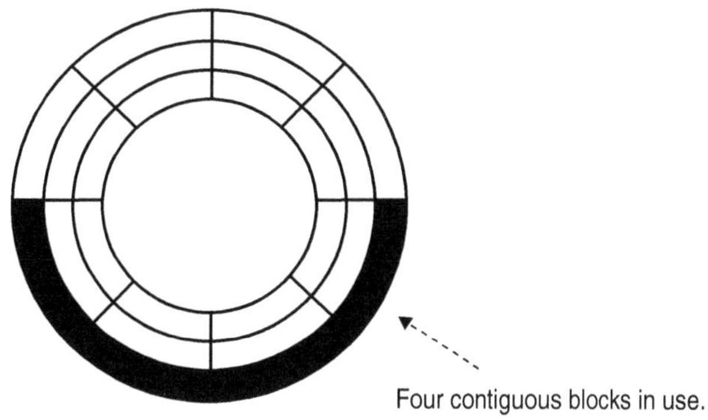


A File Is Stored on the Disk

As the disk fills up, fewer contiguous blocks of free disk space remain. As the disk fragments it becomes increasingly hard for the operating system to find open space for file storage.

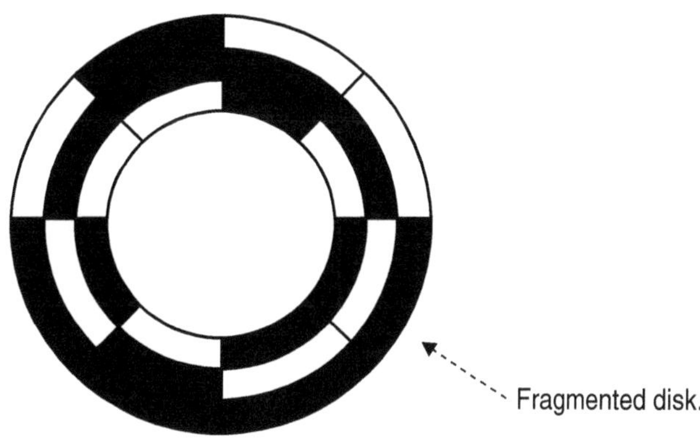


A Fragmented Disk

The solution to this problem is to **defragment** the disk. Windows includes a program called **Disk Defragmenter** which scans the entire disk drive and looks for segments of unused disk area. The segments are consolidated resulting in larger areas of contiguous space for the storage of larger files. Regular use of this program will help keep a computer running more efficiently and may prevent unexpected loss of data. It will also help the computer find files and documents faster.

**Deleting All Files from a Hard Disk** Sometimes it is desirable to delete all files from a disk. Often this is done when a previously used computer is sold or given away so that the new owner will not have access to the original user's data. Unfortunately most people believe that simply using Windows Explorer or Vista's Computer (or an equivalent program) to delete files and/or folders will do the job. This is not the case. This problem is relevant to people who sell, donate, or even throw away computers.

Explorer and Computer allow the user to manipulate entries in the disk's **directory** but do not actually allow the user to manipulate files directly. The directory is a logical list of folders and files on the disk with mapping references to the specific physical location of each file. Deleting a file does not remove the file's data from the storage device. Only the directory entry is removed.

For example, when a file is deleted it is moved to the Recycling Bin. What actually happens is that the directory entry for the file is altered to indicate that the file is now in the Recycling Bin folder. The actual physical location of the file is not changed. If the user empties the Recycling Bin the directory entries of all affected files are deleted but the files actually remain on the disk right where they were. The disk space used by the deleted file may now be re-used, but until it is re-used, a sophisticated user running a special program would be able to recover and view the "erased" data!

The solution to this problem is to use a **scrubber.** This special program overwrites each bit of data with a zero. For most users this is sufficient. For the United States Defense Department a more thorough cleansing is demanded. The DOD requires three separate overwrites, first zeros, next ones, finally a random zero or one. After scrubbing, the data truly is gone.

**Floppy Disk** A floppy disk is similar to a hard disk in that it stores data on a surface that rotates. Unlike the hard disk the platter is a flexible circular piece of metal-coated plastic. Floppy disks are considerably slower than hard disks and have limited storage capacity (1.44MB).

The main appeal of floppy disks was their portability. They were typically used to copy data or programs from one computer to another. Floppy disks were commonly used for file backup. Today floppy disks have largely been replaced by flash memory which offers portability with considerably greater storage capacity.

**Flash Memory** Flash, or solid state, memory is attractive because it is non-volatile, offers fast read access times (though not as fast as volatile RAM memory used for primary memory), has large data storage capacity (several GB is common), and has better shock resistance than hard disks. Flash memory is packaged in small portable units known as flash or jump drives which connect to the computer's USB port.

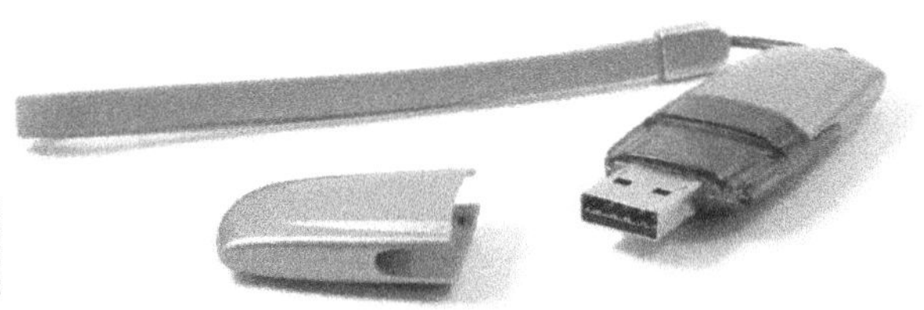



Flash Memory Packaged as a USB Drive

Although flash memory is **solid state** (an integrated circuit) and not rotational like a disk, the operating system and the flash hardware work together as if the memory were divided into track, sectors, and blocks. The flash drive is accessed by the user as if it were any **mass storage** device. Unlike a hard drive, which requires a hardware controller to operate, flash memory requires a device driver, software that allows the operating system to access the memory without consideration to its physical construction.

A flash drive consists of a circuit board encased in a plastic or metal casing, making the drive robust enough to be carried about in a pocket or on a lanyard. Only the USB connector extends from this protection, and is usually covered by a removable cap.

Flash Memory for a Digital Camera



**RAID** Redundant Array of Independent Disks (RAID) is a technique that divides or replicates data among multiple hard drives. Its benefits are increased data reliability (redundant storage) and throughput (allocation of data to separate devices). RAID is often found in fault tolerant computer systems where redundant data storage reduces the likelihood of data loss.

**Disk Mirroring** Disk mirroring is a technique that involves the replication of logical disk volumes (folder structures) onto separate hard disks in real time to ensure continuous availability of data. A mirrored volume is a complete copy of a logical disk volume. In the event of a disaster, disk mirroring can assist with recovery since the backup is a current and exact replication of the original that was lost. Mirroring is a function of the operating system and requires no manual intervention.

In a disaster recovery plan, disk mirroring can be arranged so that the mirror copy is in a different location, often at a substantial distance. Since the likelihood of disaster striking simultaneously at two distant locations is low this method provides a good level of data security.

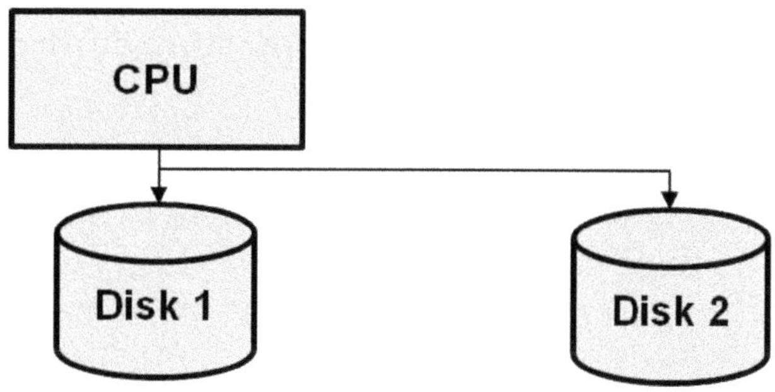


Disk Mirroring

**CD-ROM and DVD** The CD-ROM is an optical storage device that contains data accessible by a computer using a CD-Rom Drive. The compact disc format was originally designed for music storage and playback but the format was later adapted to hold any form of binary data. CD-ROMs are often used to distribute computer software, though any data can be stored on it. Unlike the hard disk which is magnetic, data is stored on the CD-ROM as a series of microscopic indentations called pits and the gaps between them called **lands**. A laser shines on the reflective surface of the disc to read the pattern of pits and lands. The pattern of the changing light intensity of the reflected beam is converted into binary data.

The storage capacity of most CD-ROMs is about 650MB of data. Originally CD-ROMs were read only devices (that is why they were called ROMs), but read/write technology has developed. The primary performance concern of CD-ROM drives is their speed. Speeds are expressed in terms of 1X, 2X, 4X, which is the number of times the drive is faster than the original CD-ROM reader.

CD-Recordable drives are usually sold with three different speed ratings, one for write-once operations, one for re-write operations, and one for read-only operations. The speeds are typically listed in that order.

DVD (Digital Versatile Disc) is also an optical rotational storage media format that can be used for storage of any type of data. DVDs appear similar to CDs because their physical dimensions are the same but they are encoded differently and at a much higher data storage density. DVDs offer considerably more storage capacity than CDs (4-5GB is common) but access speed is an issue as it is with CDs. Like CDs, DVDs can be used as rewriteable memory.

Several types of optical storage formats include:

- **CD-R**—Compact Disc-Recordable is a Write Once, Read Many (**WORM**) optical media which refers to a kind of computer storage media that can be written to once, but read from multiple times.
- **DVD-R**—Similar to CD-R but uses DVD technology and has higher capacity.

- **DVD+R**—Also DVD technology and similar to CD-R but not compatible with DVD-R.
- **CD-RW**—Compact Disc ReWritable is a rewritable optical disc CD format that is also known as CD-Erasable (CD-E).
- **DVD-RW**—A rewritable optical disc using DVD technology with equal storage capacity as a DVD-R.
- **DVD+RW**—Similar to, but not compatible with, DVD-RW.

**Zip Disk** Zip disks are a removable cartridge storage device that may be generally used to store compressed data. A zip drive has at least 100MB of storage capacity although its physical size is close to that of a floppy disk. A zip drive has considerable more tracks than a floppy (thousands compared to about 270) which results in greater storage capacity and faster access.

**Magnetic Tape** A tape drive is a data storage device that reads and writes data stored on a magnetic tape. Tape is generally used for archival storage of data stored on hard drives, and tape media generally has a lower cost per byte stored and offers longer archival stability.

Tape drives only allow for **sequential-access** of data and not random-access to data as hard disk drives do. A hard-disk drive can move its read/write head to any random part of the disk platters in a short amount of time while a tape drive spends considerable time rolling tape back and forth between reels to locate particular data. Tape drives, therefore, have slow average seek times. Despite this disadvantage, tape drives can **stream** data to tape very quickly.

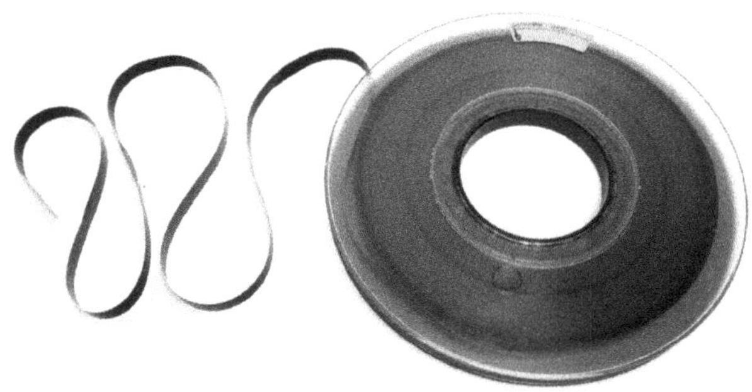



Magnetic Tape

## Pause to Review #4

### Try this:

1. If a computer has 2GB of RAM, how many bytes are in RAM?
2. Use Vista's computer to determine the capacity of your computer's hard disk.
3. What portion of your hard disk is free?

Type your answers in the window provided by Pamela.

### What do you think?

1. Why does a computer system require persistent storage?
2. What is the role of RAM in a computer?
3. Why does a disk become fragmented and why is that a problem?
4. Why does virtual memory assist in enabling multitasking?

### *Communication Devices*

Early computers were said to be stand-alone units because they were not connected to other computers and usually had no need for sharing data. The opposite is true today as almost all computers are connected to the Internet. Connectivity requires that a computer's digital signals be translated into signals that are carried by a communication network. This is usually the task of a modem. Several communication components are described here. A thorough discussion of communication and networking equipment is found in another chapter.

**Modem** A modem is a device that modulates a carrier's signal to encode a computer's digital data, and later **demodulates** the signal to decode the data at the receiving end. The purpose is to produce a signal that can be transmitted easily and decoded to reproduce the original digital data. Modems are rated by the amount of data they can send in a given time, measured in bits per second, or bps.

Historically the most common example of a modem turns the computer's digital 1s and 0s into sounds that can be transmitted over **analog** telephone lines. The process is reversed at the receiving end as **digital** signals are detected in the sounds as they are received. Modems of this type generally run up to 56Kbps (56,000 bits per second). In reality, this is a theoretical limit and a 56K bps modem will not be able to transmit at this rate.

© Anthony Berenyi, 2008, Shutterstock.

Modem with Phone In/Out Ports

Today newer modems are commonplace because the local communication backbone for computer transmission has shifted from **dial-up** to **cable** and **DSL** carriers.

Cable modems are designed to deliver **broadband** Internet access by modulating a data signal over the cable television system's infrastructure. Like DSL modems, cable modems are capable of transmitting 256Kbps or more—in fact much more.

**Digital Subscriber Line** (DSL) a technology that provides high-speed digital data transmission over the wires of the local telephone network which is known as the **local loop.** Computer signals are modulated and transmitted over the local network where they are delivered to high-speed Internet carriers. Use of this technology permits simultaneous use of a telephone line for phone calls and data transmission. Generally DSL service is not as fast as cable-based communication which relies on the television system for transmission.

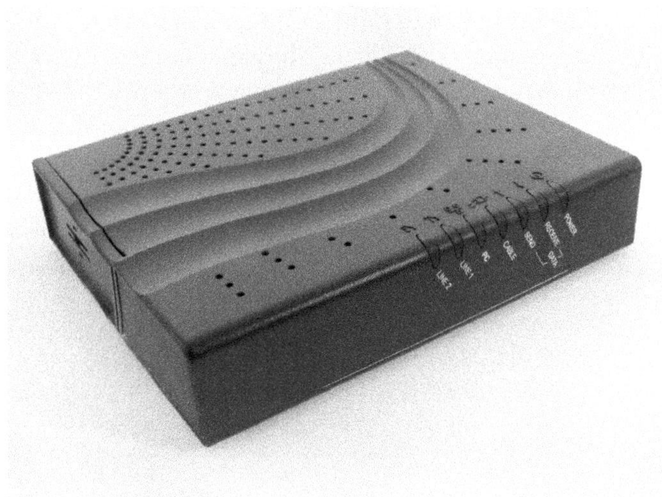



A Cable Modem

The signal delivered to the computer from the cable or DSL modem enters the computer through a network adaptor. Today virtually all new computers have the adaptor built in. In fact, the same adaptor can accept a signal from either type of modem.

**Wireless** A variation on the delivery mechanism between the modem and the computer is to use a wireless system to transmit the modem's signal to the computer which has a receiver. The modem is connected to a device known as a **wireless router** which attaches the data signal to a radio-based carrier signal for transmission to computers in the local vicinity. The router is known as an **access point** (AP). This arrangement, also known as **Wi-Fi**, provides a signal to any computer within range to receive it.

Such open signals can present a security risk for these reasons:

- **Intercepted data**—Data transmitted "over the air" can be intercepted.
- **Security breach**—Intrusions into the computer system are possible.
- **Unauthorized use**—Illegitimate use of the wireless router can slow down the transmission rates of legitimate users.

For these reasons it is best to **encrypt** wireless signals. Encryption involves disguising the bytes being transmitted so that an intruder is unable to read the bytes and to understand their content.

Wireless Router

## Computer Styles

There are several configurations that computers are found in. Today we are most familiar with personal computers, but there are **mainframes** and **super computers** as well. Personal computers, generally used by one person at a time, are available in **desktop** and **laptop** models. Mainframe computers, used typically by many people simultaneously, provide the processing power required by large organizations. Super computers are extremely powerful and expensive machines and are used for special purposes. Since personal computers are generally understood, mainframe and super computers are described here.

### Mainframe

Mainframes are computers used mainly by large organizations like government agencies, large companies, universities, the military, and research laboratories for **mission critical**

Mainframe Computer

requirements. Typically these machines are used for bulk data processing activities like census tabulation, preparation of customer statements, maintenance of student information systems, human resource record keeping, and inventory management.

The term mainframe originated during the 1960s to contrast with the newly introduced smaller computers which became known as minicomputers. As previously noted, mainframes and minicomputers generally shared the same technology but were packaged differently.

Mainframes have proven powerful and robust over the years. In fact, most mainframes operate continuously and maintenance is performed while the machines remain in operation. Dependability is a hallmark of these computers—since they are used for support of critical applications, downtime could be catastrophic. Reports of intrusive attacks against mainframes are rare even though they often support thousands of simultaneous users.

### Super Computer

A super computer is a machine that processes data exceptionally fast. Super computers are used for calculation-intensive tasks such as economic and weather **forecasting,** climate research, molecular modeling, **simulations** of physical events (like nuclear fusion experimentation and airplane wind tunnel tests), and computer-based cryptography. Major universities, military agencies, and scientific research laboratories are heavy users and may share super computers due to the high expense. Super computers are typically one-of-a-kind custom designs and often become outdated as newer and faster technology is developed.

Super Computer

## Moore's Law

Moore's Law is based on the empirical observation made in 1965 by Gordon E. Moore, a co-founder of Intel, that the number of transistors on an integrated circuit for a given cost doubles every 24 months. Moore's Law relates to the rapidly continuing advance in computing power per unit cost, because increase in transistor count is also a surrogate measure of computer processing power.

The implication of Moore's Law for computer component suppliers is significant. A typical major design project (such as a new CPU) takes between two and five years to reach production. Consequently, component manufacturers face timescale pressures to complete projects and get new products into production quickly and achieve sales.

The law also has an impact on information system developers. System development projects take a long time (usually years) and the price of computer processing power will fall between the beginning and end of a project. This is because the **price/performance ratio** of a product, which refers to a product's ability to deliver performance for its price, changes over time. This means that one dollar spent 24 months from now will buy twice the processing power than if spent today. Knowing this, a project director should attempt to defer purchase of hardware until it is absolutely needed and not early in a project.

## Source Data Automation

Did you ever use an ATM (automatic teller machine), vote at the ballpark for the major league all-star team, register for college courses by telephone, pay at the store with a bank card, or have items you wish to purchase scanned at the checkout line? If you did, then you have experienced source data automation. Simply put, it is the use of special equipment to collect data at the source and send it directly to the computer for processing.

Why is this important? Well, think about it. If your data is directly collected and sent to the computer then:

- It will get there **faster.**
- May have **fewer errors** because it does not have to be entered by an intermediary (like a bank teller).
- Will be **less expensive** (because there are no intermediaries to hire).

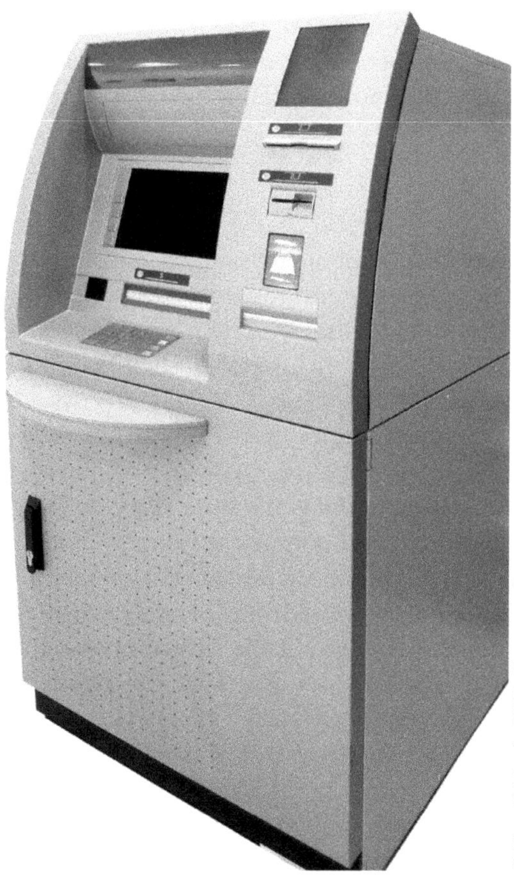



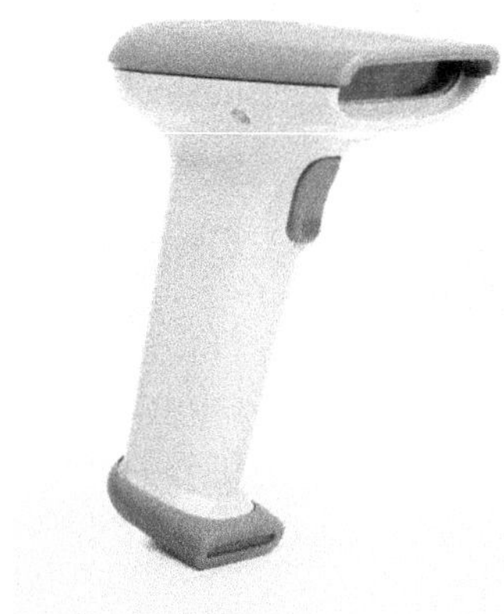



Source Data Automation

There are many uses for source data automation. Look around, you will surely think of others!

## Recycling Hardware

When hardware ceases to operate properly or when it ceases to meet your requirements, it may be disposed of in several ways.

### Donating a Computer

Organizations exist that reuse old hardware and distribute the resulting systems to those who would benefit even from an older computer. Since discarding old electronic equipment in landfills or incineration not only wastes valuable resources, but also releases potentially hazardous materials into the environment, donation should be considered. Prior to donating a computer, be sure that any personal or private data on the hard drive is permanently erased. A scrubber program should be used for that purpose.

If donation is not possible or if the equipment is beyond continued use, some companies also recycle hardware, such as discarded printers. However, unlike toner cartridge recycling, these can involve a cost to the consumer for shipping and handling.

### Toner Cartridges

Toner cartridges have a life span limited by the volume of toner they contain, and toner cartridge manufacturers design the components of their products to be able to function throughout this life span. When the toner supply is exhausted recycling is an option. All the major manufacturers of toner cartridges offer some way to recycle their cartridges, usually in the form of a prepaid mailer that comes with the cartridge.

## Chapter Review

Hardware is the physical part of a computer system. It includes the electronic circuitry, input and output devices, data and program storage devices, memory for program execution, communication equipment, and, most important of all, the processor that performs calculations and controls all equipment. It is distinguished from software programs that execute within the hardware as data is processed. A computer system's hardware is infrequently changed in contrast to software as new programs are more frequently installed and older ones updated.

Data processing using a computer follows the Input-Process-Output model. The computer's input (keyboard, mouse, etc.) and output hardware (monitor, printer, etc.) support the activities of the model. As data is processed it may be necessary to store (for later use) or retrieve additional data. Data storage is provided by persistent memory devices (hard disks, CD/DVD-ROMS, and jump drives). During the data processing activity programs are loaded into RAM (volatile memory) for execution. To assist with speeding up processing, a computer system employs special high-speed cache memory.

While electronic computers are a relatively new invention, a long history of research and development preceded their introduction around the time of World War II. Early mechanical attempts were remarkable in their time but hampered by reliance on a decimal scheme for coding data and program instructions. Electronic computers are binary machines, and data representation, using schemes like ASCII, greatly simplified and promoted interoperability among products of different vendors.

Hardware is the physical part of a computer system, but it would be impossible to process data into information with a computer alone. The operating system gives a series of instructions that command the hardware to act in specific ways. The OS facilitates the operation of application programs and provides them access to resources like files, databases, and hardware.

## Mini Quiz

Answer these questions in the window provided by Pamela.

**1.** Magnetic tape, floppy disks, and CDs are all examples of __________ devices.
   A. storage
   B. input
   C. output
   D. multimedia
   E. processing

**2.** A device that sends information into a computer is considered to be an output device.
   A. True
   B. False

**3.** A computer cannot disobey programming instructions.
   A. True
   B. False

**4.** Hardware is the sequence of instructions that tells the computer what to do.
   A. True
   B. False

**5.** Match the computer component on the left with a description on the right.

| | |
|---|---|
| A. ___ Bus | a. Provides cooling |
| B. ___ Port | b. Carries data, control signals or power |
| C. ___ Bay | c. Doorway |
| D. ___ Heat pipe | d. Holds auxiliary hardware |

**6.** Match the term on the left with a description on the right.

| | |
|---|---|
| A. ___ Machine language | a. Manager |
| B. ___ RISC | b. Reduced instruction set computer |
| C. ___ Register | c. Object code |
| D. ___ Control unit | d. Where data is stored and processed in processor |

**7.** Match the term on the left with a description on the right.

| | |
|---|---|
| A. ___ Gigabyte | a. Reduction in number of bytes to store data |
| B. ___ Data compression | b. Keyboard layout |
| C. ___ QWERTY | c. 1,000 megabytes |
| D. ___ LCD | d. Liquid crystal display |

**8.** The possibility of a computer understanding spoken input is known as:
A. Speech synthesis
B. Speech recognition
C. Channeling

**9.** Which is not a measure of printer performance?
A. DPI
B. Refresh rate
C. PPM

**10.** What type of memory is used in multitasking systems to create the appearance of more primary memory than there really is?
A. RAM
B. Jump Drive
C. Virtual
D. Tape

**11.** The speed of moving data from a random access device to the CPU is known as:
A. Seek time
B. Bus time
C. Data transfer rate
D. Rotational delay

**12.** On a disk, the intersection of a sector and track is a:
A. Byte
B. BIOS
C. Block
D. Fragment

**13.** When accessing data, what type of storage would provide fastest access?
A. RAM
B. Tape
C. Disk
D. Cache
E. Flash

**14.** Which input device does not translate physical human movements into data?
A. Keyboard
B. Mouse
C. Scanner
D. Microphone
E. Touch screen

**15.** A Terabyte is how many Megabytes?
A. 10
B. 100
C. 1,000
D. 10,000
E. 100,000
F. 1,000,000
G. 10,000,000

## Exercises

**1.** Write a description for these concepts and components:
   A. IPO model
   B. CPU
   C. Transistor
   D. Integrated circuit
   E. ASCII
   F. Motherboard
   G. BIOS
   H. Port
   I. Primary memory
   J. Secondary memory
   K. Virtual memory
   L. Mainframe
   M. Super computer

**2.** Identify and describe three each of:
   A. Input devices
   B. Output devices
   C. Storage devices
   D. Bus

**3.** Assume you are purchasing a computer system for your business. Considering Moore's Law, by what percent could you buy additional processing power if you waited 12 months to make the purchase by spending the same amount?

**4.** How many different characters would be available in a system of 5-bit bytes?

**5.** Considering ASCII codes, answer these questions:
   A. What sequence of bits is used to represent the words: July Fourth
   B. Examining the ASCII chart, can you determine the relationship between upper- and lowercase versions of the same letter?
   C. How many bits would be needed in a byte to represent all upper-case letters, 10 digits, and the punctuation keys on the keyboard?

**6.** Using the information provided in this chapter, what is the ASCII-bit pattern and decimal equivalent for these characters. Assume the first bit for each character is zero. The remaining 7 bits are to be determined by you.
   A. &
   B. +
   C. G
   D. g
   E. R
   F. t
   G. h

**7.** What is the sequence of bits that represents **Good Morning!**? Assume that the first bit for each character is a zero. The remaining 7 bits per byte should be determined by you. Provide a total of 8 bits per character. You will need to consult a complete ASCII table to answer this question.

**8.** Write a short paper that describes how the invention and implementation of the personal computer has impacted and changed the world. How has your life been changed by this technology?

**9.** Answer these questions about the early development of computing:
   A. What is the Analytical Engine and why was it important?
   B. What is the Jacquard Loom?
   C. Who was Herman Hollerith, and why is he important in the history of computing?

**10.** You have a $1,150 budget available for purchasing a computer and peripheral devices for school work. The computer is to last for four years of school. Decide what hardware and software you require. Visit retail stores or shop online and select three candidate configurations that satisfy your requirements and your budget. Identify which package is your first choice. Explain your decision-making process.

**11.** Moore's Law suggests that the price/performance ratio of hardware changes over time. Assuming that this is correct, what price would you pay in 18 months for hardware that costs $1,000 today?

**12.** Download FRAGMENTED.TXT from Pamela. The file represents a fragmented disk. Reorganize the blocks so that each file occupies contiguous space. Place the first reorganized block in sector 0 of track 0 and continue sequentially until all blocks are reorganized. Select the files in the order of blocks occupied. If two or more files occupy the same number of blocks, order the files alphabetically.

**13.** Download PUNCHCARD.DOCX from Pamela. The document displays a punch card used for data storage in earlier computers. The document also explains the significance of the arrangement of holes in the card. Translate the card's data into ASCII codes.

**14.** Cache memory is used to store copies of frequently-accessed data. Download CACHE.TXT from Pamela. The file lists data that programs have requested over the last ten minutes. It also identifies the size of storage requirements and the frequency of requests. Based on the information provided, decide what data should be maintained in cache.

## Discussion Questions

**1.** Why does data remain on a disk after the file containing it has been deleted?

**2.** Describe what disk fragmentation is and what to do about it.

**3.** What must be done to permanently delete data or information from a disk?

**4.** What is the fundamental difference between flash memory and most other types of secondary storage devices?

**5.** Suggest three possible applications for super computers.

**6.** Why would different processors each have their own unique machine language?

**7.** What is the file system?

**8.** What is the difference between memory and storage?

**9.** List the major parts of a computer and describe the function of each.

**10.** What is Moore's law? What implications does it have for system developers?

**11.** Describe three types of memory and the uses of each.

**12.** What is ASCII code and how is it used?

**13.** What are ports?

**14.** How do busses affect a computer's processing speed?

**15.** What was the significance of Jacquard's invention?

**16.** What is a mainframe?

17. Some people prefer to use online storage services. Discuss why using online storage might be desirable and identify three such services.
18. Considering the history of pre-electronic inventions that preceded the electronic computer, which do you believe contributed most significantly to the development of electronic data processing? Why?
19. Not all computer users require the same CPU power or amount of RAM or secondary storage. How would you assess the hardware needs of a user?
20. Considering secondary storage options available for data backup, what are the tradeoffs between using different storage media.
21. Considering the needs of the visually impaired, investigate hardware solutions available to assist such persons with computer usage.
22. What are the advantages of using speech recognition software? Investigate speech recognition software and discuss challenges to be overcome if it is to be widely used.

## Activities

1. Use Disk Defragmenter or another tool to determine how fragmented your computer's hard disk is, then defragment the disk.
2. Determine how much disk space is assigned as virtual memory in your computer.
3. Visit a computer lab on your campus and meet the lab director. Learn what the largest challenges facing the director are. Ask the director how software and hardware are maintained in the lab.
4. Contact an organization that accepts donations of used computers. Find out what the organization requires before accepting a computer. Also describe what you would do to ensure that your personal data was not revealed to the new user of the computer.
5. When purchasing new equipment at a retail store, a customer is usually offered an extended service contract for an additional charge. Determine the details of service contracts offered by two large retail vendors and compare the coverage provided, as well as the cost.

Software is one of three building blocks of an information system; hardware and the community of stakeholders are the other two. Each is important in its own right, and hardware and systems analysis are the subjects of other chapters. Here the topic is software which is defined as:

> **Software** – Software is data and computer programs. It is not physical and cannot be directly seen. Computer programs execute within the hardware and enable a computer to perform specific tasks. Programs include **system software** such as an operating system, which enables other software to run properly and **application software** such as a word processor or database manager, which enables a user to perform a task.

The differences between software and hardware seem straightforward, but can be confusing. Hardware is easier to understand than software. You see hardware and you see data on a computer screen, too, yet data is software. Hardware makes it possible to view data. In fact, without hardware you could not store data or computer programs.

This may help: you take notes in class and your notes are data. You use hardware (paper and pencil) to record and store your notes (data). To view your data (notes) you must take out your notebook (hardware). The same is true of computer-based data. Data (and programs) are stored on disks or on other storage devices. Disks are hardware not software.

## Software

Software is **data** and it is also **programs** that enable a computer to perform specific tasks. It is not hardware which is the physical component of the computer system. Programs include **application software** such as a word processor, which enables a user to perform a task, and such as the **operating system** (known as system software), which enables other programs to run properly by interfacing the hardware, other software, and the computer user.

**Charles Babbage** proposed the idea of reading instructions into a machine's memory for the purpose of controlling computations. His plan for the Analytical Engine was to use punch cards as the source of program and data. While Babbage's ideas of the early 1800s could not be tested until the last century, they did prove valid and modern computing environments that process data are based on his conceptualization.

Before discussing what computer programs are and what they do, how they are written, and what programming languages are available, we will investigate the relationship between programs and three important partners: hardware, data, and users. The following illustration partitions the world of software to programs and data. The focus of this chapter is computer programs; data is the subject of Chapter 8, Data and Information. For the balance of this chapter the term software will refer to computer programs. The process of writing computer programs is described in Chapter 7, Computer Programming.

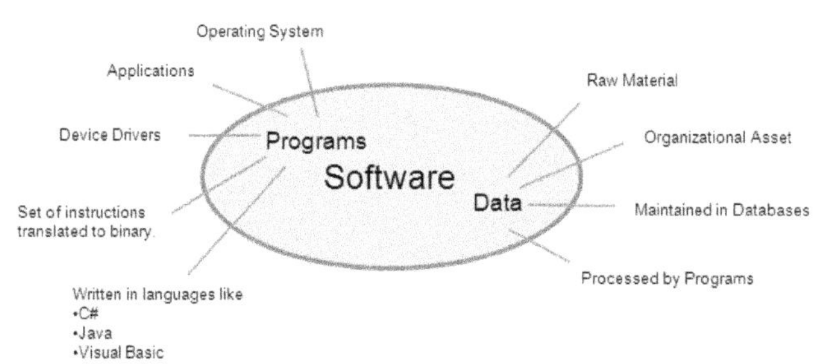


Software: Programs and Data

### Software's Relationship to Hardware

Computer software directs the actions of computer hardware. Software is loaded into memory **(RAM)** and executed in the central processing unit **(CPU).** The operating system determines when specific application programs are loaded for execution. Programs that require access to files on the disk drive communicate with the **file system** (system software) which retrieves or updates data. The file system communicates to storage devices (hardware) through special system programs known as **device drivers.** When an application program wishes to print or perform other external functions, device drivers are activated by the operating system after the application program makes a request.

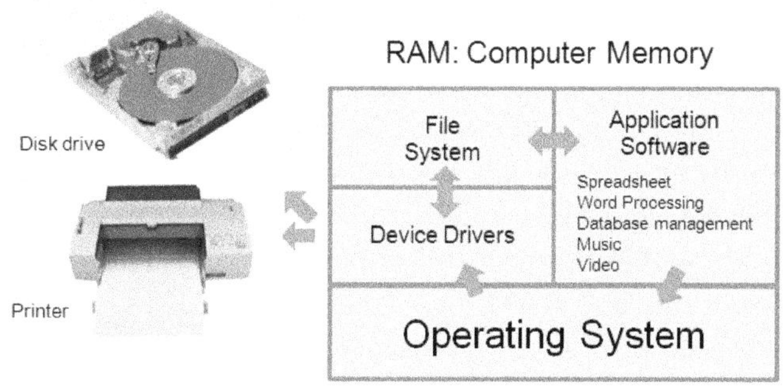


Software and Hardware

## Software's Relationship to Data

Software is the intermediary between electronic hardware and data, which hardware processes according to the sequence of instructions given in computer programs. Data is generally considered the input or output of executed software. Data is visually presented by hardware (monitor, printer, speaker, etc.); it cannot be seen by itself.

## Software's Relationship to Computer Programming

Application software is usually written in **high-level** programming languages that are easier and more efficient for humans to use than the machine's native language. These high-level languages known as **source code** are translated into **machine language**. Software at its most basic level is a collection of binary digits (1 and 0) that are defined by the machine language specific to the individual processor. Machine language is defined groups of binary digits signifying processor instructions (**object code**). Software is an ordered sequence of instructions that change the state of the hardware. The process of translating source code to machine language is described in Chapter 7, Computer Programming.

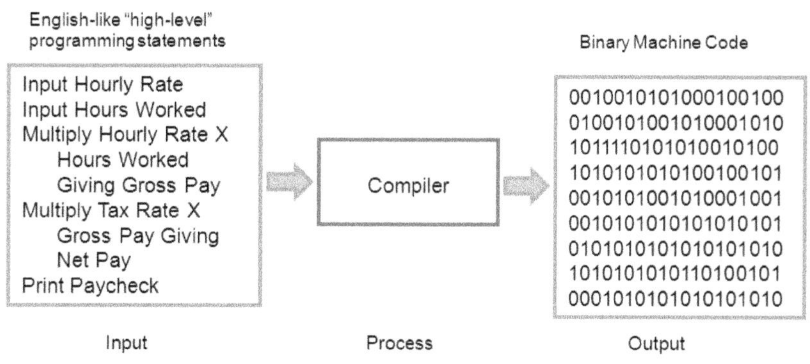


Computer Programs

## Software's Relationship to People

Programs execute because users want them to. The operating system (**OS**), a program which allows the execution of programs, runs because a person has booted a computer. When the user, interacting with the operating system's interface, requests that a program be started, the OS responds by directing the hardware to fetch the program from storage (usually a disk) and load it into RAM. It is the user who initiates these activities.

### Software's Relationships

These relationships between software and its partners can be summarized as follows:

No computer is useful without programs to give it commands. A computer cannot even run without a specific type of program called an operating system, or OS. This program is like the government in that it is in charge. Once the computer starts up, the OS tells each piece of hardware when it is allowed to act. The OS is also responsible for loading programs from disk into RAM for execution. The OS authorizes generation of the images seen on a monitor or printed on paper. Nothing happens without the approval of the OS.

The relationship between hardware, user, OS, and other programs (**application programs**) is depicted in the figure below. As you can see neither the user nor the application software directly commands the hardware. Any command given by the user, such as requesting the display of a folder's content, printing a document, or updating a database, is intercepted by the OS which then constructs a formal command for the hardware to perform.

In a spreadsheet program like Excel, each time the mouse is moved making a new cell active the spreadsheet program asks the OS to command the hardware to allow the screen to be re-drawn showing the new active cell.

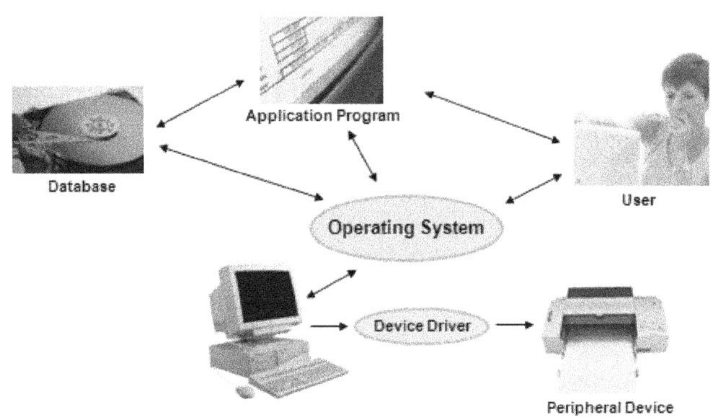


Software's Relationships

From our earlier discussion, recall that software is data and programs. Software is stored in files as a collection of bytes. Each file could be either a program or data. You probably know about data (images, sound, etc.) which is why the focus of this chapter is on the other kind of software, computer programs. This chapter discusses operating systems and application programs followed by consideration of system architecture and design.

## The Operating System

General-purpose computers, including mainframes and personal computers, have an operating system to control hardware, present a user interface, manage files, and run other programs. Examples of operating systems for personal computers include Microsoft Windows, Linux, and Mac OS X. Original electronic computers did not have operating systems. However, software tools for managing those systems appeared soon afterward, and gradually expanded in scope becoming the basis for operating systems of today.

An **operating system** (OS) is the master program controlling all resources within a computer. Control of the operating system is up to the user. A significant advantage gained by using Windows is the **graphical user interface (GUI),** making the use of the computer and associated programs visually intuitive thus eliminating the obtuse command languages of the past which required memorizing command **syntax** (*the words and grammar of a language*).

Once the computer starts up, the OS tells each piece of hardware when it is allowed to act. The OS is also responsible for loading programs from disk into **RAM** (computer memory) for execution. The OS generates the images seen on a monitor or printed on paper. Nothing happens without the approval of the OS. This process of starting the computer is known as **booting up.** When power is applied to the computer, a small program in firmware known as the **Basic Input/Output System** (BIOS), is run. Its primary function is to stabilize the machine and devices on the motherboard so that the **operating system** can be loaded and can take control of the computer.

The relationship between hardware, user, OS, and other programs (**application programs**) is depicted here. As you can see neither the user nor the application software directly commands the hardware. Any command you give is intercepted by the OS which then constructs a formal command for the hardware to perform.

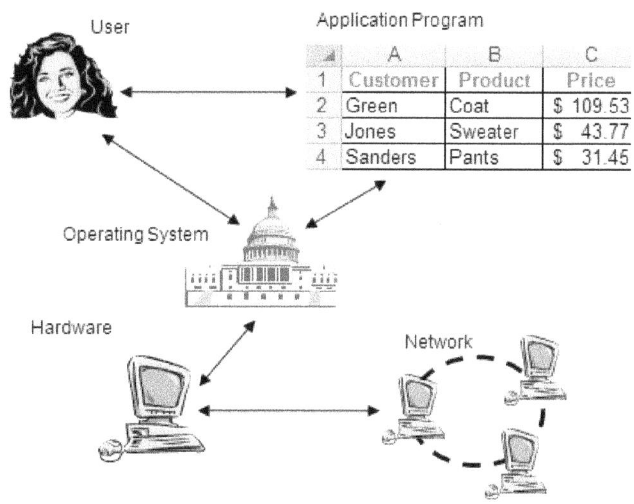


The Role of the Operating System

It may sound pretty complicated, and it is, but it does work. There are a variety of very excellent technical reasons for this arrangement. The primary reason is that by allowing the OS to know how to command each hardware device the same knowledge is not needed redundantly in each program that you use. This feature is known as **device independence.**

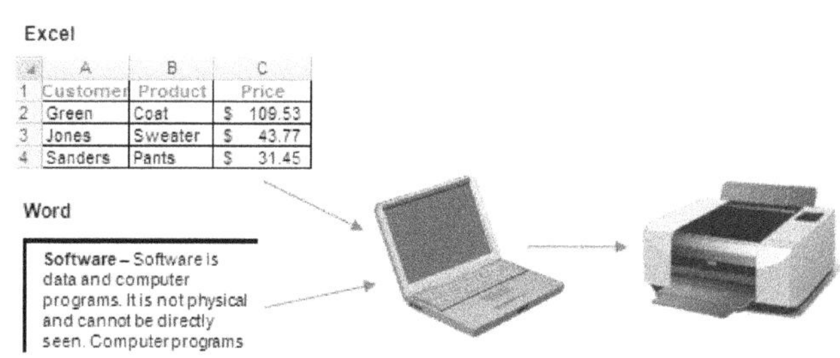


Windows Permits Device Independence

## What an Operating System Does

All operating systems perform the same collection of basic tasks. In this section those tasks are enumerated and described.

- **Process management**—The operating system runs programs and allocates memory. Every program on a computer is run as a **process.** Only one process per CPU can actually be run at a time. Modern operating systems are able to simulate the execution of many simultaneous processes by doing what is known as **multitasking.** Process management is the operating system's way of dealing with running multiple processes. Multitasking is accomplished by simply switching from one process or another quickly and is known as **context switching.** As more processes run, the time available for each diminishes and may result in the system **thrashing.** It is the responsibility of the OS to recognize this situation before it becomes a problem by prioritizing time allocations.

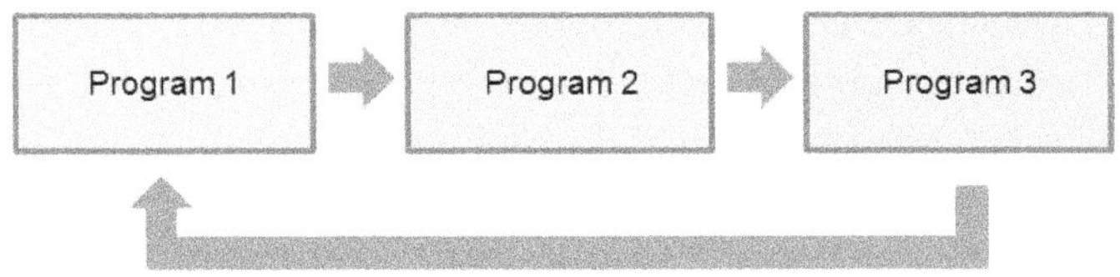


The Operating System Controls Multitasking

- **Memory management**—There are many demands for the computer's memory and the OS must allocate memory sensibly. Although there are several types of memory to manage (cache, RAM, disk), as the OS tracks what is needed and what is available it allocates and deallocates memory accordingly. One of the most important tools available to the OS is swapping between main memory and secondary memories. This is known as **virtual memory** management (described in Chapter 3, Hardware) and greatly increases the amount of memory available for a process.
- **File System**—Any operating system has thousands and possibly hundreds of thousands of files stored in directories and subdirectories that must be managed. Files are persistently stored on disk (or other storage device) and must be located, read, and copied into RAM for processing as needed. This happens frequently (even continuously) as programs execute. Keeping track of the physical location of files is an important task. Large files (especially databases) may not occupy contiguous portions of the disk (consecutive **blocks**) thus making the task more difficult to manage. As the disk fills and files are added, updated, and deleted the disk may become **fragmented** and performance suffers. The file system should provide tools like disk defragmenters for managing the disk's hygiene.
- **Mapping**—Navigation through a disk begins with the route folder and progresses until the desired content is located. **Navigation** is **logical** and not **physical.** This is because the actual (physical) location of a file on a disk is really of no concern to the user. The operating system stores files where it finds available space and not in a specific sequential order. To allow the user to navigate, the operating system's file system maintains a directory that links logical content (folders) to the physical locations of files on the on the disk. This linkage is known as **mapping.**
- **File Associations**—All files (documents) of the same type will have the same file extension. For example: all files with the extension DOCX are Microsoft Word documents. This means that they were created using Word and that Word must be used to edit or print those documents. For instance, the name of a file containing a term paper might be "English Term Paper.docx". "English Term Paper" is descriptive of the contents of the file and "docx" indicates that this is a Microsoft Word document.

The linkage between a file and a program is important. Windows handles this **association** automatically since it knows that DOCX means a Word Document, XLSX means an Excel Workbook and so on. The significance is that if you double-click an icon for an XLSX file it opens in Excel automatically. If you right click an icon for a PPTX file it displays a menu of options for a PowerPoint presentation!

Right Click on an Icon to Display a Menu Based on Associated File Type

The complete list of all file extensions is too extensive to display here—no one knows for sure how many different extensions exist because many are proprietary. Several commonly used file types and their associated extensions are listed here:

| Extension | Purpose |
|---|---|
| BMP | Image File |
| DOCX | Word Document |
| EXE | Computer Program |
| GIF | Image File |
| JPG | Image File |
| ACCDB | Access Database |
| MP3 | Music File |
| PPTX | PowerPoint Presentation |
| TXT | Text File |
| WAV | Sound File |
| XLSX | Excel Workbook |

Common File Extensions

- **Networking**—Most operating systems are capable of using networking **protocols** like **TCP/IP.** This means that systems can appear on a network and share resources such as storage devices, printers, and scanners with other computers. It also means that computers can connect to the Internet and operate as **clients** or **servers** (see Chapter 2, Internet and World Wide Web and Chapter 5, Data Communications and Networking). Some operating systems (especially mainframe systems) support older vendor specific protocols like IBM's SNA.
- **Security**—Security involves **authenticating** users (people and other computers) prior to allowing access and limiting user access to functions that are permitted. Since most computers are now attached to networks, a critical aspect of security is preventing unauthorized **intrusion** into a computer system. Common violations include: virus attachment, Trojan horse penetration, denial of service attack, being an intermediary for another attack, and spyware installation. Chapter 11, Security, Ethics, and Privacy has more information.
- **Graphical User Interfaces**—Today, most operating systems provide Graphical User Interfaces (**GUIs**, pronounced "gooey") enabling users and computer operators to command the computer using a mouse or other **pointing device.** Pictures representing objects **(icons)** make it easier to provide access to system components. Some operating systems are more graphical than others and some are more flexible in that commands may also be entered on the **command line.** The interface is more a matter of style and not an indication of the operating system's power.

- **Device drivers**—A device driver is computer software that allows interaction with hardware devices. This constitutes an **interface** for communicating with the device through the computer bus or communications system the hardware is connected to. Each device driver is specific to a particular hardware device coupled with a specific operating system.

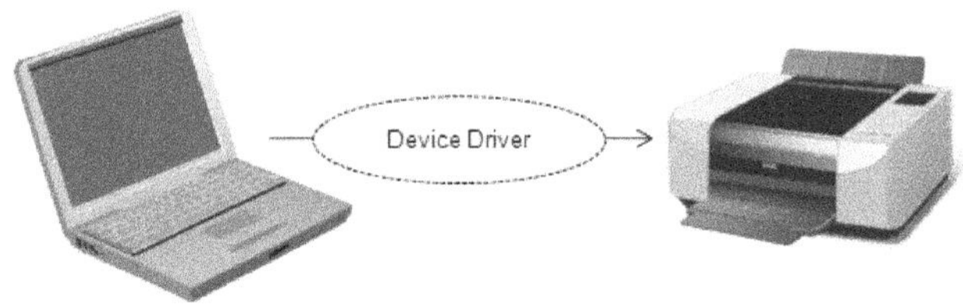


Device Driver Directs Hardware

The objective of this arrangement is **abstraction.** Every model of peripheral hardware is different (for example all printers). As newer models are released operating systems cannot be expected to know how to control every new device. To solve this problem the OS relies on the device driver to translate application requirements (print this page, store this image, etc.) to device specific actions.

## Windows

Microsoft's Windows operating system originated as a **graphical** layer on top of MS-DOS for the IBM PC. In essence the original versions of Windows were not operating systems but a shell that surrounded the challenging **syntax** of the operating system DOS. Later versions of Windows became operating systems in their own right and the DOS interface faded into obscurity. The most recent addition to the Windows family is **Windows Vista** which was released in 2007. Windows is a 64-bit operating system that runs on 32-bit and 64-bit Intel and AMD processors. Microsoft remains the dominant vendor of desktop operating system software.

Windows offers a **graphical user interface** (GUI) but did not present the first graphically oriented **point and click** environment. Apple was the first company to commercialize that concept which it borrowed from research of the 1960s at Xerox Palo Alto Research Center (PARC). The concept of the **mouse** interacting with **icons** was first developed there.

While Windows provides many excellent features (including **multitasking**—the ability to run several programs simultaneously), perhaps its most significant contribution was that it opened the computing door to many people afraid of or unable to use the command syntax and structure of DOS.

Specific operations using Windows Vista are presented in Appendix C.

### *Windows Registry*

An important component that assists Windows in remaining organized and running efficiently is the **Registry.** It is a database which stores settings and options for the operation of the computer including information about the hardware, software, and users. Changes made, for example, to **Control Panel** settings, file associations, or by software installations are reflected and stored in the registry. The Windows Registry was introduced to clean up the disorganized distribution of configuration files (INI files) that had previously been used to store configuration settings for individual programs. These files tended to be scattered all over the system, which made them difficult to keep track of.

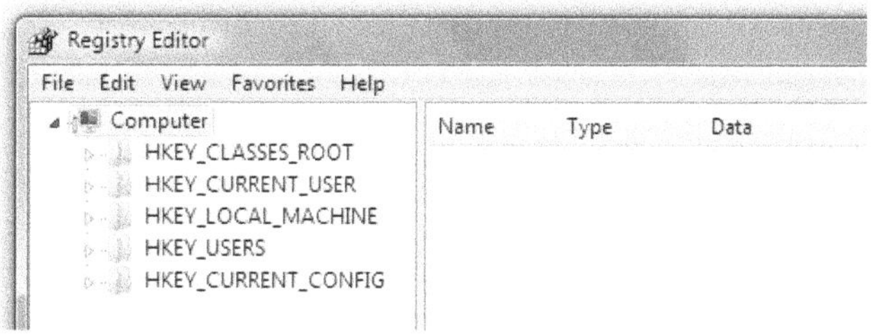


Windows Registry

## Unix

Unix or UNIX was originally developed in the 1960s and 1970s by a group of engineers at AT&T's **Bell Labs.** Although it did not initially catch on commercially, Unix gained attention in academic environments. The most notable Unix offspring, **BSD-Unix,** was created at the University of California, Berkeley and later deployed by Sun Microsystems which offers a version of Unix as its **Solaris** operating system. Today, Unix is used in both servers and workstations. The Unix environment and the client-server model that defined it were important constructs in the development of the Internet as computing became centered in networks rather than in individual computers.

The programming language **C,** also developed at AT&T and used in the development of Unix, was distributed with Unix for free to academic institutions and government agencies. The wide deployment of both caused them to be ported to a greater variety of platforms than any other operating system or programming language. Unix became synonymous with **open systems** or **free software.**

As an operating system perhaps ahead of its time, Unix was designed as portable, multitasking, and multi-user. Architecturally, Unix was assembled from a large number of small programs that were strung together as **pipes** to complete larger functions. This arrangement efficiently delivered software components as required rather then relying on larger programs that provided more functionality than was necessary. It also permitted customization of the OS installation giving more flexibility.

Unix is based on a master control program, the **kernel** which provides services to start and stop programs, handles the file system, schedules access to hardware to avoid conflicts, and provides common "high level" tasks that many programs require.

## Linux

Linux is a **Unix-like** computer operating system and is one of the most significant examples of **open source development** and **free software.** Unlike proprietary operating systems such as Windows or Macintosh OS X, all of its program code is available for anyone to use, alter, and redistribute freely.

Linux was initially developed and used by hobbyists on personal computers. Since then, however, Linux has gained the support of major corporations such as Sun Microsystems, IBM, and Novell for use in servers. It is used in numerous systems ranging from appliances like digital cameras, Sony PlayStation 3, and cell phones to mainframes and super computers.

The Linux **kernel** (the core of the operating system) was first developed by Linus Torvalds in 1991. It was originally designed only for Intel 80386 (pre-Pentium) microprocessors, but now supports a wide variety of computer architectures. Linux is one of the most widely **ported** operating systems. Linux has historically been used mainly as a server operating system as the platform for server based web development applications like **Apache** (Web server), **MySQL** (database server), **PHP** and **Python** (both programming languages).

The main concern of personal computer users wishing to base their operations on Linux is the lack of application software. Most end-user software is developed for Windows and has not been ported to other operating systems. Unlike Windows, Linux is not prone to be the target of hacking and other intrusive activities.

## Macintosh OS

Mac OS, which stands for Macintosh Operating System, is Apple Computer's graphical user interface-based operating system. It is usually given credit for popularizing the graphical user interface. It was first introduced in 1984, long before the first stable version of Windows was available. Apple actually avoided the term operating system in the Macintosh's early years because of the public perception of operating systems (like DOS) as unintuitive and difficult to use. Apple stressed the computer and not the software. Early versions of Mac OS ran on the Motorola 68000 processor but recent versions are compatible with Intel's architecture.

Mac **OS X** was introduced in 2001 and incorporated Unix-style management and multitasking to the Mac. It is derived from the BSD implementation of UNIX, and had been used as the basis for NeXTSTEP, the **object-oriented** operating system developed by Steve Jobs's NeXT company. The new OS allowed more programs to run simultaneously and virtually eliminated the possibility of one program crashing another.

## DOS

DOS or **Disk Operating System** is a generic term for a class of operating systems that were disk based. These operating systems were without graphical interface relying instead on the **command line** where the user's instructions were typed in a somewhat arcane grammar. These systems were an advance over older systems that relied only on available system memory (RAM) and could not take advantage of the additional storage provided by a disk. The most commonly known disk operating systems were **PC-DOS** (created by Microsoft for the original IBM-PC in 1981) and **MS-DOS** which Microsoft licensed to users of other systems. Neither DOS version was designed to be a multi-user or multitasking operating system.

PC/MS-DOS has effectively disappeared. It dominated the desktop computer industry from 1981 until 1995 when Windows '95 was released. Since the first several versions of Windows (95, 98, and Me) were actually shells surrounding DOS, the older operating system really powered computers until 2000 with the release of Windows 2000.

## Mainframe and Other Operating Systems

Operating systems in mainframes usually must support thousands of simultaneous users running hundreds of programs. Large databases are rapidly accessed and updated as well. Normally mainframes are too costly to be brought down for maintenance so their operating systems must handle operations while hardware components are removed, serviced, and replaced. The fundamental chores of mainframe operating systems are no different from the systems previously discussed. Several important mainframe operating systems were: MVS, VM, OS/390, TOPS-10, and TOPS-20. As noted, Unix (and Linux) are used for mainframe operations as well.

## Virtual Machine

A virtual machine essentially mimics a computer so that several copies of an operating system, for example Windows and Linux, can run on one machine at the same time. It allows computing chores to be done on fewer computers, using less electricity and taking up less space, offering a potential way to control costs. A virtual machine is implemented in software and allows multiple operating systems to be run at the same time on the same physical computer. This technology allows hardware to be shared by applications running on different operating systems.

Microsoft's **Virtual PC** permits creating separate virtual machines on the Windows desktop. Each machine (remember, the virtual machine is really just software) virtualizes the hardware of a complete physical computer. This feature allows the user to run multiple operating systems at once on a single physical computer and switch between them with a mouse click.

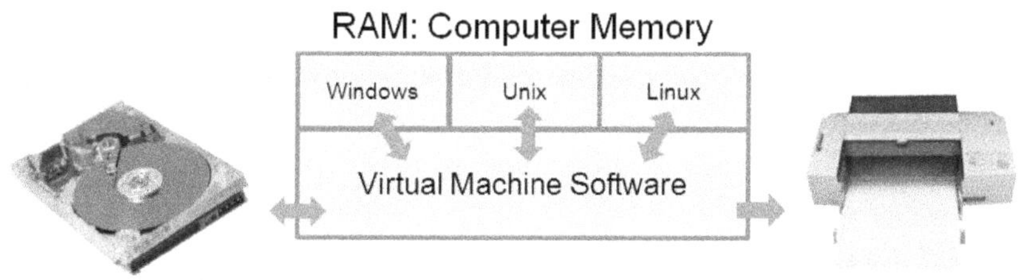


Virtual Machine

## Pause to Review #5

**Try this:**

1. A computer is a binary machine. What computer language is a binary language?
2. Match items below with definitions from the right.

| | |
|---|---|
| A. ___ Memory Management | a. Manages permanent storage |
| B. ___ Process Management | b. Links application programs with document type |
| C. ___ File System | c. Facilitates multitasking |
| D. ___ File Association | d. Permits swapping primary and secondary storage |

3. Match items below with definitions from the right.

| | |
|---|---|
| A. ___ Syntax | a. Small program in firmware |
| B. ___ BIOS | b. Relationship of physical to logical locationn in storage |
| C. ___ Mapping | c. Protocol |
| D. ___ TCP/IP | d. Grammar of a language |

4. Match items below with definitions from the right.

| | | |
|---|---|---|
| A. ___ Virtual Machine | | a. Operating system derived from Unix |
| B. ___ OS X | | b. Alternative to GUI |
| C. ___ Apache | | c. Computer runninnng multiple operating systems |
| D. ___ Command Line | | d. Web server |

Type your answers in the window provided by Pamela.

Computer programming (sometimes known as coding) is the process of writing, testing, and maintaining the code of computer programs. The code is written in programming languages like Java, Visual Basic, C, C#, or scripting languages like PHP, Perl, or VBScript. The process of writing program code requires expertise in many different subjects, including knowledge of the application domain and algorithms to implement the hardware's desired behavior.

Computer programs execute within the hardware and enable a computer to perform specific tasks. Programs include **system software** such as an operating system, which enables other software to run properly and **application software** such as a word processor or database manager, which enables a user to perform a task. System software is commercially available and necessary for the operation of a computer. Application software is commercially available, too, but it is also custom created by programmers for clients. Regardless of the type of software, computer programming follows certain techniques and principles, which is the subject of this chapter.

It would be impossible to process data into information with a computer alone. The operating system (OS) gives a series of instructions that command the hardware to act in specific ways. The OS facilitates the operation of application programs and provides them access to resources like files and databases and hardware. The computer's horsepower impacts greatly on the amount of data that can be processed in a given portion of time.

Computer programming involves writing instructions for a computer to follow as it processes data. The instructions are usually written in a **high-level language** and later translated into the computer's native language: **machine language.** There are different **programming paradigms** with object-oriented programming having become quite popular in the last decade. Numerous programming languages exist and each has its own **syntax** and form.

Who are these people who create computer programs and what do they do? Sometimes a programmer works alone but more often the programmer is part of a larger development team. Coordination among team members is, of course, essential.

- **Programmer**—A person who writes, tests, and maintains the source code of computer programs. A programmer normally follows specifications provided by an analyst.
- **Software Engineer**—A person who follows a systematic, disciplined, quantifiable approach to the development of software. This person has a broader project perspective than a programmer and must consider systems analysis, system design, and project management.

This chapter discusses what programming is as well as the issues faced by programmers. Different design and development paradigms are considered. The fundamentals of programming including data structures, logic are presented as well. Programming languages and development tools are presented with code examples in Appendix D. This chapter also teaches programming with a hands-on section. Macro programming using Microsoft Excel as a prelude to VBA and procedural programming using VBScript are included in Appendix E. Numerous automatically graded programming exercises at the end of the chapter give ample opportunity to practice the concepts and skills presented in this chapter.

In this chapter's discussion of logic and coding, no distinction is made between compiled computer programs and interpreted scripts. While the former is generally considered computer programming, applications are built with both technologies.

## Computer Programming

A **computer program** is a series of commands that instructs the computer **how to process data.** It is, in effect, a sequence of rules. Ada Lovelace's algorithms were the first example of a set of rules for processing data. Today's programs are exactly the same. Without a program running within it, a computer is nothing more than an expensive paperweight because it could not operate. The main thing to understand about computer programs is that they must be given to the computer in a language that the computer understands: **machine language** (code with only 1s and 0s). Machine language is comprised of an arrangement of 0s and 1s; it is called **binary.**

Since humans (computer programmers) do not speak binary they write computer programs in languages such as PHP, C, Java, and Visual Basic. Programs written in these **high level languages** must be translated into machine language before the computer can use them. The programmer creates **source code** which is translated into **binary code.** A special program, called a **compiler** performs this translation. The good news is that, as end-users, we do not need to know how to operate a compiler because the programs that we run have already been compiled for us and stored in the native machine language of the computer. Since each processor has a unique set of instructions designed into the chip, programmers must provide separate compilations for each processor they expect to distribute their software for. The compiling process is depicted here. Compiled programs are known as **executables** and usually have a file extension of **EXE, COM, DLL,** or **JAR.**

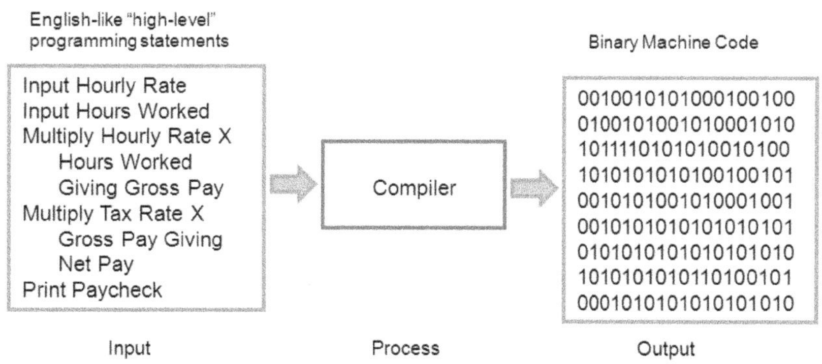


**The Compiler Translates Source Code to Binary Machine Code**

The process is actually a bit more complex because the compiled code (known as **object code**) is combined with other code already compiled that is stored on disk in libraries. Libraries contain code for many special purposes including: sorting data, displaying graphics, spell checking content, and so on.

A special program, the **linkage editor** (linker), assembles object and library code and produces an executable known as a **load module.** The load module is so named because it can be loaded into memory and executed.

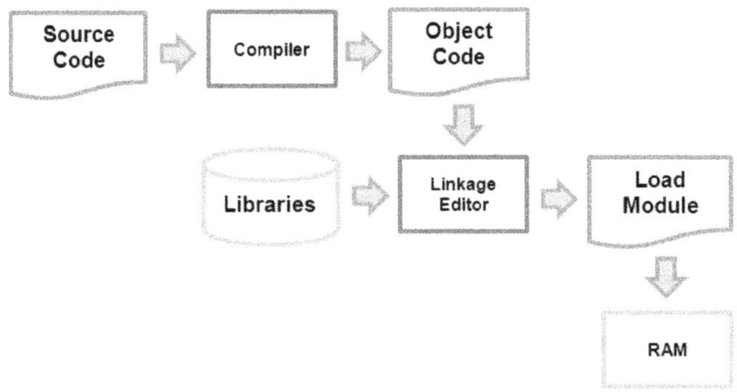


The Role of the Linkage Editor

## Interpreter Versus Compiler

An alternative approach to program execution involves interpretation of program code as the program is running. The translation is not done once and distributed to users as the product of a compiler: machine code. Here the **source code,** known as a **script,** is translated to the required binary line by line during execution. This is not a particularly efficient approach for program execution but since compiling can be a long process, using an interpreter can be quite useful during program development and debugging as software is prototyped because programmers can quickly and repeatedly test their work. Interpreted code is also valuable as a teaching tool. Some languages are always interpreted as noted below.

The interpreter is part of the operating system (OS) and some interpreters have been ported (distributed) to various operating systems. **Perl** and **PHP** are two interpreted languages that are hosted on a variety of platforms. A commonly used scripting protocol is **Active Server Pages** (ASP) which is hosted by Windows servers. The file extension of the script varies depending on the programming language used.

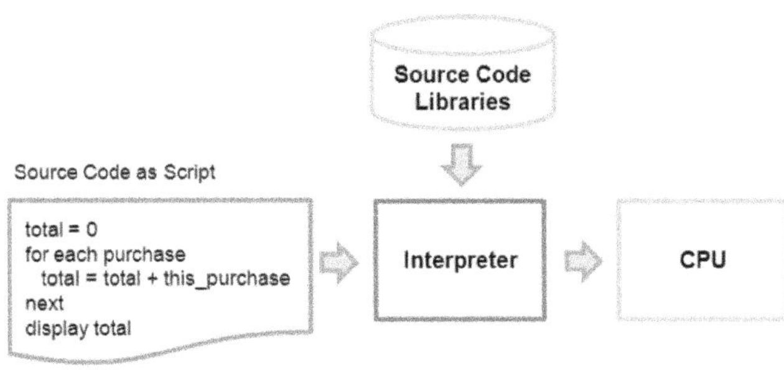


How a Script Executes

## Bytecode Interpreter

A compromise between compiling and interpretation is a **partial translation** that yields what is known as **bytecode**. The translation is not into machine code that is native to any particular processor, but instead an efficient **platform independent** representation of the program is produced and distributed that undergoes a final (and quick) translation to machine code when it runs. This process is known as **just-in-time compilation** (JIT) because the bytecode is compiled to native machine code at runtime. Since the code is ultimately rendered in machine language, the high execution speed of running native machine code is achieved. Programs written in **Java** are distributed using this approach.

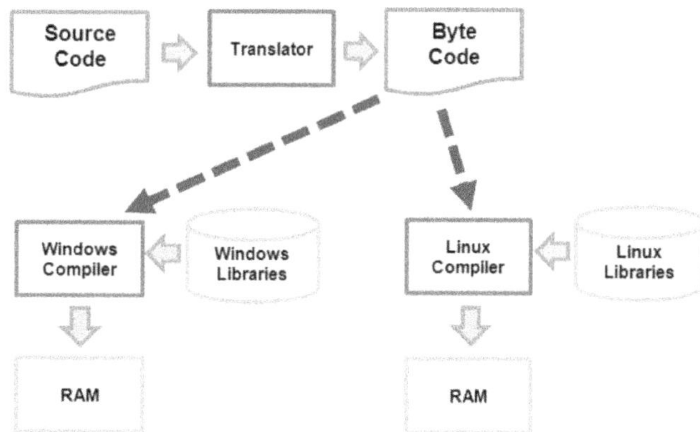


Bytecode Is Pre-Compiled

## Programming Design, Paradigms, and Architecture

Good programs are well thought out in advance. They are designed before coding begins and tested before being turned over to stakeholders for use. The design process follows the **System Development Lifecycle** or **SDLC** and the architecture of programs broadly follows established **paradigms** or style of programming.

### System Development Lifecycle

When software is developed a standard process is followed that imposes a formalized structure on the project. Here, several stages of the process are identified. Chapter 6, Systems Analysis has more complete information. As you see, once a project is complete maintenance is required because **stakeholder** needs and requirements change over time thus necessitating updates to the software.

- **Problem Definition and Analysis**—The first activity is to clearly define the problem to be solved and develop a solution that meets the needs of clients and stakeholders. This may involve negotiation between stakeholders that is facilitated by a systems analyst.
- **Program Design**—Once the solution is accepted by all parties a technical design is prepared. This document defines all technical aspects of the program or programs including: selection of programming language, design of program logic and of the database structure, interface design and design of output (reports and screen display). During this phase acceptance criteria should be established so that success can be measured.
- **Coding**—This phase is for the programmers. It is usually the most time-consuming and costly phase of the development cycle.
- **Testing**—Here work is tested and certified to meet the already established acceptance criteria. Errors that are identified must be corrected before moving to implementation.

- **Implementation**—Once the system is satisfactorily tested it is time to create user documentation, train users, and convert data for use by the software.
- **Maintenance**—It is rare that completed systems are static. Changes in business requirements, governmental regulation, and stakeholder needs demand software modification and upgrade. Program errors not detected during testing may surface as the system ages and require fixing. In the lifetime of a system considerable time and money is spent on maintenance so a good design and thorough testing is important because they could affect the cost and extent of maintenance expenditures.

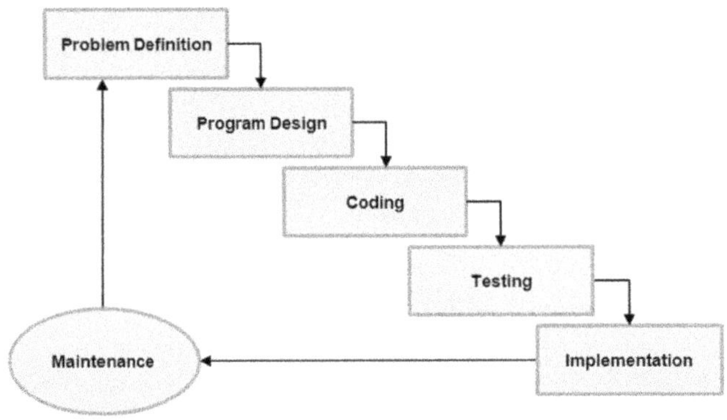


Program Development Lifecycle

The software engineer or systems analyst uses various tools to better understand system requirements and to specify the design for programmers. The system designer uses various diagramming and prototyping tools to create charts that depict the structure and flow of a system. The designer may also use tools to document the system's processing logic and even create **pseudocode** that is the basis for program code. See Chapter 6, Systems Analysis, for examples of analysis tools and pseudocode.

## Program Design Paradigms

A programming paradigm is style of programming. The relationship between programming paradigms and programming languages can be complex since a programming language can support multiple paradigms. Two of the best known paradigms are discussed here.

### *Structured Programming*

Structured programming is a task-oriented design technique. There are two approaches: Top-Down Design and Bottom-Up Design. Programmers working with this approach break larger pieces of program functionality into smaller sections called subroutines, functions, procedures, and methods. These **code blocks** are generally small, self-contained, and reasonably easy to understand. Code blocks are combined to build larger functional structures, thus the paradigm's name. The idea is to build large numbers of small program units that can be individually tested and placed into **libraries** of code **modules** affording code **reuse** as larger programs are assembled. In the structured approach data is maintained in a common area generally shared among all code blocks.

Structured programming is frequently considered a **top-down** approach to design. Programmers map out the full structure of a program in terms of smaller operations, which are implemented and tested individually and then tied together in a whole program. Each unit of code is called a **subroutine** or **function.** Each unit can be called by any number of other units. Ultimately the top level unit, the main program, orchestrates the sequence of calls and operations.

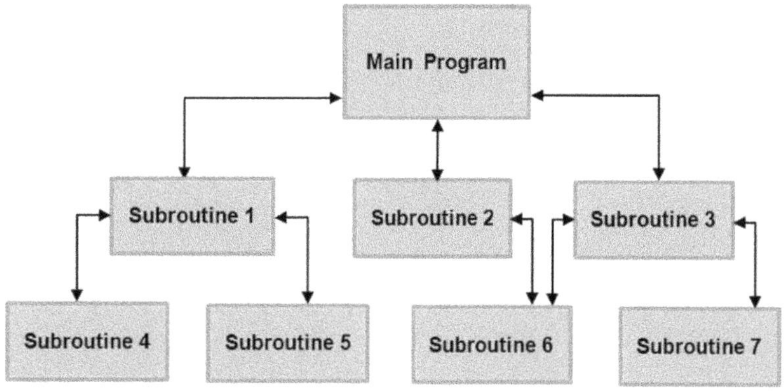


Structured Programming

**Bottom-up** design is a structured approach to a problem where the programmer uses smaller pieces, already created, in developing the larger solution to the problem.

### *Object-Oriented Programming*

The concept of object-oriented programming or **OOP** is that a computer program is a collection of individual units (**objects**) that maintain their own data and behaviors. This is different from the structured approach in which a program is considered a collection of subroutines and functions with shared data. An example of an object is a clickable button frequently found on graphical interfaces. All objects have built in functionality (known as methods) that defines certain behaviors for all **instances** of that object. Each instance of a button has common properties (screen location, size, color, etc.) and common methods (depress when clicked, take action when clicked).

## Programming Languages

Computer languages are considered to have been developed in several **generations.** The first level, or generation, is the binary language understood by the machine itself: **machine code.** In fact, programmers of the original computers were required to perform all of their work in binary. This was a tedious process using only abstract symbols: 0s and 1s. A second-generation language, **assembly,** became popular in the 1950s as a short hand version of machine language. The development of this language removed some of the abstraction of machine language, but was more or less just as tedious. The third generation of languages, **high level** languages, saw the eventual introduction of most of the popular computer languages in use today: **Java, Visual Basic,** and **C#.** The first three generations are grouped together as **procedural languages,** so named because these languages are used to tell a computer **how to behave.**

Fourth and fifth generation languages are considered to be **non-procedural** because the user tells the computer ***what to produce,*** not how to do it. These languages are used mostly by users other than programmers. When performing a database query in Microsoft Access a fourth generation **query language** is used telling Access what data is wanted but not directing the steps needed to retrieve that data. Examples of query languages are **SQL** (Structured Query Language) and **QBE** (Query by Example). A fifth generation language is very much like English and is known as **natural language.** The idea is to allow the user to converse with the computer in a comfortable (preferably spoken), non-technical form. The sequence of language introduction with examples of each is summarized here and presented fully in Appendix D.

| Generation | Language | Example | Introduced |
|---|---|---|---|
| 1 | Machine | 01100011100010 | 1940s |
| 2 | Assembler | LDX ACC | 1950s |
| 3 | High Level | pay=gross-tax | 1956 |
| 4 | Query Language | List customers in 'Spain' | 1970s |
| 5 | Natural Language | spoken English | 1980s |

Programming Language Generations

### Choosing What Language to Use

Most procedural third generation languages provide the same fundamentals: **data structures, branching,** and **iteration.** The question, therefore, of which language to select for a project depends on several other factors:

- **Integration**—The potential for integration with existing data processing systems.
- **Platform Independence**—The ability to run the application on systems governed by different operating systems.
- **Scalability**—The extent to which the language can properly handle increasingly large processing loads defined as quantity of data and number of concurrent users.
- **Distribution**—The method by which the programs can be distributed to clients is an important factor. For example, programs written in some languages are more easily embedded in a Web page and others work best on a server or as stand alone executables.
- **Programmers**—Some languages are known by more programmers and some by less. Finding sufficient seasoned staff to develop a project is an essential ingredient to successful project completion.
- **Speed**—Certain languages lend themselves more to prototype development and others to a more traditional development approach. Project deadlines can be a significant determining factor.

All programs ultimately must be represented in the computer's memory (RAM) as a sequence of binary digits (1 and 0). Digital computers are binary machines, so only two states are possible: on and off. Only machine language is exclusively binary. Programs written in all other languages are a higher level abstraction and must be translated into binary (Steinberg).

## History of C++

In the 1970s, Dennis Ritchie of Bell Laboratories was working on a project to develop a new operating system. To accomplish this he would need a programming language that produced compact and fast programs, hence the development of programming language **C**.

In 1979, Bjarne Stroustrup, a Danish- and British-trained computer scientist, also of Bell Laboratories, developed a programming language based on the **C** language called **C with Classes**. This improvement on the **C** language included object-oriented features. **C with Classes** was renamed **C++** in 1983, replacing "with Classes" with the increment operator (++).

Stroustrup stated the purpose of C++ as making writing good programs easier and more pleasant for the programmer. When he designed C++, he added Object Oriented Programming (OOP) features without significant changes to the C component, making C++ a superset of C. This means any C program is also valid as a C++ program.

C++ programming language is regarded as an intermediate-level language, comprising both high-level and low-level language features. It is heavily used for software development where performance matters, particularly with complex application development where OOP makes that complexity manageable.

C++ is implemented on a wide variety of hardware and operating system platforms. It's used in system software, application software (i.e., video games), device drivers, embedded software, and high-performance server and client applications.

There are several versions of the C++ language such as Borland C++, Turbo C++, and Code Warrior (Mac). In an attempt to maintain portability of both the C and C++ languages, the American National Standards Institute (ANSI) developed a standard of consistency called ANSI Standard.

The first commercial implementation of C++ was released in October 1985, and since then there have been many improvements. C++ continues to be one of the preferred programming languages to develop professional applications.

## Algorithms

An algorithm is a set of step-by-step detailed instructions for performing a specific task that when executed produces a predictable output.

Algorithms are essential to the way computers process data. Many computer programs contain algorithms that detail the specific instructions a computer should perform, in a specific order to carry out a specified task, such as calculating employees' paychecks or printing students' report cards.

To make a program do something, you need to do spell it out step by step. When the program executes, it follows each step mechanically to accomplish the end goal. The algorithm is the basic technique used to get the job done.

Below is an algorithm example for making a peanut butter and jelly sandwich:

1. Place bread package on the table.
2. Place knife on the table.
3. Place peanut butter jar on the table.
4. Twist peanut butter jar lid counterclockwise until it separates from jar and place it on the table.
5. Place jelly jar on the table.
6. Twist jelly jar lid counterclockwise until it separates from jar and place it on the table.
7. Remove one slice of bread from bread package and place it on the table.
8. Take the knife and spread some peanut butter from the jar onto the bread slice.
9. If peanut butter does not cover bread surface, repeat prior step.

10. Remove second slice of bread from bread package and place it on the table.
11. Take the knife and spread jelly from the jar onto the second bread slice.
12. If jelly does not cover bread surface, repeat prior step.
13. Place the jellied side of the second slice of bread on top of the peanut buttered side of the first piece of bread, lining up the edges.
14. If desired, use a sharp knife and cut the sandwich in half either vertically or diagonally. Optional: Be artistic and cut the sandwich in inventive ways.
15. Place jelly lid on jelly jar and twist clockwise until it stops.
16. Place peanut butter lid on peanut butter jar and twist clockwise until it stops.

*Chapter 2*

# Fundamental Data Types

***"Only the hand that erases can write the true thing."***

**—Meister Eckhart**

## C++ Programming Process

Programming is not a spectator "activity". The only way to learn programming is to actually do it. Before we embark on this journey, let's first learn the basics:

- The first step is to **write** the source code. You're going to need an editor to type your C++ code. This can be as simple as Notepad, or as sophisticated as an IDE (Integrated Development Environment). There are many IDE's to choose[1] from—in many factors will influence your decision—ease-of-use, cost, good debugger, etc.
- Once you have written your source code, the next step is to **compile** it. Upon successful compilation, and executable file is generated and you will recognize it because it has .exe extension. Often, the compiler will complain about syntax errors which you will need to correct and re-compile your program.
- The last step is to **execute** your program.

Let's examine the mechanics of the compilation process. There are many ways to compile a C++ program, but it basically boils down to two choices—command line compilers versus IDE compilers.

### Command Line Compilers

Command line compilers such as GNU C++ compiler (GCC, the GNU Compiler Collection, 2013) are free but little more difficult to use because you have to learn a few commands to initiate the process. These commands are typed into the command line window. For UNIX/Linux systems you don't need to do anything special except invoke the command line window and start typing. On the Windows systems, you will need to download free software such as Cygwin or MinGW which use the GNU C++ compiler. To initiate the compilation you would simply type the following command at the command line prompt:

```
g++ helloWorld.cpp
```

followed by the enter key. If your program compiles successfully, you will get an executable file called a.out. If you wanted to change the name of the output file, or to link with another

[1] http://en.wikipedia.org/wiki/Comparison_of_integrated_development_environments

library, then the command you type would be a little more complex as it would include so-called flags.[2] The list is exhaustive and you can consult the documentation for examples.

## Integrated Development Environment

Alternatively, you can use an Integrated Development Environment (IDE) which abstracts the compilation process from the programmer. There is no need to memorize any commands except few buttons (also menu options) that you need to click on. These include:

- Compile—compiles the current file. Keep in mind that you may have more than one file in your C++ project.
- Build—builds only the file that has changed. If you have multiple files in your project, and you make changes to only one of them tend that is the file that is going to be built.
- Rebuild All—as the name implies rebuild all files in your project.
- Link—this option may (or may not) be bundled with the next option (the Run option) in your IDE.
- Run—executes the program
- Debug—What is great about IDEs is that they provide a Debugger which is a very nice feature that allows you to step through the code as it executes, and view the contents of variables in real-time. Most of the time this will help you catch clues as to why your program is not running correctly. It is very important to distinguish between a syntax error and a runtime error:
  - A syntax error is simply an error in the language syntax—perhaps you forgot to put a semicolon (;) to terminate the statement, or you misspelled a keyword, variable etc. Most of the time the compiler will catch those mistakes and report them back.
  - On the other hand, runtime errors are difficult to spot as the compiler does not report them. The code compiles correctly but when executed, produces erroneous results. To catch runtime errors you need to hand trace the program, which means listing all your variables and tracing through each line of code to update the values that should be stored in your variables. This is a very tedious and time-consuming process which is why you should place high value on IDEs with good debuggers.

Usually, when compiling the code using an IDE, two versions are possible: a Debug version, and a Release version. The difference between the two versions is:

- The Debug version contains extra code that can aid in debugging the application.
- The Release version is stripped of all debugging code.

Typically you would test your program with a debug version and then once you're happy with the outcomes you want recompile only the release version, test it again and if satisfactory ship it to your client (or simply "release" it on the network for example).

## Behind the Scenes

To make things simple, we are going to use an IDE. The following figure depicts the journey of a C++ program from the source code file all the way to the executable file:

---

[2] http://gcc.gnu.org/onlinedocs/gcc/Option-Summary.html

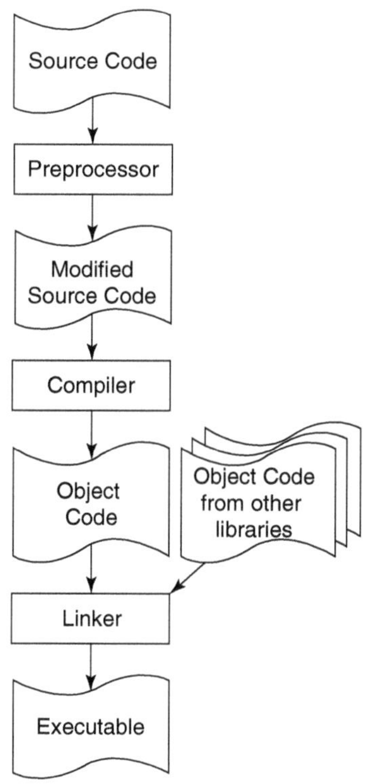


**Figure 1:** From Source Code to Executable.

The source code is first inspected by the preprocessor. The preprocessor is a program whose job is to search for "#include" directives and augment the source code with the code from these files. The resulting file (modified source code file) is forwarded to the compiler as input. The compiler checks for syntax errors and if finds any, reports them. If the compiler reports any errors, the programmer needs to correct them and recompile the source code.

Once the compiler successfully compiles the modified source code file it produces an object code file. This file typically has an extension of ".o" and is fed with object files from other programs/libraries to a program called the linker.

The linker combines all the object files and produces the executable file. This process is the same for both command line compilers and compilers bundled in an IDE.

Learning a new language programming language is similar to learning anew natural language (English, Spanish, Italian, Chinese, etc.). In the beginning, it is difficult because you lack the vocabulary and grammar rules. Thus it is normal to make a lot of grammatical and syntactical mistakes. Hopefully a native speaker can point out the mistakes and you can learn from them. In Computer science, you can think of the compiler as the native speaker that is at your disposal ready to correct your grammar and syntax every time you interact with it. However, even after you become proficient in C++, you will still have to recompile your programs several times before you get an executable file. One thing to keep in mind is that the semantics (the meaning) is yours—meaning when you're learning a natural language native speaker can correct your syntax and your grammar but you are responsible for the semantics. Similarly, in C++, the compiler can correct your syntax errors but the logic (semantics) is your responsibility. Thus getting your code to compile does not mean that you are done. It just means that there are no syntax errors and you still need to check whether your logic is correctly translated into computer code meaning that you do not have any runtime errors.

## Your 1st C++ Program

What makes a great programmer is attention to detail. It is very important to learn the basics and build a solid foundation for more complex concepts. Will start with a simple hello world program:

```
 1. // my first C++ program -Hello World
 2. #include <iostream>
 3.
 4. using namespace std;
 5.
 6. int main()
 7. {
 8.      cout << "Hello world!" << endl;
 9.      return 0;
10. }
```

**Listing 1:** Hello World

Line 1 starts with the following two characters: //. The // indicates a single line comment. Once the compiler encounters the // it ignores everything until the end of line. For multiline comments you can use the "/" followed by an asterisk "*" (/*) to mark the beginning of the comment block, and an asterisk "*" followed by a "/" to mark the end of the comment block (*/):

```
 1. /*
 2.     Programmer    : Adi Zejnilovic
 3.     Date          : 07/28/2013
 4.     Description   : This program will display the following message:
 5.                     Hello world!
 6. */
 7. #include <iostream>
 8.
 9. using namespace std;
10.
11. int main()
12. {
13.      cout << "Hello world!" << endl;
14.      return 0;
15. }
```

**Listing 2:** Hello World with Multiline Comments

In the above listing, lines 1 through six are ignored by the compiler because they are (multiline) comments.

Programming is a team effort thus you should make necessary efforts to document your source code. Not only does this help your teammates understand your source code, but it will also help you in the future in case you ever have to go back and maintain or debug your program. What should you document? Usually, functions should start with a short description indicating the date the function was written, the programmer named, and a short description of what the function does. In addition, more complex blocks of code should also be documented.

As a programmer, you should be proud of your code and take ownership of it. That starts with a comment on line 1 that contains your name. Let's dissect the rest of the program:

- The include directive: The program starts on line number 7 with a statement:

  ```
  #include <iostream>
  ```

  which is a preprocessor directive. The "io" is a short hand for input/output.

  Since the program will be displaying ("outputting") a message onto the screen, we need to include the iostream file. When the preprocessor encounters this directive it creates a new file into which it copies the contents of the source code file along with the contents of the iostream file.

  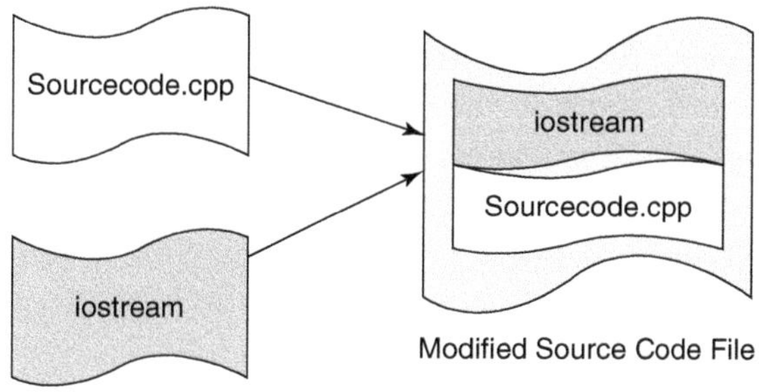
  

  **Figure 2:** The `<iostream>` **Preprocessor Directive.**

  Include files are sometimes called header files. Both terms are correct, it is a matter of personal preference.

- using namespace std; The next statement on line 9:

  ```
  using namespace std;
  ```

  specifies which namespace (in this case the namespace named "std") the program will be using. You can think of name spaces as "directories"—although they're not directories but a language feature that allows programmers to call functions that may have the same name but belong to different namespace. If you do not specify the `using namespace` directive, then you will need to precede all cout objects as follows:

  ```
  std::cout << "Hello world!" << std::endl;
  ```

- the main function. The next statement on line 9:

  ```
  int main()
  ```

is the **function header** followed by the **function body** which is a collection of statements between the opening brace "{" and the closing brace "}". Together they form a function definition:

| Function Definition | | |
|---|---|---|
| | `int main()` | Function Header |
| | `{ cout << "Hello world!" << endl; return 0; }` | Function Body |

**Figure 3:** Function Definition, Function Header, and Function Body.

The main function is a special function because every C++ program must have the main function. It starts with the keyword int which specifies the function return type. The two brackets "("and")" mark the beginning and end of the parameter list. In this case, there are no parameters The beginning of the function body is marked with the left brace "{", and the end of the function body is marked with the right brace "}". Notice that the last statement of the function is the return statement—in this instance the function returns a zero.

We can conclude that a function is a collection of statements. Besides the main function, a C++ program will have programmer defined functions which are similar to the main function.

- The cout object encountered on line 13 is defined in the iostream header file and is used to display information on the screen. In our program example, the cout object displays the string literal (the text enclosed inside of the quotes) on the screen. The cout object works in tandem with the insertion operator (<<). You can think of the string literal being fed (the arrows indicate the direction) to the cout object. Another insertion operator << feeds the endl manipulator to the cout object :

```
cout << "Hello world!" << endl;
```

The "endl" means end line—and it moves the cursor to the new line after the cout object displays the string literal.

The cout is short for "console output". A console (also known as computer or root or operator console) is a relic from the days when computer I/O was strictly character based—i.e. using computer terminals which were also known as operator consoles[3] (Wikipedia). Given the technology at the time, it was appropriate to name the object that displayed data as "console output". A cout statement does not need to be on one line. For better readability, it can be written over several lines:

```
cout << "Hello! My name is Adi"
     << "I live on 123 Main Street in "
     << "Miami, FL 33134 "
     << endl;
```

Even though, the cout is written over several lines, the output will still be displayed on one line:

```
Hello! My name is AdiI live on 123 Main Street in Miami, FL 33134

Process returned 0 (0x0)   execution time : 0.019 s
Press any key to continue.
```

[3]http://en.wikipedia.org/wiki/System_console

Keep in mind that computers "do exactly as they are told—nothing less, nothing more". If you want to add a space or a new line, then you need to specify that in the statement so that the computer can execute it. Making a few changes to the statement:

```
cout << "Hello! My name is Adi" << endl
     << "I live on " << endl << "123 Main Street in " << endl
     << "Miami, FL 33134 "
     << endl;
```

will produce correct output:

```
Hello! My name is Adi
I live on
123 Main Street in
Miami, FL 33134

Process returned 0 (0x0)   execution time : 0.014 s
Press any key to continue.
```

Note the "endl" right after the string literal "I live on" forces the new line. The point being illustrated here is that it does not matter how many lines the statement is written on in the source code. What matters is the placement of manipulators such as "endl".

In addition to the endl manipulator, it is possible to use escape sequence characters to manipulate the output. For example, the following statement:

```
cout << "Hello world!\n";
```

will also move the cursor to the next line after it displays the string literal "Hello World". Notice that there is no endl manipulator at the end. However, there is a \n inside the string literal. The \n is known as an escape sequence character, and it stands for new line. The following table[4] (http://en.cppreference.com) lists escape sequences:

| Escape Sequence | Character | Comments |
|---|---|---|
| \' | Single quote | Prints a single quote |
| \" | Double quote | Prints a double quote |
| \\ | Backslash | Prints a backslash |
| \0 | Null character | Null Character (to terminate char arrays) |
| \b | Backspace | Moves the cursor back one space |
| \a | Audible bell | Plays a predetermined sound |
| \f | Form feed (new page) | Prints a new page |
| \n | Line feed (new line) | Moves the cursor to the new line |
| \r | Carriage return | Moves the cursor to the beginning of the existing line |
| \t | Horizontal tab | Moves the cursor to the next tab stop |

**Table 1:** Escape Sequences.

Consider the following statement:

```
cout << "Hello! My name is Adi\n\nI live on\n\t123 Main Street
in \n\tMiami, FL 33134\n";
```

[4] http://en.cppreference.com/w/cpp/language/escape

It produces the following output:

```
Hello! My name is Adi

I live on
        123 Main Street in
        Miami, FL 33134

Process returned 0 (0x0)   execution time : 0.017 s
Press any key to continue.
```

Trace the escape sequence characters and the output.

Following statements demonstrates two escape sequences: a single quote and a carriage return:

```
cout << "Let\'s test this. Single Quote and Carriage return\r";
cout << "Where is the cursor?"
```

```
Where is the cursor?gle Quote and Carriage return
Process returned 0 (0x0)   execution time : 0.017 s
Press any key to continue.
```

Notice how thee first statement printed the string literal "Let's test this. Single Quote and Carriage return" and then due to \r escape sequence the cursor was to the beginning of the existing line. Single quote was printed, but we cannot see it because the next statement that prints "Where is the cursor" overrode the previous string literal starting at the cursor's position (1st character).

Finally, the last character in a statement is the semicolon (;) which marks the end of the statement.

- The last statement:

  ```
  return 0;
  ```

  returns a zero to the caller program—in this case, the operating system.

It is time to get your hands dirty! Type and compile the above program. Your output should look like this (your execution time may be different):

```
Hello world!

Process returned 0 (0x0)   execution time : 0.022 s
Press any key to continue.
```

## Programming Style

The C++ compiler does not care how neatly your program is written. Even if you wrote the entire program on one line, if you did not have any syntax errors, it was compiled and executed without any problems. However in order to successfully maintain your programs (or have someone else on your team maintain your program) it is very important to adhere to certain programming style. This includes indentations of new statements by 3 to 4 spaces and having one statement per line. It also includes maintaining the same indentation level of the beginning and ending braces which should be on separate lines. There are numerous coding style recommendations such as K&R (Kernighan and Ritchie), ANSI C,

GNU, etc. (WikiBooks). The key point is consistency which will assure program readability, maintainability, and easier debugging:

```
// K&R style
if (a > 5) {
    // statement(s);
}
// This is ANSI C++ style
if (a > 5)
{
    // statement(s);
}
// This is GNU style
if (a > 5)
  {
     // statement(s);
  }
```

**Figure 4:** Some C++ Coding Styles[5]

A program is correctly styled and documented if a layman person could read it and more or less get an idea what the program is trying to accomplish.

## Fundamental Data Types

So far, we have written a program to display a string of characters on the screen. We learned the steps C++ program goes through from a simple source code file until the executable file. We also learned that a program consists of statements and that a function is a collection of statements.

In order to write C++ statements, you will need to become familiar with the following elements of the language:

- Reserved Words: also known as Key Words, they are not available for use as identifiers. Some examples[6] of reserved words are bool, int, float, for, if, namespace, etc.
- Identifiers: are programmer defined constants, variables, types, templates, classes, functions, and namespaces. An identifier must start with a letter or an underscore and it can contain characters and numbers. An identifier cannot start with a number although.
- Operators: An operator operates on one or more operands to produce a result (a value). Some examples of operators are:
  - An assignment operator (=). For example, "x takes on the value of 5" or x = 5; What this means is that an integer literal 5 is copied to memory location called x. In other words, the compiler assigns value of 5 to memory location x.
  - Another example would be an addition operator (+):

    $$x = a + b;$$

  In this example, a, b, and x are operands, and + and = are operators.

---

[5]http://en.wikibooks.org/wiki/C%2B%2B_Programming/Programming_Languages/C%2B%2B/Code/Style_Conventions
[6]http://en.cppreference.com/w/cpp/keyword

- Punctuation: semicolon (;) signifying end of statement, a dot operator (.) used to access structure (or class) members, a comma (,) to separate list items, etc.
- Grammar: These are the language rules. All natural languages have syntax rules, for instance a subject, a predicate, an adjective, etc. and rules about correct placement of these elements when forming sentences. Similarly, computer languages have rules that specify how language elements are to be used. For example, you need to declare a variable in order to use it.

## Literals

Literals are constants. Their value is not going to change during the program run. For example, this string enclosed inside the quotes is a string literal:

```
cout << "Hello world!" << endl;
```

Recall the escape sequences we discussed earlier in the chapter? It should make perfect sense why you need an escape sequence (\") for the quote character ("). Since quotes begin and terminate string literals, if you need to print quote character as part of your string literal, then you need the escape sequence \" to tell the compiler not to treat it as the terminating (or starting) quote.

It is possible to have literals of other data types such as integers, floats, doubles, etc. The following statement contains an integer literal:

```
cout << 5 << endl;
```

which should not be confused with the string literal:

```
cout << "5" << endl;
```

The compiler automatically appends an extra character (null) at the end of string literals, so "5" is really:

| | |
|---|---|
| 5 | '\0' |

Regardless of the string literal size, the last character in always the null terminating character ('\0'):

| | | | | | | | | | | | | |
|---|---|---|---|---|---|---|---|---|---|---|---|---|
| 'H' | 'e' | 'l' | 'l' | 'o' | | 'w' | 'o' | 'r' | 'l' | 'd' | '!' | '\0' |

The reason for the terminating null character is to mark the end of the string. This is how the cout object knows when to stop displaying the string literal.

## Variables

In order for a program to "remember" something, you need to store it in a variable. Variables are nothing more than names (aliases) for memory locations. The reason they are called variables is because the contents of the memory location may change during the course of program run.

In computer's RAM, each memory cell has an address. The addresses are represented in hexadecimal base and look like:

```
0x28ff44
```

That is hard to remember for a human. Luckily, we can create a variable with a more "human-friendly" name such as "interestRate", "x" or "counter" etc. Whenever we declare a variable, it is assigned an address in the RAM. The following statement:

```
int x;
```

declares a variable called x whose data type is an integer. This is known as variable ***definition***. Also, note the semicolon (;) at the end—this simply indicates the end of the statement. It is very important to understand why we need to declare data type for a variable. The answer is simple—storage. When the compiler encounters variable definition statement, it looks at the data type and allocates (reserves) space according to the data type. In computer RAM, the lowest unit of memory measure is a bit. A byte is a sequence of 8 bits. Depending on the computer architecture different data types can have different sizes in bytes.

To better understand computer memory, let's look at the following scenario: Suppose there is a parking lot partitioned in such a way that the spaces are big enough only to accommodate parking of bicycles. To park a bicycle you would need to reserve one parking space in this parking lot. However, there is a small problem—you are not riding a bicycle, instead you are driving a sedan. In order to park your sedan you call the parking lot attendant and declare your intention to park your car. The parking attendant looks at the list of available spaces and reserves five bicycle spaces for you informing you that your assigned parking space starts at number 12855 through space 12860:

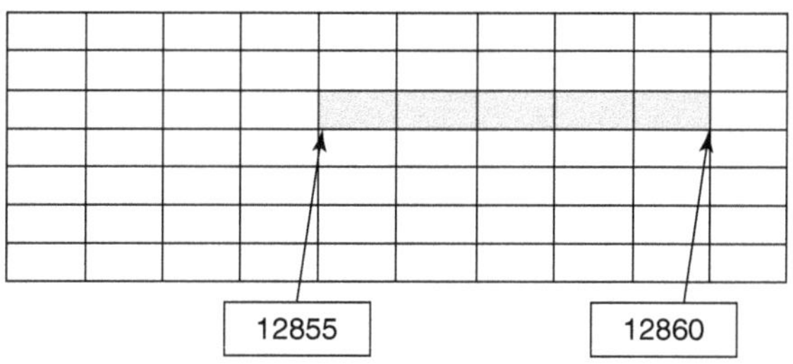


**Figure 5:** Fictitious Parking Lot Reserved Spaces.

Suppose another person driving an SUV needs to park their vehicle at this parking lot. They go through the same process of calling the attendant and they gets 8 spaces instead of five. Another person driving a bus may require 15 spaces. Instead of referring to parking spaces by their numbers, the attendant names customer parking spaces, essentially creating an alias (a variable) for their respective parking spaces.

The above described scenario is similar to how computer allocates (reserves) memory for different data types. Just like certain number of bicycle parking spaces is needed to park a car, an SUV, and a bus, different number of consecutive bytes are needs to "park" an integer, a double, a string, etc. in the RAM. Choosing the right data type depends on what you are trying to capture and store (numeric, character, true/false, etc.) as different data types have different storage requirements due to the range of values they can address. Here is an example of declaring an integer and how it is represented in memory:

```
int x;
```

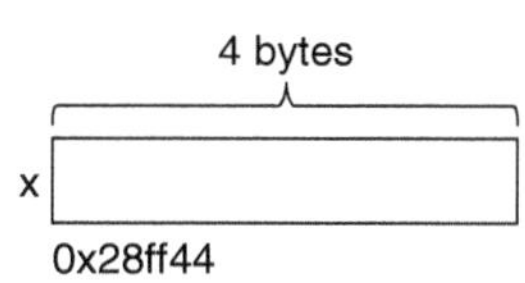


**Figure 6:** Integer Representation in Memory.

The compiler reserved 4 bytes for the variable x because it is an integer. The starting address of the 4 bytes block is located in memory address 0x28ff44.

We will discuss memory addresses in greater detail later on in the book. For now, remember that a variable is an alias for memory location and that it must be large enough to store values of particular data type.

The C++ data types can be classified as:

- Fundamental integer data types } Built-in
- Non-Fundamental data types } Built-in
- Abstract data types } Programmer Defined

We will examine them in greater detail in the following sections.

## Built-In Data Types

Built in data types do not require any include headers as they are part of the language. In C++, built in data types are Numerical data types and Non-Fundamental data types.

### *Numerical Data Types*

In C++, built in data types are:

- *Integer data types.* An integer is a whole number such as 1, −115, 2013, etc.
- *Floating point data* types. Floating point number is a number with the decimal point such as the 3.14, −191.81, 0.34, etc.

**Integer Data Types** Integer data types include:

- bool
- char
- short int (also short)
- int
- long int (also long)
- unsigned char
- unsigned short int (also unsigned short)
- unsigned int
- unsigned long int (also unsigned long)

From the above list we see that data types can be signed and unsigned. For example:

```
unsigned short x;
```

can store only positive short integers, from 0 to 65535 while

```
short x;
```

can store both negative and positive integers ranging from −32768 to 32767.

I can easily remember the lower bound for all signed data types, which is the zero. However, I can never remember the lower and upper bounds for the unsigned data types. To further complicate things, these ranges may be different on different system architectures. For example, the values will be different on a machine running Win 32 bit architecture versus a machine running Win 64 bit architecture. Fortunately, C++ provides a header file called <climits> which stores symbolic constants for different data type limits. All I have left to do is to write a short program that will report data type limits:

```
1. /*
2.     Programmer  : Adi Zejnilovic
3.     Date        : 07/28/2013
4.     Description : This program will display sizes (in bytes) and upper/lower
                     boundaries for different integer data types.
5.
6. */
7. #include <iostream>
8. #include <climits>
9.
10. using namespace std;
11.
12. int main()
13. {
14.     cout << "DATA TYPE: short & unsigned short" << endl;
15.     cout << "sizeof short: " << sizeof(short) << " bytes" << endl;
16.     cout << "short range: " << SHRT_MIN << " to " << SHRT_MAX << endl;
17.     cout << "sizeof unsigned short: " << sizeof(unsigned short)
             << " bytes" << endl;
18.     cout << "unsigned short range: " << 0 << " to " << USHRT_MAX << endl;
19.     cout << "========================================================\n";
20.     cout << "DATA TYPE: int & unsigned int" << endl;
21.     cout << "sizeof int: " << sizeof(int) << " bytes" << endl;
22.     cout << "int range: " << INT_MIN << " to " << INT_MAX << endl;
23.     cout << "sizeof unsigned int: " << sizeof(unsigned int) << " bytes"
             << endl;
24.     cout << "unsigned short range: " << 0 << " to " << INT_MAX << endl;
25.     cout << "========================================================\n";
26.     cout << "DATA TYPE: long & unsigned long" << endl;
27.     cout << "sizeof long: " << sizeof(long) << " bytes" << endl;
28.     cout << "long range: " << LONG_MIN << " to " << LONG_MAX << endl;
29.     cout << "sizeof unsigned long: " << sizeof(unsigned long)<< " bytes"
             << endl;
30.     cout << "unsigned long range: " << 0 << " to " << LONG_MAX << endl;
31.
32.     return 0;
33. }
```

**Listing 3:** Using the <climits> Header File

The program in Listing 3 includes the <climits>[7] (cplusplus, 2013) header file on line 3. Also, the program uses the sizeof operator to determine data type size in bytes. You can easily enhance the program in Listing 3 to find out sizes and ranges of other data types such as char, double, etc. Following is the output of the program in Listing 3:

---

[7]To find out more about the <climits> header file please see: www.cplusplus.com/reference/climits/

```
DATA TYPE: short & unsigned short
sizeof short: 2 bytes
short range: -32768 to 32767
sizeof unsigned short: 2 bytes
unsigned short range: 0 to 65535
==========================================================
DATA TYPE: int & unsigned int
sizeof int: 4 bytes
int range: -2147483648 to 2147483647
sizeof unsigned int: 4 bytes
unsigned short range: 0 to 2147483647
==========================================================
DATA TYPE: long & unsigned long
sizeof long: 4 bytes
long range: -2147483648 to 2147483647
sizeof unsigned long: 4 bytes
unsigned long range: 0 to 2147483647

Process returned 0 (0x0)   execution time : 0.024 s
Press any key to continue.
```

Alternatively, you can always do a little math to figure out the sizes for data types. How did the range boundaries get computed? As we have already established, a byte is a sequence of eight bits:

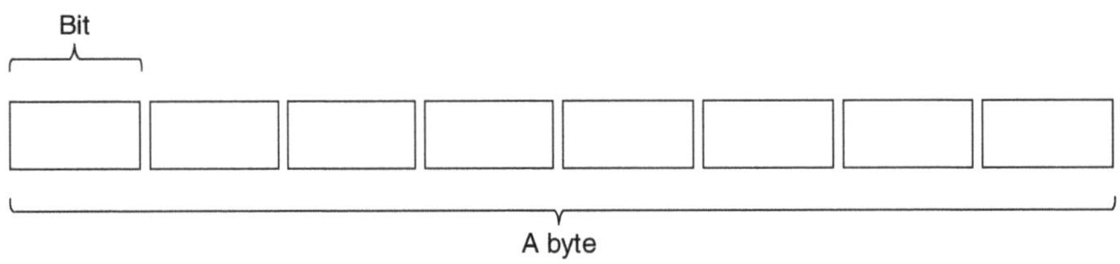


**Figure 7:** Bit vs. Byte.

A bit can store either a 0 or 1, meaning there are two possible values for each bit. Since there are eight bits in a byte that would mean that there are $2^8$ or 256 possible combinations of zeros and ones. On most systems, a short data type occupies two bytes in computer memory. Two bytes is 16 bits or $2^{16}$ possible combinations of zeros and ones, which turns out to be 65536. An integer occupies four bytes, it could possibly address $2^{32} = 4294967296$ possible combinations. All you need to know is how many bytes a particular data type requires and you can compute the range of values that the particular data type can address (support).

## Signed vs. Unsigned

The range of numbers an unsigned short can address is from 0 to 65535. Why is the range of a short from −32768 to +32,767? Why not from −3276**8** to + 32,76**8**?

The following figure depicts the problem:

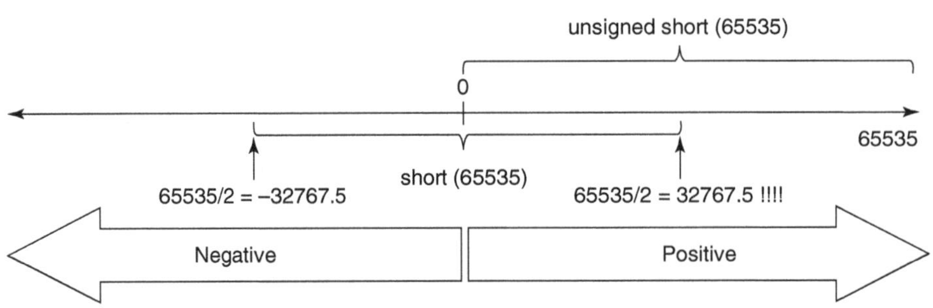


**Figure 8:** unsigned short and signed short.

From Figure 6 above, the range for both unsigned and signed short is 65535. The signed short needs to split the range (65535) equally on both negative and positive side of the number line. The problem is that 65535 divided by 2 yields 32767.5!

It turns out there is an easy solution for that! We forgot that the computer stores numbers in binary format (0's and 1's) rather than in the decimal format. Binary numbers are laid out from right to left, where the smallest digit is on the right and the largest digit is on left. This is due to the fact that each digit in a binary number is a representation of a 2 raised to some power. For example, the rightmost digit in a binary number represents $2^0$ or 1, the next digit represents $2^1 = 2$, the next digit is $2^2 = 4$, and so on:

| | | | | | | | |
|---|---|---|---|---|---|---|---|
| $2^7 = 128$ | $2^6 = 64$ | $2^5 = 32$ | $2^4 = 16$ | $2^3 = 8$ | $2^2 = 4$ | $2^1 = 2$ | $2^0 = 1$ |

For example, if we wanted to convert decimal number 65 by hand to its binary equivalent, all we need is to draw the following table:

| $2^7 = 128$ | $2^6 = 64$ | $2^5 = 32$ | $2^4 = 16$ | $2^3 = 8$ | $2^2 = 4$ | $2^1 = 2$ | $2^0 = 1$ |
|---|---|---|---|---|---|---|---|
| | | | | | | | |

Next, we need to find the largest number in the first row that is less or equal to our "target" number 65 and place a 1 in the same column in the second row:

| $2^7 = 128$ | $2^6 = 64$ | $2^5 = 32$ | $2^4 = 16$ | $2^3 = 8$ | $2^2 = 4$ | $2^1 = 2$ | $2^0 = 1$ |
|---|---|---|---|---|---|---|---|
| | 1 | | | | | | |

Next, find the largest number in the first row that when added to 64 will be less or equal to 65 and place a 1 in the corresponding column in the 2nd row. In this case that is number 1 in position 0:

| $2^7 = 128$ | $2^6 = 64$ | $2^5 = 32$ | $2^4 = 16$ | $2^3 = 8$ | $2^2 = 4$ | $2^1 = 2$ | $2^0 = 1$ |
|---|---|---|---|---|---|---|---|
| | 1 | | | | | | 1 |

Sum the two numbers and check whether the sum equals 65. If not, repeat the process. Otherwise, place 0's in the remaining cells in the 2nd row and you are done:

| $2^7 = 128$ | $2^6 = 64$ | $2^5 = 32$ | $2^4 = 16$ | $2^3 = 8$ | $2^2 = 4$ | $2^1 = 2$ | $2^0 = 1$ |
|---|---|---|---|---|---|---|---|
| 0 | 1 | 0 | 0 | 0 | 0 | 0 | 1 |

Thus number 65 base 10 is 01000001 base 2. In Computer Science, we write this as:

$$65_{10} = 01000001_2$$

The question is how do we represent negative numbers in binary number system? The answer to this question lies in the way numbers are represented in the computer which is called Two's Compliment[8] (Two's Compliment, 2013). The leftmost bit is the sign bit:

| $-2^7 = 128$ | $2^6 = 64$ | $2^5 = 32$ | $2^4 = 16$ | $2^3 = 8$ | $2^2 = 4$ | $2^1 = 2$ | $2^0 = 1$ |
|---|---|---|---|---|---|---|---|
| | | | | | | | |

[8]For more information please see : http://en.wikipedia.org/wiki/Two's_complement

To represent a negative number in binary, the leftmost bit needs to be turned on (must have a 1) and the rest remains the same. For example, $-65_{10}$ is $11000001_2$:

| $-2^7 = 128$ | $2^6 = 64$ | $2^5 = 32$ | $2^4 = 16$ | $2^3 = 8$ | $2^2 = 4$ | $2^1 = 2$ | $2^0 = 1$ |
|---|---|---|---|---|---|---|---|
| 1 | 1 | 0 | 0 | 0 | 0 | 0 | 1 |

Any negative number will have the leftmost bit set to 1 while any positive number will have the left most bit set to 0, which means that the largest positive number that can be represented using 1 byte two's compliment is $127_{10}$ ($01111111_2$) and largest negative number is $-128_{10}$($11111111_2$):

| $-2^7 = 128$ | $2^6 = 64$ | $2^5 = 32$ | $2^4 = 16$ | $2^3 = 8$ | $2^2 = 4$ | $2^1 = 2$ | $2^0 = 1$ | |
|---|---|---|---|---|---|---|---|---|
| 0 | 1 | 1 | 1 | 1 | 1 | 1 | 1 | ← 127 |
| 1 | 1 | 1 | 1 | 1 | 1 | 1 | 1 | ← −128 |

Using the two's compliment[9], it is clear why data types requiring two bytes of storage such as short can address −32768 to 32767.

Now that we know the mechanics of how integer data types are stored in computer memory, when do you use signed and when do you use unsigned numbers? In cases where you know that your data can never be negative such as rain precipitation, person's age, number of students in a class, etc. you should use unsigned integer data types. This can also flag possible errors, in case the user attempts to enter negative data.

### short vs. int

For example, if you are writing a program for an embedded system then you need to be concerned with memory allocation because such systems usually come with small memory. In that case, you should consider using short instead of an integer data type.

**The bool Data Type** The bool data type (or boolean) is named after the English mathematician George Boole[10] (George_Boole, 2013) and it is used to store values that can either be true or false. Boolean data type occupies one byte of memory. Historically, C++ interpreted value of zero as false, and non-zero as true. With the bool data type, C++ programs are more readable as it is very clear that the outcome can be one of two values (true or false). You can use integers instead of boolean as fundamentally they are not any different but instead of having only two possible outcomes you will have many possible outcomes which makes the program less readable.

Boolean data type is used as flag variables to signal that a certain condition has changed. For example, a flag could signal a condition has been met to terminate a loop.

**The char Data Type** Integers and characters are interchangeable in C++ due to the fact that characters are internally stored as integers. For every printable and the nonprintable character there is a corresponding unique number in the ASCII[11] table (Asciitable, 2013).

---

[9] A simple online Two's Compliment machine can be found at http://www.cse.yorku.ca/~peterc/2scompl.html
[10] http://en.wikipedia.org/wiki/George_Boole

According to the ASCII table, character 'A' is 65, 'B' is 66, 'C' is 67 and so on. Lower case 'a' is 97, 'b' is 98 and son. It is easy to see how the computer can distinguish between names written in upper/lower case letters.

A char data type can be used as a single character or as a string of characters (an array of characters) which we will discuss later on in the book.

**Floating- Point Data Types** Floating—point data types are used to store real numbers such as percentages, fractions etc. There are several floating-point data types in C++:

- Float
- Double
- Long double

Doubles require twice the amount of storage as floats hence the name. Some texts refer to doubles as double-precision numbers and call floats single-precision numbers. The ANSI C++ compliant compilers require that a double data type has at least the same amount of precision as a float. Long doubles need to have at least the same size as doubles. The actual sizes will depend on the compiler and the computer architecture. Then again, you can always write a program similar to the program in Listing 3. The only difference is that you will need to include the following header file <cfloat>.

**Non-Fundamental Data Types** Discuss string here etc. include which header file etc.

**String Data Type** Not exactly a fundamental data type but a class. In order to use it a program, it is necessary to include the <string> header file:

```
#include <string>
```

String data type is used to store a group of characters. Following are a few examples of strings:

```
string bestEver = "Michael Jordan";
string myAddress = "123 Main Street";
```

## Arithmetic Operators

In C++ language, there are many operators. They can be classified according to the number of operands they require. Thus we have:

- Unary operator requires only one operand. A good example is the negation operator: −10
- Binary operator requires two operands. The following table lists binary operators in C++:

| Operator | C++ Symbol | Example |
|---|---|---|
| Addition | + | 5 + 3 |
| Subtraction | – | 5.4 – 3 |
| Multiplication | * | 5 * 3.14 |
| Division | / | 5.0 / 3.0 |
| Modulus | % | 5 % 3 |

**Table 2:** C++ Operators.

[11] http://www.asciitable.com/

- Ternary operator requires three operands. Following is a general example of a ternary operator:

  ((x + 5) > 0) ? x = x + 1 : x = 10;

  if (x + 5) is greater than zero then the program is going to execute x = x + 1; otherwise it is going to execute x = 10. This is just another way of writing a conditional statement (if then else statement) and we are going to discuss it later on in the book.

## Integer Arithmetic

When working with operators, you need to be aware of few rules as the results may surprise you even if you check your results with a calculator. For example, a simple division of 5 by 3 using calculator:

**Figure 9:** Integer Arithmetic.

is not the same. The following C++ code segment produced the above output:

```
int main()
{
        cout << "5 / 3 = " << 5/3 << endl;
        return 0;
}
```

Is it possible for a simple calculator to be more accurate than a C++ program? The answer is that C++ program is just as accurate as the calculator! What is going on? The answer is the data type of the operators. Take a good look at the cout statement above. Number 5 is an integer literal and so is number 3. An **integer** divided by an **integer** results in an **integer**:

5/3=1.666666666666667

the computer actually produces the real number 1.666666666666667 but since the result has to be an integer, the decimal part is discarded.

To force real number as the quotient, you simply need to force mixed mode arithmetic which means that one of the operands has to be a double:

```
int main()
{
    cout << "5 / 3 = " << 5/3.0 << endl;
    return 0;
}
```

```
5 / 3 = 1.66667

Process returned 0 (0x0)   execution time : 0.032 s
Press any key to continue.
```

The general rule for integer arithmetic is that if both operands are integers the result will be an integer. In case one of the operands is a floating-point data type the result will always be the floating-point.

The modulus operator is the only operator that requires both operands to be of integer data type. However if you need to use floating-point data type operands, there is a function called fmod (floating-point modulus):

```
 1. #include <iostream>
 2. #include <cmath>                                    // required for fmod
 3.
 4. using namespace std;
 5.
 6. int main()
 7. {
 8.     cout << "5 / 1 = " << 5/3 << endl;             // integer / integer = integer
 9.     cout << "5 / 3.0 = " << 5/3.0 << endl;         // integer / double = double
10.
11.     // modulus
12.     cout << "5 % 3 = " << 5 % 3 << endl;           // integer % integer = integer
13.     cout << "fmod(5,3.2) = " << fmod (5,3.2); // fmod(integer,double) = double
14.
15.     return 0;
16. }
```

**Listing 4:** Integer Division and Modulus Operators

The following figure is the output of the Listing 4 program:

```
5 / 1 = 1
5 / 3.0 = 1.66667
5 % 3 = 2
fmod(5.3.2) = 1.8
Process returned 0 (0x0)   execution time : 0.019 s
Press any key to continue.
```

**Figure 10:** Listing 4 Program Run.

Calling fmod on line 4 in the above program is an example of calling a function. To call a function, you simply write its name and pass any inputs (called arguments) the function may require. How fmod computes the floating-point remainder is abstracted from us. In computer science, when the details of the function (or an object) are hidden, that is known as the "black box":

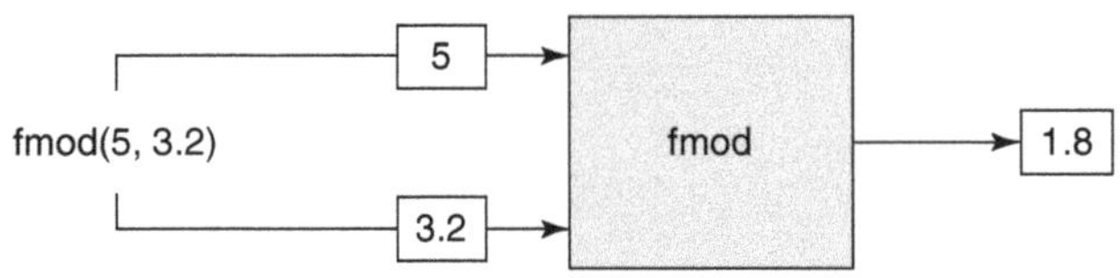


**Figure 11:** The fmod Function.

The fmod function receives integer value 5 and double value 3.2 as input. It processes these input values and returns the result (1.8).

This is an example of calling a library (built in) function. Later on when you learn how to write your own functions you will called in a similar manner.

## Operator Precedence and Associativity

The precedence rules specify the order of evaluation of operators. When there is only one operator there is no need to worry about the precedence rules. However, when there are more operators then the precedence rules determine the order of evaluation. For example:

$$3 + 5 * 10 - 20 / 2 + 5 \% 2 = 44$$

How did we arrive and that solution? The division, multiplication, and modulus operators are evaluated first. If the two operators of the same precedence need to be evaluated, they are evaluated from left to right:

| | | | | | | | | | | | | |
|---|---|---|---|---|---|---|---|---|---|---|---|---|
| 3 | + | 5 | * | 10 | - | 20 | / | 2 | + | 5 | % | 2 |
| 3 | + | 50 | | | - | 10 | | | + | 1 | | |
| 44 | | | | | | | | | | | | |

If we wanted to force different order of precedence, then we can use rules of associativity. This means grouping operations that we want to execute first inside the parentheses:

$$3 + 5 * 10 - 20 / 2 + 5 \% 2$$

| | | | | | | | | |
|---|---|---|---|---|---|---|---|---|
| (3+5) | * | (10−20) | / | 2 | + | 5 | % | 2 |
| 8 | * | -10 | / | 2 | + | 1 | | |
| -80 | | | / | 2 | + | 1 | | |
| -40 | | | | | + | 1 | | |
| -39 | | | | | | | | |

Following is the C++ statement:

```
cout << "(3+5)*(10-20)/2 + 5 % 3 = " << (3+5)*(10-20) /2 + 5% 3 << endl;
```

and the output of the program run:

```
(3+5)×(10-20)/2 + 5 % 2 = -39

Process returned 0 (0x0)   execution time : 0.018 s
Press any key to continue.
```

## Variable Assignments, Initializations, Scope

So far we have written programs using only simple cout statements and literals. Now that we have a good understanding of data types, the mechanics of how variables are allocated in computer memory we can use this newly gained knowledge to write more sophisticated programs.

### Variable Assignment

Let's write the program that will assign a letter grade to a student based on five quiz scores, a midterm, and a final exam score. Each category has different weight:

- quizzes are 60% of the grade
- midterm is 10% of the grade
- final is 20% of the grade

We start the program by declaring variables that will hold values for five quizzes. As a programmer, you need to strive to write clean, readable source code as it will make it easier to debug and maintain well written and well documented source code. It is very important to choose meaningful names for variables:

```
#include <iostream>

using namespace std;

int main()
{
     int midTermExam;
     int finalExam;
     int quiz1;
     int quiz2;
     int quiz3;
     int quiz4;
     int quiz5;
     int sum;
     double quizAvg;
     double score;
     // logic to be implemented later

     return 0;
}
```

**Listing 5:** Student Average Calculation

Listing 5 above is an incomplete program. We declared variables that will hold values for midterm exam, final exam, quizzes (5 of them), sum and average. Notice that a lot of variables are of integer data type. In situation like this, instead of declaring each variable on a separate line we can declare a single declaration:

```
int midTermExam, finalExam, quiz1, quiz2, quiz3, quiz4, quiz5, sum;
double quizAvg, score;
```

The format is data type followed by a list of variables that share the same data type. For better readability, you may want to declare some variables on separate lines even though they are of same data type.

In order to compute student average, we need to store some values in the quiz, midterm, final exam variables. That is accomplished with the assignment operator. For example, to assign a value of 100 to the variable quiz1, we need to type the following:

```
quiz1 = 100;
```

This is known as variable assignment statement. The assignment operator (=) has two operands: quiz1 and 100. It is very important to understand the operand positioning. The operand on the left hand side of the assignment operator is going to be "assigned" the value of 100. This operand is also known as the lvalue. The operand on the right-hand side of the assignment operator is known as the rvalue:

```
lvalue = rvalue;
```

The lvalue is an alias for the location in memory while the rvalue represents a value that is going to be stored in the memory location. Interestingly, rvalue can only be on the right hand side of the assignment operator, while the lvalue can also be on the right hand side of the assignment operator. The following code segment illustrates that:

```
1. int myNumber;
2. int yourNumber;
3. myNumber = 100;
4. yourNumber = 150;
5. myNumber = yourNumber;
6. cout << "myNumber = " << myNumber << endl;
```

**Figure 12:** Assignment Operator (lvalue and rvalue).

If we were to compile and run the above code segment, the output would be 150! Here is why:

On lines 4 and 5, we assign integer literals to respective memory locations (myNumber and yourNumber):

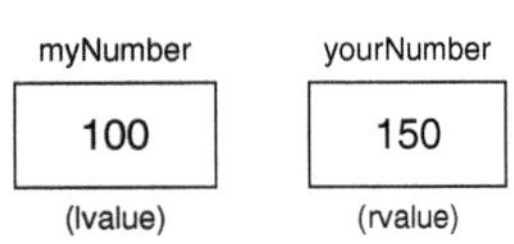


When the statement on line 5 executes, the value from yourNumber memory location is copied into the memory location that holds myNumber effectively destroying the original value in myNumber:

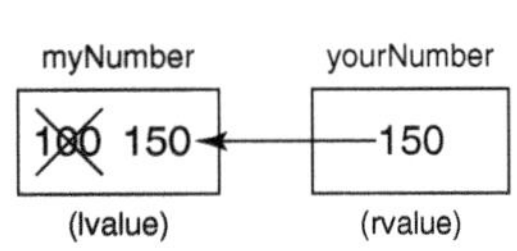


Similarly, placing a lvalue on the right hand side of the assignment operator will have the same effect:

We start with myNumber having a value of 150:

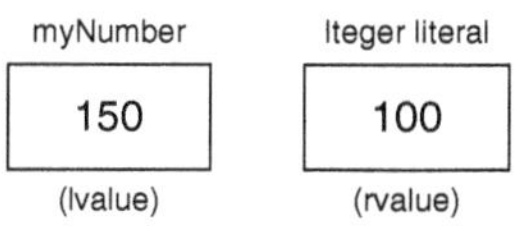


Then the following statement:

```
myNumber = myNumber + 100;
```

is executed:

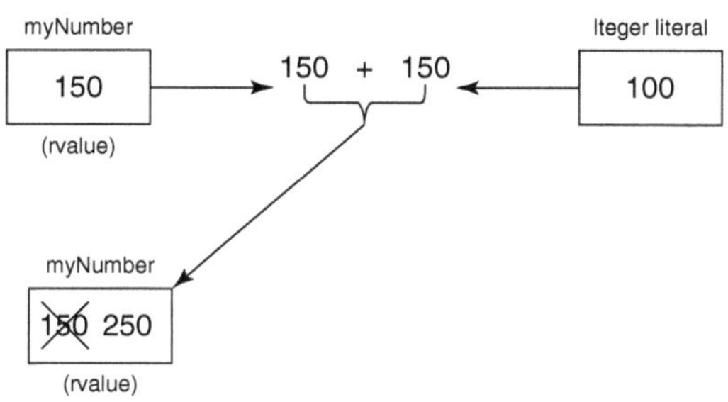


And the original value in myNumber is destroyed and the newly computed value 250 is stored into it. In essence, the instruction to the computer is to:

1. Compute the sum of the current value in myNumber and integer literal
2. Store the sum in the memory location called myNumber (at which point, the original value that was stored in the myNumber memory location is destroyed).

The above statement can be written in shorthand for the use of the C++ compound operators:

```
myNumber = myNumber + 100;
```

could be written as:

Move the + operator in front of the = operator

```
myNumber += 100;
```

The following table illustrates compound (combined) assignment operators:

| Long Version | Short Version |
|---|---|
| x = x + 10; | x += 10; |
| x = x − 10; | x −= 10; |
| x = x * 10; | x *= 10; |
| x = x / 10; | x /= 10; |

**Table 3:** Compound Assignment Operators.

## Multiple Assignment

Consider the following code segment:

```
int a, b, c;
int x = a = b = c = 10;
cout << "x = " << x << endl;
```

what would the value of x be ?

```
x = 10

Process returned 0 (0x0)   execution time : 0.009 s
Press any key to continue.
```

What about the following code segment:

```
int a=5, b=7, c=10;
int x = a = b = c;
cout << "x = " << x << endl;
```

what would the value of x be ?

```
x = 10

Process returned 0 (0x0)   execution time : 0.009 s
Press any key to continue.
```

The assignment operator works from right to left. In the above code sample:

1. The contents of the variable c would be assigned to the variable b destroying the value in the (7).
2. Next, the contents of the variable b, which now has value of 10 would be copied to the variable a, destroying the original value in the variable a (5).
3. Finally, the contents of variable a, which at this point contains value of 10 would be copied to the variable x.

## Initialization

It is possible to store values into variables at the same time when they are declared. This is known as initialization:

```
int quiz1 = 100;
```

Instead of declaring the variable first, and then initializing it in a separate statement, both operations are combined into one:

```
int quiz1;      }
quiz1 = 100;    }   int quiz1 = 100;
```

It is also possible to initialize variables in the single-line multiple declaration:

```
int quiz1=100, quiz2=90, quiz3, quiz4=88, quiz5=90;
```

In the statement above, quiz3 was simply declared but not initialized. The rest of the variables were initialized with data. If we attempt to display the contents of the variables:

```
cout << "Quiz1: " << quiz1 << endl;
cout << "Quiz2: " << quiz2 << endl;
cout << "Quiz3: " << quiz3 << endl;
cout << "Quiz4: " << quiz4 << endl;
cout << "Quiz5: " << quiz5 << endl;
```

We will get correct values for the variables that have been initialized. However, the quiz3 variable will display whatever was stored at the moment in the memory location assigned to it:

```
Quiz1: 100
Quiz2: 90
Quiz3: 8074256
Quiz4: 88
Quiz5: 90

Process returned 0 (0x0)   execution time : 0.024 s
Press any key to continue.
```

The point is that if the memory location is not initialized, it's safe to assume that it will contain some values ("garbage") that will negatively impact your program. From the example above, had we performed calculations without initializing the quiz3 variable, we would end up with an error.

When using multiple declarations on single line don't do this:

```
int quiz1, int quiz2, int quiz3; // ERROR!!!
```

There is no need to re-declare the type again as it has already been declared! Having learned all this, let's finalize the program:

```
#include <iostream>

using namespace std;

int main()
{
    int midTermExam;       // declare the midTermExam variable
    int finalExam;         // declare the finalExam variable
    int quiz1 = 100,       // initialize quiz variables
        quiz2 = 90,        // this could be done on separate lines
        quiz3 = 89,        // like this, or on one line
        quiz4 = 88,
        quiz5 = 90;
    double quizAvg, score;      // declare average and score

    midTermExam = 78;      // assign 78 to midTermExam
    finalExam = 92;        // assign 92 to finalExam

    // perform calculations (note the mixed mode arithmetic, associativity)
    // quiz variables are all integers, forcing a double by dividing
    quizAvg = (quiz1 + quiz2 + quiz3 + quiz4 + quiz5)/5.0;
    score = (quizAvg*0.60)+ midTermExam*0.10 + finalExam*0.20;
    cout << "Your score is: " << score << endl;
    return 0;
}
```

**Listing 6:** Student Average Program

The output of Listing 6 program run:

```
Your score is: 81.04

Process returned 0 (0x0)   execution time : 0.016 s
Press any key to continue.
```

Lines 7 and 8 could have been consolidated to one line multiple variable declaration since both of them are of the same data type. On lines 9 through 13, we initialized the quiz variables with some data. For improved readability we chose to list the variables on separate lines. As long as you have commas separating variables in a variable list, the compiler will not care whether the variable list is on one line or on separate lines.

On line 16, we assign some data to midterm and final exam variables and then we proceed to perform calculations. This is where he gets very interesting as some of the techniques we discussed earlier in the chapter are utilized. On line 21 we use associativity and mixed mode arithmetic. If we had the written the statement:

```
quizAvg = (quiz1 + quiz2 + quiz3 + quiz4 + quiz5)/5.0;
// correct!!!
```

without the parentheses:

```
quizAvg = quiz1 + quiz2 + quiz3 + quiz4 + quiz5/5.0;
```

the calculations would not be correct. Due to precedence rules, the division would take place first—so the result of quiz5/5.0 would be added to the sum of quiz1 through quiz4. What is peculiar is that the program will compile without any warning because the statement is syntactically correct. This would be an example of a runtime error where program compiles correctly but produces erroneous results:

```
Your score is: 257.2

Process returned 0 (0x0)   execution time : 0.022 s
Press any key to continue.
```

**Figure 13:** Erroneous Output - Run Time Error

## Scope

A variable cannot be used until it is declared. Consider the following code segment:

```
int main ()
{
    cout << "Number: " << number << endl;
    int number = 10;
    return 0;
}
```

The above code segment will not compile because, the variable number was not declared prior to the cout statement. In this case, the variable is said to be out of scope. You can think of variable scope as its lifetime:

1. A variable is declared,
2. it is used and
3. eventually destroyed

To put this in perspective, recall that program logic executes from top to bottom. As the compiler encounters statements such as variable declarations, it allocates necessary memory for them. Only after the memory has been allocated, it is possible to refer to the variable. As we have seen earlier, there may some "garbage" in the memory location but the code will be syntactically correct. Attempting to refer to a variable that is out of scope going to result in a syntax error as there is not memory location assigned to the variable.

## Named Constants

As a programmer, you will often have to anticipate requirements change. The code that we wrote the previous section has one problem that the weights associated with each grade category are hardcoded on line 22. What if those weights were to change? This is a relatively short program so the change would not be time-consuming. Imagine if your program was couple thousand lines long and you hardcoded these values all over the place. That change would be time-consuming as you would have to hunt for every line of code that contained those values.

So how do you deal with a situation like that? You could declare a variable for each one of the weights:

```
double quizCatWt = 0.60;
double midTermCatWt = 0.10;
double finalCatWt = 0.20;
```

and substitute the variables for constants in the statement on line 22:

```
score = (quizAvg* quizCatWt)+ midTermExam* midTermCatWt +
finalExam* finalCatWt;
```

This would work the only problem is that the code is not safe. Since the values for grade categories are not going to change during the program run it does not make sense to declare them as variables. As we know, variables can change during the program run. If this program is part of a large project with many programmers working on it then there is a possibility to corrupt the code with statements that affect the variables intended to hold constant values. As you can imagine this could have undesired outcomes.

To make the code safer, whenever values are not going to change during the program run you should use named constants. A named constant is a symbolic representation of a literal. The syntax for declaring a named constant is the keyword const followed by the data type, followed by the constant name, an assignment operator, and the value:

```
const dataType constantName = value;
```

Although there is no rule in C++ that states that named constant names have to be in capital letters, it is a good programming practice as it will help you distinguish between constants and variables:

```
const double QUIZ_CAT_WT = 0.60;
const double MIDTERM_CAT_WT = 0.10;
const double FINAL_CAT_WT = 0.20;
```

When you declare constants, any attempt to change them will result in an error as the following code segment demonstrates:

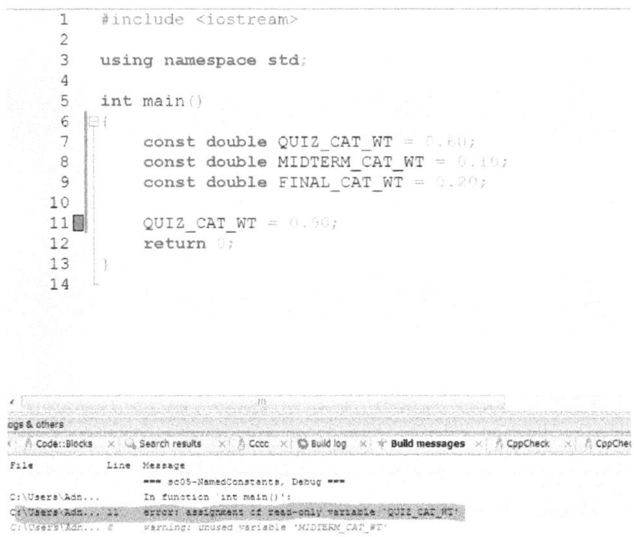


Using named constants instead of variables for values that are not going to change during the program run "hardens" the code. The following listing is the program with named constants:

```
#include <iostream>

using namespace std;

int main()
{
    // Constants
    const double QUIZ_CAT_WT = 0.60;
    const double MIDTERM_CAT_WT = 0.10;
    const double FINAL_CAT_WT = 0.20;

    // variables
    int midTermExam, finalExam; // declare midTermExam and finalExam
    int quiz1 = 100,    // initialize quiz variables
        quiz2 = 90,     // this could be done on separate lines
        quiz3 = 89,     // like this, or on one line
        quiz4 = 88,
        quiz5 = 90;
    double quizAvg, score;      // declare average and score

    midTermExam = 78;   // assign 78 to midTermExam
    finalExam = 92;     // assign 92 to finalExam

    // perform calculations (note the mixed mode arithmetic, associativity)
    // quiz variables are all integers, forcing a double by dividing
    quizAvg = (quiz1 + quiz2 + quiz3 + quiz4 + quiz5)/5.0;
    score = quizAvg * QUIZ_CAT_WT +
```

```
                 midTermExam * MIDTERM_CAT_WT +
                 finalExam * FINAL_CAT_WT;

        cout << "Your score is: " << score << endl;
        return 0;
}
```

**Listing 7:** Using Named Constants

## Legacy C/C++ Directives

As you interact with C++ legacy code, you will encounter the #define preprocessor directive:

```
#define QUIZ_CAT_WT 0.60
```

This was the way constants used to be defined in C/C++ programs. Note that there is no ";" at the end of the directive.

This is simply a preprocessor directive kind of like a macro (Stroustrup, 2009) and not a true constant. Unlike the constant declaration, no memory gets allocated for the #define preprocessor directive. Since it is a preprocessor directive, the preprocessor performs text substitutions. By the time the augmented source code is passed on to the compiler, the name QUIZ_CAT_WT will never be parsed by the compiler and placed into the symbol table. What if there is a conflict due to an import header file that has a constant with the same name? The compiler will report (Meyers, 1997) it as 0.60 rather than the QUIZ_CAT_WT conflict! Looking for 0.60 in a 10,000+ lines program will definitely test your patience.

Even worse, imagine making a simple mistake as adding the ";" (Gaddis, 2012) at the end of the preprocessor #directive:

```
#define QUIZ_CAT_WT 0.60;
#define MIDTERM_CAT_WT 0.10
#define FINAL_CAT_WT 0.20
```

The ";" becomes part of the text pattern that is going to be inserted by the preprocessor anywhere it finds `QUIZ_CAT_WT`! After the text substitution, the statement which uses the constant defined with the #directive would look like:

```
score = quizAvg * 0.60; + midTermExam * 0.10 + finalExam *
FINAL_CAT_WT;
```

Mistakes like this are easily made, especially when coding under pressure and trying to meet the deadline. Keep in mind that errors like this could produce hard-to-resolve compilation issues and unexpected results. Whenever possible, avoid the #define preprocessor directive and use the constant declaration.

## Overflow and Underflow

When performing math operations on variables of numeric data types, the programmer needs to be careful not to cause overflow and underflow. These phenomena occur when adding (or subtracting) to (from) a variable whose value is close to the limit of the data type. Consider the following code segment:

```
short myUpperNumber = 32767;
myUpperNumber = myUpperNumber + 1;
cout << myUpperNumber;
```

compiling and running this code segment is not going to produce 32767:

```
-32768
Process returned 0 (0x0)   execution time : 0.011 s
Press any key to continue.
```

The compiler would not flagged any errors, however the result may surprise you. This is an example of an overflow which means the number (result) simply wrapped around to the other end of the data type range:

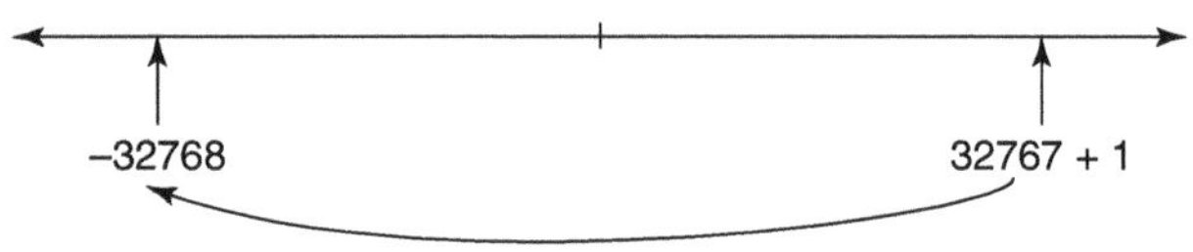


The underflow works the same way—if we were to attempt to subtract a number on the other end of the data type range at −32768, the resulting value would be 32767 because there is no −32769 in the short data range so the value would wraparound to the other end of the range (32767).

## End of Chapter Questions

### True/False

Indicate whether the statement is true or false.

**1.** The C++ programming process consist of writing, compiling, and writing the code.
**2.** Syntax error is simply an error in the language syntax.
**3.** Runtime errors are easy to spot because it produces erroneous result.
**4.** The preprocessor is a program whose job is to search for "#include" directives and augment the source code with the program file.
**5.** Every C++ must have a main function.
**6.** The C++ compiler cares how neat your program is written.
**7.** The elements of the C++ language are as follow: Reserved words, identifiers, operators, punctuation, and grammar.
**8.** Literals are values that change during the program run.
**9.** The compiler does not append an extra character call NULL at the end of a string literal.
**10.** Variables are names (aliases) for memory location.
**11.** int x declares a variable called x whose data type is an integer.
**12.** C++ data types can be classified as fundamental integer data types, non-fundamental data types, and abstract data type.
**13.** In C++, the precedence rules does not specify the order of evaluation of operator.

**14.** A variable can be used even though is not declared.

**15.** It is possible to store values into variables at the same time when they are declared.

## Exercises

**1.** Age limit

Write a program that asks the birth date of a person and calculates the age of the person. The program should ask the user for their birthdate and calculates how old they are.

**2.** Zoo Park Rates

A zoo park likes to generate welcome booklets for their customers; the booklet shows the family members' names, the price for each ticket. The program should ask how many adults and children tickets are needed (the price for an adult is $32.00 and $15.00 for a child).

**3.** Princess/Pirate theme birthday e-card

Write a program that asks the user for the following information:

- His or her name
- His or her age

The program is going to display the following e-card

Happy Birthday to you! Happy Birthday NAME!! Happy Birthday NAME!! You are age!! years old.

*Chapter 3*

# Interactive Input, Expressions, and Formatting

***"The only Zen you find on the tops of mountains is the Zen you bring up there"***

***—Robert M. Pirsig***

## Interacting with the User

### The `cin` Object

All the programs that we have written so far have used hardcoded data. What is wrong with that? For starters, you are limited to only one set of data. If you need to change the data set, that means you have to edit your program, save it, recompile it, and run it again. There's no input from the user. In this chapter are going to learn how to interact with the user.

We're going to write a program that will prompt the user to enter some data, will capture the data and store it in a memory location, and display it back.

```
int main()
{
    int myNumber;    // to store user input
    cout << "Enter your favorite number (1-100): " << endl;
    cin >> myNumber;

    cout << "You entered : " << myNumber << endl;
    return 0;
}
```

**Listing 1:** Interacting with the User

Since we're asking the user to enter a number, we declare a variable myNumber of integer data type. We capture user input with the help of an object called cin. The cin object uses what is known as stream extraction operator (>>) to store the data into the integer variable myNumber. What stream are we extracting this data from? To help understand that, let's review user interaction with the program in Listing 1. When we compile and run the program, the first thing the user is going to see is the prompt asking him or her to enter a favorite number. The user will type in the number and press the enter key. How does our program know to capture user input? Through the cin object? Yes, that is correct, but how does the cin object capture user input? The answer is through the keyboard buffer. There is a buffer called the keyboard buffer in the RAM that is allocated for user input. It is nothing more than a block of memory reserved for user input. The cin object reads from this block of memory (stream) through the >> operator, also called the stream extraction operator because it extracts the data from the keyboard buffer and stores it into the variable as instructed by the program.

Let's compile and run the above program:

```
Enter your favorite number (1-100):
5
You entered : 5

Process returned 0 (0x0)   execution time : 3.265 s
Press any key to continue.
```

What happens if you enter a double instead of an integer? The program still outputs an integer:

```
Enter your favorite number (1-100):
5.32
You entered : 5

Process returned 0 (0x0)   execution time : 3.769 s
Press any key to continue.
```

This is due to the fact that the cin object was instructed to read an integer from the keyboard buffer. What happens to the decimal part?

| 5.32↵ |
|---|

**Figure 1:** Keyboard Buffer after the User Enters the Data.

It remains in the keyboard buffer as illustrated below:

| 0.32 ↵ |
|---|

**Figure 2:** Keyboard Buffer after the cin Statement Executes.

To better understand this, let's change the above program to include the following lines:

```
int main()
{
    int myNumber;          // to store user input
    double yourNumber;     // to store 2nd user input

    cout << "Enter your favorite number (1-100): " << endl;
    cin >> myNumber;

    cout << "Enter another number: " << endl;
    cin >> yourNumber;

```

```
12.     cout << "myNumber : " << myNumber << endl;
13.     cout << "yourNumber: " << yourNumber << endl;
14.     return 0;
15. }
```

**Listing 2:** Modified Program from Listing 1

We added another variable on line number 4, and we added another prompt on line 9, followed by another cin object attempting to read the new value entered by the user. Finally, on lines 12 and 13 we display the contents of the two variables in the program. Compiling and running this program will result in the little surprise:

```
Enter your favorite number (1-100):
5.32
Enter another number:
myNumber : 5
yourNumber: 0.32

Process returned 0 (0x0)   execution time : 4.166 s
Press any key to continue.
```

First of all, instead of entering an integer for the first prompt we entered a double (5.32). When the program prompted for another number, we never had the chance to enter it. Instead the program displayed the contents of myNumber and the contents of yourNumber. However, we never entered any data for the second number (yourNumber)! What is going? The answer lies in the keyboard buffer:

- The first cin statement on line 7 was instructed to read an integer. It did precisely that—read an integer!
- The .32 was left in the keyboard buffer. The second cin statement on line 10 was instructed to read a double. Value .32 was left in the keyboard buffer, and .32 is a real number so the cin statement extracted it and stored it into the yourNumber variable.

We will learn later on how to mitigate these type of situations. If we were to change the above program to read two integers or two doubles, the program would work just fine. This is because the cin object does exactly what is told to do and nothing more or less.

## Reading Multiple Input

The cin object does not have to be written as a separate statement. In in fact, several cin reads could be accomplished using one line of code:

```
cin >> myNumber >> yourNumber;
```

If written this way, the user can enter the first number, press the space bar, and then enter the second number. One thing to keep in mind is that user behavior is unpredictable and that you cannot count that they will do exactly as told.
Another issue that can arise from using one of cin statement to read multiple values is that some users may enter these values backwards. For example:

```
cout << "Enter your age, press the space bar, and then enter
your weight: " << endl;
cin >> age >> weight;
```

Most users will follow the directions and enter age followed by the weight. However, small percentage will not follow directions. Some people may enter data backwards—first the weight, then enter the age, which could have disastrous consequences if people are performing certain calculations.

This type of input collection is okay in a controlled environment—if you're testing your program or other operation. For programs geared towards general public use, where you don't have much control of your user's actions, you need to write more robust code where you would prompt the user for each value and read each value with its own cin statement:

```
cout << "Enter your age: ";
cin >> age;
cout << "Enter your weight: ";
cin >> weight;
```

## Strings and Character Input

The cin object has some intelligence built in so that it can distinguish between different data types and capture user input. However, the cin object has its some limitations. Suppose you are writing a program that needs to capture person's full name:

```
int main()
{
    string fullName;

    cout << "Please enter your full name: ";
    cin >> fullName;

    cout << "Your full name is : " << fullName << endl;
    return 0;
}
```

**Listing 3:** Using cin with string Objects

Compiling and running this program will have a little surprise:

```
Please enter your full name: Adnan F. Zejnilovic
Your full name is : Adnan

Process returned 0 (0x0)   execution time : 7.584 s
Press any key to continue.
```

What happened to the rest of my name? The answer is that it was left in the keyboard buffer:

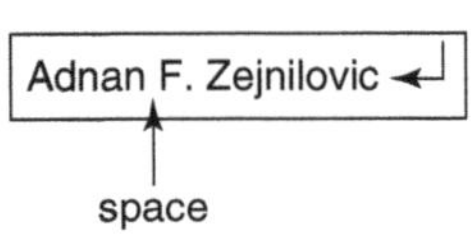


**Figure 3:** Keyboard Buffer after the User Enters the Data.

The cin object terminates reading from the keyboard buffer the moment it encounters what is known as the white space (space, tab, newline, carriage return, etc.).

In order to successfully capture user input that contains white space characters, C++ provides a function called getline. Instead of the cin statement on line 6, we can use the following statement

```
getline(cin, fullName);
```

in the above statement, to get one function takes two arguments (the cin object, and the string variable fallName). With the help of the getline function begins successfully read person's full name:

```
Please enter your full name: Adnan "Adi" F. Zejnilovic
Your full name is : Adnan "Adi" F. Zejnilovic

Process returned 0 (0x0)   execution time : 17.262 s
Press any key to continue.
```

Suppose that we want to gather some additional information from the user. Let's assume that the user is a student and we will capture and their GPA and their major. We declared several variables to store the information:

```
int main()
{
    string fullName, studentMajor;
    double studentGPA;

    cout << "Please enter your full name: ";
    getline(cin, fullName);

    cout << "Please enter your GPA: ";
    cin >> studentGPA;

    cout << "Please enter your major: ";
    getline(cin, studentMajor);

    cout << "Your full name is : " << fullName << endl;
    cout << "Your major is : " << studentMajor << endl;
    cout << "Your GPA is : " << studentGPA << endl;
    return 0;
}
```

**Listing 4:** Using the getline function to Capture User Input

If we compile and run this program, it will not work properly:

```
Please enter your full name: Adnan "Adi" Zejnilovic
Please enter your GPA: 3.9
Please enter your major: Your full name is : Adnan "Adi" Zejnilovic
Your major is : Adnan "Adi" Zejnilovic
Your GPA is : Adnan "Adi" Zejnilovic

Process returned 0 (0x0)   execution time : 18.581 s
Press any key to continue.
```

This is certainly not the output that matches programming statements in our source code. What is going on? Wasn't the getline function supposed to solve the user input capture problems? It turns out it did, but the order of information being captured throws a challenge. We know that the user input for the first variable (fullName) is captured correctly with the getline function. It seems that the second prompt for the GPA creates this new challenge. In order to rise to the challenge, we need to review what information is stored in this point in the keyboard buffer.

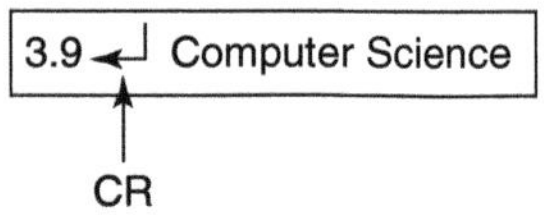


**Figure 4:** Keyboard Buffer Contents.

Analyzing the information in the keyboard buffer, we see that there is a carriage return character (caused by pressing the enter key on the keyboard) in the keyboard buffer followed by students major. Using the cout statement on line 10, the program extracts 3.5 from the keyboard buffer and stores it into the studentGPA variable. The carriage return (CR) character is left in the keyboard buffer. The next statement is a prompt to enter the major. The subsequent statements on line 13 is the call to the getline function. The getline function consumes the carriage return from the keyboard buffer, so the major is never extracted from the keyboard buffer and stored it into the variable allocated for it.

How do we correct this situation? The cin object provides member function ignore to deal with situations like this. The ignore member function clears leftover character in the keyboard buffer:

```
 1. int main()
 2. {
 3.       string fullName, studentMajor;
 4.       double studentGPA;
 5.
 6.       cout << "Please enter your full name: ";
 7.       getline(cin, fullName);
 8.
 9.       cout << "Please enter your GPA: ";
10.       cin >> studentGPA;
11.       cin.ignore();
12.       cout << "Please enter your major: ";
13.       getline(cin, studentMajor);
14.
15.       cout << "Your full name is : " << fullName << endl;
16.       cout << "Your major is : " << studentMajor << endl;
17.       cout << "Your GPA is : " << studentGPA << endl;
18.       return 0;
19. }
```

**Listing 5:** Using the cin.ignore Member Function

Compiling and running the above program produces correct output:

```
Please enter your full name: Adi Zejnilovic
Please enter your GPA: 3.9
Please enter your major: Computer Science
Your full name is : Adi Zejnilovic
Your major is : Computer Science
Your GPA is : 3.9

Process returned 0 (0x0)   execution time : 11.348 s
Press any key to continue.
```

The output looks great, so we are done, right? Not so fast! Let's run one more test. When prompted for the GPA, enter something like 3.92 space, space, perhaps a tab character, and then some numbers, and the program will not perform correctly:

```
Please enter your full name: Adi Zejnilovic
Please enter your GPA: 3.91  891        11
Please enter your major: Your full name is : Adi Zejnilovic
Your major is :  891    11
Your GPA is : 3.91

Process returned 0 (0x0)   execution time : 19.148 s
Press any key to continue.
```

Why are we entering erroneous input? The reason is that users are unpredictable, and maybe in the middle of a phone call while interacting with your program. Or they may be searching for something and mistakenly press extra keys that you did not anticipate. How do we get this program to run?

The member function ignores only one character. There are a few overrides that can be used to clear "x" number of characters, but we do not know how many characters we need to clear—5,10, or 100? So we engage help of another cin member function called sync:

```
cin.ignore();
cin.sync();
```

and finally we get the program to perform correctly:

```
Please enter your full name: Adi Zejnilovic
Please enter your GPA: 3.9      89  11
Please enter your major: Computer Science
Your full name is : Adi Zejnilovic
Your major is : Computer Science
Your GPA is : 3.9

Process returned 0 (0x0)   execution time : 20.972 s
Press any key to continue.
```

To read single characters and not be affected by the white space, the cin object provides the get function with the following syntax:

```
char myChar = cin.get();
```

This is another override that you can use:

```
cin.get(ch);
```

You can mix to cin>> and cin.get(), but you have to be very careful because this can cause some problems. Remember that cin >> leaves characters in the keyboard buffer and the cin.get() ignores them. Unless you are extracting the same data type for multiple variables—i.e., integers—then you should use the cin.ignore() followed by the cin.sync() after the cin>> to remove leftover characters in the keyboard buffer.

## Mathematical Library Functions

In order to implement more sophisticated mathematical functions, you need to use C++ math library functions. For example, C++ does not have a way to square a number. Hence you need to use the pow function from the math library. In order to use the math library, you need to include the following header file:

```
#include <cmath>
```

Some of the most common C++ math library functions are listed in Table 1.

**Table 1:** Most Common Built-In Math Functions.[1]

| Function Name | Description |
|---|---|
| abs(a) | Absolute value |
| exp(a) | Exponent |
| sqrt(a) | Square root |
| pow(a,n) | Variable a raised to the power of this n |

The following code segment demonstrates the sqrt and the pow functions:

```
int main()
{
    int number,        // to hold user  number
        myExponent,    // to hold user exponent
        myPower;       // to hold the result of number ^ myPower
    double myRoot;     // to hold the result of sqrt(myRoot)

    cout << "Demonstrating the pow function: " << endl;
    cout << "Enter a number: ";
    cin >> number;
    cout << "What power would you like to raise " << number << " ? :";
    cin >> myExponent;
    myPower = pow(static_cast<double>(number), myExponent);
    cout << number << " ^ " << myExponent
         << " = " << myPower << endl;

    cout << "\n\n\nDemonstrating the sqrt function: " << endl;
    myRoot = sqrt(myPower);
    cout << "sqrt(" << myPower << ") = " << myRoot << endl;

    return 0;
}
```

**Listing 6:** Using pow and sqrt Math Library Functions

[1]For more information, please see www.cplusplus.com/reference/cmath

Compiling and running the program produces the following output:

```
Demonstrating the pow function:
Enter a number: 3
What power would you like to raise 3 ? :4
3 ^ 4 = 81


Demonstrating the sqrt function:
sqrt(81) = 9
```

## Type Conversion

C++ data types are ranked in the following hierarchy:

**Table 2:** C++ Data Type Rankings.

| | |
|---|---|
| **HIGHEST** | long double |
| | double |
| ↑ | float |
| | unsigned long |
| | long |
| | insigned int |
| | int |
| | unsigned short |
| | short |
| **LOWEST** | char |

When C++ is working with an operator, if the operands are of different data type, it tries to convert them to the same type. This is called implicit (automatic) conversion. It is also referred to as type coercion.

Just like in the military, corporate world, or any organization where there is a hierarchy, moving from lower rank to high rank is called promotion. The opposite process,moving from the higher rank to the lower rank, is called demotion. In C++, when lower-ranked data types are converted to a higher-rank data type, they are promoted. Demoting a value means converting is to the lower data type. The C++ language uses three rules when it comes to type coercion:

- Rule 1: char, short, and unsigned short are automatically promoted to int.
- Rule 2: When an operator works with two operands of different data types, the lower-ranking operand is promoted to the data type of the higher-ranking operand.
- Rule 3: When the final value of an expression is assigned to a variable, it is converted to the data type of the variable regardless of the data type rank.

Consider the following code segment:

```
int x;
double y = 3.141376;
x = y;
```

```
cout << "This is y:  " << y << endl;
cout << "This is x:  " << x << endl;
```

which will produce the following output:

```
This is y: 3.14138
This is x: 3

Process returned 0 (0x0)   execution time : 0.007 s
Press any key to continue.
```

## Type Casting

Consider the following statement:

```
double myNumber = 2.25;
```

It declares a variable of data type double and initializes it with a value of 2.25. Suppose you need to convert it to an integer, but you do not want to introduce any other variables. How would you do that?

It turns out that this is quite easy to do in C++ through static cast. The syntax is as follows:

```
static_cast<DataType>(value)
```

Now that you know the syntax, you could type the following:

```
cout << "The integer part of " << myNumber << " is : " << static_cast<int>(myNumber);
```

This works with variables is in the statement above; it also works with literals: Instead of myNumber, we could have passed a double literal:

```
cout << "The integer part of " << myNumber << " is : " << static_cast<int>(2.25);
```

Do not forget to put parentheses around the data dates your typecasting to a different cast. Where is this useful? You would use static_cast when you need to programmatically force certain data type:

```
int main()
{
    const int numTests = 3;
    int test1=85, test2=100, test3=87;
    double average;

    average = (test1+test2+test3)/numTests;
    cout << "Your average is : " << average << endl;
    return 0;
}
```

**Listing 7:** Simple Average

Compiling and running the above program produces the following output:

```
Your average is : 90

Process returned 0 (0x0)   execution time : 0.015 s
Press any key to continue.
```

How is this possible given that the variable average was declared as a double? The problem is that variables test1, test2, and test3 are declared as integers. In addition, the constant numTests is declared as an integer constant. Thus the result of integer over integer will be an integer, which means that any decimal part that is a result of the consultation will be discarded prior to the number being converted to a double (the data type of the variable average to which this result is being assigned). To make sure the calculations are correct, you can static cast either the numerator or the denominator (but not both):

```
average = static_cast<double>(test1+test2+test3)/numTests;
```

or

```
average = (test1+test2+test3)/static_cast<double>(numTests);
```

which will force mixed-type arithmetic and therefore generate the correct result. The result is stored in the average variable and displayed with the cout statement on line 8:

```
Your average is : 90.6667

Process returned 0 (0x0)   execution time : 0.015 s
Press any key to continue.
```

One of the most common mistakes made by programmers is to static cast the entire quotient:

```
average = static_cast<double>((test1+test2+test3)/numTests);
```

The statement above will not result in a double because the operation inside of the parentheses will take place first, meaning test scores (integer) would be summed and divided by numTests (integer), resulting in an integer. As a consequence of integer arithmetic, any fraction will be discarded (i.e., showing a result of 90 instead of 90.6667), so static casting to double will not have much effect except to convert an integer to a double.

## Legacy Casts

If you work on a project that calls legacy functions, you may encounter casts in the following format:

```
average = (test1+test2+test3)/(double)numTests; // C cast syntax
average = (test1+test2+test3)/double (numTests); // C++ cast syntax
```

Whenever possible, use the static_cast rather than the legacy casts.

## Expressions

We have encountered expressions in this book, but we have not formally defined them. An expression is anything that evaluates to numeric value. An expression can be a combination of values and operators, but it always results in a value. Following are some examples of expressions:

- A Literal constant such as 85 assigned to a variable:

  ```
  test1 = 85
  ```

  In order to evaluate this expression, a literal constant is assigned to the variable test1. As a result, whatever value was in memory location called test1 was destroyed. If the assignment operation completes successfully, the expression will evaluate to 1 (true).

  Expression could also be "expression statements":

  ```
  test1 = 85;
  ```

  When you add the semicolon at the end, the expression became a statement.

- A Symbolic constant, such as

  ```
  const int numTests = 3;
  ```

  which is also an expression statement, evaluates to the value assigned to it when it was defined. In this case it would be integer number 3.

- Expressions can use arithmetic operators (with associativity rules), which we have seen in Chapter 2:

  3 + 5 * 2

  3 + (12 – 4) * ((14/2 – 8)*3)

  An expression could be evaluated inline in a cout statement:

  ```
  cout << "3 + 5 * 2 is : " << 3 + 5 * 2 << endl;
  ```

  In computer science, when an expression is evaluated as part of another statement, it is called "inline" evaluation because the calculations take place and the result is not stored in a variable but it is returned to the statement (inline) in the same line. Alternatively, you could have:

  ```
  int result = 3 + 5 * 2;

  cout << "3 + 5 * 2 is : " << result << endl;
  ```

  which is not inline because the calculations were performed first in the statement prior to the cout statement.

- A variable, which evaluates to the value assigned to it by the program. In the previous section, we have computed the average by using the following statement:

  ```
  average = (test1+test2+test3)/static_cast<double>(numTests);
  ```

To better understand these expressions we need to elaborate on the relational operators.

# Operators

In addition to the assignment and arithmetic operators, the C++ language also has relational operators and logical operators. We covered the assignment operator and introduced arithmetic operators in Chapter 2. In this section, we will expand on the arithmetic operators.

## Arithmetic Operators

In Chapter 2, we have learned that depending on the number of operands, arithmetic operators can be classified as:

- Unary
- Binary
- Ternary

We have also learned about the operator precedence and associativity rules.

### *Unary Operators*

Unary operators require only one operand. We have seen the negation operator (–) in Chapter 2. It simply changes the sign of the value.

In addition to the negation operator, the increment (++) and decrement (– –) operators are also unary operators:

**Table 3:** Increment and Decrement Operator.

| Operator | C++ Symbol | C++ |
|---|---|---|
| Increment | ++ | ++x, x++ |
| Decrement | – – | – –x, x– – |

Depending on the position of the operator in reference to the operand, the outcome will be different. If the operator is in front of the operand, this is called the prefix:

```
++x;
```

And it is equivalent to:

x = x + 1; ( which can also be written as x+=1;)

Similarly, the decrement operator can be in prefix mode:

```
--x;
```

Which is equivalent to:

```
x = x - 1; (or x-= 1;)
```

When the operator is in prefix mode, the arithmetic operation on the operand takes place first, then the operand is used.

The postfix mode works differently because the operand is first used, then the increment (or decrement) operator modifies the operand. Following are a few examples of prefix and postfix modes and their outcomes as the following code segment demonstrates:

```
 1. int x = 5;
 2.
 3. // prefix increment operator
 4. cout << "PREFIX operator demo" << endl;
 5. cout << "This is x before: " << x << endl;
 6. cout << "This is x after: " << ++x << endl;
 7.
 8. // postfix increment operator
 9. cout << "\n\n\nPOSTFIX operator demo " << endl;
10. cout << "This is x before: " << x << endl;
11. cout << "This is x after: " << x++ << endl;
12. cout << "This is x after the cout statement: " << x << endl;
```

**Listing 8:** Prefix and Postfix Operator

Compiling and running the above program will produce the following output:

```
PREFIX operator demo
This is x before: 5
This is x after: 6



POSTFIX operator demo
This is x before: 6
This is x after: 6
This is x after the cout statement: 7

Process returned 0 (0x0)   execution time : 0.022 s
Press any key to continue.
```

The program starts by declaring an integer variable x and initializing its value to 5. When the prefix operator executes inline in the cout statement on line 6, it first performs the arithmetic operation (x=x+1) on the operand x. This is why the cout object displays x=6.

On the other hand, when the increment operator is in the postfix mode, if will first use the operand x, then perform the increment operation. At this point, x contains value of 6, which is what the cout statement on line 11 displays. After the cout statement displays the contents of x, the increment takes place and x becomes 7, which is displayed by the last cout statement (on line 12).

### Binary Operators

Binary operators require two operands, hence the name. The following table lists C++ binary operators:

**Table 4:** C++ Binary Operators.

| Operator | C++ Symbol | Example |
|---|---|---|
| Addition | + | 5 + 3 |
| Subtraction | - | 5.4 – 3 |
| Multiplication | * | 5 * 3.14 |
| Division | / | 5.0 / 3.0 |
| Modulus | % | 5 % 3 |

As discussed in Chapter 2, the rules of operator precedence and associativity apply to binary operators.

## Relational Operators

In our everyday lives, we make a lot of decisions. For example, if we shop for an item, we do price comparison and make decisions based on that comparison. In C++, we can compare numeric and character values with the aid of relational operators.

An expression containing a relational operator evaluates to either true or false. There are six relational operators in C++:

**Table 5:** C++ Relational Operators.

| Operator | C++ Symbol | Example | Means | Evaluates[2] |
|---|---|---|---|---|
| Equal | == | x == y | Is operand x equal to operand y? | False |
| Greater than | > | x > y | Is operand x greater than operand y? | True |
| Less than | < | x < y | Is operand x less than operand y? | False |
| Greater or equal | >= | x >= y | Is operand x greater or equal to operand y? | True |
| Less or equal | <= | x <= y | Is operand x less or equal to operand y? | False |
| Not equal | != | x != y | Is operand x not equal to operand y? | False |

Do not confuse the assignment operator (=) with the equal operator (==)!

```
 1. int x = 5;
 2. int y = 20;
 3.
 4. cout << "Operator EQUAL == " << endl;
 5. cout << "x == y: " << (x==y) << endl;
 6. cout << "x: " << x << endl;
 7. cout << "y: " << y << endl;
 8. cout << "\n\n\nAssignment Operator = " << endl;
 9. cout << "x = y: " << (x=y) << endl;
10. cout << "x: " << x << endl;
11. cout << "y: " << y << endl;
```

**Listing 9:** Operator == (equal) vs. = (assignment)

On line 5, we test whether x is equal to y, and the program correctly responds with a 0 (false). On line 9, we assign the value of y to the value of x, destroying the original value of x (5):

[2]Assuming x = 5 and y =3

```
Operator EQUAL ==
x == y: 0
x: 5
y: 20


Assignment Operator =
x = y: 20
x: 20
y: 20

Process returned 0 (0x0)   execution time : 0.061 s
Press any key to continue.
```

Any expression will evaluate to either true or false as illustrated by the following code segment:

```
int x = 5;
int y = 20;
bool result = x < y;
cout << "x: " << x << endl;
cout << "y: " << y << endl;
cout << "x < y = " << result << endl;
```

And the output:

```
x: 5
y: 20
x < y = 1

Process returned 0 (0x0)   execution time : 0.020 s
Press any key to continue.
```

Relational operators are mainly used to test create conditions (expressions) whose evaluation will influence program logic in if statements.

## Conditional Statements

So far we have written only programs that operated on variable constants, gathered input from the user, performed calculations, and displayed results. These programs were sequential programs because they executed all the statements in sequence. That is great for simple programs. In order to write more sophisticated programs, we need to use conditional statements. Conditional statements, as the name implies, execute only if a certain condition is met.

### The `if` Statement

An if statement has the following syntax:

```
if (expr)
    statementA;
statementB;
statementC;
```

There is no semicolon (;) at the end of the if statement!

The statement starts with the keyword "if" followed by an expression in parentheses.

Based on how the expression evaluates (true or false), the subsequent statement (statementA) may (or may not) execute. If the expression evaluates to true, statementA will execute. Otherwise, statementA will not execute—it will be skipped over. Regardless, the statement(s) that follow (statementB, statementC) will execute. In other words, the execution of the statementA is tied to the evaluation of the expression in the if statement.

It is customary to indent the statement to the if statement 3 to 4 spaces for better program readability, maintainability, and debugging. The compiler does not care about the indentations; however, it is much easier to read well formatted source code.

Consider the following code segment:

```
int main()
{
    int x = 25;
    int y = 20;
    if (x < y)
        cout << x << " is less than " << y << endl;
    return 0;
}
```

**Listing 10:** Simple if Statement

When compiled, the program will output the following:

```
Process returned 0 (0x0)   execution time : 0.021 s
Press any key to continue.
```

Let's add several more lines of code, namely changing the value of x so that the expression evaluates to true in order to trigger the execution of the cout statement:

```
1. int main()
2. {
3.     int x = 5;
4.     int y = 20;
5.     if (x < y)
6.         cout << x << " is less than " << y << endl;
7.
8.     cout << "Have a nice day!" << endl;
9.     return 0;
10. }
```

**Listing 11:** Simple if Statement Modified

If we compile and run this program, the expression on line 5 will evaluates to true, triggering the execution of the cout statement on line 6. We added one more line of code, a cout statement displaying a message "Have a nice day," on line 8, which will display regardless of how the expression in the if statement evaluates:

```
5 is less than 20
Have a nice day!

Process returned 0 (0x0)   execution time : 0.030 s
Press any key to continue.
```

If we initialize variable x with a value so that it is greater than 20, the cout statement on line 6 will not execute. The cout statement on line 8 will execute regardless because it is not influenced by the if statement:

```
 1. int main()
 2. {
 3.     int x = 25;
 4.     int y = 20;
 5.     if (x < y)
 6.         cout << x << " is less than " << y << endl;
 7.
 8.     cout << "Have a nice day!" << endl;
 9.     return 0;
10. }
```

**Listing 12:** Simple if Statement (expression evaluates to false)

If we compile and run the code example above, we can definitely see that the if statement affects only the execution of the statement following it.

```
Have a nice day!

Process returned 0 (0x0)   execution time : 0.022 s
Press any key to continue.
```

We can use a flowchart[3] to depict the logic of conditional statements (see Figure 6).

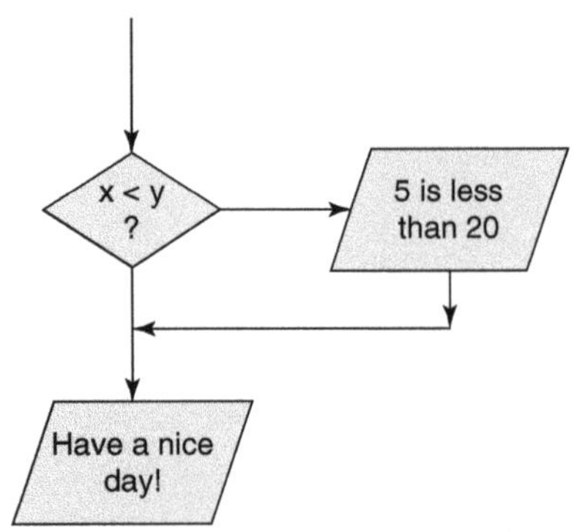


**Figure 5:** Flowchart for a Simple if Statement.

[3]For more information, please see http://en.wikipedia.org/wiki/Flowchart and www.farshadoo.com/ic/tutorials/flowchart-diagrams.php

In Figure 5, the decision is represented with a diamond shape. Depending on the evaluation, if it evaluates to true, then the program logic branches to the right and executes the phrase "5 is less than 20," and returns to execute the next statement "Have a nice day!" Otherwise, if the decision in the diamond evaluates to false, the next statement ("Have a nice day!") is executed. Flowcharts are very useful tools to visualize the program flow and are used in the design phase of software projects.

### *Block of Code*

We have seen an if statement that influences execution of only one statement. What if more than one statement depended on the if statement? In that case, we can specify a block of code that depends on the if statement. Consider the following code:

```
1. int main()
2. {
3.      int x = 5;
4.      int y = 20;
5.      if (x < y)
6.      {
7.          cout << x << " is less than " << y << endl;
8.          cout << "This is a block of code." << endl;
9.          cout << "All the statements in this block execute together." << endl;
10.     }
11.
12.     cout << "Have a nice day!" << endl;
13.     return 0;
14. }
```

**Listing 13:** Block of Code Dependent of the if Statement

In Listing 13, curly brace { on line 6 specifies the beginning of the block of code where all statements inside of that block are treated as one. The block is terminated by the right curly brace } on line 10. If the expression on line 5 evaluates to true, then the entire block will execute as demonstrated below:

```
5 is less than 20
This is a block of code.
All the statements in this block execute together.
Have a nice day!

Process returned 0 (0x0)   execution time : 0.016 s
Press any key to continue.
```

If the expression on line 5 evaluates to false, the entire block will not execute; only the statement following the block of code will be executed. To accomplish that, simply change line 5 in the listing above to the following if statement:

```
if (x == y)
```

and you will see the following output:

```
Have a nice day!

Process returned 0 (0x0)   execution time : 0.023 s
Press any key to continue.
```

The flowchart for an if statement followed by a block of code is shown in Figure 6.

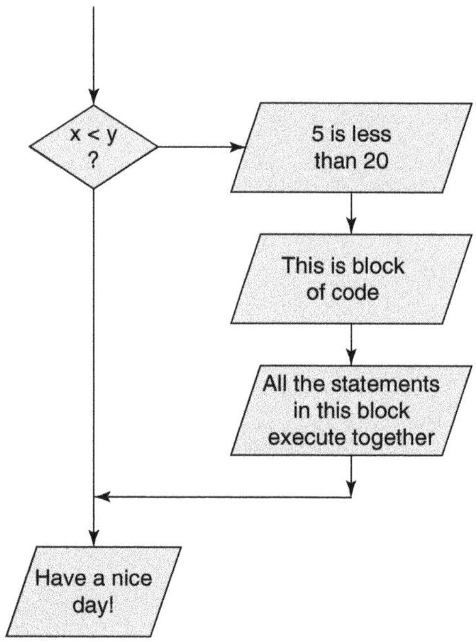


**Figure 6:** Flowchart for if Statement Followed by a Block of Code.

### *Some Common Mistakes to Avoid*

Using the same code from Listing 13, let's change the statement on line 5 to:

```
if (x = y)
```

What statements would execute in this case? The answer is that the entire block of code would execute:

```
5 is less than 20
This is a block of code.
All the statements in this block execute together.
Have a nice day!

Process returned 0 (0x0)   execution time : 0.016 s
Press any key to continue.
```

Notice that the expression is actually not testing whether the contents of x are equal to the contents of y. Instead, x is being assigned the value of y, which will evaluate to true. This is one of the most common mistakes made by novice programmers, and it is very difficult to debug.

Please make a note of this and don't confuse the assignment operator with the equal operator.

Another typical mistake novice C++ programmers make is to put a semicolon (;) at the end of the if statement (line 5 below):

```
1. int main()
2. {
3.     int x = 25;
4.     int y = 20;
5.     if (x < y);
6.     {
7.         cout << x << " is less than " << y << endl;
8.         cout << "This is a block of code." << endl;
9.         cout << "All the statements in this block execute together." << endl;
10.    }
11.
12.    cout << "Have a nice day!" << endl;
13.    return 0;
14. }
```

**Listing 14:** Common Mistake: No Semicolon at the End of if Statement

The compiler will not flag a syntax error, instead it will execute the block of code following the if statement even though the expression evaluated to false!

```
5 is less than 20
This is a block of code.
All the statements in this block execute together.
Have a nice day!

Process returned 0 (0x0)   execution time : 0.042 s
Press any key to continue.
```

How is that possible? Well, placing the semicolon at the end of the if statement instructs the compiler to do nothing. You can think that there is an "invisible command to do nothing" between the right parenthesis and the semicolon:

```
if (x < y) <invisible "do nothing">;
```

In fact, with the semicolon at the end of the if statement, the "invisible do nothing" is the statement that is tied to the condition tested in the if statement and is the only statement that will (or will not) be executed if the expression evaluates to true. The block of code in this scenario is not tied to the expression evaluation and will be executed regardless.

This is another very simple mistake that is very difficult to debug.

### *Comparing Floats with the Help of Conditional Statements*

Due to how floating-point numbers are stored internally, you should avoid comparing them with the == operator. The reason is that you can never be sure of the levels of precision for floating-point numbers. For example, if you have the following declarations:

```
float x = 1.125f;
```

then the following comparison may not work:

```
if (x == 1.125)
```

The reason is that the compiler may store x as 1.12334576898011 so the comparison between the number and the 1.125 produce correct result.

What you need to do instead is the following[4]:

- Define a small floating-point constant:

```
const float DELTA = 0.000001;
```

- Take the absolute value of the difference between the x and 1.125 and test to see if it is smaller than constant DELTA:

```
if ( abs(x-1.125) < DELTA)
```

If the expression evaluates to true, then the difference between the two numbers is so insignificant that they are highly likely the same number.

### The `if-else` Statement

***"When you arrive at a fork in the road, take it."***[5]

***—Yogi Berra***

Sometimes you will need to shape your logic so that only one of the two statements executes. In that case you need to use the if-else statement. The syntax for the if-else statement is as follows:

| Single Statement | Block of Code |
|---|---|
| `if (expr)` | `if (expr)` |
| `    statementA;` | `{` |
| `else` | `    statement(s);` |
| `    statementB;` | `}` |
| | `else` |
| | `{` |
| | `    statement(s);` |
| | `}` |

It is kind of like a fork in the road. Notice how the statements are indented 3 to 4 spaces. This makes the program more readable and improves its maintainability. Figure 7 shows a flowchart for the `if-else` statement:

There are two possibilities, and only one of them will execute. In Figure 6 x is either greater than y or it is not. Implementing this logic in the source code is depicted in Listing 15.

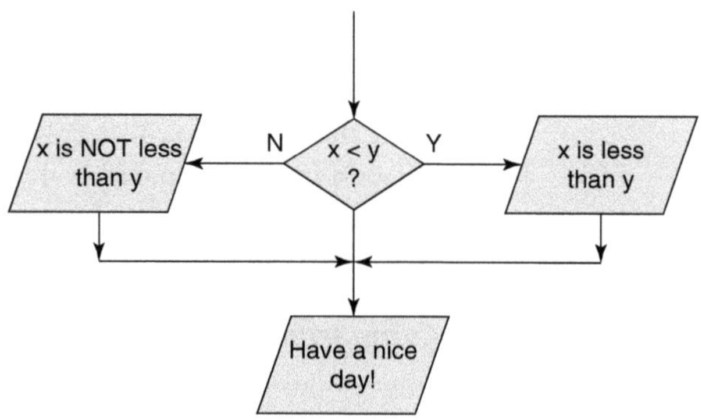


**Figure 7:** Flowchart for the if-else Statement.

[4]To find out more please see www.cygnus-software.com/papers/comparingfloats/comparingfloats.htm
[5]www.brainyquote.com/quotes/authors/y/yogi_berra.html

```
int main()
{
    int x, y;       // to hold the 1st and 2nd number

    // Prompt the user to enter the 1st number
    cout << "Please enter a number: ";
    cin >> x;   // capture the 1st number
    cout << "Please enter another number: ";
    cin >> y;   // capture the 2nd number
    cout << "I will compare the two numbers and let you know"
         << " which one is bigger!" << endl;
    if (x > y)
        cout << x << " is bigger than " << y << endl;
    else
        cout << x << " is NOT bigger than " << y << endl;

    return 0;
}
```

**Listing 15:** The **`if-else`** Statement

Compiling and running the program from Listing 11 will produce the following output:

```
Please enter a number: 10
Please enter another number: 25
I will compare the two numbers and let you know which one is bigger!
10 is NOT bigger than 25

Process returned 0 (0x0)   execution time : 4.225 s
Press any key to continue.
```

Let's try executing the program with different set of numbers:

```
Please enter a number: 25
Please enter another number: 15
I will compare the two numbers and let you know which one is bigger!
25 is bigger than 15

Process returned 0 (0x0)   execution time : 7.256 s
Press any key to continue.
```

### *Using `if-else` Statements*

In general, when writing software programs, it is always a good practice to employ defensive programming techniques such as validating user input. For example, suppose that in your program logic you need to perform a division operation. Your program is interactive, and you need to protect your code from possible bad user input. How do you do that? How do you make sure that user input will not crash your program? The division operation could crash if the denominator is 0. You cannot control what the user enters, but you can inspect the input before storing it into the denominator variable. If the value entered as the denominator is 0, simply display a message that this is not a valid input, and ask the use to try again. Otherwise, perform the calculation:

```
int main()
{
    int numerator;    // to hold the numerator
    int denominator; // to hold the denominator

    cout << "Please enter the Numerator Value: ";
    cin >> numerator;
    cout << "Please enter the Denominator Value: ";
    cin >> denominator;
    if (denominator==0)
    {
        cout << "Error! The denominator cannot be a 0.";
        cout << "Please run the program again!";
    }
    else
    {
        cout << numerator << "/" << denominator
             << " = " << numerator/static_cast<double>(denominator)
             << endl;
    }

    return 0;
}
```

**Listing 16:** Defensive Programming Using if-else Statement

Entering acceptable input values produces the following output:

```
Please enter the Numerator Value: 3
Please enter the Denominator Value: 4
3/4 = 0.75

Process returned 0 (0x0)   execution time : 2.749 s
Press any key to continue.
```

On the other hand, if the user enters a 0 for the denominator value, the output is different:

```
Please enter the Numerator Value: 3
Please enter the Denominator Value: 0
Error! The denominator cannot be a 0.Please run the program again!
Process returned 0 (0x0)   execution time : 5.458 s
Press any key to continue.
```

As an exercise, try the program without the if-else statement. What is the outcome?

## Multiple Options

Sometimes the if statements will not be adequate to model the logic used to solve a particular problem. For those situations, C++ provides alternatives such as nested if statements and if-else-if statements.

### *Nested `if` Statements*

When using if-else statements, it is possible that one of the statements in either branch could itself be an if statement:

**Table 6:** Nested if Statements.

| Original if-else | Possible Statement | Expanded |
|---|---|---|
| `if (expr)`<br>`  statementA;`<br>`else`<br>`  statementB;` | `What if statementA is`<br>`if (expr1)`<br>`  statementC;` | `if (expr)`<br>`  if (expr1)`<br>`    statementC;`<br>`  else`<br>`    statementB;` |
| `if (expr)`<br>`  if (expr1)`<br>`    statementC;`<br>`  else`<br>`    statementB;` | `What if statementC is`<br>`if (expr2)`<br>`  statementD;`<br>`else`<br>`  statementE;` | `if (expr)`<br>`  if (expr1)`<br>`    if (expr2)`<br>`      statementD;`<br>`    else`<br>`      statementE;`<br>`  else`<br>`    statementB;` |

From Table 6, we can see that any statement can be substituted for an if or if-else statement. Let's illustrate the point by writing a short program. The program is going to:

- Prompt the user to enter an integer number between 1 and 999.
- If the user enters a number outside the range, the program will display an error message and terminate.
- If the user enters a number inside the acceptable range, the program will determine whether the number has 1, 2, or 3 digits and display a message stating that.

We start with a flowchart:

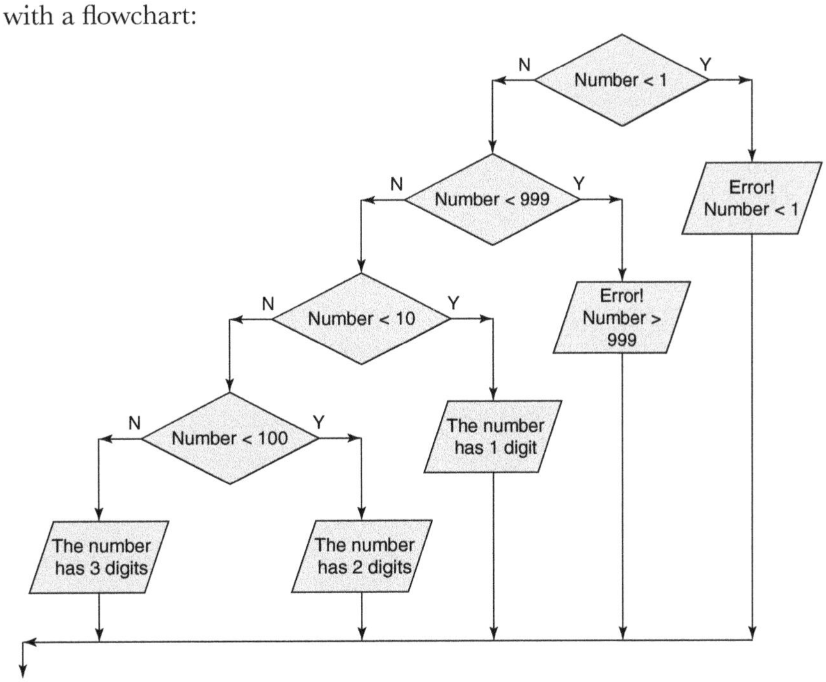


**Figure 8:** Flowchart for Nested if Statements.

Listing 17 contains the source code for the program:

```
1. int main()
2. {
3.      int number;
4.      cout << "Enter a number between 1 and 999: ";
5.      cin >> number;
6.      if (number < 1 )
7.      {
8.          cout << "ERROR! The number is less than 1! " << endl;
9.      }
10.     else
11.     {
12.         if (number > 999)
13.         {
14.             cout << "ERROR! The number is greater than 999! " << endl;
15.         }
16.         else
17.         {
18.             if (number < 10)
19.                 cout << "The number has ONE digit." << endl;
20.             else
21.             {
22.                 if (number < 100)
23.                     cout << "The number has TWO digits. " << endl;
24.                 else
27.                     cout << "The number has THREE digits. " << endl;
30.             }
31.         }
32.     }
33.     return 0;
34. }
```

**Listing 17:** Nested if Statements

After prompting the user for a number between 1 and 999, the program captures user input and stores it into an integer variable number. It performs a series of checks through nested if and if-else statements from lines 6 through 32.

The following table displays several test cases and their outcomes:

It is always a good programming practice to test the upper and lower boundaries of the numeric range (if there is one), to make sure that the program works within the specified limits. In addition, the program should be tested for other specific values. In our case, these were tests to determine whether a number contains one, two, or three digits.

For better readability, easier debugging, it is very important to align beginning and ending braces signifying the beginning and end of block statements when working with nested if statements. This is accomplished through indentations for every new level of nesting. It is customary for new nesting levels indent 3 to 4 spaces.

**Table 7:** Test Cases for Program in Listing 13.

| **Input value** | **Purpose** | **Outcome** |
|---|---|---|
| `number = -1` | `Test the lower boundary of the range` | `Enter a number between 1 and 999: -1`<br>`ERROR! The number is less than 1!` |
| `number = 1001` | `Test the upper boundary of the range` | `Enter a number between 1 and 999: 1001`<br>`ERROR! The number is greater than 999!` |
| `Number = 5` | `Test 1 digit number` | `Enter a number between 1 and 999: 5`<br>`The number has ONE digit.` |
| `number = 15` | `Test 2 digit number` | `Enter a number between 1 and 999: 15`<br>`The number has TWO digits.` |
| `number = 899` | `Test 3 digit number` | `Enter a number between 1 and 999: 899`<br>`The number has THREE digits.` |

### *The `if-else-if` Statements*

Nested if statements could become complex, resulting in difficult-to-understand source code. Fortunately, there is an easier way to implement the same logic through the if—else—if statements. The syntax is as follows:

```
if (expr1)
{
     statement(s);
}
else if(expr2)
{
     statement(s);
}
   . . .
   . . .
   . . .
  else
  {
     statement(s);
  }
```

```
Many more
  else if (exprN)
  {
     statement(s)
  }
```

**Figure 9:** if-else-if Statement Syntax.

The idea is to test each expression and if it evaluates to true, enter the block of code that is associated with that particular if statement (expression). If the expression does not evaluate to true, the program tests another expression (else-if statement). The last block of code is an else statement and is used as a catch all blocks of code that execute if all the tests fail. This else statement is also known as the trailing else and is optional.

```
if (exprA)
{
    Astatement(s)
}
```

**The first test is exprA. If it evaluates to true, only the block of code "Astatement(s)" associated with that if statements will execute.**

```
else if (exprB)
{
    Bstatement(s)
}
```

**If not, the program attempts the exprB. If the expression evaluates to true, then only the block of code associated with this (else if) statement will execute.**

```
else if (exprN)
{
    statement(s)
}
```

**This process is repeated for as many blocks as listed in the if–else–if statement.**

```
else
{
    statement(s)
}
```

**If no expressions evaluate to true, the trailing else statement, if present will execute.**

**Figure 10**

Most of the time, it will be possible to rewrite nested if statements as if-else-if statements, resulting in more readable code, which is easier to debug and maintain.

Following is the program from Listing 13 written using the if-else-if statements:

```
int main()
{
    int number;
    cout << "Enter a number between 1 and 999: ";
    cin >> number;

    if (number < 1 )
    {
        cout << "ERROR! The number is less than 1! " << endl;
    }
    else if (number > 999)
    {
        cout << "ERROR! The number is greater than 999! " << endl;
    }
    else if (number < 10)
    {
        cout << "ERROR! The number has 1 digit." << endl;
    }
    else if (number < 100)
    {
```

```
        cout << "The number has 2 digits. " << endl;
    }
    else
    {
        cout << "The number has 3 digits. " << endl;
    }

    return 0;
}
```

**Listing 18:** Program Using if-else-if Statements

Compiling and running the Listing 18 produces the same results as the program in listing 13 (written with nested if statements). However, the program in listing 14 is more readable and easier to understand.

Another use of if-else-if statements is for menus. For example, let's say you need to write a program that displays a menu of options. Each menu option could be an if-else if block of code. Listing 19 demonstrates that.

```
int main()
{
    cout << "Welcome to my ATM" << endl;
    cout << "1. Check your balance " << endl;
    cout << "2. Withdraw           " << endl;
    cout << "3. Depostit " << endl;
    cout << "4. Exit" << endl;
    cout << "Your choice: ";

    int userChoice;

    cin >> userChoice;

    // Valid selection
    if (userChoice == 1)
    {
        cout << "Check account balance" << endl;
    }
    else if (userChoice == 2)
    {
        cout << "Withdraw" << endl;
    }
    else if (userChoice == 3)
    {
        cout << "Deposit" << endl;
    }
```

```
    else if (userChoice == 4)
    {
        cout << "Thank you for using my ATM" << endl;
        cout << "Exiting..." << endl;
    }
    else    // trailing else
    {
        cout << "Please enter 1, 2, 3, or 4" << endl;
    }

    return 0;
}
```

**Listing 19:** Menu Program Using if-else-if Statement

Table 8 displays test cases for the program in Listing 15:

**Table 8:** Test Cases for Program in Listing 19.

| Input value | Purpose | Outcome |
|---|---|---|
| userChoice = -1 | Test the lower boundary of the range | Welcome to my ATM<br>1. Check your balance<br>2. Withdraw<br>3. Depostit<br>4. Exit<br>Your choice: -1<br>Please enter 1, 2, 3, or 4 |
| userChoice = 5 | Test the upper boundary of the range | Welcome to my ATM<br>1. Check your balance<br>2. Withdraw<br>3. Depostit<br>4. Exit<br>Your choice: 5<br>Please enter 1, 2, 3, or 4 |
| userChoice = 1 | Test Check Account Balance | Welcome to my ATM<br>1. Check your balance<br>2. Withdraw<br>3. Depostit<br>4. Exit<br>Your choice: 1<br>Check account balance |
| userChoice = 2 | Test Withdraw | Welcome to my ATM<br>1. Check your balance<br>2. Withdraw<br>3. Depostit<br>4. Exit<br>Your choice: 2<br>Withdraw |

| **Input value** | **Purpose** | **Outcome** |
|---|---|---|
| `userChoice = 3` | `Test Deposit` | `Welcome to my ATM`<br>`1. Check your balance`<br>`2. Withdraw`<br>`3. Depostit`<br>`4. Exit`<br>`Your choice: 3`<br>`Deposit` |
| `userChoice = 4` | `Test Exit` | `Welcome to my ATM`<br>`1. Check your balance`<br>`2. Withdraw`<br>`3. Depostit`<br>`4. Exit`<br>`Your choice: 4`<br>`Thank you for using my ATM`<br>`Exiting...` |

## The Switch Statement

The switch statement is very similar to the if-else-if statement. The only difference is that the switch statement works only with integer (char) data types. The syntax of the switch statement is as follows:

```
switch(expr)
{
    case value1:
        statement(s);
        break;
    case value2:
        statement(s);
        break;
    . . . . . . .
    . . . . . . .
    case valueN:
        statement(s);
        break;
    default:
        statement(s);
}
```

The switch statement starts with the keyword switch followed by an expression inside of parentheses. The left brace "{" marks the beginning of the switch statement, and the right brace "}" marks the end of the switch statement. The expression is evaluated against each of the cases. The order of evaluation is sequential, meaning from top to bottom. Each case starts with the keyword case followed by an integer constant followed by a colon. Inside each case there is a statement or statements depending on the logic being modeled.

There could be any number of cases in any order in the switch statement. If the value of the integer expression being compared does not match any of the case constants, then the optional default (two's catchall) case is executed.

Only the code in one of the case statements will execute. In case there is no default, and there is no match, none of the case statements will execute.

The break statement is responsible for the terminating the case and transferring the program control to the statement following the switch statement. If the options for some case statements are the same, then it is possible to stack these case statements by omitting the break statement:

```
switch(number)
{
    case 1:
        cout << "Check Account Balance" << endl;
        break;
    case 2:
    case 3:
    case 4:
        cout << "To be implemented later" << endl;
        break;
}
```

In essence, there are only two case statements in the above code segment: case 1 and combined case 2, case 3, and case 4. This is because the break statement has been omitted between case 2, case 3, in case 4. We could rewrite the above statement as follows:

```
switch(number)
{
    case 1:
        cout << "Check Account Balance" << endl;
        break;
    case 2:
        cout << "Withdraw" << endl;
        break;
    case 3:
        cout << "Deposit" << endl;
        break;

    case 4:
        cout << "Thank you for using my ATM" << endl;
        cout << "Exiting..." << endl;
        break;
    default:
        cout << "Please enter 1, 2, 3, or 4" << endl;
}
```

In this example, there are four distinct cases with an optional default case that is equivalent to the trailing else statement.

The switch statement is an excellent choice for processing menu choices as long as they are either integers or characters. The following program demonstrates switch statement with character data type:

```
switch(userChoice)
{
    case 'a':
    case 'e':
    case 'i':
    case 'o':
    case 'u':
        cout << "Vowel" << endl;
        break;

    default:
        cout << "Consonant" << endl;
}
```

## Logical Operators

Logical operators provide a mechanism to combine two or more relational expressions into a single expression that evaluates either to true or false. Table 9 lists C++ logical operators:

**Table 9:** C++ Logical Operators.

| Operator | C++ Symbol | Example |
|---|---|---|
| AND | && | (expressionA && expressionB) |
| OR | \|\| | (expressionA \|\| expressionB) |
| NOT | ! | !expressionA |

Using logical operators makes it possible to create more complex conditions by combining two or more simple expressions.

### *The Logical AND (&&) Operator*

The logical AND (&&) operator is a binary operator used to combine the two or more relational expressions into one expression. The AND operator produces the following output:

**Table 10:** The Logical AND Truth Table.

| Operand1 | Operand2 | Operand1 && Operand2 |
|---|---|---|
| T | T | T |
| T | F | F |
| F | T | F |
| F | F | F |

The operands are expressions. For example, if the first operand (a relational expression) evaluates to true and the second operand (another relational expression) evaluates to true as well, then using the logical AND operator we can test for two conditions at the same time.

The following code example prompts the user to enter a number within a certain range, let's say between 1 and 100. Once this code captures the user input, it tests it to see if it is within the specified range:

```
int main()
{
    int number;

    cout << "Please enter a number between 1 and 100: ";
    cin >> number;

    if (number >=1 && number <=100)
        cout << "Correct Range" << endl;
    else
        cout << "Incorrect range!" << endl;
    return 0;
}
```

The logical AND operator requires both of its operands to be true in order to evaluate the expression as true. If any of the operands is false, then the logical AND operator will evaluate the expression as false.

**Lazy Evaluation** The logical AND operator performs so-called lazy evaluation of its operands. Since it requires only one operand to be false in order for the entire expression to be false, it evaluates the first operand (the first expression) and if it evaluates to false, the evaluation process stops as there is no point of evaluating the rest of the expressions.

The logical AND operator is a very good choice of operator when attempting to determine whether a number is inside a certain range. It also can be used to simplify nested if statements. *Hint: Rewrite the program in listing 13 using the logical AND operator.*

### *The Logical OR (||) Operator*

The logical OR operator is also a binary operator that takes two expressions as its operands and evaluates them according to Table 11:

**Table 11:** The Logical OR Operator Truth Table.

| Operand1 | Operand2 | Operand1 \|\| Operand2 |
|---|---|---|
| T | T | T |
| T | F | T |
| F | T | T |
| F | F | F |

The logical OR operator requires only one of the operands to be true in order for it to evaluate the entire expression as true. It will evaluate the expression as false if both of the operands are false. The logical OR operator is a very good choice when attempting to determine whether a certain number is outside specified range.

### *The Logical NOT (!) Operator*

The logical NOT operator is unary operator. It is used to reverse the truth of an expression. If an expression evaluates to true, placing a logical NOT operator in front of it will result in it evaluating to false:

**Table 12:** The Logical NOT Operator Truth Table.

| Operand1 | !Operand1 |
|---|---|
| T | F |
| F | T |

The following code segment will not execute the cout statement even though the expression (x < y) evaluates to true. The logical NOT operator "!" Placed before the expression reverses the expression to its opposite side:

```
int x = 10;
int y = 20;
if (!(x < y))
   cout << x << "is less than " << y << endl;
```

### *Logical Operator Precedence*

There is a hierarchy of execution among logical operators. The logical NOT operator has the highest precedence, followed by the logical AND, followed by logical OR. Table 13 displays operator precedence hierarchy:

**Table 13:** Precedence among Logical Operators.

| Precedence | Operator | | | | |
|---|---|---|---|---|---|
| 1 | ! | - | ++ | -- | |
| 2 | * | / | % | | |
| 3 | + | - | | | |
| 4 | < | <= | > | >= | |
| 5 | == | != | | | |
| 6 | && | | | | |
| 7 | \|\| | | | | |
| 8 | = | += | -= | *= | /= |

## Formatting Output

Now that we have learned about expressions and conditional statements, the last thing left in this chapter is to learn how to display data. The same data can be printed in many different ways. For example, the following numbers have the same value but they are formatted differently:

255

255.0

255.0000

The cout object has limited way of formatting data. Consider the Listing 19, which displays the rows of data with spaces between them:

```
int main()
{
    string name1 = "Joe Montana";
    string name2 = "Dan Marino";
    string name3 = "Jerry Rice";

    double avg1 = 88.34;
    double avg2 = 98.88;
    double avg3 = 90.78;

    int yearsPro1 = 15;
    int yearsPro2 = 18;
    int yearsPro3 = 20;

    cout << name1 << " " << name2 << " " << name3 << endl;
    cout << avg1 << " " << avg2 << " " << avg3 << endl;
    cout << yearsPro1 << " " << yearsPro2 << " " << yearsPro3 << endl;
    return 0;
}
```

**Listing 20:** Formatting Data

Unfortunately, the data did not line up nicely:

```
Joe Montana Dan Marino Jerry Rice
88.34 98.88 90.78
15 18 20
```

This is because some of the values occupy more spaces—i.e., names versus integer data such as years spent as a NFL pro.

To correct this, the cout object provides a manipulator called setw, which allows programmers to specify the width for each field. You simply insert the setw manipulator inline in the cout statement:

```
int fieldWidth = 25;
cout << setw(fieldWidth) << name << endl;
```

This will print a variable name in the field of 25 spaces. If the value of the name is less than 25 spaces, the manipulator will pad the extra positions with blank spaces. The padding occurs from left to right, thus the value displayed appears to be right justified.

In order to use the setw manipulator, we need to include the following header:

```
#include <iostream>
```

Listing 20 demonstrates the setw manipulator:

```
#include <iostream>
#include <iomanip>    // needed for the setw


using namespace std;

int main()
{
    string name1 = "Joe Montana";
    string name2 = "Dan Marino";
    string name3 = "Jerry Rice";

    double avg1 = 88.34;
    double avg2 = 98.88;
    double avg3 = 90.78;

    int yearsPro1 = 15;
    int yearsPro2 = 18;
    int yearsPro3 = 20;

    cout << setw(11) << name1 << setw(11) << name2 << setw(11) << name3
         << endl;
    cout << setw(11) << avg1 << setw(11) << avg2 << setw(11) << avg3
         << endl;
    cout << setw(11) << yearsPro1 << setw(11) << yearsPro2 << setw(11)
         << yearsPro3 << endl;
    return 0;
}
```

**Listing 21:** Using the setw Manipulator

Notice that setw was used in front of each field (variable). This is necessary because setw creates a field only for the value that immediately follows it. After that value displays, the cout object reverts back to its default way of printing. Compiling and running the program in Listing 20 produces the following output:

```
Joe Montana Dan Marino Jerry Rice
      88.34      98.88      90.78
         15         18         20
```

Notice how everything is right justified because of the padding? Be careful not to specify a width that is too small for the field that is being printed because in that case the cout object will override the setw manipulator and revert to printing in the default style.

When working with floating point data, you need to count the decimal point as a space when setting the width for the setw manipulator.

## The setprecision Manipulator

Floating-point data can be manipulated to display certain degrees of precision with the setprecision manipulator:

```
#include <iostream>
#include <iomanip>

using namespace std;

int main()
{
    double number = 1.234567;

    cout << setprecision(6) << number << endl;
    cout << setprecision(5) << number << endl;
    cout << setprecision(4) << number << endl;
    cout << setprecision(3) << number << endl;
    cout << setprecision(2) << number << endl;
    cout << setprecision(1) << number << endl;
    return 0;
}
```

**Listing 22:** Using setprecision Manipulator

Listing 22 will produce the following output:

```
1.23457
1.2346
1.235
1.23
1.2
1

Process returned 0 (0x0)   execution time : 0.031 s
Press any key to continue.
```

If the value of a number is expressed in fewer digits of precision than specified by set precision, the manipulator will have no effect. In the following statements the displayed value will remain unchanged:

```
double myNumber = 19.95;
cout << "no setprecision: " << myNumber << endl;
cout << "with setprecision(5): " << setprecision(5) << myNumber
     << endl;
```

as seen in the following output:

```
no setprecision: 19.95
with setprecision(5): 19.95
```

The setprecision manipulator does not need to be set for each value. It is sufficient to set it to once and then every value from that point forward will be displayed with the same precision until a new setprecision manipulator is declared.

## The fixed Manipulator

If a number is too large to print using the number digits specified with setprecision, many compilers will display output in scientific notation. For example, a large number like this one:

```
double amount=1234567.99;
 cout << "Amount: " << amount << endl;
```

will be displayed using the scientific notation:

```
Amount: 1.23457e+006

Process returned 0 (0x0)   execution time : 0.013 s
Press any key to continue.
```

To prevent this, you can use the fixed stream manipulator, which indicates that floating point output should be printed in decimal and not in scientific notation. The syntax is as follows:

```
cout << fixed << "Amount: " << amount << endl;
```

```
Amount: 1234567.990000

Process returned 0 (0x0)   execution time : 0.017 s
Press any key to continue.
```

If used in conjunction with the setprecision manipulator:

```
cout << fixed << "Amount: " << setprecision(2) << amount
     << endl;
```

it will produce decimal notation with specified precision:

```
Amount: 1234567.99

Process returned 0 (0x0)   execution time : 0.020 s
Press any key to continue.
```

## The Showpoint Manipulator

This is another very useful manipulator, which forces the decimal point to be printed for a floating-point number, even if the value being displayed does not have any digits after the decimal point. Consider the following code segment:

```
double amount = 25.0;
cout << "Amount: " <<  amount << endl;
```

Compiling and running this code segment produces the following output:

```
Amount: 25

Process returned 0 (0x0)   execution time : 0.044 s
Press any key to continue.
```

Even though the variable amount is declared as a double, it does not have any numbers beyond the decimal point except zero, therefore it is displayed without the decimal point. To force the decimal point, you can use the showpoint manipulator:

```
double amount = 25.0;
cout << showpoint << "Amount: " <<  amount << endl;
```

which would produce the following output:

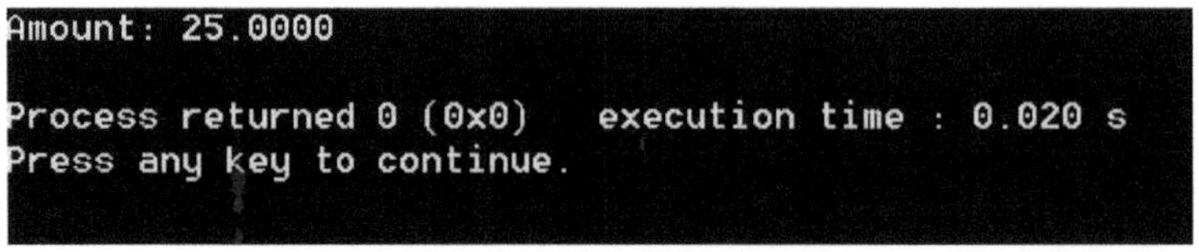


This output can then be manipulated with fixed and setprecision manipulators to display the desired number format.

### The left and right Manipulators

By default, output is right justified. As we have seen in the setw manipulator examples, if the field is larger than the value that is being displayed, the value is right justified and padded with blanks from left to right. Sometimes you may need to left justify your data. To accomplish that, you can use the left manipulator. It remains in effect until you use a right manipulator to set it back to default. Both left and right manipulators can be used on any data type. Following is the syntax of the left stream manipulator:

```
cout << left << showpoint << "Amount: " <<  amount << endl;
```

## End of Chapter Questions

### True/False

Indicate whether the statement is true or false.

1. The cin object is only used to store user input.
2. Unary operators require two operands.
3. Increment and decrement operators are also unary operators.
4. By default the setw stream manipulator displays data left justified.
5. Logical operator NOT (!) has the highest precedence.

### Exercises

1. What are the three classifications of operands?
2. List the three rules of data coercion and elaborate on each one of them.
3. Write a short C++ program that will display your name in ASCII.
4. Write a C++ program that will prompt the user for a character and run tests on it to determine whether it is a digit, a capital letter, or a lowercase letter.

**5.** You were hired by a T-shirt store to write a program to help them sell T-shirts online. They are running a special with the following discounts:

| T-Shirt Quantity | Discount |
|---|---|
| 5–10 | 5% |
| 11–20 | 10% |
| 21–30 | 15% |
| 31+ | 20% |

Assuming $10 price for a T-shirt, write a program that will ask the user for the number of T-shirts he or she wishes to purchase and then calculate the discount and the total and present it to the user:

```
12 T-shirts @ $10 each = $120
Discount 10%           = $ 12
Total                  = $108
Thank you for your business!
```

## Chapter 4

# Loops

***"Your Treasure House is in yourself, it contains all you need"***

***—Hui Hai, Zen Teaching of Instantaneous Awakening***

Loops are repetitive statements that keep executing as long as certain condition is true. There are several different loop types and they are commonly classifies into pre-test and post-test loops. The pre-test loops basically first evaluate the condition to determine whether the body of the loop should execute at all. The post-test loop is guaranteed to execute at least once after which the condition that determines future iterations (repetitions) is evaluated. Depending on that test, the post-test loop may terminate at that point or continue executing until the condition is no longer true. The while and the for loop are known as pre-test loops. The do-while is the post-test loop.

## While Loop

### `While` Loop Basics (loop control variable)

The while loop's format is as follows:

```
while (expression)
  statement(s);
```

As long as the expression evaluates to true the statement or statements will continue to execute until the expression evaluates to false. Here is an example of a while loop:

```
#include <iostream>
using namespace std;
int main()
{
  int i = 0;

  while (i < 5)
    cout << "Hello world";
  return 0;
}
```

Will produce the following output:

```
o worldHello worldHello worldHello worldHello worldHello worldHello worldHello w
orldHello worldHello worldHello worldHello worldHello worldHello worldHello worl
dHello worldHello worldHello worldHello worldHello worldHello worldHello worldHe
llo worldHello worldHello worldHello worldHello worldHello worldHello worldHello
 worldHello worldHello worldHello worldHello worldHello worldHello worldHello wo
rldHello worldHello worldHello worldHello worldHello worldHello worldHello world
Hello worldHello worldHello worldHello worldHello worldHello worldHello worldHel
lo worldHello worldHello worldHello worldHello worldHello worldHello worldHello 
worldHello worldHello worldHello worldHello worldHello worldHello worldHello wor
ldHello worldHello worldHello worldHello worldHello worldHello worldHello worldH
ello worldHello worldHello worldHello worldHello worldHello worldHello worldHell
o worldHello worldHello worldHello worldHello worldHello worldHello worldHello w
orldHello worldHello worldHello worldHello worldHello worldHello worldHello worl
dHello worldHello worldHello worldHello worldHello worldHello worldHello worldHe
llo worldHello worldHello worldHello worldHello worldHello worldHello worldHello
 worldHello worldHello worldHello worldHello worldHello worldHello worldHello wo
rldHello worldHello worldHello worldHello worldHello worldHello worldHello world
Hello worldHello worldHello worldHello worldHello worldHello worldHello worldHel
lo worldHello worldHello worldHello worldHello worldHello worldHello worldHello 
worldHello worldHello worldHello worldHello worldHello worldHello worldHello wor
```

What just happened here? To understand this we need to analyze the source code. Line number 7 in the source code above tests whether the value stored in variable i is less than 5. We initialized i is an integer and set its value to zero. We are not updating that value ever so therefore the expression in line number nine is always going to evaluate to true thus our while loop will continue to execute forever. In order to make our while loop execute only five times we need to control the expression (loop condition). We do that by incrementing or decrementing the variable whose value we're comparing to a constant in this case number five. So the following change in the source code will result in our loop executing only five times:

```
#include <iostream>
using namespace std;

int main()
{
  int i = 0;
  while (i < 5)
  {
    cout << "Hello world" << endl;
    i++;
  }

  return 0;
}
```

Resulting in the following output:

```
Hello world
Hello world
Hello world
Hello world
Hello world

Process returned 0 (0x0)   execution time : 0.017 s
Press any key to continue.
```

In the example above, the variable i is considered a so-called loop control variable. With each iteration of the loop the value of i gets incremented by one and then tested against the constant (number 5) in the expression. Once the value of i became equal to five the expression evaluated to false and the program was able to break out of the loop and complete. Notice that only five statements were printed.

## User Input and Ranges

### *Simple User Input Filter for a Range*

Suppose you want to filter user input. For example, you are writing a program that will collect student quiz scores. The acceptable range of score is from 0 through 100 and you would like to your program to accept only the values that are in that range. How do you do it? One way to do this would be to use a conditional statement and test user input for validity so that it is within the desired range.

The following code segment accomplishes that:

```
 1. #include <iostream>
 2. using namespace std;
 3. int main()
 4. {
 5.    int quizScore; // declare a variable to hold the quiz score
 6.
 7.    cout << "Please enter your score: <0-100 only> :";
 8.    cin >> quizScore;
 9.    if (quizScore <0 || quizScore >100)
10.    {
11.        cout << "Invalid quiz score! Please enter 0-100 only:";
12.        cin >> quizScore;
13.    }
14.    cout << "You entered: " << quizScore;
15.    return 0;
16. }
```

The only problem that we have now is that this code segment will execute only once. As the program follows the top-down execution path, if the user enters a value that is outside of 0 to 100 range the statement in line number eight will test the user entered value (score) to determine whether it is within the range of zero through 100. If that is not the case, the user will see a warning message and be prompted to enter the correct value again. The statement in line number 11 will read whatever the user enters at this point without testing it so the program again is not accomplishing its task to test and verify user input. You did it correctly once but as you can see from the above code it is unable to verify the range of acceptable values the second time around. Thus we need a better mechanism to accomplish this. A simple change online number eight from an if statement to a while loop will correct that:

```
int quizScore;
cout << "Please enter your score: <0-100 only> :";
cin >> quizScore;
```

```
while (quizScore < 0 || quizScore > 100)
{
    cout << "Invalid quiz score! Please enter 0-100 only:";
    cin >> quizScore;
}
cout << "You entered: " << quizScore << endl;
```

The idea is to keep the user in the while loop as long as they are providing the input that is outside the range of acceptable values. Recall that logical OR requires only one of its inputs to be true in order for the result to be true. In the above code example, the condition

```
while (quizScore < 0 || quizScore > 100)
```

is going to evaluate to true if either **`quizScore < 0`** evaluates to true **`OR quizScore > 100`** evaluates to true. So the code segment will work and we are done, right? Well, not quite. The code will work correctly only for the numeric input. The moment the user enters a letter for example, the above code will result in an infinite loop as depicted below:

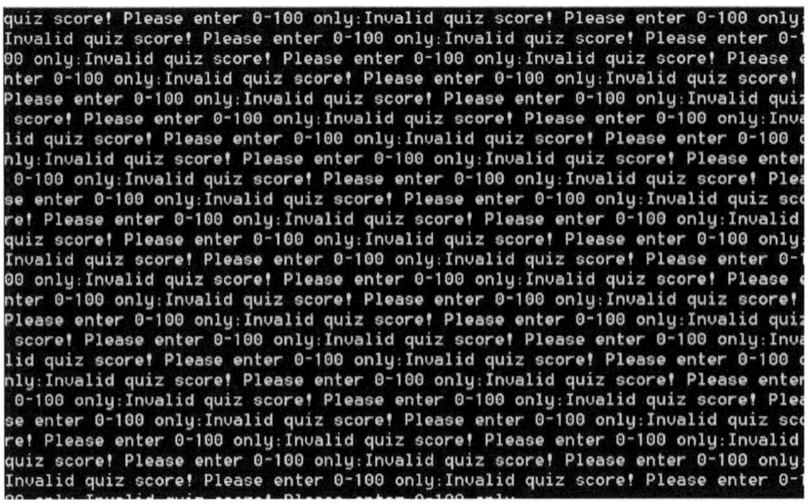


As you can see from the above screenshot, the program is in an infinite loop. Why is this happening and how do we correct it?

### *Bullet-Proof Code*

To prevent our program from going into the infinite loop every time the user enters anything other than a whole number, we need to write a few more lines of code. Before we do that we need to reflect on how the cin object works. Take a look at the following code segment:

```
1. int number;
2. cout << "Enter a number: ";
3. cin >> number;
```

What does the line #3 evaluate to when the user enters let's say 5? How about a 10? What about 4.23? What about if the user enters an exclamation point?

Recall from the earlier chapters that the cin object has some intelligence built it in a sense that it "knows" how to read user input. How does it know that? The variable number was declared of data type integer and the cin object is expecting an integer. If the user enters an integer the statement cin >> number will evaluate to true. If the user enters 4.23, the cin will read the integer portion of the input (number 4) and leave .23 on the keyboard buffer and return true as it accomplished the task (read an numeric value (whole number) and stored it into the memory location we call number that can hold an integer). However, once the user enters non numeric input such as an exclamation point, a letter, etc., the cin object will return false as it will not be able to populate the memory location aliased as number.

Why is this important for us if we are trying to write a while loop? Well, for one, while is a pre-test loop and needs a condition to evaluate whether the loop will even execute. So we can capitalize on that and write the following:

```
int number;
cout << "Enter a number: ";
while(cin >> number)
{
    cout << "Thank you for entering a number" << endl;
}
cout << "Have a nice day!" << endl;
```

So now it is clear that as long as the user enters numeric input the body of this loop will execute. The moment they enter a non-numeric input, the condition (`cin>>number`) fails so the loop does not execute and the next statement, `cout << "Have a nice day!" << endl;` will execute.

So how do we use this information to keep the user in a loop as long as they enter non-numeric input?

How about reversing the condition in the while loop with a NOT:

```
while(!(cin >> number))
int number;
cout << "Enter a number: ";
while(!(cin >> number))
{
    cout << "Wrong data type. Please enter a number:" << endl;
}
cout << "Have a nice day!" << endl;
```

The above program is far from perfect, as if the user enters non-numeric input the program will end up in an infinite loop as there is nothing in the body of the loop that will change the condition. For now that is OK, as we still need to make a few changes:

```
int number;
cout << "Enter a number: ";
while(!(cin >> number))
{
    cin.clear();
    cout << "Wrong data type. Please enter a number:" << endl;
    char ch;
    while(cin.get(ch) && ch != '\n'); // infinite loop
}
cout << "This is what you entered: " << number << endl;
cout << "Have a nice day!" << endl;
```

Now the code is rock solid:

```
Please enter a number :a
Wrong data type. Please enter numbers only: b
Wrong data type. Please enter numbers only: s
Wrong data type. Please enter numbers only: c
Wrong data type. Please enter numbers only: e
Wrong data type. Please enter numbers only: 22
You entered: 22
Process returned 0 (0x0)   execution time : 8.747 s
Press any key to continue.
```

## Counters

Sometimes you will need to count how many times you loop executes. For example, let's say you want to determine how many years will it take for a certain amount of money (principal) to reach maturity. For each year that the bank keeps your money, they give you interest on your capital. So for example, if the interest rate was 1.5%, and you put down $1,000, the first year you would earn $15 in interest. Your capital (principal) will thus grow to $1,015. Then next year (iteration) you will earn 1.5% on $1,015 which is $15.225 and your capital will become $1030.225. To determine number of years it would take an amount to reach certain value, we need to implement a counter:

```
#include <iostream>
using namespace std;
int main()
{
    const double TEN_K = 10000.00;
    const double INTEREST = 0.015;   // 1.5% interest
    int numYears = 0; // counter
    double principalAmt, initialAmt, interest;
    cout << "Enter your initial deposit: ";
    cin >> initialAmt;
    principalAmt = initialAmt; // copy initialAmt
      to principalAmt for the purpose of reporting
    while (principalAmt < TEN_K)
    {
      interest = principalAmt * INTEREST;
      principalAmt = principalAmt + interest;
      numYears++;
    }
    cout << "Assuming " << INTEREST * 100 << "% Interest rate, it will take you " << numYears
         << " years to grow $" << initialAmt << " to $" << TEN_K << endl;
    return 0;
}
```

```
Enter your initial deposit: 1000
Assuming 1.5% Interest rate, it will take you 155 years to grow $1000 to $10000
You will have: $10051.6

Process returned 0 (0x0)   execution time : 3.332 s
Press any key to continue.
```

One characteristic that counters have incommon is that they need an initial value which is defined outside of the loop. Inside of the loop the counter's value is incremented (or decremented). The initial value is usually (but not always) set the zero.

## Accumulators (Running total)

Accumulators are identical to counters with one difference. Both counters and accumulators must have initial value which is then incremented or decremented in the loop depending on programming logic. However, accumulators are used to keep the running total so when their value is incremented/decremented, it is incremented/decremented by the value of the variable being accumulating which is not the case with counters as their value is incremented/decremented by value of one.

## Sentinels

A Sentinel is a special value that is used to mark the end of user input. Usually this is a value that is not typical for the data being collected. For example, let's say we are tracking number of customers that visit a retail store and the amount of money they spend. Thus, we're going to use a counter (to track number of customers) and an accumulator (to track amount of profit) to implement our solution. Since we don't know how many customers will arrive in that particular store in one day we need a way to signal to our program went to terminate. This can be accomplished by entering data such as negative number for the amount spent to signal the end of input. The following program illustrates that:

```
#include <iostream>

using namespace std;
const int MY_SENTINEL = -99;        // sentinel
int main()
{
    double billAmt,
           totalProfit = 0.0;       // accumulator
    int    numCustomers = 0;        // counter
    cout << "Enter the bill amount: ";
    cin >> billAmt;

    while (billAmt != MY_SENTINEL)
  {
```

```
15.         totalProfit += billAmt;
16.         numCustomers++;
17.         cout << "Enter the bill amount: ";
18.         cin >> billAmt;
19.     }
20.
21.     cout << numCustomers << " customer visits. Total profit: " << totalProfit << endl;
22.     return 0;
23. }
```

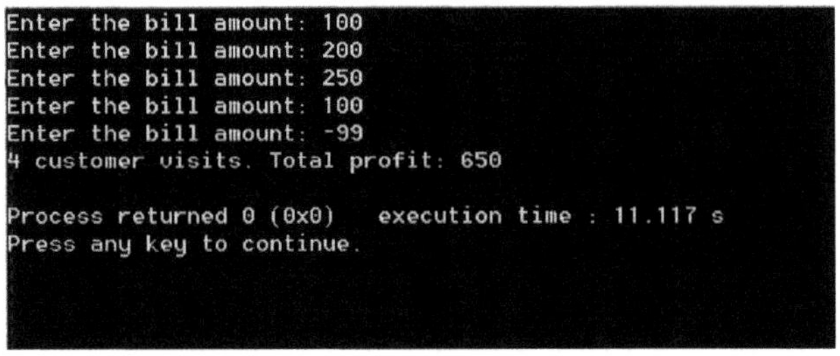


### *Priming Read*

In the above program, we also used what is known in computer science "priming read" (prime read). You will notice in lines 10 and 11 that the program prompts the user to enter some data ahead of the loop. So this data that we capture is then used to test the loop expression and based on that test we either enter the loop over you don't. In case we entered the loop we still need to read the data again for the next iteration and we do that in lines 17 and 18.

## Do While Loop

The general format of the do while loop is:

```
do
{
   statement(s);
} while (expression);
```

This loop is a so called post-test loop and is guaranteed to execute at least once. Since the program logic executes from top to bottom, all the statements after the keyword "do" execute, and then the program tests for the validity of the expression. If the expression evaluates to true, then the statements following the o keyword are executed again and so on.

### Used With Menus

The do-while is best suited for menus. You want to present a menu to the user and then test the expression against the user input. The following program illustrates that:

```
#include <iostream>
using namespace std;
int main()
{
    int userChoice;
    do
    {
        cout << "1. Withdraw" << endl;
        cout << "2. Deposit" << endl;
        cout << "3. Check Balance" << endl;
        cout << "4. Exit" << endl;
        cout << "Your choice: ";
        cin >> userChoice;
    }while(userChoice !=4);

    switch(userChoice)
    {
    case 1:
        cout << "Withdraw selected" << endl;
        break;
    case 2:
        cout << "Deposit selected" << endl;
        break;
    case 3:
        cout << "Check balance selected" << endl;
        break;
    case 4:
        cout << "Thank you for using XYZ Bank ATM" << endl;
        break;
    default:
        cout << "Please enter 1,2,3, or 4 only!" << endl;
    }
    return 0;
}
```

So we present the menu to the user and we prompt them to make a choice. We capture that choice and based on that choice we either execute the loop again or we don't in which case the programming logic simply executes the next statement.

## For Loop

The while and the do-while loops are conditional loops because they will keep executing as long as the condition evaluates to true. For example if you want to capture monthly precipitation for your city then you know that you need to prompt the user to enter the data once for each month thus your loop will execute exactly 12 times. When you know ahead of time how many iterations your program is going to needs to accomplish certain task can use a so-called count controlled loop. In addition to classifying loops as pretest and posttest loops we can classify loops as conditional and count controlled loops.

The for loop syntax is:

```
for (initialization¹; test²; update⁴)
{
  statement(s)³;
}
```

The superscripts in the above for loop syntax denote the components of the for loop in the order of execution. The initialization takes place first and this is where the loop control variable gets initialized. Next, the test expression determines whether the statement (or statements) in the body of the loop will execute. Should the test evaluate to true, the statement or statements inside of the loop body execute. After the statements execute, the loop control variable is updated and the process is repeated again without the initialization step. When the condition evaluates to false, the loop terminates and the programming logic shifts the program execution to the next statement after the body of the loop. Here's an example of the for loop:

```
for (int i=0; i<10; i++)
{
    cout << "Hello world" << endl;
}
```

- The int i=0; is the initialization section.
- The condion is i<10;
- The statement is cout << "Hellow world" << endl;
- i++ is the update

The above loop with execute 10 times. First, variable i is declared it initialized to zero, then it is tested whether that i is less than 10; if so, the cout statement is executed after which the i is updated. Since the i is 0, which is less than 10 the loop with continue to execute and update until the condition $i < 10$ is no longer true. That is how the variable i is used to control the number of executions of the loop .

We could have declared the variable i before the loop and then initialized inside of the loop as follows:

```
int i;
for (i=0; i<10; i++)
{
    cout << "Hello world" << endl;
}
```

The difference between the two code segment is that in the first code segment where we declared and initialized variable I in the loop header, the variable i was local (in scope) to the block of code/body of the for loop. In the second example, variable i was declared outside of the block of code that is associated with the for loop so it will retain its value after the for loop finishes its execution. A lot of times you will need to print the counter, in other words display how many times you went through the loop, so in that case it's better to declare the loop control variable prior to the for loop and then simply initialize it in the loop header. This way the variable will be in scope even after the loop terminates.

In the examples above, the for loop tested the condition prior to executing the statement in its body. Thus the for loop is classified as the pretest (count controlled) loop.

Suppose we want to compute the average points per game for a basketball player over a number of games. We could ask the user to provide the number of games they wish to track the points and then use the for loop to compute the average:

```
#include <iostream>
using namespace std;
int main()
{
    int numGames;           // to hold number of games tracked
    int points;             // to hold individual points
    int totalPoints =0;     // accumulator, used to track total
                               points scored
    double avg;             // average ppg
    cout << "How many games do you want to track: ";
    cin >> numGames;
    // collect the data
    for (int counter = 0; counter < numGames; counter++)
    {
        cout << "Game #" << counter + 1 << " points: ";
        cin >> points;
        totalPoints += points;
    }
    // calculate the average
    avg = static_cast<double>(totalPoints)/numGames;
    cout << "The player averaged " << avg << " points in "
         << numGames << " games" << endl;
    return 0;
}
```

## Omitting the expressions

You could omit sections (initialization, test, or update) and still have your loop execute. For example, if you want to run an infinite loop than simply omit all three sections:

```
#include <iostream>
using namespace std;
int main()
{
    for (;;)
    {
        cout << "Hello world!" << endl;
    }
    return 0;
}
```

In order to get out of this loop, you could use the break statement, just like the break statement that was used in the switch statement. So one way to break out of this loop would be to test a condition inside the body of the loop and when it evaluates to true simply invoke the break statement:

```
#include <iostream>
using namespace std;
int main()
{
    int i=0;
    for (;;)
    {
        i++;
        cout << "Hello world!" << endl;
        if (i==5)
            break;
    }
    return 0;
}
```

You would simply declare and initialize a variable that will be used to break out from the loop once the condition evaluates to true. In the example above, we use an integer variable i, which in this case was used as a counter and once its value became equal to five we broke out of the loop.

```
Hello world!
Hello world!
Hello world!
Hello world!
Hello world!

Process returned 0 (0x0)   execution time : 0.008 s
Press any key to continue.
```

It is possible to automate other sections of the for loop. For example, the following for loop does not have the initialization section in the loop header:

```
int i=0;
for (;i<5;i++)
{
    cout << "Hello world!" << endl;
}
```

Generally, this is not a good coding practice. As a programmer, you always need to be in control of your called so unless you have a very good reason to permit a section of the for loop don't do it. The following section will elaborate on few other "do nots".

## What not to do

Here a couple of things that you should not do:

### *do not put a ";" at the end of the loop header*

```
for (int i=0; i<10; i++);
```

usually, novice programmers tends to put a; as in the example above. You can think of the above for loop as of a for loop without the body due to the; immediately following the loop header. So the loop will execute the initialization, then in this case 10 times test and the update but no statements will execute, as there is no body of the loop.

### *Do not re-declare loop control variables in nested loops*

```
for (int i=0; i<5; i++)
{
   for (int i=0; i<5; i++)    // variable i just got
     re-declared!!!
   {
       //statements here….
   }
}
```

### *Do not update the loop control variable in the body of the loop*

```
for (int i=0; i<10; i++)
{
   cout << "Hello world" << endl;
   i+=5;
}
```

you want to control your code at any time. So the best place to increment your loop control variable is in the update section. For example, if you want to print "Hello world" on every fifth iteration of the loop then you should write your for loop as follows:

```
for (int i=0; i<10; i+=5)
{
   cout << "Hello world" << endl;
}
```

## For Loop and While Loop

Since the for loop and while loop are both pretest loops it is possible to rewrite a for loop is a while loop and vice versa:

| for loop | Equivalent while loop |
|---|---|
| `for (int i=0; i<20; i++)` | `i=0;                      // initialization` |
| `{` | `while(i<20)               // test` |
| `    cout << "Hello world" << endl;` | `{` |
| `}` | `    cout << "Hello world" << endl; // statement` |
| | `    i++;                  // update` |
| | `    }` |

Note the initialization, test expression, statement, and the update (section/component) in the while loop.

## Nested Loops

Suppose you want to print your data in tabular fashion, for example a multiplication table. How would you go about it? One way to do it would be to use nested loops:

```
#include <iostream>
using namespace std;
int main()
{
    for (int i=0; i<3; i++)    // outer for loop
    {
        for (int j=0; j<3; j++) // inner for loop
        {
            cout << (i+1)* (j+1) << " ";
        }
        cout << endl;
    }
    return 0;
}
```

In the example above, for each iteration of the outer for loop, the inner for loop completes all of its iterations producing the following multiplication table:

```
1 2 3
2 4 6
3 6 9

Process returned 0 (0x0)   execution time : 0.018 s
Press any key to continue.
```

Nested loops can be used to print patterns. In the early days, before proliferation of graphical user interface operating systems, the only way to represent data graphically lost to print patterns. The following program prints a square with stars:

```
#include <iostream>
using namespace std;
int main()
{
    for (int i=0; i<5; i++)    // outer for loop
    {
        for (int j=0; j<5; j++) // inner for loop
        {
            cout << "*";
```

```
        }
        cout << endl;
    }
    return 0;
}
```

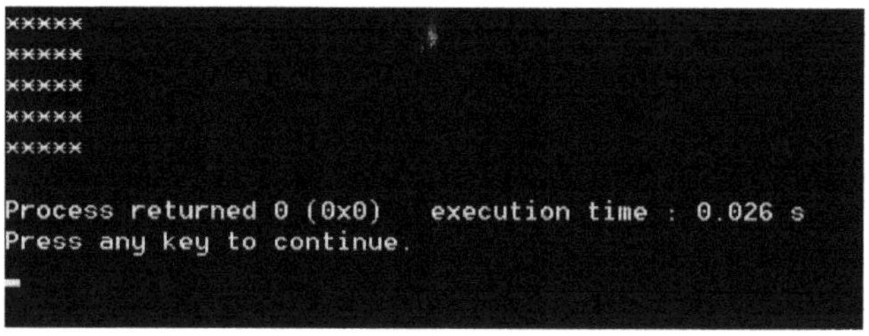


We could easily manipulate the output simply by tweaking loop control variables. Here's a short program that prints a triangle:

```
#include <iostream>
using namespace std;
int main()
{
    // triangle top
    for (int i=0; i<10; i++)
    {
        for (int j=0; j<i; j++)
        {
            cout << "*";
        }
        cout << endl;
    }
    return 0;
}
```

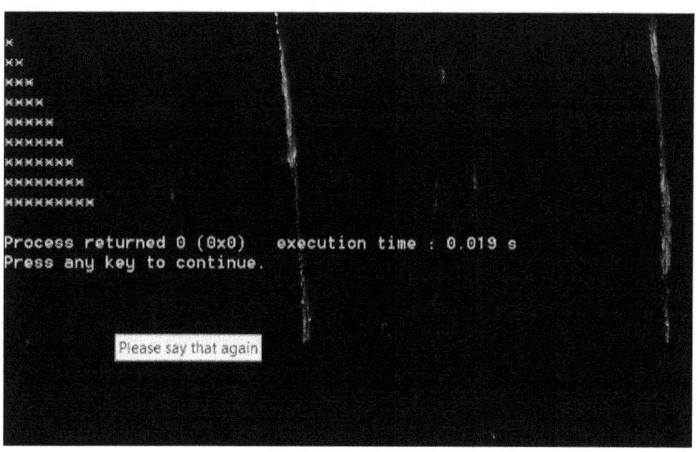

What if we want to print a triangle on the bottom?

```
#include <iostream>
using namespace std;
int main()
{
    // triangle top
    for (int i=0; i<10; i++)
    {
        for (int j=0; j<i; j++)
        {
            cout << "*";
        }
        cout << endl;
    }
    // bottom triangle
    for (int i=0; i<10; i++)
    {
        for (int j=10; j>i; j--)
        {
            cout << "*";
        }
        cout << endl;
    }

    return 0;
}
```

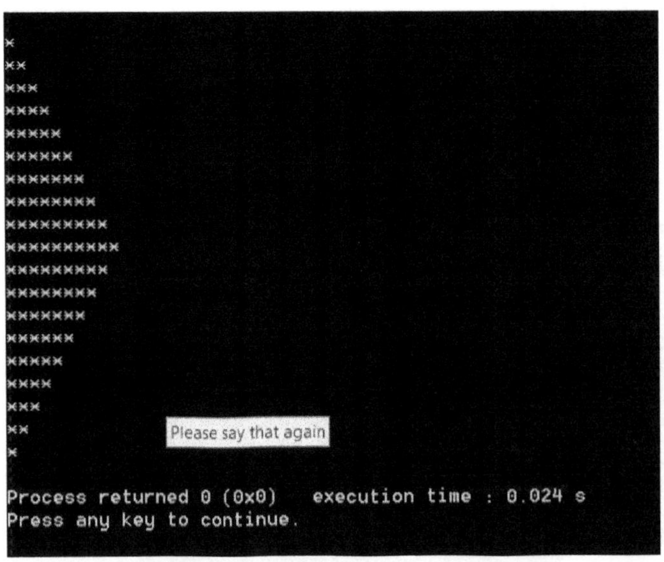


Finally, we can use control statements inside of the for loop to determine what pattern gets printed under what condition:

```
#include <iostream>
using namespace std;
int main()
{
    for (int i=0; i<10; i++)
    {
        for (int j=0; j<i; j++)
        {
            if (i==(j+1))
               cout << "*";
            else if (i==9)
               cout << "*";
            else
               cout << " ";
        }
        cout << endl;
    }
    return 0;
}
```

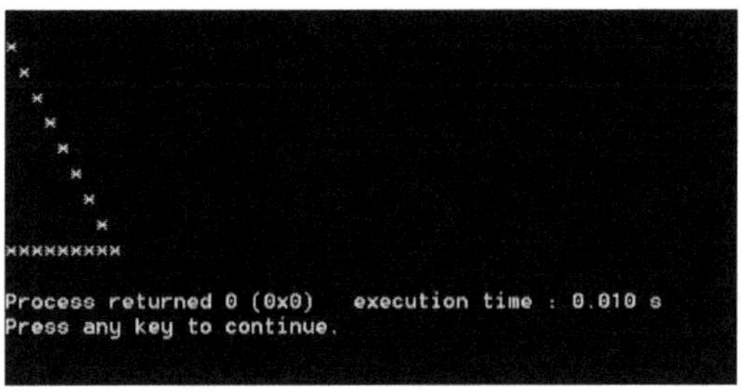


Printing data using patterns is not the only application of nested loops. As we saw nested loops could be used for tabular data or for data that is somehow related to another data. For example, an application that tracks student grades for a class of students. Throughout the semester each student takes quite a few quizzes, exams, and other types of assignments. To write this application, we would need to have a note to loop that will loop through all students. Then for each student, we would have inner loops that will be used to collect data for every assignment such as quizzes, exams, exercises etc. So the algorithm would look something like this:

```
for each student
{
     for each quiz
     {
       accumulate quiz scores
     }
     compute quiz average
     for each exam
     {
       accumulate exam scores
     }
```

```
        compute exam eaverage
        compute total average (quiz avg + exam avg)
    }
```

# End of Chapter Questions

## True/False

Indicate whether the statement is true or false.

1. Loops are repetitive statements that allow you to keep executing as long as certain condition is true.
2. In a while loop as long as the expression evaluates to false the statement or statements will continue to execute.
3. One characteristic that counters have in common is that they need an initial value which is defined outside of the loop.
4. Accumulators do not have to be initialized.
5. The difference between counters and accumulators is that accumulators are used to keep the running total.
6. A sentinel is a special value that is used to mark the end of the user input.
7. The do-while loop is called a post-test loop and is guaranteed to execute at least once.
8. Both the while and do-while loops are conditional loops.
9. A for loop is an example of a conditional loop.
10. In a for loop, initialization takes place first and this is where the loop control variable gets initialized.

## Exercises

1. Rent Fee Increase

   An apartment complex, which currently charges $1,000 per month for a two-bedroom, has announced it will increase its monthly charge by 3% for the next 3 years. Write a program that uses a loop to display the projected rates for the next three years.

2. Video Game Rental

   Write a program that calculates the purchase for video game sales, new games are $9.95 and all others $7.95. If a customer buys more than 3 video games, the fourth one is free. Ask the user how many video games the customer is purchasing. Ask the user whether the video game is a new release. Then display the total of the purchase.

3. Programming Team Training

   Write a program that calculates the total problems solved over a series of trainings by a member. The user enters a series of problems solved, and then enters -1 when finished.

4. Write a C++ program that will output the following:

   ```
   ////////////////
   // Hello C++ //
   ////////////////
   ```

   *Note: there are 16 '/' characters in the top and the bottom row.*

**5.** Random Grade Generator

Write a program that asks the user to enter the number of students in his/her class and then calculates and displays number of A's, B's, C's, D's, and F's for the entire class. Each student is graded on the following categories:

- 10 programming Exercises (progEx)
- 1 Midterm (midTerm)
- 1 Final Exam (final)

For each student, use random number generator to generate scores for each category. You need to make sure that the random number generator returns value in the range 1–100 for each of the grade book categories. So for each student you need to calculate their grade using the following formula:

```
numericGrade = (progEx Average *.70) + (midTerm *.15)+(final *.15)
```

The program needs to compute the letter grade equivalent according to the following chart:

| numericGrade (range) | letterGrade |
|---|---|
| 0–59 | F |
| 60–69 | D |
| 70–79 | C |
| 80–89 | B |
| 90–100 | A |

Once letter grade has been computed, update the count for that letter grade. When the program finishes the loop, it should display the following information:

| Number of students who received each letter grade: | |
|---|---|
| 10 | A |
| 14 | B |
| 6 | C |
| 4 | D |
| 4 | F |

Chapter 5

# Streams—Input, Output, and Customization

*"Preoccupied with a single leaf you won't see the tree."*

*—Vagabond*

## The Basics

What are streams? Streams are like buffers that can hold data. There are input and output streams. Input streams hold the data that was entered via keyboard, a file from the disk, or data that is coming from the network. In contrast, output streams hold the data that needs to be written to a screen, a file, a printer, or other location. The bottom line is that a process produced some data, and to this data is "parked" in a stream awaiting further processing.

So far we have been using stream extraction operator >> to "extract" (read) user input from input streams. We also used the stream insertion operator << to insert (output) the data for the purpose of presenting it to users. The cin object is tied to the standard input, which is normally the keyboard. The cout object is typically associated with an output device such as monitor.

Similar to console I/O streams, file streams could be input file streams and output file streams.

The process of reading from and writing to a file is very much similar to reading and writing from the standard console I/O. One difference between the standard console I/O stream and streams is how and when they are created. For example, the console iostreams are global in nature to your program and are created when your program starts. File streams, on the other hand, need to be created explicitly by the programmer.

In addition to input and output streams, some files could simultaneously be both input and output streams. Streams are an abstraction from how the operating system actually interacts with files and or networks. The only thing the programmer needs to learn is how to interact with a stream. Whether that stream is a local file or a network device such as printer is irrelevant.

Let's elaborate on the process of reading and writing to (and from) streams. When working with streams, the program views data in the streams as a series of bytes. Moreover, each bite is interpreted as a character. When we extract the data with the cin object, a translation from character to appropriate data type as requested by the cin object takes place. For example, if we declare a variable of integer data type called myNumber:

```
int myNumber;
cout << "Enter a number: ";
cin >> myNumber;
```

When the user enters input, even if it is a decimal number such as 13.5, it is stored in the keyboard buffer (I/O stream) as bunch of characters. At this point, the cin object sees the data as bunch of characters. Also, in this example, the cin object is instructed to read an integer. Thus, the cin object will read characters from the I/O stream until it encounters the first non-numeric character. Next, the cin object converts the two characters it read into a binary representation of an integer and stores it in the memory location called myNumber.

If the cin object was instructed to read any other data type, such as double, the process would be the same exactly the same with the exception that in this case the cin object would read the dot "." and the numeric characters following the dot until it encountered the white space character that signals the end of reading.

The process of writing to a stream is the opposite. The data that is stored in binary format in the RAM is converted to a characters before it's displayed (" written") to the stream.

The above-described process takes place in the console I/O (keyboard buffer and display device). This process is identical when working with file streams. The good news is that you already know how to read and write to and from the console I/O; therefore, reading and writing to and from files should not be much different.

Before we dive deeper into this topic, we need to become familiar with files and file types.

### File Types

Files are used to store data between program runs. Without files, the only way to run programs would be in real time. These are the type of programs we have written thus far. They required reentering of the data each time the program ran. With files it is possible to save a particular state of a program to a disk, and the data will remain on the desktop enough for the program to finish its execution. The data can be retrieved and used at a later date.

There are different file types, such as binary files and text files. Binary files contain data in the raw format. What this means is that the conversion that takes place from the way data is stored in the RAM (binary format) to the way data is stored in a stream (character format) was omitted in case of binary files. Many files are not readable by humans unless you are Mr. Data from Star Trek.

The text files, on the other hand, can be read by humans because they contain the data in character format. In other words, the data was translated from its binary format into the character format.

The intricacies of how files are formatted depends on the underlying operating system, which keeps track of creating, deleting, moving, and updating files.

## How to Read/Write from/to Files Programmatically

The following steps are necessary in order to successfully read/write files programmatically:

1. Include the header file #include `<fstream>`.
2. Declare a file handle variable(s) of appropriate data type:
   a. ofstream data type for output files.
   b. ifstream data type for input files.

**3.** Associate the file handle with the actual file by opening the file.
**4.** Read/write from/to the file.
**5.** Close the file.

In order for a computer program to interact with a file located on a computer disc or some other storage medium device, the program needs to specify to the filestream object how it intends to use that file. Typically, this means asking the operating system to connect the stream object to the file by telling the stream to "open" the disk file whose name is supplied. In this chapter we are going to explore text files.

## Writing to a File

Listing 1 illustrates how to write to a text file:

```
#include <iostream>
#include <fstream>

using namespace std;

int main()
{
    ofstream myOutFile;
    myOutFile.open("StudentNames.txt");
    myOutFile << "Joe" << endl;
    myOutFile << "Jill" << endl;
    myOutFile << "Jake" << endl;
    myOutFile.close();
    return 0;
}
```

Step 1
Step 2
Step 3
Step 4
Step 5

### *Listing 1 Writing to a Text File*

Several things are worth mentioning here:

- `myOutFile` in Listing 1 is a variable (file handle) of the data type ofstream. Since ofstream is an object, we can access its member functions via the dot (".") operator. Thus the statement

  ```
  myOutFile.open("StudentNames.txt");
  ```

  calls the open member function to which we supply filename StudentNames.txt.
- Notice that we did not specify the directory path where the file resides. The default is the project directory. If we do not specify the path, then the ofstream object is first going to look for the file in the project directory. If the file does not exist, it will be created. If the specified file exists, then it will be opened and its contents will be erased. Technically, the file pointer, which is the current position in the file, will simply be moved to the beginning of the file. There are ways to control how the data already in the file can be treated. It is possible to:
  - **Append** data to existing data in a file.
  - For now, accept that the data in the file will be **erased**.

- You will also notice another call to a member function called close( ). Even if we do not close the file, eventually the operating system will close it. However, it is a good programming practice to close files that are opened to reduce potential deadlocks. Deadlocks occur when more than one process is attempting to utilize a resource, in this case StudentNames.txt file, which could lead to undesired outcomes.
- Notice the stream insertion operator << on line 10 (also on lines 11 and 12). With the exception of ofstream variable`myOutFile,` there is little difference between the cout statement and this statement:

  ```
  cout << "Joe" << endl;
  ```

  The only difference is that myOutFile is used instead of the cout.

## Reading from a File

Reading data from standard console I/O is accomplished with the aid of the stream extraction operator >>. Similarly, the stream extraction operator is used to read data from a file. We need to instruct the stream object to open the file, then we read the data from the file, and finally we close the file. The process is almost identical to writing to a file with one crucial difference: In order to read from a file, the file <u>must exist</u> on the storage medium in the specified directory. If the file does not exist, the rest of the programming logic, which depends on the data to be read from the file, could produce undesirable results.

```
#include <iostream>
#include <fstream>
using namespace std;
int main()
{
    ifstream myInFile;                        // declare a variable of data type ifstream
    myInFile.open("StudentNames.txt");        // open the file for reading
    // be safe
    if (!myInFile)
    {
        cout << "Could not open data file.\nExiting..." << endl;
        exit(0);
    }
    string studentName;                       // to hold student names read from the file
    while(myInFile >> studentName)            // as lon as this is true keep reading
    {
        cout << studentName << endl;
    }
    // close the input file
    myInFile.close();
    return 0;
}
```

### *Listing 2*

In Listing 2, lines 9 through 13 are ensuring that the rest of the programming logic, which hinges on successful file opening and reading the data from it, is not compromised. Line 15 is also very interesting because it is the while loop condition. Given that myInFile is a stream object, it has the same logic built in as the cin object, which means that it is capable of signaling when a failure occurs. We are capitalizing on this built-in feature and using it to control the while loop, which is used to read the data from the file. The condition `myInFile >> studentName` is going to evaluate to true as long as there is data in the file. Once we reach the end of the file, the condition no longer holds true and the loop terminates.

## Reading Characters

It is possible to read one character at the time by calling the get function:

```
char ch;
myInFile.get(ch);
```

Unlike the >> operator, the get function is capable of reading white-space characters. This means that all the newlines, spaces, and tabs will be read. The following program reads data from a file one character at a time and writes it to output file:

```
#include <iostream>
#include <fstream>

using namespace std;
int main()
{
    ifstream myInFile;          // input file
    ofstream myOutFile;         // output file
    char     ch;                // to hold ch read from file

    myInFile.open("StudentNames.txt");
    if (!myInFile)              // safe programming
    {
        cout << "Could not open data file.\nExiting..." << endl;
        exit(0);
    }

    myOutFile.open("StudentNamesCopy.txt");  // open output text file

    while (myInFile.get(ch))    // read a char from input text file
    {
        myOutFile.put(ch);      // write it to the output file
    }
    myOutFile.close();          // close output file
    myInFile.close();           // close input file
    return 0;
}
```

### *Listing 3*

## Reading Lines

As long as the data does not contain whitespaces, reading and writing it from and to files using the stream extraction (>>) and stream insertion (>>) operators are not an issue. However, once the data contains whitespace characters, then the stream insertion and stream extraction operators are not the best option. The getline function is a much better choice as the following program illustrates:

```
#include <iostream>
#include <fstream>

using namespace std;

int main()
{
    ifstream inFile;    // input file handle
    inFile.open("Heat.txt");

    // defensive programming
    if (!inFile)
    {
      cout << "Invalid file. Terminating the program!" << endl;
      exit (0);
    }

    // Now that we are sure we have a valid file, let's
    // read from it.
    string line;
    while (getline(inFile, line))
    {
        cout << line << endl;
    }

    inFile.close();
    return 0;
}
```

### *Listing 4*

The program would display the following output:

```
34,Ray Allen,G,6-5,205
11,Chris Andersen,F-C,6-10,228
50,Joel Anthony,C,6-9,245
31,Shane Battier,F,6-8,225
1,Chris Bosh,C-F,6-11,235
15,Mario Chalmers,G,6-2,190
30,Norris Cole,G,6-2,175
40,Udonis Haslem,F,6-8,234
6,LeBron James,F,6-8,250
22,James Jones,G-F,6-8,215
9,Rashad Lewis,F,6-10,230
3,Dwyane Wade,G,6-4,220

Process returned 0 (0x0)   execution time : 0.016 s
Press any key to continue.
```

However, if we wanted to parse the input with the comma (,) as the delimiter, then a simple change on line 17 would suffice:

```
while (getline(inFile, line,','))
```

This would tell the getline that the comma is the delimiter. In this case the output would be different:

```
34
Ray Allen
G
6-5
205
11
Chris Andersen
F-C
6-10
228
50
Joel Anthony
C
6-9
245
31
Shane Battier
F
6-8
225
1
Chris Bosh
C-F
6-11
235
```

## Miscellaneous File Functions

Detecting and the file is a useful function and in C++ that is accomplished by calling the following member function:

```
inFile.eof()
```

assuming `inFile` was a file handle.

In simple programs in this chapter we hardcoded filenames. This is not a very good programming practice. Instead, the program should prompt the user to enter the filename, perhaps even the location of the file, in order to provide flexibility to users.

# Chapter 6

# Functions

***"It is easy to believe we are each waves and forget we are also the ocean."***

***—Jon J. Muth***

## What Is a Function?

Let's start this chapter by asking couple of questions:

- What is a function?
- What functions are you familiar with?
- What functions have you used - not only in Computer science, but also in math?
- How about sqrt, pow? int main()?

Before we answer the first question what is a function, let's take a look at a few examples of functions:
$f(x) = x^2 – 7$
if we substitute number 3 for x what would be the answer?
$f(3) = 3^2 – 7$
$f(3) = 9 – 7$
$f(3) = 2$
The above example illustrates a function. From it we can conclude that there is a left-hand side followed by an equal sign followed by an expression (rule) on the right-hand side. We could have simply used a letter such as "y" to denote f (3). However, using this notation f(x) is easier to see how functions work. We simply substitute a value for x and obtain the results by performing the calculation.

We have also used the following functions inside of C++ programs:

```
y = pow(3.0, 2);
```

```
#include <iostream>
#include <cmath>
using namespace std;
int main()
{
    int y = pow (3.0, 2);
    cout << "3 Squared is : " << y << endl;
    return 0;
}
```

**Listing 1:** Using a Built-in Function

From the above two examples, we can conclude that a function operates on some kind of input according to some rules. Raising a value to a particular exponent is a rule. The data/input is the value that we provide.

Thus we can graphically represent a function as an input that is manipulated by some rules producing an output:

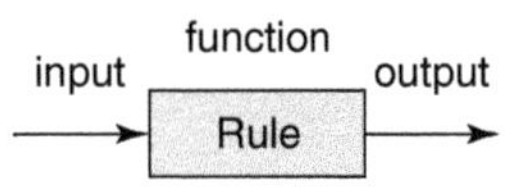


More specifically, the math example used above can be graphically represented as follows:

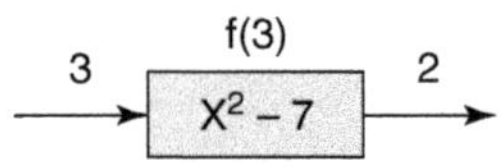


And finally, the power function in the C++ code example can be generalized as follows:

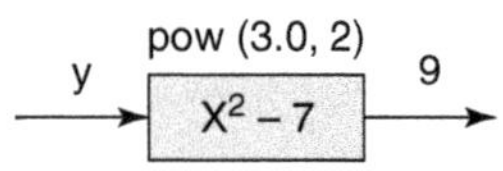


We can also reflect on one function that we have used all along in C++:

```
int main()
```

or more specifically:

```
int main(int argc, char* argv[])
```

This is a special function and it is required for a C++ program to run. Without this function, no C++ program will run. This function also follows the same pattern as described above as it has an input in the form of two arguments argc of data type integer, and argv which is an array of characters.

The int is the return type and the main is the name of the function which is followed by the parentheses inside of which we normally have a list of arguments that are passed to the function. Each function has a beginning brace and an ending brace:

```
int main()
{
     Statement1;
     Statement2;
     Statement3;
     .........
     .........
     Statementn;
     return 0;
}
```

## Benefits of Using Functions

So far we have also written all our logic inside of this special function. Sometimes this entailed writing repetitive statements making programs very long. Here is an example of that:

```
 1. #include <iostream>
 2.
 3. using namespace std;
 4.
 5. int main()
 6. {
 7.     int x, y, z, sum;
 8.
 9.     cout << "Enter the first digit:";
10.     cin >> x;
11.     cout << "Enter the second digit: ";
12.     cin >> y;
13.     cout << "Enter the third digit: ";
14.     cin >> z;
15      sum = x + y + z;
16.     cout << x << "+" << y << "+" << z << "=" << sum << endl;
17.     return 0;
18. }
```

**Listing 2:** Repetitive Statements

As you can see from the above program, interacting with the user in obtaining three numbers and adding them and displaying the sum requires quite a few lines of code. Suppose we need to compute a sum for another three digits and we do not know how to use loops we would have to repeat lines 9 through 16:

```
 1. #include <iostream>
 2.
 3. using namespace std;
 4.
 5. int main()
 6. {
 7.     int x, y, z, sum;
 8.
 9.     cout << "Enter the first digit:";
10.     cin >> x;
11.     cout << "Enter the second digit: ";
12.     cin >> y;
13.     cout << "Enter the third digit: ";
14.     cin >> z;
15.     sum = x + y + z;
16.     cout << x << "+" << y << "+" << z << "=" << sum << endl;
17.     cout << "Enter the first digit:";
```

```
    cin >> x;
    cout << "Enter the second digit: ";
    cin >> y;
    cout << "Enter the third digit: ";
    cin >> z;
    cout << x << "+" << y << "+" << z << "=" << sum << endl;
    return 0;
}
```

**Listing 3:** More Repetitive Statements

Fortunately, we know how to use loops. So we can simplify this code as follows:

```
1. #include <iostream>
2.
3. using namespace std;
4.
5. int main()
6. {
7.      int x, y, z, sum;
8.      for (i = 0; i<2; i++)
9.      {
10.          cout << "Enter the first digit:";
11.          cin >> x;
12.          cout << "Enter the second digit: ";
13.          cin >> y;
14.          cout << "Enter the third digit: ";
15.          cin >> z;
16.          sum = x + y + z;
17.          cout << x << "+" << y << "+" << z << "="
                  << sum << endl;
18.      }
19.      return 0;
20. }
```

**Listing 4:** Using Loops to Eliminate Repetitive Statements

That looks much better, as we have put the statements that repeat into a block of code (lines 9 through 18). We use the for loop to call this block of code repeatedly. What if we were able to give a name to the block of code that repeats? Would that improve the readability of our source code? Let's try:

```
#include <iostream>

using namespace std;

int main()
{
    for (i=0; i<2; i++)
```

```
 8.     {
 9.         myFunction();
10.     }
11.     return 0;
12. }
```

Function call

**Listing 5:** Using Functions to Eliminate Repetitive Statements

Even the code example without the for loop would look more elegant if we were to call myFunction:

```
 1. #include <iostream>
 2.
 3. using namespace std;
 4.
 5. int main()
 6. {
 7.         myFunction();
 8.         myFunction();
 9.         return 0;
10. }
```

Function call

**Listing 6:** Calling Multiple Functions

## Function Calls

Even though the source code has been simplified, and it looks more elegant, the attempt to compile it would result in a syntax error because the compiler would not know how to interpret what myFunction is. Fortunately, there are some rules that we need to abide by in order to isolate source code statements into a separate unit, or a function and tell the compiler how to use it.

First, we need to learn what a **function call** is. The code that is isolated into a function will execute when a function is called. Function main is a very special function and it is automatically executed when a C++ program is run. All other functions needs to be called in order to execute the statements that comprise the function. In the for loop example above, line number 9 contains a function call. Similarly, the code segment without the for loop contains function calls on lines number 7 and 8. To call a function we simply write its name followed by parentheses and the semicolon. The statement in line number 9 (7 and 8 in the other example) will cause the function to execute.

## Function Definition

Second, we need to provide **function definition**. A function definition contains:

- the return type (void in our case )
- function name (myFunction)
- parameter list inside of brackets. In our case, there are no parameters.

- Function body which starts with a open brace "{" and ends with a closed brace "}". In between the beginning and ending brace are the statements:

```
 1. void myFunction()
 2. {
 3.     int x, y, z, sum;
 4.     cout << "Enter the first digit:";
 5.     cin >> x;
 6.     cout << "Enter the second digit: ";
 7.     cin >> y;
 8.     cout << "Enter the third digit: ";
 9.     cin >> z;
10.     sum = x + y + z;
11.     cout << x << "+" << y << "+" << z << "=" << sum << endl;
12. }
```

**Listing 7:** Isolating a Block of Code Into a Function

Lines 4 through 11 are nothing more than the block of code that we used in the for loop. We also added variable declarations for x, y, z and sum in line number 3.

This function is very similar to the int main() function:

- It has a return type called **`void`** instead of **`int`**;
- it has a name (myFunction); and it has beginning and ending braces on lines to and 2 and 12 respectively.
- The function myFunction does not have any arguments (parameters) between the parentheses.

Let's discuss the return type of our function (myFunction) - what is void? In the case of int maine(), the return type is an an integer. Other functions may return different data types such as double, char, float, a string, etc., but what is the void return type? A function returning a void is not returning anything to the caller program.

```
#include <iostream>
using namespace std;
void myFunction()
{
    int x, y, z, sum;
    cout << "Enter the first digit:";
    cin >> x;
    cout << "Enter the second digit: ";
    cin >> y;
    cout << "Enter the third digit: ";
    cin >> z;
    sum = x + y + z;
    cout << x << "+" << y << "+" << z << "=" << sum << endl;
}
int main()
{
    for (int i=0; i<2; i++)
    {
```

Function definition

```
19.         myFunction();
20.     }
21.     return 0;
22. }
```

**Listing 8:** Function Example

In the above code segment, lines 3 through 14 are the function definition for myFunction(). Thus this program contains two functions: the necessary main function and myFunction() which is called from the main function, specifically on line 19. The program flow starts in function main. The statements will execute sequentially from the top. When statement on line 19 is encountered, the program execution will jump from function main (which is the **caller** of function myFunction in this case) to myFunction() (see line 3). All the statements in myFunction() will be executed sequentially and the execution will return to the caller (the main function).

Key points to remember when it comes to function headers and function calls are:

- A function header contains the return data type, function name and parameter list (if any) inside of parentheses: **`void myFunction()`**

  Notice that there is no semicolon at the end of the function header due to the fact that the body of the function follows the function header.
- A function call consists of the function name followed by parameter (list if any), and because it is just like any other C++ statement, it must end with a semicolon: **`myFunction();`**

Since C++ programs execute sequentially (from top to bottom), it is necessary to put the function definitions prior to the main function in order to successfully compile and execute the code. Here is an example of that:

```
#include <iostream>
using namespace std;

void goodMorning()
{
    cout << "Good morning!" << endl;
}

void goodAfternoon()
{
    cout << "Good afternoon!" << endl;
}

void goodEvening()
{
    cout << "Good evening!" << endl;
}
int main()
{
    goodMorning();
    goodAfternoon();
```

```
    goodEvening();
    return 0;
}
```

**Listing 9:** Function Bodies Before the main() Function

## Function Prototypes

Here is the same program with function prototypes:

```
#include <iostream>

using namespace std;

// Function prototypes
void goodMorning();
void goodAfternoon();
void goodEvening();

int main()
{
    goodMorning();
    goodAfternoon();
    goodEvening();
    return 0;
}

// function definitions
void goodMorning()
{
    cout << "Good morning!" << endl;
}
void goodAfternoon()
{
    cout << "Good afternoon!" << endl;
}
void goodEvening()
{
    cout << "Good evening!" << endl;
}
```

Function prototypes

**Listing 10:** Function Prototypes

The reason for placing function prototypes before the main function is to let the compiler know:

- The function return type
- Parameters (if any) and their data type

This way the compiler will not issue a syntax error when it encounters a function call in the main function. Also, listing function prototypes prior to the main function makes source code more readable. A word of caution, listing only function prototypes without corresponding function definitions will result in syntax errors when trying to compile the program.

Because the execution of the program starts with the main function, it makes sense that it is the first function in the source code. We can clearly see that a function prototype is nothing more than the first line of the function definition followed by a semicolon:

```
// Function prototypes
void goodMorning();
void goodAfternoon();
void goodEvening();
```

A function prototype is also known as a **function declaration** because a function is declared prior to being used (called). In the example above the functions did not contain any parameters. In case a function contains a parameter list, the only requirement is to list the data types of each parameter but not the parameter names. We will see an example of this later on in this chapter.

When implementing more complex software such as object-oriented software, function prototypes are usually isolated in header files which have extension ".h". The implementation (function definitions) is isolated into source code files which have extensions ".cpp".

## Passing by Value

One of the big benefits of breaking down programs into functions is code reusability. In order to successfully reuse code, it is necessary to pass data to functions. This is accomplished through b and **parameters**. It is necessary to make a distinction between an argument and a parameter.

In the caller program, when executing a function call, sometimes data is passed into a function. This value that is passed into a function is called an argument. Suppose we have the following program that calls the function which converts degrees Fahrenheit into degrees Celsius:

```
#include <iostream>
using namespace std;

// function prototypes
void fahren2Celsius(double);

int main()
{
    double tempF;
    cout << "Enter the temperature in degrees Fahrenheit:";
    cin >> tempF;
    fahren2Celsius(tempF);
    return 0;
}
```

**tempF is an argument passed to the function**

**Listing 11:** Passing by Value

The argument tempF could have also been a double literal:

```
fahren2Celsius(81.0);
```

in any case, either variable or a literal it is a value that is part of the main function and is being passed to the function fahren2Celsius as an argument. To successfully write this function we need to know how to convert from one temperature scale to another. The formula to convert degrees Fahrenheit to degrees Celsius is:

$$C = \frac{5}{9} * (F - 32)$$

where C is temperature in degrees Celsius, and F is temperature in degrees Fahrenheit. Given a temperature in degrees Fahrenheit we can substitute and obtain equivalent temperature in degrees Celsius.

So the function fahren2Celsius needs to be able to receive a value representing temperature in degrees Fahrenheit:

```
1. void fahren2Celsius(double fahren)
2. {
3.       cout << fahren << "degrees Fahrenheit is"
4.            << 5.0/9 * (fahren - 32)
5.            << "degrees Celsius"
6.            << endl;
7. }
```

**This is the parameter that will receive the value (argument) passed in from the caller program**

**Listing 11:** Function Receiving Values Through a Parameter

In the code example above, on line 1, the variable of data type double called **fahren** is a parameter that will receive the data passed to the function in the caller program. We have simplified the function logic by writing the formula in line of the cout statement.

When we analyze what takes place behind the scenes, we see that the function main allocated a variable called tempF of data type double. Similarly, the function fahren2Celsius allocated the variable called fahren also of data type double. The actual passing of the data to function is as simple as copying the contents of the argument variable to the memory location of the parameter variable. The following figure illustrates that:

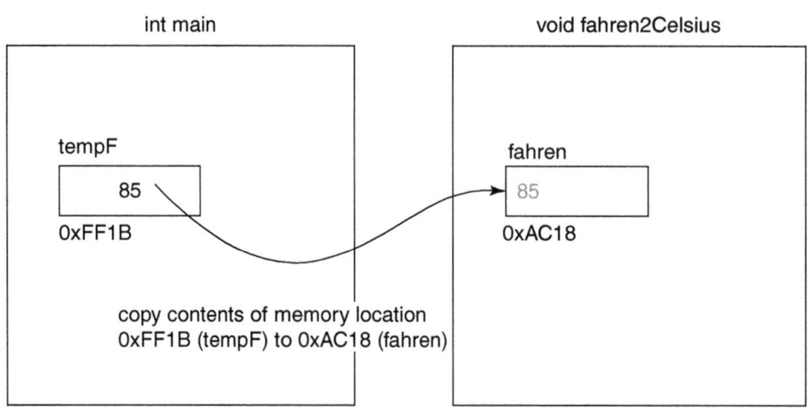


**Figure 1:** Copying Contents of an Argument Variable to the Parameter Variable

In the above figure, the argument tempF is allocated in memory location 0xFF1B and corresponding parameter fahren is allocated in 0xAC18. When the main function calls fahren-2Celsius (line 12), the contents of memory location 0xFF1B are copied to the memory location 0xAC18. This is known as passing data by value or simply **pass by value**.

When passing data by value, it is important to remember the following:

- if we are passing a literal (integer, double, float, etc.) then we simply put that value inside of the parentheses as an argument in the caller program:

```
fahren2Celsius(85.8);
```

- if we are passing a variable as an argument, then we simply put the variable name inside of the parentheses:

```
fahren2Celsius(tempF);
```

  And we never put the data type inside of the parentheses:

```
fahren2Celsius(double tempF);
```

  as this would result in compiler error.

- The data type of the parameter in function prototype and in function definition needs to match.
- Passing arguments whose data type is not the same as the parameter's data type will result in promotion or demotion of arguments data type:

```
fahren2Celsius(85);
```

  85 will be promoted to 85.0 (a double).

- A copy of the argument is made, so the original values of the arguments are not affected:

```
#include <iostream>
using namespace std;
void fahren2Celsius(double);

int main()
{
    double tempF;
    cout << "Enter the temperature in degrees Fahrenheit:";
    cin >> tempF;
    cout << "---- BEFORE --- the function call" << endl;
    cout << "Value of tempF: " << tempF << endl;
    fahren2Celsius(tempF);
    cout << "---- BACK --- in the int main function"<< endl;
    cout << "Value of tempF: " << tempF << endl;
    return 0;
}

void fahren2Celsius(double fahren)
{
    cout << "---- INSIDE --- the function fahren2Celsius"
        << endl;
    cout << "Received value: " << fahren << endl;

    // purposely add 10 to the received value
    fahren = fahren + 10;
    cout << "Received value + 10: " << fahren << endl;
```

```
26.
27.      cout << fahren << "degrees Fahrenheit is"
28.           << 5.0/9 * (fahren - 32)
29.           << "degrees Celsius"
30.           << endl;
31. }
```

**Listing 13:** Pass by Value

The output of this program run reveals that the function received a copy of the argument (value of 85). Next, we added 10 to the parameter and computed the temperature in $^0$C for the new value 95 (85 + 10). When the function returns to the main function, the cout statement on line 14 reveals that the value of the argument is still 85 which proves that the function did not alter the value of the original argument.

```
Enter the temperature in degrees Fahrenheit:85
---- BEFORE --- the function call
Value of tempF: 85
---- INSIDE --- the function fahren2Celsius
Received value: 85
Received value + 10: 95
95 degrees Fahrenheit is 35 degrees Celsius
---- BACK --- in the int main function
Value of tempF: 85

Process returned 0 (0x0)   execution time : 3.039 s
Press any key to continue.
```

The following figure illustrates what took place behind the scenes:

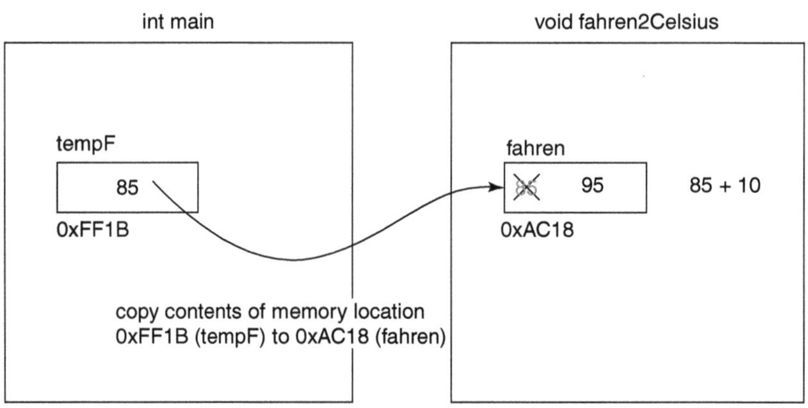


**Figure 2:** Contents of the Argument Variable are not Affected by Math Operations on Parameter Variables

## Functions with Multiple Parameters

It is possible to pass multiple values to functions. Here's a function that is designed to receive two values:

```
#include <iostream>

using namespace std;

// Function prototypes
void sumOfTwo(int, int);
```

```
 7.
 8. int main()
 9. {
10.     sumOfTwo(5,10);
11.     return 0;
12. }
13.
14. void sumOfTwo(int a, int b)
15. {
16.     cout << a << " + " << b << " = " << a + b;
17. }
```

**Listing 14:** A Function with Multiple Parameters

Key points to remember when using functions with multiple parameters is to match the order of parameters with arguments. In the example above, integer literal five is passed (copied) to memory location where integer variable a is allocated. Similarly, integer literal 10 is copied to memory location where integer variable B is allocated. If we were to reverse the order of arguments in the caller program, specifically online 10 and call the function sumOfTwo with arguments 10 and 5, then a would receive 10 and be with receive 5. In the example above sumOfTwo, the reversal of arguments would not impact the overall result. However, for some functions reversing the order of arguments could have undesired consequences:

```
 1. #include <iostream>
 2.
 3. using namespace std;
 4.
 5. // function prototypes
 6. void division(double, double);
 7. int main()
 8. {
 9.     division(5,2);
10.     division(2,5);
11.
12.     return 0;
13. }
14.
15. void division(double numerator, double denomenator)
16. {
17.     double quotient;
18.     quotient = numerator/denomenator;
19.     cout << numerator << " / " << denomenator << " = "
20.          << quotient << endl;
21. }
```

**Listing 15:** The Order of Arguments in a Function Call is Important

Calling the division function in line 9 and line 10:

```
 9.     division(5,2);
10.     division(2,5);
```

will yield different results. What would happen if the denominator (the 2nd value) in either function call was a 0?

## Pass by Reference

Pass by reference is a very powerful feature of the C++ language. In order to better understand it, let's first become familiar with the concept of references.

### What is a Reference?

A reference is an alias for an object. For example, it is possible to declare a reference to an object (in this case an integer variable):

```
#include <iostream>

using namespace std;

int main()
{
    int x = 10;
    int &refX = x;

    cout << "This is refX: " << refX << endl;

    refX = refX + 1;
    cout << "This is X <after>: " << x << endl;

    return 0;
}
```

**Listing 16:** A Reference

Thus working on x or refX is in reality the same as refX is just another name for the variable x. The following figure is an output of the above program and it illustrates that x and refX are indeed the same variable:

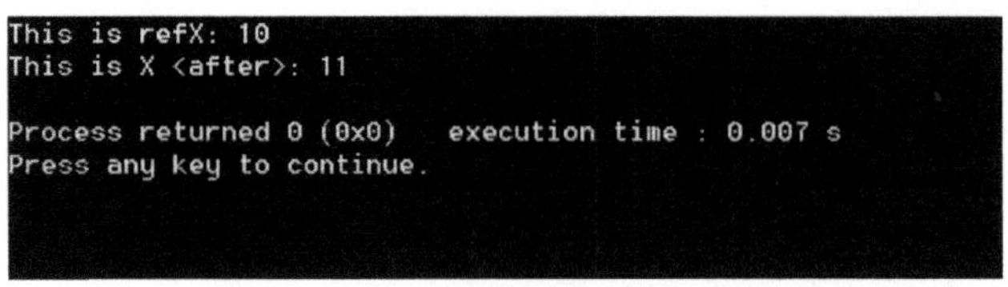


The following illustration depicts what takes place behind the scenes, in computer memory:

**Figure 3:** Reference Depicted

The int variable x is allocated in the memory location 0x28FF44 and the reference, refX is also referring to the same memory location.

## Pass by Reference

Why is this important when essentially these are the same? The answer is that sometimes you will need to work on the original argument rather than the copy of the variable. It makes sense to pass arguments as reference in cases when the object (data type) is large and making a copy of it would be less efficient than working on the original.

The function call whether it is pass by reference or pass by value is identical. In the function definition, more specifically in the function header, the parameters that receive data as a reference are preceded by an "&" to denote that the parameter is a reference to the original argument. The programmer needs to be careful as in this scenario, he/she is working on the original argument, and any changes to the reference parameter in the function will be reflected in the original argument:

```
#include <iostream>
using namespace std;
// Function prototype
void fahren2Celsius(double &);

int main()
{
    double tempF;
    cout << "Enter the temperature in degrees Fahrenheit:";
    cin >> tempF;
    cout << "---- BEFORE --- the function call" << endl;
    cout << "Value of tempF: " << tempF << endl;
    fahren2Celsius(tempF);
    cout << "---- BACK --- in the int main function" << endl;
    cout << "Value of tempF: " << tempF << endl;
    return 0;
}

void fahren2Celsius(double &fahren)
{
    cout << "---- INSIDE --- the function fahren2Celsius"
         << endl;
    cout << "Received value: " << fahren << endl;

    // purposely add 10 to the received value
    fahren = fahren + 10;
    cout << "Received value + 10: " << fahren << endl;

    cout << fahren << " degrees Fahrenheit is "
         << 5.0/9 * (fahren - 32)
         << "degrees Celsius"
         << endl;
}
```

**Note the "&" in the parameter list signifying a reference parameter**

**Function call**

**Reference parameter. Think of "fahren" as a nickname (an alias) for tempF.**

**Listing 17:** Passing by Reference

Compiling and running the above example would result in the following output:

```
Enter the temperature in degrees Fahrenheit:85
---- BEFORE --- the function call
Value of tempF: 85
---- INSIDE --- the function fahren2Celsius
Received value: 85
Received value + 10: 95
95 degrees Fahrenheit is 35 degrees Celsius
---- BACK --- in the int main function
Value of tempF: 95

Process returned 0 (0x0)   execution time : 4.192 s
Press any key to continue.
```

Note the change in the original value tempF (last cout statement)—it is not 85, but 95. The function received 85, but on line 25:

```
25      fahren = fahren + 10;
```

The function added 10 to the received (original) value resulting in the change to the value of the original argument (tempF).

## Pass by Constant Reference

Sometimes the programmer will need to pass a large object to a function but not necessarily risk having function change the value of the original argument. An example of that would be passing a large object to a function but not wanting that function to make any changes to the object. In this case, it is necessary to pass this object by constant reference.

The syntax for passing by constant reference is as follows:

```
#include <iostream>

using namespace std;

// Function prototype
void fahren2Celsius(const double &);

int main()
{
    double tempF;
    cout << "Enter the temperature in degrees Fahrenheit:";
    cin >> tempF;
    cout << "---- BEFORE --- the function call" << endl;
    cout << "Value of tempF: " << tempF << endl;
    fahren2Celsius(tempF);
    cout << "---- BACK --- in the int main function" << endl;
    cout << "Value of tempF: " << tempF << endl;
    return 0;
}

```

**Note the "const" in the parameter list**

**The function call is still the same**

```
void fahren2Celsius(const double &fahren)
{
      cout << "---- INSIDE --- the function fahren2Celsius"
           << endl;
      cout << "Received value: " << fahren << endl;

      // purposely add 10 to the received value
      fahren = fahren + 10;
      cout << "Received value + 10: " << fahren << endl;

      cout << fahren << " degrees Fahrenheit is "
           << 5.0/9 * (fahren - 32)
           << "degrees Celsius"
           << endl;
}
```

**Everything is the same; only "const" is in the parameter list**

**Listing 18:** Passing const References

The program above would not compile because of the constant reference parameter in the function. This is illustrated in the following screenshot of the attempted copulation of the program:

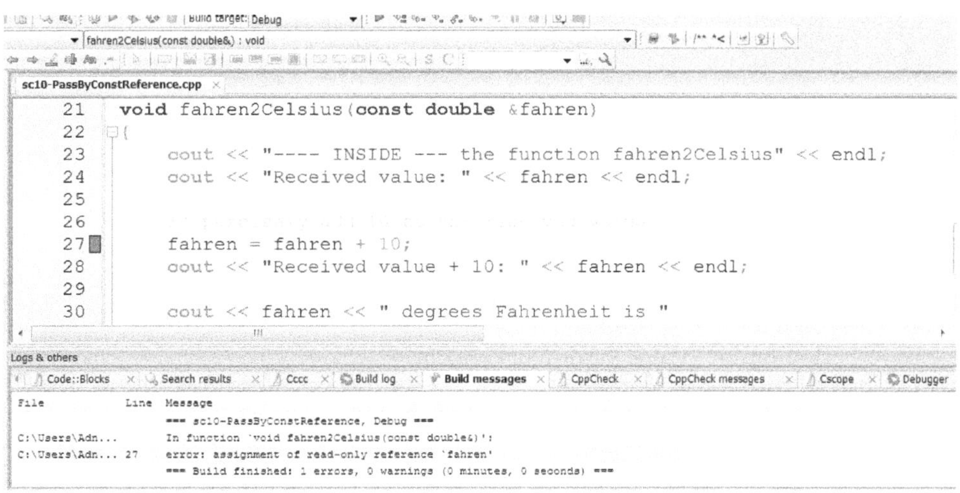


**Figure 4:** Error Message When Attempting to Change the const Reference

This is one way C++ has to ensure efficient passing of large objects to functions without changing the contents of the original object. Any attempt to change the value of the constant parameter will result in compiler error.

## Value Returning Functions

So far, we have only used void functions. Many functions return results of the tasks they were designed to accomplish. Case in point, the main function returns an integer which signals to the operating system the outcome of main functions execution.

When writing value returning functions, it is necessary to specify the return type which is going to be something other than void. In addition, in the caller program it is necessary to capture the value returned from a function if it needs to be processed further. Having functions return values makes source code more readable as illustrated in the following example:

```
1. #include <iostream>
2.
3. using namespace std;
4.
5. // Function prototype
6. double fahren2Celsius(double );
7.
8. int main()
9. {
10.     double tempF;
11.     cout << "Enter the temperature in degrees Fahrenheit:";
12.     cin >> tempF;
13.
14.     cout << tempF << " degrees Fahrenheit is : "
15.          << fahren2Celsius(tempF)
16.          << " degrees Celisus." << endl;
17.     return 0;
18. }
19.
20. double fahren2Celsius(double fahren)
21. {
22.     double cels;  // to hold the computed value that will
23.                   // be returned back to the caller
24.     cels = 5.0/9 * (fahren - 32);           // formula
25.     return cels;
26. }
```

**Note the return type in the prototype**

**Function returns a value that can be used inline in the cout statement**

**The function code is much cleaner. It computes the value and returns it. Note the return statements on line 25.**

**Listing 19:** Value Returning Function

Value returning functions usually do not have any cout statements instead they return a value back to the caller program. This simplifies the code as the function performs the task it was designed to perform which is usually some kind of computation.

The caller program receives computed value back from the function and it can use it for additional computations which could be in the main function, or it could pass the computed value to another function. Following code segment is an example of how value returning functions could be used in a menu-based program:

```
#include <iostream>

using namespace std;

// Function prototypes
void displayWelcomeMessage();
void displayMenu();
int getUserChoice();
double fahren2Celsius(double);
```

```
double celsius2Fahrenheit(double);
void displayConversion(double, double, char);

int main()
{
    int userChoice;
    double tempF, tempC;

    displayWelcomeMessage();

    do
    {
        tempF = 0.0;
        tempC = 0.0;
        userChoice = getUserChoice();
        switch(userChoice)
        {
        case 1:
            cout << "Enter the temperature in degrees Fahrenheit:";
            cin >> tempF;
            tempC = fahren2Celsius(tempF);
            displayConversion(tempF, tempC, 'F');
            break;
        case 2:
            cout << "Enter the temperature in degrees Celsius:";
            cin >> tempC;
            tempC = celsius2Fahrenheit(tempC);
            displayConversion(tempC, tempF, 'C');
            break;
        case 3:
            cout << "Thank you for using the conversion utility!" << endl;
            break;
        default:
            cout << "Wrong choice. Please enter 1, 2, or 3 only" << endl;
        }
    }while (userChoice !=3);


    return 0;
}

void displayWelcomeMessage()
{
    cout << "Welcome to temperature conversion program!" << endl;
}
void displayMenu()
{
```

```
    cout << "1. Fahrenheit to Celsius" << endl;
    cout << "2. Celsius to Fahrenheit" << endl;
    cout << "3. Exit" << endl;
    cout << "Your choice: ";
}

int getUserChoice()
{
    int choice;
    displayMenu();
    cin >> choice;
    return choice;
}

double fahren2Celsius(double fahren)
{
    double cels;     // to hold the computed value that will
                     // be returned back to the caller
    cels = 5.0/9 * (fahren - 32);  // formula
    return cels;
}

double celsius2Fahrenheit(double celsius)
{
    double fahren;
    fahren = celsius * 9.0/5 + 32;
    return fahren;
}

void displayConversion(double tF, double tC, char conversion)
{
    cout << "\n";
    if (conversion == 'F') // fahrenheit 2 celsius
    {
        cout << tF << "degrees Fahrenheit is: "
             << tC << "degrees Celisus." << endl;

    }
    else if (conversion == 'C')
    {
        cout << tC << "degrees Celisus is: "
             << tF << "degrees Fahrenheit."<< endl;

    }
    cout << "\n";
}
```

**Listing 20:** Value Returning Functions in a Menu-Based Program

The program starts by calling the displayWelcomeMessage function on line 18. Next, user choice is obtained by calling the getUserChoice function, which in turn calls the displayMenu function. The returned value from the getUserChoice function is stored in the userChoice variable. Depending on the user's choice the program will either perform conversion from degrees Fahrenheit to degrees Celsius or vice versa. The switch statement (line 25) is used to accomplish this. The user is prompted to enter temperature in one scale and then appropriate conversion function is called. In case 1 of the switch statement the fahren2Celsius function is called and temperature Fahrenheit is passed to it. It computes the equivalent temperature in degrees Celsius and returns it to the main program. This return value is captured in the variable tempC. Both tempF and tempC are passed to the displayConversion function. This function takes one additional parameter which specifies the conversion that is taking place. For example, if the conversion is from degrees Fahrenheit to degrees Celsius, then this parameter is 'F'. Otherwise, it is 'C'. The role of the third parameter is to simplify the body of the displayConversion function.

## void Functions and the return Statement

Unlike value returning functions, void functions do not need to end with a return statement. Following code is an example of a simple sum function:

```
#include <iostream>

using namespace std;

// function prototypes
void sum(int, int);

int main()
{
    int a, b;
    cout << "Number: ";
    cin >> a;
    cout << "Number: ";
    cin >> b;
    sum(a,b);
    return 0;
}

void sum(int x, int y)
{
    int mySum;
    mySum = x + y;
    cout << x << " + " << y << " = " << mySum << endl;
}
```

**Listing 21:** void Functions and the return Statement

Compiling this program will result in sum of two numbers:

```
Number: 2
Number: 5
2 + 5 = 7

Process returned 0 (0x0)   execution time : 2.957 s
Press any key to continue.
```

However, if we were to insert a return statement in anywhere before the cout statement in the function, the outcome would be different. The moment the return statement was executed, the program control would immediately be transferred to the caller (in this case the main) function:

```
1. #include <iostream>
2.
3. using namespace std;
4.
5. // function prototypes
6. void sum(int, int);
7.
8. int main()
9. {
10.     int a, b;
11.     cout << "Number: ";
12.     cin >> a;
13.     cout << "Number: ";
14.     cin >> b;
15.     sum(a,b);
16.     return 0;
17. }
18.
19. void sum(int x, int y)
20. {
21.     int mySum;
22.     return;          <- return to main
23.     mySum = x + y;
24.     cout << x << " + " << y << " = " << mySum << endl;
25. }
```

**return to main**

**These two statements would never execute**

**Listing 22:** The return Statement Implications

The statements in lines 23 and 24 would never execute because the function would terminate and the control would return to the caller:

```
Number: 5
Number: 2

Process returned 0 (0x0)   execution time : 3.555 s
Press any key to continue.
```

Use caution when using return statements to abruptly terminate functions.

## Default Arguments

Default arguments are a safety measure incorporated into the C++ language to give programmers an option to use default values for parameters should the caller program omit passing the arguments to a function. Default arguments are specified in function prototypes:

```
void displayValues(int=10, int=20);   // function header
```

When calling this function, if the arguments are omitted in the caller program then the first parameter will be assigned a value of zero and the second parameter will be assigned a value of 100:

```
displayValues();
```

Otherwise, if the arguments are provided in the function call then those values are copied to function parameters:

```
displayValues(500, 1102);
```

In this case, the first parameter will receive 500 and the second parameter will receive 1102. Here is a sample program that illustrates default arguments:

```
#include <iostream>

using namespace std;

// Function prototypes
void displayValues(int = 10, int=20 );
int main()
{
    displayValues();
    return 0;
}

void displayValues(int first, int second)
{
    cout << "This is the first parameter: " << first << endl;
    cout << "This is the second parameter: " << second << endl;

}
```

**Listing 23:** Default Arguments

would result in the following output:

```
This is the first parameter: 10
This is the second parameter: 20

Process returned 0 (0x0)   execution time : 0.017 s
Press any key to continue.
```

A couple of rules to remember when using default parameters:

- Default arguments must be specified in the function prototypes because due to the nature of C++ programs where statements are executed sequentially, this is the logical place (the earliest occurrence of the function name) to specify default arguments. In case the programmer is not using function prototypes, then default arguments need to be specified in the function header.

- Default arguments consist of an equal sign (=) and a literal—i.e. line number 6 in the above listed program.
- Skipping default arguments is possible but only from left to right and in order. This means that if there are two arguments, it is possible to omit the second one rather than the first one:

  displayValues(150);

  this is OK, and the 150 would be copied to the 1st parameter, the 2nd parameter will be assigned 20 (default value).

  However,

```
displayValues(,10); //not correct and would result in a
syntax error.
```

The statement above is incorrect even though it would be nice to be able to omit the first argument and assign default value to it, and assign some value (10 in this case) to the 2nd argument.

Default arguments are not very flexible, and should be used with extreme caution. The next section, Overloading Functions, discusses a similar feature of the C++ language.

## Overloading Functions

Overloading functions means to have a function with the same name but different parameter list:

```
void displayValue (int);    // int parameter
void displayValue (double); // double parameter
```

the compiler would make a distinction between the two functions by looking ahead into the data type being passed to a function:

```
displayValue(85); // would call the function that takes an
integer
displayValue(85.75); // would call the function that takes a
double
```

Similarly if there is more than one parameter the compiler can make the distinction by looking at the number of parameters as well as their data types:

```
int sum(int, int);
```

versus

```
int sum(int, int, int);
```

Overloaded functions simplify source code. Since writing software programs is both art and science, the "art part" is choosing a good name for a function. Without the overloading capability of the language, a programmer would possibly have to write one function called sumOfTwo and another function called sumOfThree. Calling these functions in the caller program would make the code less readable:

```
sumOfTwo(1,17);
sumOfThree(1,17,19);
```

Even though the logic of these functions is very simple—they perform the same task which is adding the values passed to them. When choosing function name, a programmer needs to think in abstract terms, meaning they need to be clear of what is the task a function performs. A good rule to follow when designing functions is "one function, one task". Thus choosing a good name for a function is very important. In the example above, `sumOfTwo` and `sumOfThree` initially seem to be good names. However, having the number of arguments be of part of the function name is redundant. With function overloading feature there is no need to complicate the source code with complex function names. Simply call each function sum and have different parameter list so that the compiler can pick the appropriate function based on the number of values in the function call:

```
result = sum (1,17);     // would call "sumOfTwo" function
result = sum(1,17,19);    // would call "sumOfThree" function
```

## Scope

In C++ program, variables go through a process—they are declared, initialized, incremented/decremented and eventually destroyed. Scope refers to the "lifetime" of a variable. It is also very important where in the program a variable has been declared. For example, the following program will compile without a problem:

```
#include <iostream>

using namespace std;

int main()
{
    int x;      // declare a variable
    x = 10;     // initialize it with a value

    // display it
    cout << "This is x: " << x << endl;
    return 0;
}
```

**Listing 24:** Correct Program

However, if we were to slightly change the order of the statements in this short program:

```
#include <iostream>

using namespace std;

int main()
{
    // display it
    cout << "This is x: " << x << endl;

```

```
10.     int x;      // declare a variable
11.     x = 10;     // initialize it with a value
12.     return 0;
13. }
```

**Listing 25:** Out of Scope

Then the program would not compile. Why? The reason is because on line 8, the program is trying to display the contents of the variable x, but the variable has not been declared yet. In this example, x is said to be "out of scope".

A variable is said to be in scope right after its declaration. In Listing 1 above, variable x is declared on line 7 and from that point on, until the end of the program (the return statement on line 12) any time it is referred to, the compiler will not complain as the variable is in scope. This is also known as the **global scope**. File scope begins after the declaration of a variable and it is in effect until the end of the file.

There is another type of scope, called the **block scope**. Take a look at the following code:

```
1. #include <iostream>
2.
3. using namespace std;
4.
5. int main()
6. {
7.      int x;          // declare an integer variable
8.      x = 10;         // initialize it with a value of 10
9.
10.     {
11.         int y; // beginning of a block - perfectly legal
12.         y = 15;
13.     }           // end of a block
14.
15.     cout << "This is x: " << x << endl;
16.     cout << "This is y: " << y << endl;
17.     return 0;
18. }
```

**Listing 26:** Block Scope

This code would not compile because variable y was declared on line 11 which is part of a block of code that starts on line 10 and ends on line 13. Because of this, y "goes out of scope" on line 14 with the block of code it belongs to. This can be confusing to novice programmers especially because y was declared before the cout statement in line 15. The answer lies in the fact that y is part of a block of code. This block of code can be viewed as its own self-contained unit. Anything declared inside of that unit is part of that unit and is not available to the code outside of the unit.

Now that we just cleared that, take a look at the following code segment:

```
1. #include <iostream>
2.
3. using namespace std;
4.
5. int main()
6. {
7.     int x;                          // declare an integer variable
8.     x = 10;                         // initialize it with a value of 10
9.
10.    {                               // beginning of a block - perfectly legal
11.        cout << "Inside the block of code: This is x: " << x << endl;
12.        int y;
13.        y = 15;
14.    }                               // end of a block
15.
16.    cout << "This is x: " << x << endl;
17.    //cout << "This is y: " << y << endl;
18.    return 0;
19. }
```

**Listing 27:** Block Scope w File Scope

In both listings, variable x was declared on line 7 and it has global scope, which means it is in scope until the return statement on line 18. Since we now know about the block scope, we commented out line 17 to allow for successful program compilation:

```
Inside the block of code: This is x: 10
This is x: 10

Process returned 0 (0x0)   execution time : 0.231 s
Press any key to continue.
```

Everything compiles and executes correctly. The question is, why was x in scope inside of the block of code? Isn't that block of code supposed to act as a separate unit? The answer is that the variable x was declared in before the block of code, and it has file scope—which means that it is "visible" to the code that follows it. The block of code is below (after) starting on line 10 so x will be in scope in the block of code. However, y which was declared inside of the block of code is in scope just within the block of code. Once the block of code goes out of scope, all the variables declared in that block go out of scope.

## Function Prototype Scope

A **function prototype scope** refers to the function parameters visibility. For example, parameters passed to a function are in scope for the lifetime of the function—until the function returns to the caller program at which point the parameters go out of scope:

```
1.  #include <iostream>
2.
3.  using namespace std;
4.
5.  // function prototypes
6.  void myFunction(int);
7.  int myFunction2(int, int);
8.
9.  int main()
10. {
11.     myFunction1(10);
12.     myFunction2(25);
13.     return 0;
14. }
15.
16. void myFunction1(int x)
17. {
18.       // x is in scope until the end of the
19.       // function
20.       cout << "This is x: " << x << endl;
21. }
22.
23. int myFunction2(int a, int b)
24. {
25.       cout << "This is a: " << x << endl;
26.       cout << "This is b: " << y << endl;
27.       return a * b;
28. }
```

**Listing 28:** Function Prototype Scope

In Listing 5, both functions receive data through parameter lists. The function myFunction1 is a void type of function which receives an integer value through its parameter called x. The variable x is in scope until the end of the function on line 21.

Similarly, the function myFunction2 receives data through parameters and b. Both of these are in scope until the end of the function which is the return statement on line 27.

### *Statement scope*

Statement scope refers to the visibility of variables that are declared in the loop header:

```
#include <iostream>

using namespace std;

int main()
{
```

```
7.        for (int counter = 0; counter<10; counter++)
8.        {
9.             cout << "Counter: " << counter << endl;
10.       }
11.
12.       return 0;
13.    }
```

**Listing 29:** Statement Scope

The program executes correctly:

```
Counter: 0
Counter: 1
Counter: 2
Counter: 3
Counter: 4
Counter: 5
Counter: 6
Counter: 7
Counter: 8
Counter: 9

Process returned 0 (0x0)   execution time : 0.015 s
Press any key to continue.
```

However, if we try to print the counter variable after the loop finished its execution, the compiler will signal an error, as the variable is out of scope at this point (line12):

```
5    int main()
6    {
7        for (int counter = 0; counter<10; counter++)
8        {
9            cout << "Counter: " << counter << endl;
10       }
11
12       cout << "Counter after the loop: " << counter << endl;
13       return 0;
14   }
15
```

```
Logs & others
Code::Blocks | Search results | Cccc | Build log | Build messages | CppCheck | CppCheck messages | Cs

File              Line  Message
C:\Users\Adn...         In function 'int main()':
C:\Users\Adn...   12    error: name lookup of 'counter' changed for new ISO 'for' scoping
C:\Users\Adn...   7     error:   using obsolete binding at 'counter'
                        === Build finished: 2 errors, 0 warnings (0 minutes, 0 seconds) ===
```

**Listing 30:** Syntax Error—Variable counter Out of Scope

Variable counter is in scope from line 7 (where it was declared) through line 10 at which point the loop terminates.

## Namespace and Namespace Scope

Namespace is a C++ mechanism for organizing functions, data, types, etc. into a grouping in order to prevent name clashes. So far, we have used namespace std in our programs. If a name is defined inside the namespace then it is said to have the **namespace scope**. **Global scope** is in essence a namespace scope but the namespace in this case was not given a name.

It is very important to understand the scope concept as it is a stepping stone to understanding global variables and local variables.

## Global Variables and Global Constants

As the name implies variables can hold different values at different times. Moreover, global variables are in scope for the entire program. There is no need to pass global variables from function to function. Novice programmers usually write code that relies on global variables because they are unsure how to pass data to functions. The problem with this approach is that any function has access to global variables and therefore can change its contents. This makes debugging very difficult because it is impossible to determine which function changed the contents of a global variable. In a short program, this would not be that much of an issue. However, in larger programs it becomes impossible to determine which function changed the contents of a global variable.

Working with global variables also affects code portability. Functions that use global variables cannot be ported to other programs because of the dependency on these global variables.

You should not use global variables at all. This is a very bad programming practice. Instead declare your variables locally and pass them to functions as needed. With this approach, if there's a bug in the code it to be easy to isolate the location (function) where the problem is occurring.

Global constants, as the name implies cannot be changed. Thus it is okay to declare constants as global constants because they are all placed at the top of the program which makes it easy to find them. Also by declaring constants global they are in scope throughout the entire program.

Following is an example of a program that uses global constants:

In Listing 8, global constants are listed in statements on lines 5 through 9. These constants are used as menu choices in the program. Notice the location where global constants are declared—before function prototypes. This way, global constants are in scope throughout the entire program.

```
 1. #include <iostream>
 2.
 3. using namespace std;
 4.
 5. const int CHOICE_ADD = 1;
 6. const int CHOICE_SUBTRACT = 2;
 7. const int CHOICE_MULTIPLY = 3;
 8. const int CHOICE_DIVIDE = 4;
 9. const int CHOICE_EXIT = 5;
10.
11. // function prototypes
12. void displayMenu();
13. int getANumber();
14. int getSum(int, int);
```

```
void displayResults(int, int, int, char);

int main()
{
    int userChoice;
    int number1 = getANumber();
    int number2 = getANumber();
    int sum;

    do
    {
        cout << "\nNow what do you want to with the numbers: " << endl;
        displayMenu();
        cin >> userChoice;

        switch(userChoice)
        {
            case CHOICE_ADD:
               sum = getSum(number1, number2);
               displayResults(number1, number2, sum,'+');
               break;
            case CHOICE_SUBTRACT:
               break;
            case CHOICE_MULTIPLY:
               break;
            case CHOICE_DIVIDE:
               break;
            case CHOICE_EXIT:
              cout << "Thank you. GO watch a Heat game" << endl;
               break;
            default:
               cout << "Please enter 1,2,3,4, or 5 only" << endl;
        }

    }while (userChoice != CHOICE_EXIT);

    return 0;
}

void displayResults(int n1, int n2, int result, char operation)
{
    cout << n1 << " "
         << operation <<" "
         << n2 << " = "
         << result
```

```
          << endl;

}

int getSum(int n1, int n2)
{
    int sum;
    sum = n1 + n2;
    return sum;
}
int getANumber()
{
    int number;
    cout << "Please enter a number: ";

    // good/defensive programming techiques should be utilized
    cin >> number;
    return number;

}
void displayMenu()
{
    cout << "1. Add" << endl;
    cout << "2. Subtract" << endl;
    cout << "3. Multiply" << endl;
    cout << "4. Divide" << endl;
    cout << "5. Exit" << endl;
    cout << "Your choice: ";
}
```

**Listing 31:** Using Global Constants and Local Variables

## Local Variables

Local variables are confined to the functions in which they are defined. Unlike global variables which are in scope throughout the entire program, local variables are in scope only inside the function where they are defined. No other function can access local variables. The following listing demonstrates a local variable and its scope:

```
#include <iostream>

using namespace std;

// function prototypes
void sum(int, int);

```

```
 8. int main()
 9. {
10.     int a, b;
11.     cout << "Number: ";
12.     cin >> a;
13.     cout << "Number: ";
14.     cin >> b;
15.     sum(a,b);
16.     cout << "mySum is: " << mySum << endl;
17.     return 0;
18. }
19.
20. void sum(int x, int y)
21. {
22.     int mySum;
23.     mySum = x + y;
24.     cout << x << " + " << y << " = " << mySum << endl;
25. }
```

**This would result in a syntax error as mySum is not in scope in the mail function**

**mySum is local to the function sum**

**Listing 32:** Local Variable Scope

Local variable lifetime is tied to the lifetime of the function in which they are defined. When the above code executes, local variable mySum is created in the memory when the function sum is called (line 15) by the main function. When the function sum returns to the main function, local variable mySum is destroyed in memory along with any values that may have been stored there.

## Shadowing

Programmers need to be careful when naming local variables. The compiler will report syntax errors if local variables are named the same name as the parameters. This is known as shadowing:

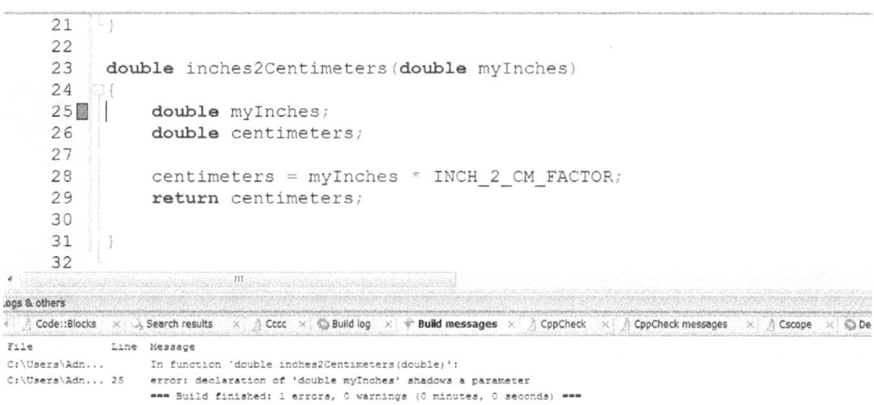


**Figure 5:** Local Variable Shadowing.

It is important to distinguish between different types of shadowing. Since the parameter is a local variable, having another local variable with the same name results in a syntax error as depicted in the figure above.

There is another type of shadowing that takes occurs when a local variable (parameter as well) is named the same name as the global variable or global constant. In this situation, the compiler does not issue a syntax error and the local variable shadows the global variable. What that means is that the values contained in the local variable will be used instead of the values in the global variables with the same name. This could lead to unpredictable outcomes.

```
#include <iostream>
// global constants
const double INCH_2_CM_FACTOR = 2.54;  // INCHES to CM conversion factor
                                       // 1 inch = 2.54 CM
// global variables
double inches;                         // avoid global variables at all cost
using namespace std;
// function prototypes
double inches2Centimeters( );
int main()
{
     double centimeters;
     cout << "Enter length in inches: ";
     cin >> inches;              // this is global variable inches!!!
     centimeters = inches2Centimeters();
     cout << inches << " inches is " << centimeters << " centimeters." << endl;
     return 0;
}
// Function inches2Centimenters. No need to pass inches to the function
// as inches was declared as a global variable, therefore the function
// should have access to it.
double inches2Centimeters()
{
     double inches = 17.5;     // local inches variable. Initialized to 17.5
     double centimeters;
     centimeters = inches * INCH_2_CM_FACTOR;
     return centimeters;
}
```

**Listing 33:** Global Variable Shadowing

Compiling and running the above program and entering 1 inch when prompted for the data will produce wrong output because the local variable inches (declared on line 30) shadows the global variable inches (declared on line 7):

```
Enter length in inches: 1
1 inches is 44.45 centimeters.

Process returned 0 (0x0)   execution time : 1.817 s
Press any key to continue.
```

The output is completely wrong, because 1 inch is 2.54 cm, yet the compiler never signaled any errors. The program is correct because the local variable inches which was set to 17.5 was used in the calculation. So 17.5 × 2.54 = 44.45, therefore the program is producing correct calculation.

To prevent shadowing from taking place, follow these simple rules:

- Avoid global variables as best as you can
- Capitalize the names of your global constants, and use lowercase (camel back notation) for your variables. This way, variables and constants will be easily distinguished from each other. Also, if they happen to have the same name, shadowing will not be possible

## Static Local Variables

Static local variables act as global variables but are declared locally. To specify that a variable is static, keyword "static" must precede the data type:

```
static int numPoints;
```

Static variables keep values between function calls, so in that sense they act as global variables but are only accessible from the function in which they are declared. To better understand static variables, let's take a look at the following program:

```
#include <iostream>

using namespace std;
// function prototypes
void displayNumber();

int main()
{
    displayNumber();
    // Finishes its execution. What is X at this point?
    displayNumber();
```

```
            //
    displayNumber();
            //
    displayNumber();
            //
    displayNumber();
            // Finished its execution
    return 0;
}

void displayNumber()
{
     int x = 0;      // initialize x to 0
     x = x + 1;      // add 1 to it and store the result back into x
     cout << "This is x: " << x << endl;
}
```

**Listing 34:** Simple Program

Listing 11 is a simple program that calls function displayNumber() five times. In the function, there is an integer variable x which was initialized to zero and incremented. The function also contains one cout statement where the value of this variable is displayed. When we compile and run the above program, this is the output that it will generate:

```
This is x: 1
This is x: 1
This is x: 1
This is x: 1
This is x: 1

Process returned 0 (0x0)   execution time : 0.020 s
Press any key to continue.
```

The program output is correct, because with each new function call locally declared integer variable X is created and set to zero, incremented by 1, and its contents displayed. Every time the function returns to the main program (function displayNumber() goes out of scope) local variable X is destroyed.

Changing the way local variable X is declared, by preceding it with keyword static, will change the way this program runs:

```
#include <iostream>

using namespace std;
// function prototypes
void displayNumber();
```

```

int main()
{
    displayNumber();
    // Finishes its execution. What is X at this point?
    displayNumber();
              //
    displayNumber();
              //
    displayNumber();
              //
    displayNumber();
              // Finished its execution
    return 0;
}

void displayNumber()
{
     static int x = 0;    // initialize x to 0
     x = x + 1;            // add 1 to it and store the result back into x
     cout << "This is x: " << x << endl;
}
```

**Listing 35:** Static Local Variable

In Listing 12, local integer variable X is declared as static. When we compile and run this program this is the output that will be generated:

```
This is x: 1
This is x: 2
This is x: 3
This is x: 4
This is x: 5

Process returned 0 (0x0)   execution time : 0.021 s
Press any key to continue.
```

How is this possible? Isn't the local variable X initialized to zero each time the function displayNumber gets called? The answer is yes and no. Because the X is declared as static, the compiler initializes it only during the first function call. Static local variables are designed to retain their values between function calls, so every time the function displayNumber is called by the main function, X is incremented by one (and it retains its values). Thus, statically allocated local variables act as if they were global variables because they retain values between function calls the program is easier to debug because only the function in which the variable was allocated can modify its value. The following figure demonstrates that behavior:

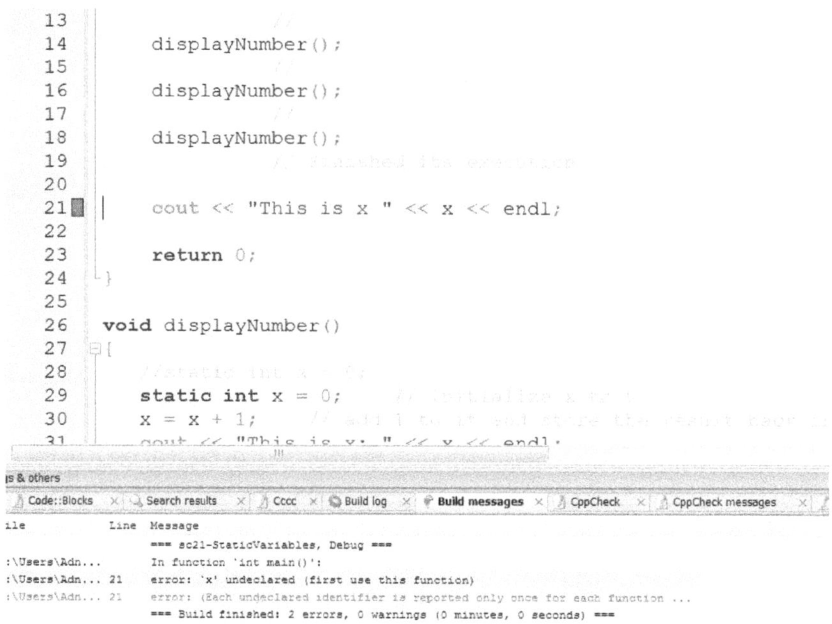


**Figure 6:** Syntax Error

The compiler generated a syntax error on line 21.

## The exit(0) Function

Given the nature of software program execution from top to bottom, sometimes execution of certain statements will be critical for the execution of the entire program. For example, the entire program could hinge on successful opening of a file so that the data can be read into programs memory and processed. What happens if that file does not exist? One of the easiest ways to mitigate this situation is to call the exit function. The exit function abruptly terminates program execution. In that regard it is similar to the return statement with one exception:

- The return statement shifts program control to the caller program.
- The exit function terminates the function / program.

The exit function should be used in extreme cases, for example when the program encounters an error from which it cannot recover. In such a case a good programming technique would be to inform the user that something terribly went wrong and that the program is going to shut down. This is better than having the program crash.

## Stubs and Drivers

Divide and Conquer is a good programming technique used to solve more complex problems. Stubs and drivers are programs used to test functions. A stub is a stripped down version of the actual function and it is generally used to determine whether the function has been correctly called from the caller program. In addition, a stub normally displays the parameters that have been passed into it. This way the programmer can test to make sure that the caller program is providing correct data to the function.

A driver is a program that is designed to test functions. To thoroughly test the function, programmer needs to send different data to the function. For example, if the function was performing some kind of division, then one of the tests would be to determine whether the function handles division by zero correctly.

Java programs could be simply used to test different functions and once the function is pass all the tests then the functions are moved to the actual program. It is not uncommon to convert the driver program to act as the main program.

## End of Chapter Questions

### True/False

1. $F(x) = X^3 + x + 3$ is an example of a function.
2. Each function does not need to have a beginning brace and an ending brace.
3. One of the benefits of using function is code reusability.
4. The code that is isolated into a function will execute when a function is called.
5. A function definition only contains a function name, function body, and parameter list.
6. A function header contains the return data type, function name and parameter list (if any) inside of parentheses.
7. A function prototype is also known as a function declaration.
8. Passing data by value is as simple as copying the contents of the argument variable to the memory location of the parameter variable.
9. When we pass by value, the original value is affected.
10. It is not possible to pass multiple values to functions.
11. A reference is an alias for an object.
12. A function call is different whether it is pass by reference or pass by value.
13. Many functions return results of the tasks they were designed to accomplish.
14. Void functions do not need to end with a return statement.
15. A local variable is not tied to the lifetime of the function in which they are defined.

### Exercises

1. Sports Protein

   Diego wants to open a shop that sells protein powder shakes. He wants to sell three different sizes, 2 pound powder, 5 pound powder, and 12 pound powder. The price for the small size is $10.00, medium size is $15.00, and the large is $18.00. Write a menu-driven program that displays the option to see the total sales for the day, how much Diego has sold of the small, medium, and large sizes.

2. Gross weekly pay

   Write a program that calculates the gross weekly pay for a part-time hourly paid employee or a salaried employee paid a daily rate. The program should ask the user if he/she wants to calculate a part-time employee or salaried employee. A menu should display P (Part-Time) or S (Salaried Employee) for the user to select either P or S. The output should display the pay rate and the gross weekly pay or annual salary and gross weekly pay.

Input Validation: Do not accept negative values for the hourly rate, hours worked, and annual salaried rate.

**3.** Calculate Areas

Write a program that calculates the area of a circle. The program should have the following functions.

- getRadius()—This function asks the user to enter the radius of the circle, and then return it.
- getArea()—This function should accept the circle radius and the value of $\pi$, and return the area of the circle.
- displayArea()—This function should accept the radius, the value of $\pi$, and area as arguments, and display them with an appropriate message.

**4.** Modify problem 3 by using reference parameter.

*Chapter 7*

# Arrays and Vectors

***"Not thinking about anything is Zen. Once you know this, walking, sitting, or lying down, everything you do is Zen."***

**—Bodhidharma, *The Zen Teaching of Bodhidharma***

## What Is an Array?

Suppose you want to write a program that will collect data for student quiz scores, test scores and homework scores and to determine student grade based on the following criteria:

- the quizzes account for 30% of the overall grade
- the tests account for 20% of the overall grade and
- the homework assignments are 80% of the overall grade

How would you go about it? One of the design questions that need to be posed is how many scores for each category. Suppose there are 10 quizzes, 3 tests, and 10 homework assignments. Next you would have to compute the average grades for each category and then assign the weights as specified above. How would you go about writing this program?

Obviously, you would need to gather some information from the user. Thus, you would need to prompt the user to enter the data for 10 quizzes, 3 tests, and 10 homework assignments. The question is where would you store the information you gathered from the user? One answer would be to have 10 variables to hold scores for 10 quizzes, 3 variables to hold scores for three tests, and 10 variables to hold scores for 10 homework assignments:

```
int quiz1, quiz2, quiz3, quiz4, quiz5, quiz6, quiz7, quiz8, quiz9, quiz10;
int test1, test2, test3;
int hw1, hw2, hw3, hw4, hw5, hw6, hw7, hw8, hw9, hw10;
```

That is a lot of variables !

Worse yet, suppose you were hired to write a program that will track points per game for a professional basketball player. There are 82 games in an NBA season! So we would have to declare 82 variables in order to capture the data for each game.

This would be very difficult to maintain but fortunately there is a C++ mechanism called arrays that is more elegant way to approach problems that require gathering data. Rather than declaring separate variables to store multiple values of same category (data type) an array can be used.

In the previous chapters, we learned that variables are names for memory locations. An array is exactly that with the exception that instead of one memory location, there are multiple memory locations and they are contiguous:

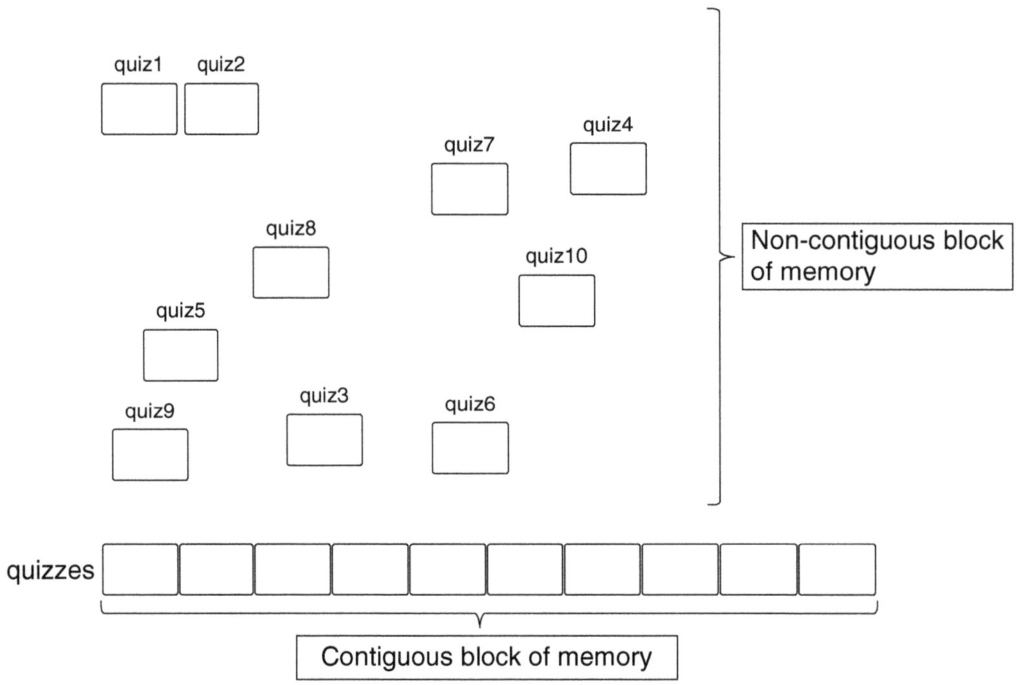


**Figure 1:** Variables vs. an Array

Figure 1 depicts how 10 integer variables could be allocated in computer memory in order to store 10 quiz scores and how an array is allocated to accomplish the same. When allocating individual variables, most of the time they're not allocated in a contiguous block of memory. In the array on the other hand is always allocated in a contiguous block of memory. This is why it's possible to have one variable for the entire block and refer to individual elements through an index. The index is nothing more than the position of an array element in the block. In C++, the index of the first array element is in position 0:

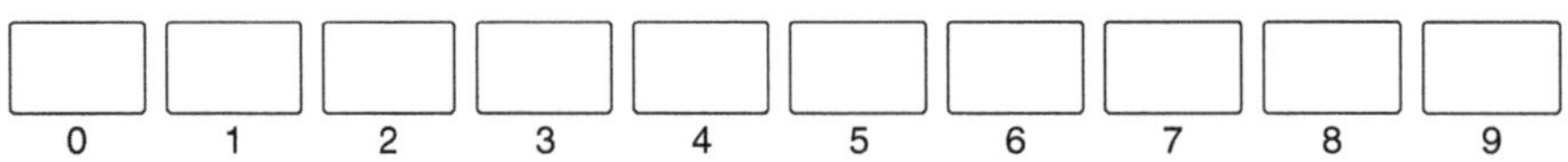


**Figure 2:** Array in Memory

One thing array elements share in common is that they are all of the same data type. Depending on the computer architecture, and the C++ compiler different data types have different sizes. For example, if an integer on a particular system is 4 bytes then for the array depicted in figure 2 above, the compiler would allocate 40 bytes. It is not possible to mix different data types in an array. All elements of an array must be of the same data type.

Now that we understand how arrays are allocated in memory, let's learn how to declare one.

## Declaring an Array

To declare an array, it is necessary to specify the data type of the elements the array will be holding, array name and the size of the array. The following statement declares an array of 10 integer elements:

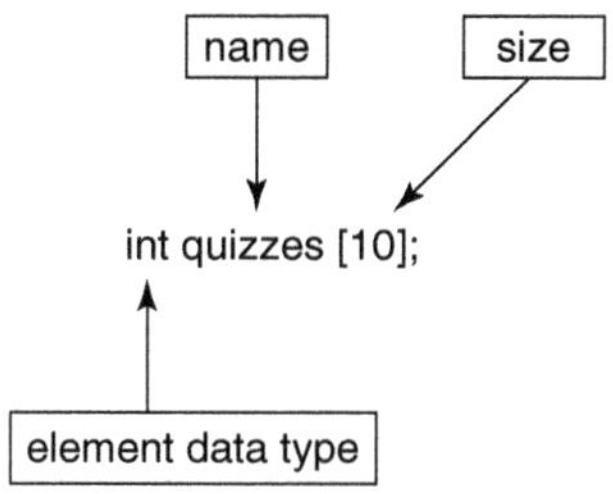


**Figure 3:** Declaring an Array of 10 Integers

Similarly, it is possible to declare an array of different data types:

```
char alphabet[26];            // assuming a char is 1 byte, 26 x 1 = 26 bytes
short points[82];             // assuming a short is 2 bytes, 82 x 2 = 164 bytes
double temperatures[31];      // assuming a double is 8 bytes, 31 x 8 = 248 bytes
```

The actual size of allocated memory is a product of number of elements in an array and the element size.

```
#include <iostream>

using namespace std;

// Global constants
const int SIZE = 5;    // array size

int main()
{
    double amountSpent[SIZE];

    amountSpent[0] = 10.15;
    amountSpent[1] = 89.25;
    amountSpent[2] = 11.95;
    amountSpent[3] = 99.85;
    amountSpent[4] = 101.03;

    cout << "The amount spent on day 1: " << amountSpent[0] << endl;
    cout << "The amount spent on day 2: " << amountSpent[1] << endl;
```

```
20.     cout << "The amount spent on day 3:  " << amountSpent[2] << endl;
21.     cout << "The amount spent on day 4:  " << amountSpent[3] << endl;
22.     cout << "The amount spent on day 5:  " << amountSpent[4] << endl;
23.     return 0;
24. }
```

**Listing 1:** Simple Program with an Array

The above listing, demonstrates how to allocate an array, populate it with values, and how to display those values. Following is the output of the program run:

```
The amount spent on day 1: 10.15
The amount spent on day 2: 89.25
The amount spent on day 3: 11.95
The amount spent on day 4: 99.85
The amount spent on day 5: 101.03

Process returned 0 (0x0)   execution time : 0.012 s
Press any key to continue.
```

It is important to understand that unlike individual variables which can be printed simply by providing the variable name to the cout statement, an array cannot be printed in the same manner. The reason for this is that there are multiple values stored in an array, so the cout statement needs to be told which particular value to display.

How does the compiler know where one element of the array begins and ends? The element size is crucial in order to understand how compiler distinguishes between array elements. Since the array is designed to hold data of the same type, each element will require same amount of memory to be allocated for it. Another thing to remember is that array elements are allocated in a contiguous block of memory. Knowing the data type, meaning knowing the size of each element makes it easy to determine the position and the contents of each element.

```
double amountSpent[SIZE];
```

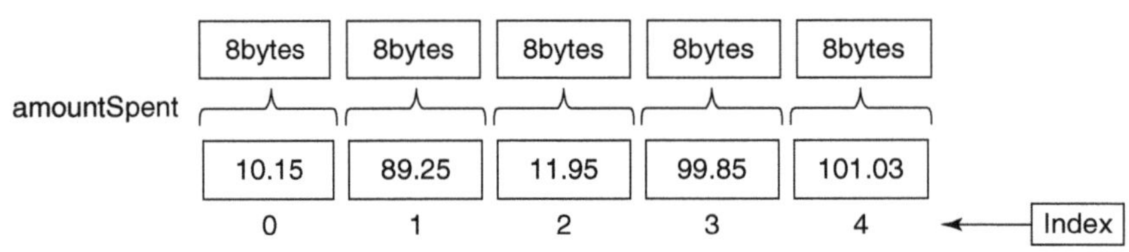


**Figure 4:** An Array of doubles

In our example above, we declared an array of doubles. Assuming computer architecture where double is 8 bytes, the first eight bytes would be reserved for the first value, the next eight bytes would be reserved for the second value, and so on. All of the values in the array are commonly referred to as amountSpent which is the variable name. Individual elements are accessed through their respective location (index). In Listing 1, when displaying the contents of the array in lines 18 through 22, were accessing individual elements through their location.

Listing one was a rudimentary program used to demonstrate array concept. Given the nature of arrays it is logical to use loops when working with arrays. The following listing is an improved program that was presented in listing one:

```
1. #include <iostream>
2.
3. using namespace std;
4.
5. // Global constants
6. const int SIZE = 5;     // array size
7.
8. int main()
9. {
10.     double amountSpent[SIZE];
11.
12.     amountSpent[0] = 10.15;
13.     amountSpent[1] = 89.25;
14.     amountSpent[2] = 11.95;
15.     amountSpent[3] = 99.85;
16.     amountSpent[4] = 101.03;
17.
18.     for (int index=0; index<SIZE; index++)
19.     {
20.         cout << "The amount spent on day "
21.              << index + 1 << ": " << amountSpent[index] << endl;
22.     }
23.     return 0;
24. }
```

**Listing 2:** Arrays and Loops

The for loop starting on line 18 through line 22 demonstrates the use of the loop to display contents of an array. Since the array index starts at position zero, it is necessary to add one to the index on line 21 to avoid displaying "The amount spent on day 0".

In Listing 1 (and Listing 2) we hardcoded values for array elements in lines 12 through 16. Normally, data gathering would be interactive, meaning the user would be prompted to enter the data. In case of large data sets, the data would be read from a file. The following program demonstrates how to gather data from the user interactively and store the values into an array:

```
#include <iostream>

using namespace std;

// Global constants
const int SIZE = 5;     // array size

```

```
int main()
{
    double amountSpent[SIZE];

    // gather the data from the user and store it in an array
    for (int i=0; i<SIZE; i++)
    {
        cout << "Amount spent on day "
             << i+1
             << ": ";
        cin >> amountSpent[i];
    }

    // display the contents of the array
    for (int index=0; index<SIZE; index++)
    {
        cout << "The amount spent on day "
             << index + 1
             << ": "
             << amountSpent[index] << endl;
    }
    return 0;
}
```

**Listing 3:** Interacting With the User

When gathering data from the user and storing it into an array, the programmer needs to be cognizant of the location of the array element that is storing the data. This is accomplished through the array index:

```
cin >> amountSpent[i]; // Correct
```

The following cin statement would not work:

```
cin >> amountSpent; // Incorrect
```

## Array Initialization

In addition to hard coding the data, and obtaining the data through user interaction, it is possible to initialize an array through an initialization list:

```
#include <iostream>

using namespace std;

// global constants
```

```
 6. const int SIZE = 12;
 7.
 8. int main()
 9. {
10.     string months[SIZE] = {"January", "February", "March",
11.                            "April", "May", "June",
12.                            "July", "August", "September",
13.                            "October", "November", "December"};
14.
15.     // display the contents of the array
16.     for (int i=0; i<SIZE; i++)
17.     {
18.         cout << months[i] << endl;
19.     }
20.     return 0;
21. }
```

**Listing 4:** Array Initialization

In listing 4 above, on lines 10 through 13, the information between braces is called an initialization list. This is a form of hard coding information. It makes no difference whether the information in the initialization list is entered one entry at a time, or as in our case, three entries per line. Array elements are assigned corresponding values from the initialization list. In the example above, January is the first element in the list therefore it will be the first element in the array. Thus, the array would contain the following information after the initialization:

| January | February | March | April | May | June | July | August | September | October | November | December |
|---|---|---|---|---|---|---|---|---|---|---|---|
| 0 | 1 | 2 | 3 | 4 | 5 | 6 | 7 | 8 | 9 | 10 | 11 |

**Figure 5:** The months Array

Compiling and executing the program would result in the following output:

```
January
February
March
April
May
June
July
August
September
October
November
December

Process returned 0 (0x0)   execution time : 0.012 s
Press any key to continue.
```

The number of elements in an initialization list needs to be equal or less to the number of elements of the array that is being initialized. If the number of elements in the initialization list is greater than the array size, then an attempt to compile the code would result in a syntax error.

## Partial Array Initialization

If the number of elements in the initialization list is less than the array size then it is possible to perform the partial array initialization.

The following code segment partially initializes an array called months:

```
#include <iostream>

using namespace std;

// global constants
const int SIZE = 12;

int main()
{
    string months[SIZE] = {"January", "February", "March", "April"};
    // display the contents of the array
    for (int i=0; i<SIZE; i++)
    {
        cout << "Month[" << i+1 << "]:  " << months[i] << endl;
    }
    return 0;
}
```

**Listing 5:** Partial Array Initialization

Program Run Output:

```
Month[1]:  January
Month[2]:  February
Month[3]:  March
Month[4]:  April
Month[5]:
Month[6]:
Month[7]:
Month[8]:
Month[9]:
Month[10]:
Month[11]:
Month[12]:

Process returned 0 (0x0)   execution time : 0.015 s
Press any key to continue.
```

Using initialization list, it is not possible to skip some members, as the compiler indexes list members starting with position zero, so when the initialization takes place then the index of the list members corresponds to the index of the array that's being initialized. The following figure shows an attempt to partially initialize an array by skipping list entries for the month of May, June, and November:

**Figure 6:** Syntax Errors Due to Skipping Elements in a List

The result is syntax errors. If we need to partially initialize an array using an initialization list, then elements from the end of the list can be omitted.

## Implicit Array Sizing

Array size is a constant and it cannot change during the program lifetime. It is always a good programming practice to declare arrays a little bit larger than necessary at the expense of wasting some computer memory. For example, if we need to write the program to track student names for a particular classroom, due to the nature of student registrations, it is impossible to know ahead of time how many students will sign up for the class. Suppose the classroom has capacity of 40 seats, and due to low interest, only 15 students sign up for the class on the first day. At the end of the first week of classes, another 10 students sign up for the. If we designed our program to handle 15 to 20 students, it would not be useful because 25 students signed up for the class. To avoid having to rewrite the program again, it is always good to err on the side of caution and write a program that can accommodate the largest number of students that could physically be present in the classroom. In this case, it would be good programming practice to declare an array of 40 students because this is the physical limitation of the classroom. This would leave enough room to handle late sign-ups. In case only a couple of students signed up for the class, then our program would not be very efficient because declaring an array of 40 would be wasting a lot of memory for only a couple of students. However, wasting a few memory locations is nothing in comparison to having to rewrite the program because the array was not big enough to accommodate the data.

There's one exception to this rule and it is called implicit array sizing, which is a form of initialization list. This is not a very flexible programming technique mainly because the data is hardcoded. Here's an example of the implicit array sizing:

```
string days[] = {"Monday", "Tuesday", "Wednesday", "Thursday", "Friday", "Saturday", "Sunday" };
```

It is very important to remember the square brackets following the array name and to omit the size of the array that would normally be placed inside of the square brackets. The second important component for implicit array sizing is an initialization list. The compiler looks at the list and the array data type and then allocates enough memory (number of list elements x data type size) to accommodate each list member. Suppose we have an array of integers and the following initialization list:

```
int numbers[] = {1,2,3,4,5,6,7,8,9,10,11,12,13,14,15 };
```

Assume the size of the integer data type to be four bytes and there are 15 members in the initialization list, the compiler would allocate 15 x 4 = 60 bytes for the numbers array.

## Bounds Checking

There is no array bounds checking in C++. Thus programmers have to be very careful as it is possible to access memory beyond the boundaries of the declared array:

```
1. #include <iostream>
2.
3. using namespace std;
4.
5. // global constants
6. const int SIZE = 5;
7. const int DOUBLE_SIZE = 10;
8.
9. int main()
10. {
11.     int myArray[SIZE] = {1, 2, 3, 4, 5};
12.
13.     for (int index=0; index<DOUBLE_SIZE; index++)
14.     {
15.         cout << "myArray[" << index << "]: " << myArray[index] << endl;
16.     }
17.
18.     return 0;
19. }
```

**Listing 6:** No Bounds Checking

In the above listed program there are two global constants, SIZE and DOUBLE_SIZE declared on lines 6 and 7. The array, myArray is dimensioned with the constant SIZE and was initialized with the initialization list of integers 1 through 5. The for loop that starts on line 13, is designed to repeat DOUBLE_ SIZE number of times which would go beyond the boundaries of myArray. However, no syntax errors were reported by the compiler. In fact, the program compiles successfully and executes producing the following output:

```
myArray[0]: 1
myArray[1]: 2
myArray[2]: 3
myArray[3]: 4
myArray[4]: 5
myArray[5]: 5190672
myArray[6]: 122
myArray[7]: 2
myArray[8]: 2686792
myArray[9]: 1971691060

Process returned 0 (0x0)   execution time : 0.021 s
Press any key to continue.
```

As it can be seen from the program run output, the initialized array locations were displayed correctly along with the memory locations located outside array boundaries. What makes this code dangerous is that there were no syntax errors, nor any kind of warnings from the compiler. In order to avoid undesired results, you as a programmer have to ensure you are:

- Storing values within array boundaries. Writing to memory locations beyond array boundaries could have unpredictable results in case another program/process owns those memory locations and has data in those locations.
- Displaying values within array boundaries when you need to display the array's stored values.

## Array Operations

Operations on array elements are no different than the operations performed on regular variables. The only thing to remember is to refer to array elements through an index. Thus it is possible to perform math operations, copy arrays, compare arrays, etc.

### Math Operations

Performing math operation on array elements is equivalent to performing math operation on any other variables. The only thing to remember is that math operations take place on individual array members:

```
int mySampleArray[SIZE] = {10, 2, 8, 13, 25};
int doubleTheFirstMember = mySampleArray[0] * 2;
int trippleTheLAstMember = mySampleArray[4] * 3;
```

In the example above, the first element of the array was doubled and the last element was multiplied by 3. The key point to remember is to refer to individual array members through the array index.

Suppose you want to perform conversion from US dollars to Euros. According to the exchange rate one US Dollar equals 0.77 Euros.

```
#include <iostream>

using namespace std;

// Global constants
const int SIZE = 5;              // array size
const double USD_EUR = 0.77;     // US $ EURO exchange rate

int main()
{
    double amountSpent[SIZE]={10.15, 89.25, 11.95, 99.85, 101.03};

    // display the contents of the array
    for (int index=0; index<SIZE; index++)
    {
```

```
16.         cout << "The amount spent on day "
17.              << index + 1 << ": $" << amountSpent[index]
18.              << " equals EUR: " << amountSpent[index] * USD_EUR
19.              << endl;
20.     }
21.     return 0;
22. }
```

**Listing 7:** Performing Math Operations on Array Elements

In the above program, we have an array initialized with some values representing an amount spent in US Dollars. The conversion rate is represented by a constant `USD_EUR` (line 7). The conversion calculation is performed in the for loop which begins on line 14. Notice how we are referring to each array member through their respective index:

```
amountSpent[index] * USD_EUR
```

Following is the output of the program run:

```
The amount spent on day 1: $10.15 equals EUR: 7.8155
The amount spent on day 2: $89.25 equals EUR: 68.7225
The amount spent on day 3: $11.95 equals EUR: 9.2015
The amount spent on day 4: $99.85 equals EUR: 76.8845
The amount spent on day 5: $101.03 equals EUR: 77.7931

Process returned 0 (0x0)   execution time : 0.015 s
Press any key to continue.
```

## Prefix and Postfix

When working with increment and decrement operators, same rules for prefix and postfix apply:

```
#include <iostream>

using namespace std;

// Global constants
const int SIZE = 5;             // array size

int main()
{
    double mySampleArray[SIZE]={10, 20, 30, 40, 50};

    // increment the value stored in array member
    ++mySampleArray[0];
    mySampleArray[1]++;
    --mySampleArray[2];
```

```
    for (int i = 0; i<SIZE; i++)
    {
        cout << "mySampleArray[" << i <<"] :"
              << mySampleArray[i] << endl;
    }
    return 0;
}
```

**Listing 8:** Using Prefix and Postfix to Increment Array Contents

Compiling and running the above program would produce the following output:

```
mySampleArray[0] :11
mySampleArray[1] :21
mySampleArray[2] :29
mySampleArray[3] :40
mySampleArray[4] :50

Process returned 0 (0x0)   execution time : 0.052 s
Press any key to continue.
```

In the above program the operations were performed on the contents of array elements. Using increment or decrement operator on the index has a different effect—it never affects the value stored in an array element—it simply moves from one array elements to another. The following statement:

```
int index = 0;
mySampleArray[index++];
```

is equivalent to:

```
mySampleArray[1];
```

This is one of the common mistakes inexperienced programmers make using increment and decrement operators on array elements.

## Copying Arrays

Copying contents from one of variable to another variable is accomplished by a simple assignment:

```
int x=10;
int y;
y = x;   // y takes on the value of x
```

Following the above logic, where contents of one memory location (variable X) copied to another memory location (variable Y), it would make sense to copy contents of one array to another array:

```
int myArray[SIZE] = {1,2,3,4,5};
int yourArray[SIZE];
yourArray = myArray;   // would not work!
```

This would not work as copying contents of one array to another array needs to be done member by member:

```
int myArray[SIZE] = {1,2,3,4,5};
int yourArray[SIZE];
for (int i=0; i<SIZE; i++)
{
    yourArray[i] = myArray[i]; // This is correct
}
```

## Comparing Arrays

Comparing the contents of two memory locations is accomplished by using comparison operator:

```
int x = 10;
int y = 20;
if (x == y)
    cout << x << " and " << y << " are equal! " << endl;
elseif (x < y)
    cout << x << " is less than " << y << " !" << endl;
```

In the above listed code segment the comparison operator compares the contents of memory location x (contains 10) and memory location y (contains 20).

Comparing two arrays involves comparing member by member. Programmers need to be very careful when comparing arrays because C++ will allow statements such as:

```
int myArray[SIZE] = {1,2,3,4,5};
int yourArray[SIZE] = {10, 20, 30, 40, 50};
if (myArray == yourArray)
    cout << "Arrays are equal!" << endl;
else
    cout << "Arrays are NOT equal!" << endl;
```

This would produce output: `"Arrays are NOT equal!"`. Before we jump to the conclusion that array comparison can be accomplished by simply comparing array variables, let's take a look at the following code segment:

```
int myArray[SIZE] = {1,2,3,4,5};
int yourArray[SIZE] = {1, 2, 3, 4, 5};
if (myArray == yourArray)
    cout << "Arrays are equal!" << endl;
else
    cout << "Arrays are NOT equal!" << endl;
```

Compiling and running this code segment produces the following output:

```
Arrays are NOT equal!

Process returned 0 (0x0)   execution time : 0.017 s
Press any key to continue.
```

How is that possible? The two arrays should be equal as they are both initialized with the same initialization list. What is going on? The answer to this puzzle lays in the way C++ compares arrays. The array variables represent a block of memory, more precisely the starting address of the memory block where an array has been allocated. Comparing two array variables is in essence comparing two memory addresses and not the contents of these memory addresses. Since the two arrays are not allocated in the same memory location, they have different memory addresses therefore the comparison operator returns false.

In order to correctly compare arrays, it is necessary to compare them member by member as the following code segment demonstrates:

```
#include <iostream>

using namespace std;

// global constants
const int SIZE = 5;
const int DOUBLE_SIZE = 10;

int main()
{
    int myArray[SIZE] = {1, 2, 3, 4, 5};
    int yourArray[SIZE] = {10, 20, 30, 40, 50};
    bool isEqual = true;    // boolean flag

    for (int index=0; index<SIZE; index++)
    {
        if (myArray[index] != yourArray[index])
            isEqual = false;
    }

    if (isEqual)
        cout << "Arrays are equal" << endl;
    else
        cout << "Arrays are NOT equal" << endl;

    return 0;
}
```

**Listing 9:** Correct Way to Compare Arrays

The output is now correct:

```
Arrays are NOT equal

Process returned 0 (0x0)   execution time : 0.009 s
Press any key to continue.
```

## Arrays and Functions

Passing arrays to functions is quite simple. There are a few things to remember:

- An array is never passed by value to a function. This is by design to avoid making a copy of an array. In case of a small array consisting of a few elements making a copy would not be time-consuming. However, in case of a large array this could be very expensive in terms of memory cycles (time).
- When passing an array to a function, the starting address of the array is passed to the function. Thus it is more like passing by reference as the changes to the array in the function will be reflected in the original. There is a special relationship between arrays and pointers. Pointers are a very powerful C++ feature which will be discussed later in the book.
- In the function parameter list, an array parameter needs to have square brackets to denote that the parameter is an array rather than a single value:

```
void displayArray(int arr[], int size)
{
        for (int i = 0; i< size; i++)
        {
          cout << arr[i] << endl;
        }
}
```

  Notice that we passed the second parameter called size. Passing the size of an array to a function is a good programming practice to make it easy to loop through the array. In case array size was declared as a global constant, then it is not necessary to pass the size parameter.
- In the caller program, simply pass the name of the array (no square brackets). The following statement demonstrates a function call:

```
// Function prototypes
void displayArray(int [], int );
int main(int argc, char *argv[])
{
      int myArray[MAXSIZE] = {100, 8, -4, 10, 95};
      displayArray(myArray, MAXSIZE);
}
```

- It is possible to pass individual elements of an array to a function. In this case, they are passed just like any other variable:

```
int main(int argc, char *argv[])
{
      int myArray[MAXSIZE] = {100, 8, -4, 10, 95};
      fahren2Celsius(myArray[0]);
}
```

## Using const Array Parameter

Since arrays are always passed by reference one way to ensure that a function does not change contents of the original array is to use keyword const in front of the array parameter:

```
void displayArray(const int arr[], int size)
{
     for (int i = 0; i< size; i++)
     {
       cout << arr[i] << endl;
     }
}
```

This way any attempts to change the contents of the array inside of the displayArray function would be flagged as a syntax error by the compiler.

## Typical Array Functions (Max, Min, Average, Sum, etc.)

Using arrays to capture data set is just the beginning. Often you will need to perform additional operations on the data such as finding the maximum, minimum value in the data set. Perhaps you will need to find an average of all the values in data set. Or you might be asked to sum all the elements in the array. The following program demonstrates some of the most common functions used with arrays:

```
#include <cstdlib>
#include <iostream>

using namespace std;

// Function prototypes
void displayArray(const int [], int );
int sum(const int [], int size);
double avg(const int [], int );
int getMin(const int [], int );
int getMax(const int [], int );

int main(int argc, char *argv[])
{
    // Local constant
    const int MAXSIZE = 5;

    int myArray[MAXSIZE] = {100, 8, -4, 10, 95};

    displayArray(myArray, MAXSIZE);
```

```
    cout << "The sum of the values in the array is: "
         << sum(myArray, MAXSIZE)
         << endl;
    cout <<"The avg of the values in the array is: "
         << avg(myArray, MAXSIZE)
         << endl;
    cout <<"The min of the values in the array is: "
         << getMin(myArray, MAXSIZE)
         << endl;
    cout <<"The max of the values in the array is: "
         << getMax(myArray, MAXSIZE)
         << endl;

    system("PAUSE");
    return EXIT_SUCCESS;
}

int getMin(const int arr[], int size)
{
    int min = arr[0]; // set the min to the 1st element of the array

    for (int i = 1; i< size; i++)
    {
        if (arr[i] < min)
            min = arr[i];
    }

    return min;
}

int getMax(const int arr[], int size)
{
    int max = arr[0];  // set the max to the 1st element of the array

    for (int i = 1; i< size; i++)
    {
        if (arr[i] > max)
            max = arr[i];
    }

    return max;
}

double avg(const int arr[], int size)
{
    double avg = 0.0;
```

```
    avg = sum(arr, size)/static_cast<double>(size); // forcing a double
    return avg;
}


int sum(const int arr[], int size)
{
    int sum = 0;

    for (int i = 0; i< size; i++)
    {
      sum = sum + arr[i];
    }

    return sum;
}

void displayArray(const int arr[], int size)
{
     cout << "Displaying the array: " << endl;
     for (int i = 0; i< size; i++)
     {
       cout << arr[i] << endl;
     }

     cout << "--------------------------" << endl;
}
```

**Listing 10:** Most Common Functions Used With Arrays

Compiling and executing the above program would produce the following output:

```
Displaying the array:
100
8
-4
10
95
--------------------------
The sum of the values in the array is: 209
The avg of the values in the array is: 41.8
The min of the values in the array is: -4
The max of the values in the array is: 100
Press any key to continue . . .
```

## Parallel Arrays

So far, the problems we encountered that required using arrays to gather data where relatively simple problems. Generally, they required only gathering data of the same type. More complex problems usually require gathering data of different types. Since arrays are designed to hold multiple data of the same data type, they do not appear to be suitable to hold data from these types of problems.

Let's look at a student record. A student record consists of student ID number, student name, address, Social Security number, major, courses taken, date of birth, age, sex, GPA, letter grade, and many other attributes. Glancing at the attributes that comprise a student record we see different data types—student ID is probably a string, a student name also a string, age is a number, etc. For the sake of simplicity were going to consider only a few attributes such as student ID, name, GPA, letter grade. The goal is to write a program that will keep track of these attributes for several students. What we want is something like this:

| ID | Name | GPA | Letter Grade |
|---|---|---|---|
| V123401 | George Washington | 2.8 | C |
| X987234 | Martha Washington | 4.0 | A |
| C987001 | Ben Franklin | 3.7 | B |
| G451222 | Abe Lincoln | 2.3 | D |

**Figure 7:** Student Records

In the above figure, each row is considered a student record. Each student record has four attributes (fields): student ID, student name, GPA, and letter grade. Clearly, these are different data types. How do we keep track of this information? Could we use arrays? The answer to the second question is yes we could use arrays, more specifically parallel arrays.

We should define several arrays, each one designated to keep track of a particular attribute in student record. We're going to have:

- An array of strings to hold student ID. Will call this array studentID
- An array of strings, called names to hold student names
- An array of doubles, called gpa to hold the GPA for each student
- An array of characters, called grade to hold the letter grade

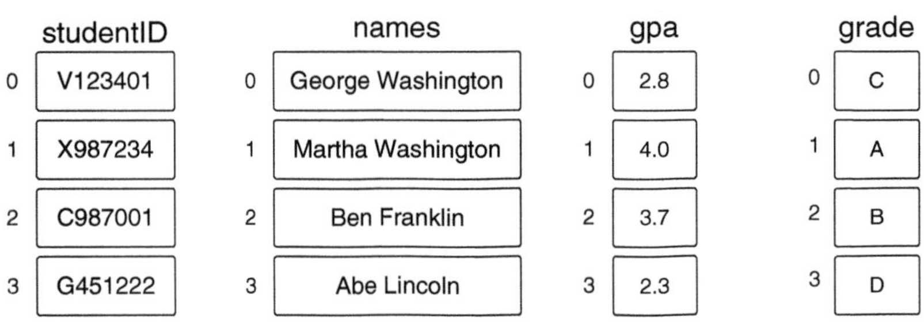


**Figure 8:** Parallel Arrays

Figure 5, depicts the four arrays discussed earlier. The arrays may have different data types but they share one thing in common and that is the index. The contents of the location referenced by index zero in the studentID array contains the student ID for a student whose name is George Washington (referenced by index zero in the names array), whose GPA is 2.8 (index zero in the gpa array), who earned a letter grade of C (reference by index zero in the grade array). By looking at the figure 5 above it is easy to see that the arrays are related to each other through the index.

The following listing is the implementation of the above design:

```
#include <cstdlib>
#include <iostream>
#include <iomanip>

using namespace std;

// Function prototypes
void getStudentNames(string [], int );
void getStudentGPAs(double [], int );
void setGrades(double [], char [], int );
void displayHeader();
void displayStudentRecord(string [], double [], char [], int );

int main(int argc, char *argv[])
{
    // local constant
    const int SIZE = 5;    // MAX number of students

    string names[SIZE];    // to hold the names of students
    double gpa[SIZE];      // to hold the gpa
    char  grade[SIZE];     // to hold the letter grade

    getStudentNames(names, SIZE);
    getStudentGPAs(gpa, SIZE);
    setGrades(gpa, grade, SIZE);
    displayStudentRecord(names, gpa, grade, SIZE);
    return 0;
}
void displayHeader()
{
    cout << setw(20) << "Student Name"
         << setw(5) << "GPA"
         << setw(10) << "Grade"
         << endl;
}

void displayStudentRecord(string arr[], double gradesAvg[], char grades[], int size)
{
    displayHeader();
    for (int i=0; i<size; i++)
    {
        cout << setw(20) << arr[i]
             << setw(5) << gradesAvg[i]
```

```
                 << setw(8) << grades[i] << endl;
      }
}

void getStudentNames(string arr[], int size)
{
      for (int i=0; i<size; i++)
      {
         cout << "Student " << i+1 << " name: ";
         getline(cin, arr[i]);
         cin.clear();
         cin.sync();
      }
}

void getStudentGPAs(double arr[], int size)
{
      for (int i=0; i<size; i++)
      {
         cout << "Student " << i+1 << " GPA: ";
         cin >> arr[i];
      }
}
void setGrades(double gpa[], char grades[], int size)
{
     for (int i = 0; i<size; i++)
     {
         if ((gpa[i] >= 0.0) && (gpa[i] <= 0.9))
             grades[i] = 'F';
         else if (gpa[i]>= 0.66 && gpa[i] <= 1.66)
                 grades[i] = 'D';
         else if (gpa[i]>= 1.67 && gpa[i] <= 2.66)
                 grades[i] = 'C';
         else if (gpa[i]>= 2.67 && gpa[i] <= 3.66)
                 grades[i] = 'B';
         else if (gpa[i]>= 3.67 && gpa[i] <= 4.00)
                 grades[i] = 'A';
     }
}

```

**Listing 11:** Complete Implementation

## Two Dimensional Arrays

We live in a three-dimensional world. Every object around us, including ourselves has a height, width and depth. However, some of this could be abstracted in two dimensions. For example, maps could be represented in two dimensions. Let's take a look at the coordinate system:

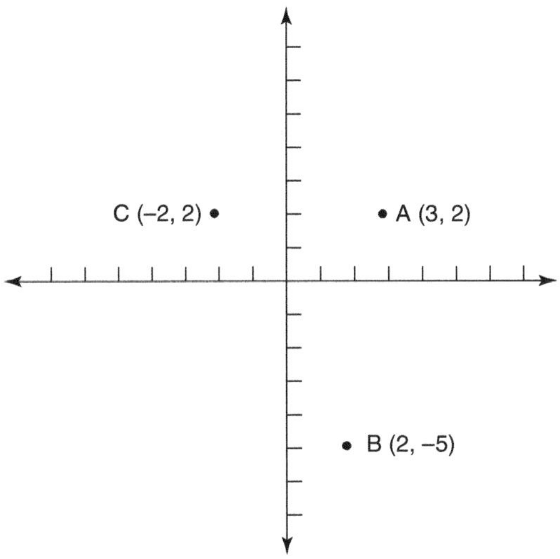


**Figure 9:** Coordinate System

In the Figure 6 above, there are a couple of points with coordinates—A(3,2), B(2,–5), C(–2,2). Another 2-D example would be a game where the object could move up, down, left, and right. Another example would be a city plan where a city could be divided into NW, NE, SE, and SW sections:

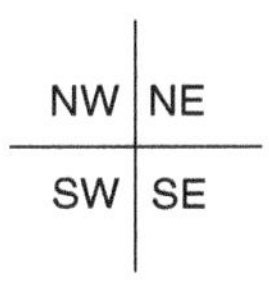


So how do we represent this in a computer program? Do we use multiple arrays? The answer is that we do not need to use multiple arrays because that would be very tedious to maintain. Instead, we use 2-D arrays.

## 2-D Array Syntax

A two-dimensional array will consist of elements of the same data type and it will have it will have two dimensions, i.e. rows and columns:

```
const int NUM_ROWS = 3;
const int NUM_COLUMNS = 4;

int myTwoDArray[NUM_ROWS][NUM_COLUMNS];
```

**Element Data Type** — **Array Name**

You can think of a 2-D array as an array of arrays. In those terms, the array declared above contains 3 arrays and each of these arrays contains 4 elements:

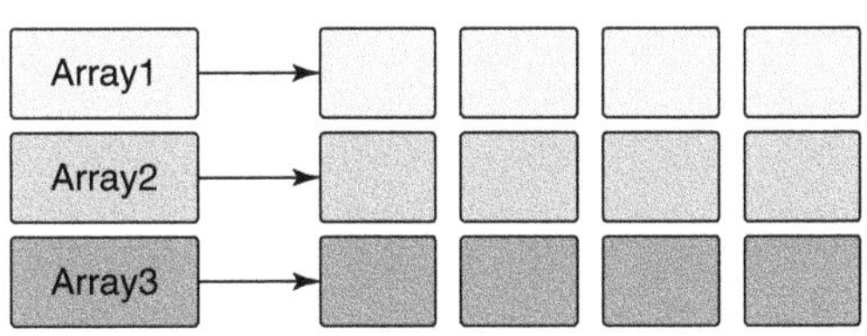


**Figure 10:** A 2-D Array

## 2D Array Initialization

A 2-D array can be initialized with an initialization list:

```
const int NUM_ROWS = 3;
const int NUM_COLUMNS = 4;

int myTwoDArray[NUM_ROWS][NUM_COLUMNS] = {
                                          {10,5,8,9},
                                          {3,2,15,7},
                                          {4,6,19,21},
                                          {11,13,4,6}
                                         };
```

**Initialization list start**

**Individual rows**

**Initialization list end**

The initialization list begins with the left curly brace ("{") and ends with right curly brace ("}"), followed by a semicolon. Individual array rows each start with the "{", followed by data (columns) separated by commas. The end of individual array row is marked with a "}" followed by a comma to signify the end of a row of data. The last row of data in initialization list is not followed by a comma.

It is not necessary to start the initialization list on one level (row) and put each row on a new line. For all practical purposes the entire initialization list could be written on one line. However, to make code more readable, it is a good practice to put rows on separate line.

To quickly initialize an array with all zeros (not any other value) you can use the following initialization list:

```
const int NUM_ROWS = 3;
const int NUM_COLUMNS = 4;
int myTwoDArray[NUM_ROWS][NUM_COLUMNS] = {{0}};
```

The type of quick array initialization works only when setting all the elements to 0 which means the array cannot be initialized with any other values.

Following is a short program that demonstrates a quick initialization:

```
#include <iostream>

using namespace std;
const int ROWS = 3;
const int COLS = 4;

int main()
{
     int my2DArray[ROWS][COLS] = {{0}};

     for (int i=0; i<ROWS; i++)
     {
          for (int j=0; j<COLS; j++)
          {
               cout << my2DArray[i][j]<< " ";
```

```
            }
            cout << endl;
        }
        return 0;
}
```

**Listing 12:** Initialize All Elements in a 2D Array to 0

and the program output:

```
0  0  0  0
0  0  0  0
0  0  0  0

Process returned 0 (0x0)   execution time : 0.011 s
Press any key to continue.
```

### *Omitting Dimensions*

When declaring a two-dimensional (or a multidimensional array such as 3-D, 4D etc.) the only dimension you can omit is the first one:

```
int my2DArray[][COLS] = {
                            {0, 1, 2, 3},
                            {4, 5, 6, 7},
                            {8, 9, 10, 11}
                        };
```

However, this is not correct:

```
int my2DArray[][] = {
                        {0, 1, 2, 3},
                        {4, 5, 6, 7},
                        {8, 9, 10, 11}
                    };
```

and will result in a syntax error.

### *Memory Requirements*

To determine memory requirements for a 2-D array simply multiply the size of the data type by the number of elements. Consider a 3 × 4 array of integers:

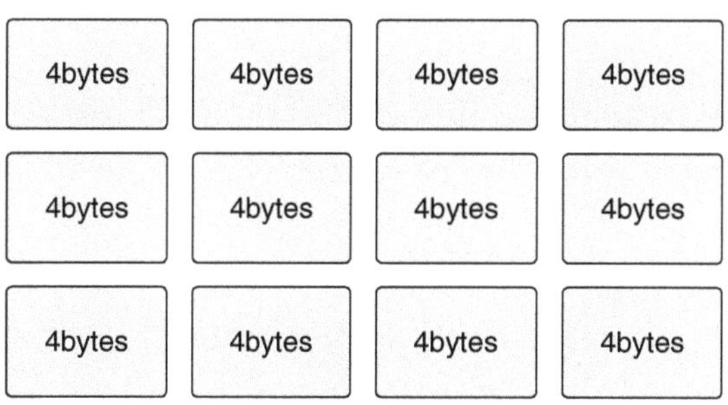


**Figure 11:** A 3 x 4 integer Array

Assuming an integer is four bytes then the total number of RAM needed would be 3 × 4 × 4 = 48.

## Accessing 2D Array Elements

Elements in a two-dimensional array are accessed through an index. The index is a zero-based just like index for one-dimensional array:

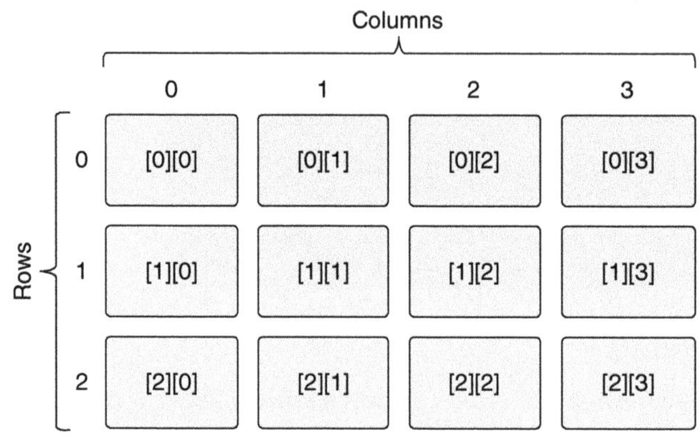


**Figure 12:** 2D Array Cells

Suppose a 2-D array, called my2DArray, was populated with the following data:

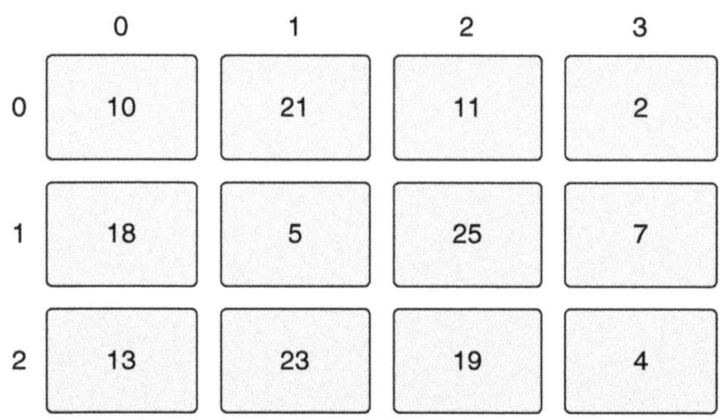


**Figure 13:** A 2-D Array Populated With Data

To access data in row 2 and column 1, it is necessary to reference a row and column:

```
cout << my2DArray[2] [1]<< endl;
```

this would display 19.

Similarly to write data to a 2-D array it is necessary to reference row and column where the data is to be placed. For example, to change the contents of array cell located in row 0 and column 3 (in the example above the cell contains value 2) to 101, write the following statement:

```
my2DArray[0] [3]  = 101;
```

## How Are 2D Arrays Stored in Memory?

2-D arrays are not stored as a matrix in computer memory. Consider the following array:

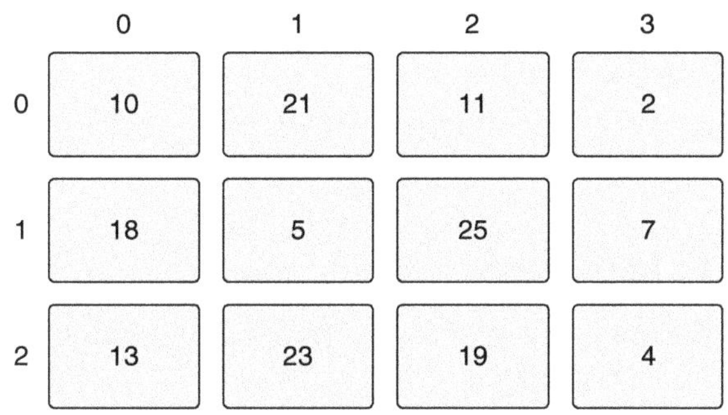


**Figure 14:** Logical Representation of an Array

That is the logical representation of the array. Computer memory is not two-dimensional—RAM is one-dimensional collection of bytes. When the compiler attempts to allocate memory for an array, it looks for a contiguous block of memory. Therefore an array (one or multi-dimensional) is stored in one contiguous block:

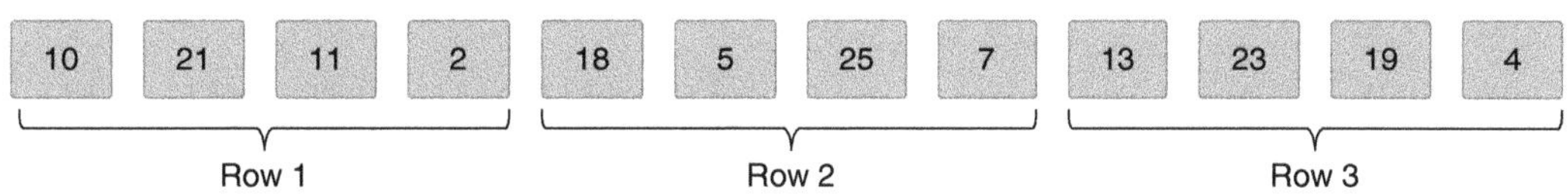


**Figure 15:** Actual Array Allocation in Memory

Recall that when initializing an array via initialization list it is possible to skip the row dimension but not the column dimension. All the compiler needs to know is where one row begins and where it ends (how many columns are in a row). That is why it is very important to provide the column (the second) dimension for a 2-D array when initializing a 2-D array.

## Iterating Through a 2-D Array

A 2-D array is a collection of rows each of which contains columns. To iterate through a 2-D array, for each row it is necessary to iterate through all the columns for that row. This is accomplished with nested loops:

```
const int NUMROWS = 3;
const int NUMCOLS = 4;
int myArray[NUMROWS][NUMCOLS];

   for (int rows=0; rows < NUMROWS; rows++)     <- Outer for loop
   {
       for (int cols =0; cols < NUMCOLS; cols++)  <- Inner for loop
       {
           cout << "Enter a Value: " ;
           cin >> myArray[rows][cols];
       }
   }
```

**Listing 13:** Iterating Through a 2D Array

The program segment in listing 12 prompts the user to enter a value, and stores that value into myArray array. For each row, the program will prompt the user to enter values for all the columns for that arrow. To move from row to row, the program uses the outer for loop. The inner for loop is used to iterate through columns. In Listing 12 the outer loop starts on line 5 and the inner loop starts on line 7.

Understanding how arrays are represented in computer memory is very important, especially when it comes to multidimensional arrays and passing 2-D arrays to functions.

## Passing 2D Arrays to Functions

When passing one dimensional arrays to functions the programmer needs to specify the size of the array in a separate parameter:

```
void displayArray(int numArr[], int size)
```

When passing two-dimensional arrays to functions it is necessary to specify how many columns the array has:

```
void display2DArray(int numArr[][NUMCOLS], int rows)
```

This is because of how two-dimensional arrays are stored in a single contiguous block of memory (single dimension).

Novice programmers often attempt to pass a 2-D array to a function in the following manner:

```
void display2DArray(int numArr[][], int rows, int cols) // ERROR!!!
```

This is incorrect, because the compiler needs to know how to distinguish between rows in the contiguous block of memory that was allocated for the array.

```
#include <cstdlib>
#include <iostream>

using namespace std;

const int NUMROWS = 3;
const int NUMCOLS = 4;

// Function prototypes
void display2DArray(int [][NUMCOLS], int );

int main(int argc, char *argv[])
{
     int myArray[NUMROWS][NUMCOLS] = {
                                       {1, 2, 3, 4},
                                       {5, 6, 0, 9},
                                       {9, 8, 6, 1}
                                     };

```

**Function prototype**

```
20.
21.     display2DArray(myArray, NUMROWS);
22.     system("PAUSE");
23.     return EXIT_SUCCESS;
24. }
25.
26. void display2DArray(int numArr[][NUMCOLS], int rows)
27. {
28.    for (int r=0; r < rows; r++)
29.    {
30.         for (int c =0; c < NUMCOLS; c++)
31.         {
32.             cout << numArr[r][c] << " ";
33.         }
34.         cout << endl;
35.     }
36.
37. }
```

**Function call** (line 21)

**Function definition** (line 26)

**Listing 14:** Passing 2-D Array to a Function

Listing 13 demonstrates how to pass an array to a function and how to call the function. Of particular interest are the following lines:

- Function prototype on line 9. Notice the second dimension (`NUMCOLS`). The compiler has been notified at the first instance of the function of the size of each row.
- Function call on line 21. Only the array name is passed as the first argument to the function. The second argument contains number of rows.
- Function definition on line 26. Notice the array parameter—it has array element type, array name, empty row dimension, and column dimension.

When compiled and executed, the above program produces the following output:

```
1 2 3 4
5 6 0 9
9 8 6 1
Press any key to continue . . .
```

## Vectors

Arrays are not the most efficient data structure. Programmers often end up wasting a lot of memory because they declare arrays bigger than the anticipated data set. Despite best guesses, sometimes the data set turns out to be much bigger than the allocated array. In this situation programmers are faced with having to allocate another array, much larger than the original, and having to copy the contents from the original to the new array. This is costly in terms of programming cycles.

Fortunately, C++ comes with a library (Standard Template Library or STL) that contains additional data types such as containers, iterators, and some algorithms. The STL data types are not part of the C++ language.

Vector is a container data type and it acts like an array as it can hold values in a contiguous block of memory. Vector elements can be accessed in the same manner as array elements—through the subscript ([ ]) operator. To declare a vector, the following header needs to be included:

```
#include <vector>
```

With the header included, defining a variable of data type vector is simple:

```
vector<int> quizzes;
```

The declaration starts with the keyword vector, followed by the data type of the collection which is enclosed in diamond (< >), followed by a variable name. In the statement above, quizzes is defined as a vector that can hold an integer data type. You don't have to provide the dimension of the vector collection, this is dynamically handled by the compiler. As elements are added to the vector, it expands, and vice versa as elements are deleted from the vector, it contracts. If you do not provide the size dimension, the vector size is set to 0.

It is possible to specify the initial size of a vector:

```
vector<int> quizzes(5);
```

The above statement defines an integer vector called quizzes with initial size of 5. Here is an example of a vector capable of storing strings with initial size of 15:

```
vector<string> names(15);
```

It is possible to initialize a vector with a particular value:

```
vector<int> homework(10,100);
```

In the above statement, homework is defined as an integer vector, whose initial size is set to 10, and all values are initialized to 100.

## Vector Member Functions

Vector is an object and it has a lot of built-in member functions. Member functions are accessed through the dot notation—normally vector object variable name followed by a period followed by the function name.

### *Size vs. Capacity*

At any time it is possible to determine the size of the vector by calling member function size:

```
int numElements = names.size();
```

The size function represents the number of elements inserted into the vector. The capacity function represents the maximum number of elements the vector can hold:

```
int canHold = names.capacity();
```

The capacity function specifies how large the size can get before the vector needs to relocate additional memory.

### *Function "at" and Subscript Operator*

One of those functions called "at" can be used to access vector elements:

```
for (int i=0; i<names.size(); i++)
{
    cout << names.at(i) << endl;
}
```

Another way to access vector elements is through the subscript operator ([ ]). This is very much so the way array elements are accessed:

```
for (int i=0; i<names.size(); i++)
{
    cout << names[i] << endl;
}
```

### *push_back and pop_back()*

To add an element to the vector use the pushback function:

```
vector <int> numbers;
for (int i=0; i<SIZE; i++)
{
    numbers.push_back(i + 10);
}
```

the push_back member function adds an element to the end of the vector. Each time a value is added to a vector, vector size is increased by one. To remove and element from a vector, pop_back member function can be used:

```
numbers.pop_back();
```

The statement above removes the last element of a vector. At the same time, vector size decreases by 1.

Other notable vector functions are:

- Clear—removes all elements from a vector:

  ```
  names.clear();
  ```

  would clear out the names vector.
- Empty—returns true if the vector contains no elements. Otherwise returns false:

  ```
  if (names.empty())
      cout << "There are no stored names" << endl;
  ```
- Reverse—reverses the order of the elements in the vector.

## End of Chapter Questions

### True/False

Indicate whether the statement is true or false.

**1.** When declaring an array, it is not necessary to specify the data type of the elements.

2. Arrays are designed to hold data of the same type and the memory allocation is the same for each element.
3. When initializing an array, if the number of elements is greater than the array size, compiling would generate a syntax error.
4. When performing partial list initialization of an array, leaving empty items anywhere in the list is possible.
5. Writing to memory locations beyond array boundaries could have unpredictable results in case another program/process owns those memory locations and has data in those locations.
6. An array is always passed by value to a function.

## Exercises

1. Which would be correct when storing user input into array amountSpent?

   a. `cin >> amountSpent[i];`

   b. `cin >> amountSpent;`

   c. `Both a and b are correct`

2. Which is the correct array initialization statement for the days in a week?

   a. `string days[5] = {"Monday", "Tuesday", "Wednesday", "Thursday", "Friday", "Saturday", "Sunday" };`

   b. `string days[] = {"Monday", "Tuesday", "Wednesday", "Thursday", "Friday", "Saturday", "Sunday" };`

   c. `string days = {"Monday", "Tuesday", "Wednesday", "Thursday", "Friday", "Saturday", "Sunday" };`

3. Assume the following array has been declared:

   int data[] = {10,20,30,40,50,60,70,80,90};

   What is the correct way to pass the 3rd array element to the function myFunction defined as:

   void myFunction(int value);

   a. `myFunction(data[3]);`

   b. `myFunction(data, 3);`

   c. `myFunction(data(2));`

   d. `myFunction(data[2]);`

4. When declaring a vector, what header needs to be included?

5. How do you pass a 2D array to a function?

   a. Pass array name only

   b. Pass array name and number of rows

   c. Pass array name and number of columns

   d. None of these

# Chapter 8

# Pointers

***"When you blame, you open up a world of excuses, because as long as you're looking outside, you miss the opportunity to look inside, and you continue to suffer."***

**—Donna Quesada,** ***Buddha in the Classroom: Zen Wisdom to Inspire Teachers***

## Intro to Pointers

Pointers are an integral part of C++ and one of the features that separates C++ from other programming languages such as Java. Pointers are widely used in other languages such as Java virtual machine but only in the background. Similarly, Microsoft's .NET platform relies heavily on pointers. One of the fastest databases in the world, called Ctree by company called FairComm is using nothing but pointers. This database is the best choice for real-time applications such as stock market quotes where there is need for speed. Even though Java and .net platform rely on pointers in the background, programmers using these tools will not directly be able to use pointers. In C++, programmers can use pointers and write very efficient code. However, not knowing how to use pointers correctly could result in program crashes and slow program execution.

## Pointer Variables

Every byte in RAM has an address. The addresses range from zero to the maximum address of installed RAM in the computer. For example, if your computer has 4 GB of RAM then every byte (memory location) of those 4 GB will have a unique address. When declaring variables of certain data type in C++ program, we basically give a name to memory location. For example:

```
int number = 101;
cout << "This is the value stored in variable number: " << number << endl;
// to get the address, simply add "&" in front of the variable
cout << "This is the address of variable number: " < < &number << endl;
```

**Listing 1:** An Address of a Variable

To get the memory address of the variable, simply prepend an ampersand (&) to the variable name:

```
cout << "This is the address of variable number: " << &number << endl;
```

if we were to place the above code segment in a C++ program and compile it this is what the program run would output:

```
This is the value stored in variable number: 101
This is the address of variable number: 0x28ff44

Process returned 0 (0x0)   execution time : 0.015 s
Press any key to continue.
```

Placing an & before the variable name gets the address of the named memory location (variable). In the example above, the address is used inline in the cout statement. Thus after the cout statement executes we have no way of referring to that address other than through & number. To capture an address of a memory location and use it somewhere in the program, C++ provides pointer variables. A pointer is a variable that can hold an address of memory location. It cannot hold a value, only an address. The following figure illustrates that:

**Figure 1:** Pointer Variable Depicted

In Figure 1 above, variable num has been allocated space (4 bytes, because it is an integer) in RAM starting at the address of 0x28ff44. Another variable, ptrNum, which is capable of holding an address, has been allocated two bytes starting at the RAM address of 0x2ff40. Notice the contents of the first memory address? It would it contains number 101. What about the location of the second memory address? It is not holding a value—instead it is holding an address effectively pointing to the memory address of 0x28ff44.

The syntax for declaring a pointer variable consists of a data type, followed by an asterisk (*), followed by a variable name. The location of the asterisk is not important. It could be next to the data type, it could be in between the data type and the variable name; or it could be next to the variable name:

```
int* ptrNum;
int * ptrNum;
int *ptrNum;
```

If a pointer variable cannot hold a value, why is it important to declare it of certain data type? The data type is actually the data type of the location to which the pointer variable is pointing to.

The following code segment demonstrates pointer variable:

```
#include <iostream>

using namespace std;

int main()
{
    int num = 101;
    cout << "Value stored in variable num: " << num << endl;
    cout << "The address of variable num: " << &num << endl;
    int *ptrNum;
    ptrNum = &num;
    cout << "This is the address of variable number: "  << ptrNum << endl;
    return 0;
}
```

**Listing 2:** Pointer Variable

In Listing 1 above, on line 7, we declared a variable called num and assigned value of 101 to it. On line 9, the program displays the address of the memory location where variable num has been allocated. Again, & preceding the variable name instructs the cout object to display the address of the variable. On line 10 we declared a pointer variable called ptrNum:

```
int *ptrNum;
```

and assigned it the address of the variable num.

Compiling and running the above code will result in the following output:

```
Value stored in variable num: 101
The address of variable num: 0x28ff44
This is the address of variable number: 0x28ff44

Process returned 0 (0x0)   execution time : 0.037 s
Press any key to continue.
```

from which we concede that the pointer variable ptrNum is pointing to the same memory location where num is located. If he wanted to find out the memory location where ptrNum is allocated, we simply needs to precede it with the & symbol in order to get its address. So the general rule is:

- variable name means contents of memory location
- & followed by a variable name means the address of memory location

```
#include <iostream>

using namespace std;

int main()
{
    int num = 101;
    cout << "Value stored in variable num: " << num << endl;
    cout << "The address of variable num: " << &num << endl;

    int *ptrNum;
    ptrNum = &num;

    cout << "The contents of memory location ptrNum: " << ptrNum << endl;
    cout << "The address of of ptrNum: " << &ptrNum << endl;
    return 0;
}

```

**Listing 3:** Working with Pointer Variables

And the output of the above program:

```
Value stored in variable num: 101
The address of variable num: 0x28ff44
The contents of memory location ptrNum: 0x28ff44
The address of of ptrNum: 0x28ff40

Process returned 0 (0x0)   execution time : 0.021 s
Press any key to continue.
```

## Dereferencing Pointers

Dereferencing a pointer means to display or to change the contents of the memory location to which the pointer variable is pointing to.

### Displaying the Content of Memory Location

To display contents of the memory location to which a pointer variable is pointing to choose the following syntax: `*ptrNum`. Following example demonstrates how contents of the memory location to which the pointer points to can be displayed simply by dereferencing the pointer variable:

```
int num = 101;
int *ptrNum = &num;
cout << "The contents of the cell ptrNum points to: " << *ptrNum
     << endl;
```

This code segment would output number 101.

### Changing the Content of Memory Location

Use the * notation to change the content of the memory location a pointer variable is pointing to:

```
int num = 101;
int *ptrNum = &num;
*ptrNum = 3;       // to change the contents, use "*"
cout << "The contents of the cell ptrNum points to: " << *ptrNum
     << endl;
```

the above code segment would print number 3 instead of 101.

When you declare a pointer you cannot assign a value to it:

```
int *p;
*p = 10;
cout << "This is p " << *p << endl;
```

because it will cause program to crash. A pointer variable has to points to an address. When changing the contents of memory location, to pointer variable the contents in the location to which the pointer is pointing to will change:

```
int num = 101;
int *ptrNum = &num;
*ptrNum = 3;       // to change the contents, use "*"
cout << "The contents of the cell ptrNum points to: "
     << *ptrNum << endl;
cout << "The contents of the cell ptrNum points to: " << num
     << endl;
```

in this example, whether you `ptrNum` or `num` the output will be the same as demonstrated above because `ptrNum` points to the memory address where num is located.

## Pointers and Arrays

As we have seen in the chapter on arrays, arrays and pointers are closely related. For example, supplying only the array name to the cout statement would result in cout outputting the starting address of the block of memory occupied by array:

```
int numbers[] = {10, 20, 30, 40, 50};
cout << "This is myArray: " << numbers << endl;
```

compiling and running the above code segment would print the following output:

```
This is myArray: 0x28ff20

Process returned 0 (0x0)   execution time : 0.013 s
Press any key to continue.
```

to print the contents of array location we need to use an index:

```
cout << "This is myArray[0]: " << numbers[0] << endl;
```

Since the data stored in array is all of the same data type, which means that each array member occupies same amount of memory, and assessing the starting address of the array, we could traverse array elements by using pointers to accomplish this task:

```
int numbers [] = {10, 20, 30, 40, 50};
int ptrNumbersAddress0 = &numbers[0];
int ptrNumbersAddress1 = &numbers[1];
int ptrNumbersAddress2 = &numbers[2];
int ptrNumbersAddress3 = &numbers[3];
int ptrNumbersAddress4 = &numbers[4];
cout << *ptrNumbersAddress0 << endl;
cout << *ptrNumbersAddress1 << endl;
cout << *ptrNumbersAddress2 << endl;
cout << *ptrNumbersAddress3 << endl;
cout << *ptrNumbersAddress4 << endl;
```

**Listing 4:** Displaying Array Contents Through Pointer Variables

In the example above, there are five pointer variables, each one is pointing to a member of the numbers array. This was done to illustrate the point, however in reality there is no need for all these pointer variables as one would suffice. The following program demonstrates more efficient way to use pointer variables to traverse an array:

```
int numbers[] = {10, 20, 30, 40, 50};
int *ptrNumbers = numbers;  // get the starting address of the array

for (int i=0; i<5; i++)
{
     cout << *ptrNumbers << endl; // display the contents of memory address
     ptrNumbers++;                // go to the next memory address
}
```

**Listing 5:** Traversing an Array With a Pointer

The code segment starts by declaring an array and populating it through an initialization list. Next, we declare a pointer variable of data type integer and point it to the starting address of the array (line 2). Notice that there is no & in front of the array variable name. That is because the array name is nothing more than a pointer to the starting memory location for the entire array. We finish off the code segment by looping through the array by using the pointer which we advance (line 7) every time we output the contents (line 6). Notice the dereference operator (*) on line 6.

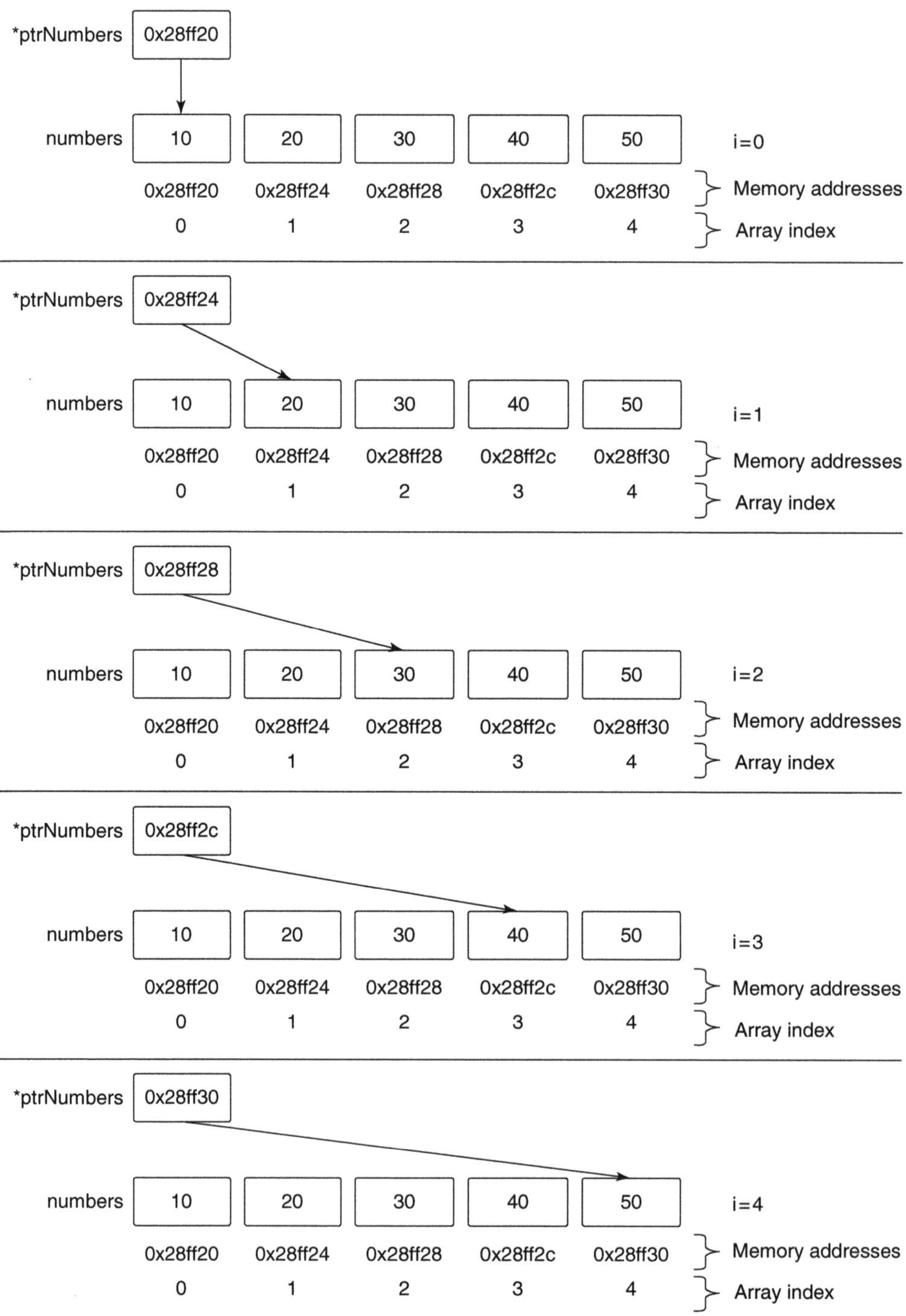


**Figure 2:** Traversing an Array with a Pointer Depicted

What is interesting is what takes place in computer memory as the program iterates through the array:

Note different addresses stored in*ptrNumbers variable for each iteration. Since *ptrNumbers was declared as a pointer variable capable of pointing to an integer data type when the statement on line 7 (in Listing 2 above) is encountered, the computer advances 4 bytes (assuming an integer is four bytes from that system) to the next memory location.

Since the array name is a pointer, we should not need a separate pointer variable. We could have accomplished the same outcome by using the array name:

```
for (int i=0; i<5; i++)
{
    cout << *(numbers + i) << endl;    // display the contents of memory address
    ptrNumbers++;                      // go to the next memory address
}
```

**Listing 6:** Dereferencing Array Name

We know that numbers is the starting address of the array. To get the contents, we need to dereference this pointer:

```
*numbers  which is the same as *(numbers + 0)
```

to move from one memory location to another, we simply need to increment the address and then dereference it:

```
*(numbers + i)
```

Numbers is the starting address—and i is the loop control variable which ranges from 0 through 4. Adding a value to the starting address of an array really means adding sizeof(integer) bytes to the starting memory address. An integer is implied because the array was declared as an array of integers. Normally an integer is four bytes. Thus adding 1 to the memory address is equivalent to adding four bytes to the starting memory location. Adding 2 to the starting memory address is equivalent to adding 2* sizeof(integer) bytes. In essence the computer is calculating the offset from the starting memory location by adding number of bytes.

Having to dereference array name (pointer) is a bit tricky because it depends on where the parentheses are placed. That's why it is easier to declare a separate pointer variable assigned it the starting point of the array and use it to traverse the array. With the separate pointer variable, working with arrays it's a little bit easier. The only rule that we need to remember is that if we want the contents of the memory location we need to dereference the pointer variable. Otherwise the pointer variable will always refer to an address. We do not need to worry about the offset as we need to when working with the array name which is also a pointer.

## Pointer Arithmetic

Let's try to print the array once and then print it in reverse using the same pointer variable *ptrNumbers:

```
#include <iostream>

using namespace std;

int main()
```

```
{
    int numbers[] = {10, 20, 30, 40, 50};
    int *ptrNumbers = numbers;          // get the starting address of the array

    for (int i=0; i<5; i++)
    {
        cout << *ptrNumbers << endl;  // display the contents of memory address

        ptrNumbers++;                 // go to the next memory address
    }


    // loop to print the array in revers
    cout << "Printing in reverse" << endl;
    for (int i=0; i<5; i++)
    {
        cout << *ptrNumbers << endl;
        ptrNumbers--;
    }
    return 0;
}
```

**Listing 7:** Printing in Reverse

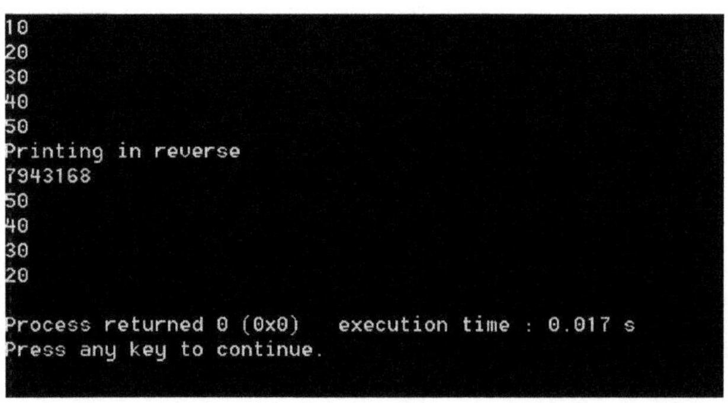


The output of the code has a surprise! What is the longest number above? Also the program failed to print the first element of the array? A careful study of the source code segment in Listing 7 reveals that the pointer is incremented after the contents of the memory cell are displayed. This means that after the loop finishes executing, the pointer variable *ptrNumbers will be pointing to an address beyond the boundaries of the numbers array:

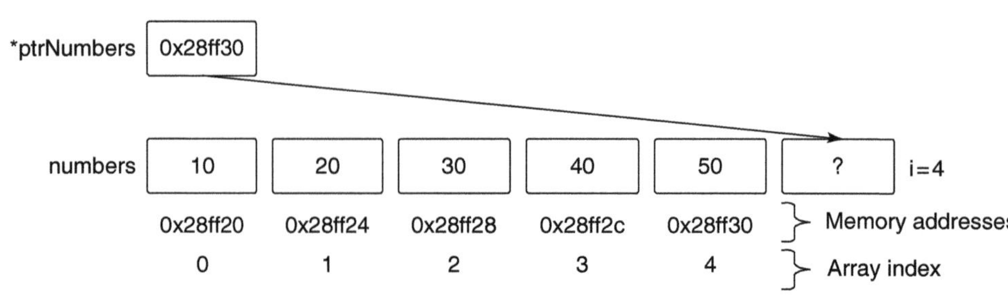


**Figure 3:** Out of Bounds Location

The large number we are displaying is the contents of the memory location beyond array boundaries. To correct that, in the loop used to display the array in reverse order we need to decrement the pointer before the cout statement (swap lines 23 and 22). We could decrement the pointer before the loop as well - right after line 19:

```
// loop to print the array in revers
cout << "Printing in reverse" << endl;
ptrNumbers--;
for (int i=0; i<5; i++)
{
    cout << *ptrNumbers << endl;
    ptrNumbers--;
}
```

Or swap the lines:

```
// loop to print the array in revers
cout << "Printing in reverse" << endl;
for (int i=0; i<5; i++)
{
    ptrNumbers--;
    cout << *ptrNumbers << endl;
}
```

## Comparing Pointers

Computer memory is a series of consecutive bytes. We have established that every byte has an address and these addresses reflect the offset from the starting address of RAM. Thus it is possible to compare memory addresses—the memory locations that are closer to the start of RAM will be considered lower than the memory addresses that are closer to the end of RAM. We have seen an example in figure 2 where each array location had a different memory address.

It is possible to compare pointers using standard C++ relational operators such as : >, >=, <, <=, !=. However, comparing pointers using relational opearators means comparing their addresses and not the contents. For example:

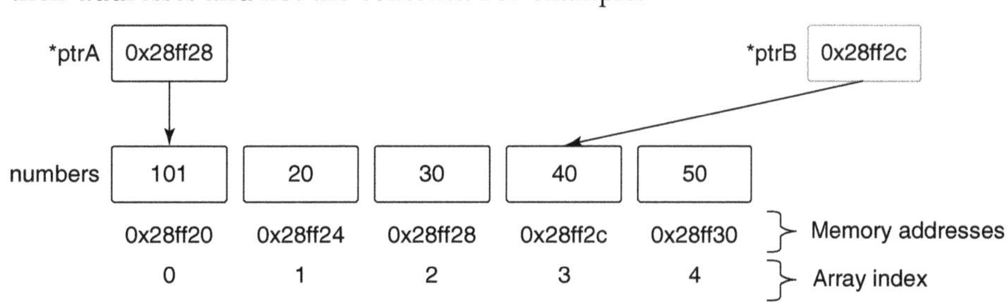


**Figure 4:** Comparing Pointers

ptrA and ptrB are two pointer variables. Pointer ptrA points to the address 0x28ff20 and pointer ptrB points to the address 0x28ff2c which is higher than 0x28ff20. So the following expression will return true:

```
if (ptrA > ptrB)
```

it is like asking if 0x28ff20 greater than 0x28ff2c (and it is not). To compare the contents of these two memory locations we would first need to dereference both pointers:

```
if (*ptrA > *ptrB)
```

The above statement is equivalent to asking if 101 (the contents of the memory cell at address 0x28ff20) is greater than 50 (contents of the memory cell at address 0x28ff2c). Clearly, 101 is greater than 50 so the expression would evaluate to true.

## Pointers and Functions

Passing pointers to functions as arguments is similar to passing references to functions. This means that the value of the argument is going to be affected by the function.
The following code segment demonstrates how a caller program would call a function whose parameters are pointers:

```
#include <iostream>

using namespace std;

// Function prototypes
void swapContents(int *, int *);

int main()
{
     int valueA = 10;
     int valueB = 20;

     cout << "Before the function call" << endl;
     cout << "valueA : " << valueA << endl;
     cout << "valueB : " << valueB << endl;

     // Function call
     swapContents(&valueA, &valueB);  // & is necessary
                                      //because the arguments
                                      // are pointers
     cout << "After the function call" << endl;
     cout << "valueA : " << valueA << endl;
     cout << "valueB : " << valueB << endl;
     return 0;
}

void swapContents(int *x, int *y)
{
     int temp;

     temp = *x;
     *x =*y;
     *y = temp;
}
```

**Function call. Note the & so that the address is passed**

**Parameters are pointers**

**Listing 8:** Function with Pointer Parameters

The output of the above program is:

```
Before the function call
valueA : 10
valueB : 20
After the function call
valueA : 20
valueB : 10

Process returned 0 (0x0)   execution time : 0.009 s
Press any key to continue.
```

The same program in listing 4 written using references:

```
#include <iostream>

using namespace std;

// Function prototypes
void swapContents(int &, int &);  // Notice the & instead of *

int main()
{
    int valueA = 10;
    int valueB = 20;

    cout << "Before the function call" << endl;
    cout << "valueA : " << valueA << endl;
    cout << "valueB : " << valueB << endl;

    // Function call
    swapContents(valueA, valueB);  // Note the arguments in the call!!!
    cout << "After the function call" << endl;
    cout << "valueA : " << valueA << endl;
    cout << "valueB : " << valueB << endl;
    return 0;
}

void swapContents(int &x, int &y)
{
    int temp;

    temp = x;
    x =y;
    y = temp;
}
```

**Listing 9:** Using References

Notice the difference in two programs? They are:

- The first difference is in the function prototypes where pointer parameters are denoted by *, and reference parameters are denoted by an &.
- Another difference is in the function call, on line 18. When calling the function that has pointer parameters it is necessary to include the address of arguments (valueA and valueB). When calling the function that has reference parameters, there is no need to provide the address, only the variable names.
- Finally, in the function swapContents, the pointer code is little more complex because of the dereferencing.

References are easier to work with as they are a higher abstraction than pointers. When working with references, instead of a programmer handling all the details of dereferencing, the compiler handles those tasks. Thus novice programmers can work with large data sets efficiently by using references. Let's examine the differences between pointers and references in greater detail. So what is the difference between a pointer and a reference?

## Pointers vs. References

A reference is an alias for a variable name, which means that there is no separate object for a reference. In other words, a reference is the original with a different name. On the other hand, a pointer is a separate object (variable) with its own address in memory. The following code segment illustrates that:

```
#include <iostream>

using namespace std;

int main()
{
    cout << "-------------------- POINTER ------------------" << endl;
    int y = 100;      // declare an integer and store value 100 in it
    int *ptrY;        // declare a pointer
    ptrY = &y;        // make the pointer point to y
    cout << "Address of y                     : " << &y << endl;
    cout << "Contents of y                    : " << y << endl;
    cout << "Address of ptrY                  : " << &ptrY << endl;
    cout << "Contents of ptrY                 : " << ptrY << endl;
    cout << "Contents of where ptrY points to: " << *ptrY << endl;

    cout << "-------------------- Reference ------------------" << endl;
    int x = 10;       // declare an integer and store value of 10
    int &refX = x;    // declare a reference to this object

    cout << "Address of x                     : " << &x << endl;
    cout << "Contents of x                    : " << x << endl;
    cout << "Address of refX                  : " << &refX << endl;
```

```
    cout << "Contents of refX                    : " << refX << endl;
    return 0;
}
```

**Listing 10:** Pointers vs. References

Compiling and running this program produces the following output:

```
------------------- POINTER ----------------
Address of y                   : 0x28ff44
Contents of y                  : 100
Address of ptrY                : 0x28ff40
Contents of ptrY               : 0x28ff44
Contents of where ptrY points to: 100
------------------- Reference ----------------
Address of x                   : 0x28ff3c
Contents of x                  : 10
Address of refX                : 0x28ff3c
Contents of refX               : 10

Process returned 0 (0x0)   execution time : 0.010 s
Press any key to continue.
```

The above program clearly demonstrates that there is no memory allocation for references. In case of a pointer, memory is allocated for the pointer variable (0x28ff40) and also for the integer variable y (0x28ff44).

References a little bit easier to work with then pointers because pointers require additional steps by the programmer such as dereferencing. However, references are not as flexible as pointers. For example, a pointer variable can be reassigned to point to a different memory location and it will not affect the original variable:

```
#include <iostream>

using namespace std;

int main()
{
    int x = 10;
    int *ptrX = &x;

    cout << "Contents of x: " << x << endl;
    cout << "Address of x : " << & x << endl;
    cout << "Contents of ptrX: " << ptrX << endl;
    cout << "Address of ptrX: " << &ptrX << endl;
    cout << "Contents of memory location where ptrX points to: " << *ptrX
         << endl;

    int y = 20;
    ptrX = &y;
    cout << "-------ptrX was reassingned to point to y----------" << endl;
    cout << "Contents of y: " << y << endl;
    cout << "Address of y : " << &y << endl;
```

```
    cout << "Contents of ptrX: " << ptrX << endl;
    cout << "Address of ptrX: " << &ptrX << endl;
    cout << "Contents of memory location where ptrX points to: " << *ptrX
         << endl;

    cout << "------------- x is unchanged ---------------------" << endl;
    cout << "Contents of x: " << x << endl;
    return 0;
}
```

**Listing 11:** Reassigning Pointers Does Not Affect the Original Pointee

Listing 10 above is a simple program that demonstrates how reassigning a pointer to a different memory location does not affect/change the contents of the original memory location to which the pointer was pointing ("pointee").

The program starts by declaring an integer variable x and assigning value 10 to it. Next, a pointer *ptrX variable is declared and assigned the address of variable x. The contents and addresses are displayed and then a new variable y is declared and assigned a value of 20. In this point, ptrX is assigned the address of the variable y. The contents and addresses are displayed. Also the original pointee (variable X) is displayed and is unchanged:

```
Contents of x: 10
Address of x : 0x28ff44
Contents of ptrX: 0x28ff44
Address of ptrX: 0x28ff40
Contents of memory location where ptrX points to: 10
------ptrX was reassingned to point to y----------
Contents of y: 20
Address of y : 0x28ff3c
Contents of ptrX: 0x28ff3c
Address of ptrX: 0x28ff40
Contents of memory location where ptrX points to: 20
------------- x is unchanged --------------------
Contents of x: 10

Process returned 0 (0x0)   execution time : 0.012 s
Press any key to continue.
```

Rewriting the above program using references:

```
int x = 10;
int& refX = x; // declare a reference to x

// display it
cout << "Contents of x: " << x << endl;
cout << "Address of x : " << &x << endl;
cout << "Contents of refX : " << refX << endl;
cout << "Address of refX: " << &refX << endl;

int y = 20;     // declare another variable
refX = y;       // reassign the reference refX to y

cout << "-------ptrX was reassigned as a reference to y ---" << endl;
```

```
14. cout << "Contents of y: " << y << endl;
15. cout << "Address of y : " << &y << endl;
16. cout << "Reference to y: " << refX << endl;
17. cout << "Address of refX: " << &refX << endl;
18.
19. cout << "------------- is x unchanged ? ---------------------" << endl;
20. cout << "x is now: " << x << endl;
```

**Listing 12:** Listing 10 Rewritten Using References

will have surprising output:

```
Contents of x: 10
Address of x : 0x28ff44
Contents of refX : 10
Address of refX: 0x28ff44
-------ptrX was reassigned as a reference to y ---
Contents of y: 20
Address of y : 0x28ff3c
Reference to y: 20
Address of refX: 0x28ff44
------------- is x unchanged ? ---------------------
x is now: 20

Process returned 0 (0x0)   execution time : 0.013 s
Press any key to continue.
```

The original value of x has been changed!!! The following statement on line 11, in listing 11:

```
refX = y;
```

is responsible for the change. Further investigation offers some clues - the memory address of the reference variable refX is still pointing to the memory address of the variable x (in this example, 0x28ff44). Even after the assignment statement, when refX was supposedly assigned to refer to the variable y, refX still had the same address as the variable x(0x28ff44) which means that the contents of X were assigned the value of variable y (20).

The above examples demonstrate differences between pointers and references. How does a programmer decide when to use references and when to use pointers? The answer is it depends—it depends on what you're trying to accomplish. When passing data to functions, in particular built-in data types such as integers, chars, doubles, floats, etc., pointers are generally preferred. A lot of built-in functions in C++ library, specifically functions that deal with characters are using pointers. When passing abstract data types (programmer defined datatypes) which were going to discuss later on in the book, use references as this makes the code more readable.

## Constant Pointers and Pointers to Constants

If you do not want a value to change, or you do not want a pointer to point to another memory location, then you should make it a constant. This can be accomplished with the keyword const. Consider the following declarations:

```
int x = 10;
const int * myPtr = &x;
int * const myPtr = &x;
const int * const myPtr = &x;
```

Each declaration is correct as they all assign the address of variable x to an integer pointer. However the trick is figuring out what is a constant.

- The first declaration:

```
const int * myPtr = &x;
```

  declares a pointer to a constant integer. This pointer can be used to change the contents of the memory location to which the pointer points to:

```
int x = 10;
const int * myPtr = &x;
*myPtr = 20;        // ERROR!!!
```

  The last statement is attempting to change the value of the memory location to which myPtr is pointing to and it would result in an error.

- The second declaration:

```
int * const myPtr = &x;
```

  declares a constant pointer to an integer which means that you cannot change where the pointer points to:

```
int x = 10;
int y = 20;
int * const myPtr = &x;
myPtr = &y; // ERROR!
```

  An attempt to reassign the pointer to another memory location would result in an error.

- The third declaration:

```
const int * const myPtr = &x;
```

  declares a pointer to an integer for both the pointer value and the value being pointed to will not change.

Constant pointers and pointers to constants come in very handy when passing data to functions through parameters. If you do not want the function to change the data then use a pointer to a constant. The reason being is that sometimes the caller program (function) could declare data as non-constant. If you have a function that receives data through a pointer parameter and the function does not needs to change the data it receives, it is a good practice to declare the receiving pointer parameter as a pointer to a constant. This is a safe coding practice assuring that the function will not change the data and it can receive both constant and it non constant data.

## Dynamic Memory Allocation

When C++ programs execute the compiler reserves computer memory in the following manner:

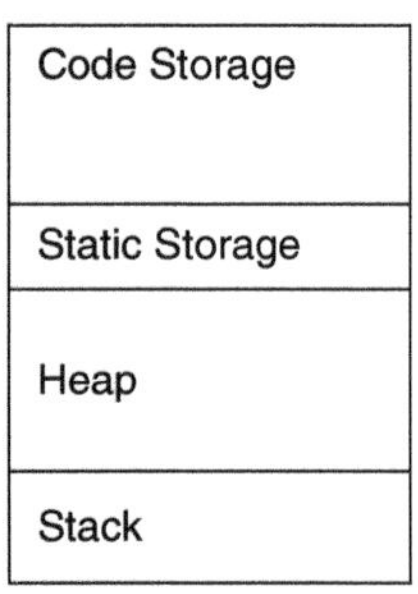


- **Code Storage:** used to store the source code. Another word for code storage is text storage
- **Static Storage:** used to store global variables and global constants.
- **Heap (free store):** used for everything else—this is why it's called the free store.
- **Stack Storage:** used for calling functions and their parameters and local variables

C++ programs can dynamically allocate memory via the new operator. This allocated memory is a "borrowed" from the Heap. The following statement demonstrates dynamic memory allocation:

```
int *myPtr = new int[5];
```

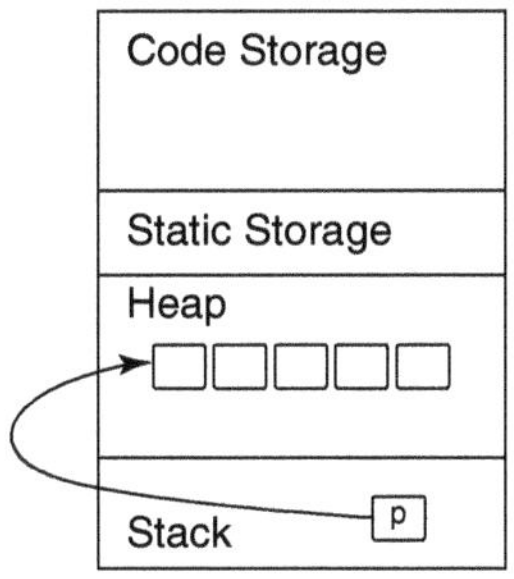


The operator new returns a pointer to the starting address of the object it created. The object needs to be of the same data type as the pointer as illustrated in the drawing.

In the above example the pointer *`myPtr` can only point to an array of integers. The new operator can allocate arrays or individual data types such a single integer, single double, single character etc.

One of the issues with dynamic memory allocation is that there is a finite number of memory cells in the heap (free store). All dynamically allocated memory should be deleted once it has served its purpose. In C++ this is accomplished with the delete operator:

```
#include <iostream>

using namespace std;

const int SIZE = 5;

// Function prototypes
double getAVG(const int *, int );

int main()
{
     int * myPtrArr = new int[SIZE];
     double average;

     myPtrArr[0] = 10;
     myPtrArr[1] = 2;
     myPtrArr[2] = 13;
     myPtrArr[3] = 21;
     myPtrArr[4] = 11;

     average = getAVG(myPtrArr,SIZE); // Notice that it is not necessary
                                      // to supply & because this is already
                                      // a pointer (an address)
     cout << "The average is: " << average << endl;
     delete []myPtrArr;
     return 0;
}
```

```
double getAVG(const int *myArray, int size)
{
    double avg=0.0;
    int sum =0;
    for (int i=0; i<size; i++)
    {
        sum = sum + myArray[i];
    }

    avg = sum/static_cast<double>(size);
    return avg;
}
```

**Listing 13:** Dynamic Memory Allocation and Deallocation

Compiling and running the above program will result in the following output:

```
The average is: 11.4

Process returned 0 (0x0)   execution time : 0.017 s
Press any key to continue.
```

The statement on line 25 in Listing 12 above contains the delete operator. By using the delete operator, the "borrowed" memory from the heap is returned back to the heap. Exit this is known as deallocating memory. Notice the square brackets [ ] preceding the pointer name? That is necessary due to the fact that the pointer is pointing to an array of integers. Had this been a single memory cell (not an array) then they would be no need for the square brackets:

```
int ptrMyInt = new int;
*ptrMyInt = 10;
cout << "ptrMyInt contents: " << *ptrMyInt << endl;
delete ptrMyInt;
```

A lot of novice programmers forget to deallocate the "newed" memory. This is not a big problem for small programs. However if memories allocated dynamically in a loop, eventually the program will run out of available memory in the heap. The consequence is performance degradation of the program. In relatively small programs these type of errors can be found and corrected. On a larger scale programs this task becomes very difficult. In order to prevent this type of predicament a programmer needs to be very diligent when allocating memory dynamically and to deallocate it when the not needed anymore.

## Returning Pointers from Functions

Since dynamically allocated memory resides on the heap if it is allocated inside of a function it will be lost along with all of its data once the function goes out of scope. To prevent this you can return a pointer to the address of dynamically allocated data. The following program illustrates that:

```
#include <iostream>

using namespace std;
```

```
// Function Prototypes
int* getStudentQuizScores(int );
double getAVG(const int *, int );
void displayQuizscores(const int *, int );


int main()
{
    const int QUIZ_COUNT = 5;
    int *ptrMyQuizzes;

    // assign the address of the dynamically allocated memory to
    // to ptrMyQuizzes
    ptrMyQuizzes = getStudentQuizScores(QUIZ_COUNT);
    cout << "\nQuiz Scores: \n";
    displayQuizscores(ptrMyQuizzes, QUIZ_COUNT);

    cout << "\nQuiz Average: " << getAVG(ptrMyQuizzes, QUIZ_COUNT)<< endl;

    // deallocate memory
    delete [] ptrMyQuizzes;
    return 0;
}

int* getStudentQuizScores(int numQuizzes)
{
    // dynamically allocate memory
    int *ptrQuizzes = new int[numQuizzes];

    // prompt the user and store the quiz data in the newly allocated
    // array
    for (int i=0; i<numQuizzes; i++)
    {
        cout << "Quiz " << i+1 <<": ";
        cin >> ptrQuizzes[i];
    }

    // return the address of the dynamically allocated memory
    return ptrQuizzes;

}

void displayQuizscores(const int *myArray, int size)
{
    for (int i=0; i<size; i++)
```

```
50.     {
51.         cout << "Quiz " << i + 1 << ": " <<  myArray[i] << endl;
52.     }
53.
54. }
55. double getAVG(const int *myArray, int size)
56. {
57.     double avg=0.0;
58.     int sum =0;
59.     for (int i=0; i<size; i++)
60.     {
61.         sum = sum + myArray[i];
62.     }
63.
64.     avg = sum/static_cast<double>(size);
65.     return avg;
66. }
```

**Listing 14:** Dynamically Allocating Memory

The program in listing 13 above demonstrates dynamic allocation of an array inside of a function. The function

```
int* getStudentQuizScores(int numQuizzes)
```

returns a pointer to an integer. The array `ptrQuizzes` is dynamically allocated inside of the function getStudentQuizscores. Next the array is populated with the data obtained from the user. Since the array has been declared as a local variable it would go out of scope the moment the function getStudentQuizscores goes out of scope. However the function is designed to return a pointer (an address) to the dynamically allocated memory. Just before the function goes out of scope its returns the address of the dynamically allocated array (line 43).

In the caller program, this address is captured in an integer pointer variable *`ptrMyQuizzes`:

```
int *ptrMyQuizzes;
// assign the address of the dynamically allocated memory to
// to ptrMyQuizzes
ptrMyQuizzes = getStudentQuizScores(QUIZ_COUNT);
```

and is then passed to other functions such as getAVG, and displayQuizScores:

```
    ptrMyQuizzes = getStudentQuizScores(QUIZ_COUNT);
    cout << "\nQuiz Scores: \n";
    displayQuizscores(ptrMyQuizzes, QUIZ_COUNT);
cout << "\nmQuiz Average: " << getAVG(ptrMyQuizzes, QUIZ_COUNT)<< endl;
```

Finally, the memory that was dynamically allocated inside of the getStudentQuizScores function is deallocated ) before the main function terminates—on line 25:

```
delete [] ptrMyQuizzes;
```

compiling and running this program produces the following output:

```
Quiz 1: 75
Quiz 2: 85
Quiz 3: 88
Quiz 4: 68
Quiz 5: 100

Quiz Scores:
Quiz 1: 75
Quiz 2: 85
Quiz 3: 88
Quiz 4: 68
Quiz 5: 100

mQuiz Average: 83.2

Process returned 0 (0x0)   execution time : 10.921 s
Press any key to continue.
```

## End of Chapter Questions

### True/False

**1.** Consider the following 2D array:

```
int numbers[2][3] = {{16,18,20},
                     {25,26,27}};
```

The following pointer notation:

*(*(numbers+1)+1) will point to the memory cell that contains the value of 26?

**2.** Consider the following 2D array:

```
int numbers[2][3] = {{16,18,20},
                     {25,26,27}};
```

The following pointer notation:

*(*(numbers+1)+ 1) will point to the memory cell that contains the value of 26?

**3.** **Static Storage:** used to store global variables and global constants.

**4.** The following statement is the correct way to delete a dynamically allocated array:

```
delete []myPtrArr;
```

**5.** **Stack Storage:** used for calling functions and their parameters and local variables

**6.** When you declare a pointer you cannot assign a value to it:

```
int *p;
*p = 10;
```

### Exercises

**1.** Write a program that uses pointers to set each element of an array to zero.

**2.** Write a function that takes a single string as its argument and returns a pointer to the first nonwhite character in the string.

## Chapter 9

# Handling Text

***"Man suffers only because he takes seriously what the gods made for fun."***

**—Alan Wilson Watts**

When writing command line programs in C++, interacting with the user is usually done via menus. Menu choices are either numeric or alpha (characters). Often, it is necessary to keep the program running until the user selects the exit menu option. A good programming practice (albeit annoying at times) is to provision for errors such as mistyped keys and ask the user whether they are sure they want to exit for example. Their response is usually a single character such as 'y' or 'n'.

Other times, when collecting data from users such as names, addresses, places etc., the program needs to correctly capture user input. Sometimes user input will consist of multiple strings separated by spaces, commas, or some other characters.

In this chapter we are going to explore ways to accomplish this with C++.

## Character Testing

The `<ctype.h>` (site, 2013) header contains functions for character testing:

| Function | Description |
|---|---|
| `int isalnum(int c)` | Returns non-zero (true) if c is an uppercase or lowercase letter. Otherwise, returns a zero. |
| `int isalpha(int c)` | Returns non-zero (true) if c is a digit, uppercase, or lowercase letter. Otherwise, returns a zero. |
| `int iscntrl(int c)` | Returns non-zero (true) if the c is a control character. Otherwise, returns a zero. |
| `int isdigit(int c)` | Returns non-zero (true) if the c is a digit character. Otherwise, returns a zero. |
| `int islower(int c)` | Returns non-zero (true) if the c is the lowercase character. Otherwise, returns a zero. |
| `int isprint(int c)` | Returns non-zero (true) if the c is a printable character including space. Otherwise, returns a zero. |
| `int ispunc(int c)` | Returns non-zero (true) if the c is a printable character except space, letter, or digit. Otherwise, returns a zero. |
| `int isspace(int c)` | Returns non-zero (true) if the c is a white-space character. Otherwise, returns a zero. |
| `int isupper(int c)` | Return non-zero (true) if the c is the uppercase character. Otherwise, return a zero. |

**Table 1:** Character Testing Functions

The above functions have an integer parameter through which they receive an ASCII code for the character that is being tested.

In addition to character testing functions, the `<ctype.h>` also contains function that can be used to convert characters from lowercase to uppercase letters and vice versa. The following table describes these character conversion functions:

| Function | Description |
|---|---|
| `int tolower(int c)` | Converts c to lowercase letter and return the lowercase of c. If c is already a lowercase letter, then returns it |
| `int toupper(int c)` | Converts c to uppercase letter and returns the uppercase of c. If c is already an uppercase letter, then returns it |

**Table 2:** Character Conversion Functions

Following is an example program that showcases some of the functions described above:

```
#include <iostream>
#include <cstdlib>
#include <ctype.h>

using namespace std;

// function prototypes
void menu();

int main()
{
    char userChoice;    // to hold user choice
    char yesOrNo;       // to hold user answer whether they want to continue

    do
    {
        do
        {
            menu();
            cin >> userChoice;

            if (toupper(userChoice) == 'A' )
                cout << "You chose the Checking Account" << endl;
            else if (toupper(userChoice) == 'B')
                cout << "You chose the Savings Account" << endl;
            else if (toupper(userChoice) == 'C')
                cout << "You chose the Money Market Account" << endl;
            else if (toupper(userChoice) == 'D')
            {
                cout << "Are you sure you want to exit(Y/N)?:";
                cin >> yesOrNo;
```

```
            }
            else
            {
                cout << "Please enter A, B, C, or D only!" << endl;
                cout << "Your choice:";
                cin >> userChoice;
            }
        }while (toupper(userChoice) != 'D');
    }while(tolower(yesOrNo) != 'y');        // purposely using tolower

    return 0;
}

void menu()
{
    cout << "M E N U " << endl;
    cout << "A. Checking Account" << endl;
    cout << "B. Savings Account" << endl;
    cout << "C. Money Market" << endl;
    cout << "D. Exit" << endl;
    cout << "Your choice:";
}
```

**Listing 1:** Using <ctype.h> Functions

Compiling and running the code produces the following output:

```
M E N U
A. Checking Account
B. Savings Account
C. Money Market
D. Exit
Your choice:a
You chose the Checking Account
M E N U
A. Checking Account
B. Savings Account
C. Money Market
D. Exit
Your choice:d
Are you sure you want to exit(Y/N)?:n
M E N U
A. Checking Account
B. Savings Account
C. Money Market
D. Exit
Your choice:d
Are you sure you want to exit(Y/N)?:y

Process returned 0 (0x0)   execution time : 14.707 s
Press any key to continue.
```

Note how user input is in the above program output all in lowercase. Without toupper (or tolower) function, we would need to perform extra check in the code:

```
while (userChoice != 'D' || userChoice !='d');
```

Using <ctype.h> header functions definitely simplifies code which makes it easier to debug and maintain. Next, we discuss strings which are nothing more than series of characters.

## C-Style Strings

The C++ programming language was originally labeled "C with Classes" by Bjarne Stroustrup (Wikipedia) who set out to augment the C language with object oriented features. Thus there are two types of strings in C++, the C-style strings and C++ style strings.

C-Style strings are a null terminated character arrays. Declaring an array of characters is no different than declaring an array of any other data type. The only difference is that for character arrays (C-Style strings), the last element of the array is null (a zero). For example, the following character array:

```
char name[] = "Joe";
```

is represented in memory in the following manner:

**name**

| 'J' | 'o' | 'e' | '\0' |
|---|---|---|---|
| 0 | 1 | 2 | 3 |

**Figure 1:** char Array name Represented in Memory

The null character is extremely important because it signals the end of input to functions (discussed a little bit later on in this chapter) designed to perform a variety of operations on C style strings. Some literature represents the null character as '\0' but in reality a character array is terminated with a zero. How is it possible to mix data types because a zero (0) is an integer? Recall, that integers and characters are interchangeable due to the fact that each character has an ASCII code which is an integer. The contents of the name array are stored in memory as:

**name**

| 74 | 111 | 101 | '\0' |
|---|---|---|---|
| 0 | 1 | 2 | 3 |

**Figure 2:** Contents of the char Array name Represented in Memory

Where 'J'=74, 'o' = 111, 'e' = 101, followed by the 0 (null).

## Correctly Dimensioning Character Arrays

As a programmer, you must ensure adequate size for your character arrays including the null (terminating) character. Consider the following array declarations:

```
const int SIZE = 5;
int numbers[SIZE];
char make[SIZE];
```

number

| | | | | |
|---|---|---|---|---|
| 0 | 1 | 2 | 3 | 4 |

make

| | | | | |
|---|---|---|---|---|
| 0 | 1 | 2 | 3 | 4 |

**Figure 3:** Arrays in Memory

Both arrays consist of five members. The difference is that in an integer array the last array member can be used to store data, whereas in the character array and the last member is used for the null character.

number

| 10 | 20 | 30 | 40 | 50 |
|---|---|---|---|---|
| 0 | 1 | 2 | 3 | 4 |

make

| 'F' | 'i' | 'a' | 't' | '\0' |
|---|---|---|---|---|
| 0 | 1 | 2 | 3 | 4 |

**Figure 4:** Array Contents

What is the difference between the following two declarations?

```
char name[] = "Joe";
char make[SIZE];
```

In the first declaration (the name array), the compiler implicitly allocates memory for the array based on the size (length) of the string literal that is being assigned to the address of the array. In fact, all string literals, such as "Hello World", "Please enter your name", etc., are always terminated with a null character. The compiler allocates the necessary memory for string literals and appends the null character at the end.

```
char greeting[] = "Hello world!";
```

The compiler would allocate enough memory to store each character in the string literal "Hello world!" plus one extra character for the null terminating character. These are character arrays so it is possible to initialize the array with character initialization list:

```
char greeting[] = {'H','e','l','l','o',' ', 'w','o','r','l','d','!','\0'};
```

Note the null character at the end.

Back to the question of difference between the two array declarations, the make array is limited by the SIZE constant. Even though the string literal "Fiat" contains four characters and the make array is large enough to accommodate the string literal and the terminating null character the compiler would throw a syntax error:

```
const int SIZE = 5;
char make[SIZE];
make = "Fiat";   // this is illegal!!!
```

This is due to the fact that you can never assign string literals to character arrays after that have been created and dimensioned (given a size):

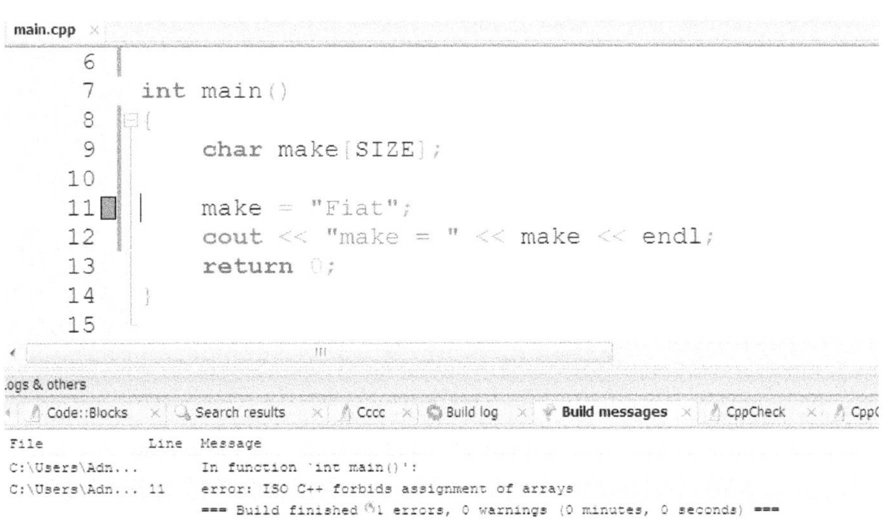


**Figure 5:** Assigning a String Literal to an Array Results in a Syntax Error

Instead, you need to use the getline function to copy the contents of a string literal into the array:

```
cin.getline(make, SIZE);
```

You could accomplish the same thing with the following statement:

```
cin >> make;
```

Recall how the cin object reads from standard input. If the user were to input single words, the above statement would capture user input correctly. The problem arises when the user enters input that contains white space such as "Mercedes Benz" for example. The cin object would capture only the first word and stop reading from the standard input when it encountered the white space. To read user input correctly, use the getline function.

## Conversion Functions

As a programmer, you will often need to convert the data from one format to another. For example, your program may read the data from an input file which contains strings that look like numbers:

```
"100.56"
"20"
```

The data types would not be an issue if you were to simply read the data from a comma delimited file and display the data neatly formatted on the screen. However, the reality is that most of the time, you will need to write programs that perform some kind of operations on the input.

Similarly, you may need to convert your numeric data to a string for the purpose of displaying it, or simply because of the requirements of the project. Perhaps your program's output is an input to another program that expects the data as strings.

Whatever the case may be, the C++ language has libraries to help with such tasks. For type conversions, you need to include the <cstdlib> library.

```
#include <iostream>
#include <cstdlib>

using namespace std;

int main()
{
    char myNumberAsString[] = "12345";
    int number = atoi(myNumberAsString);

    cout << "This is my number as a string  : " << myNumberAsString << endl;
    cout << "This is my number as an integer: " << number << endl;
```

```
13.
14.     cout << "Number after adding 10: " << number + 10 << endl;
15.     return 0;
16. }
```

**Listing 2:** Conversion Functions

On line 8 in the above program listing a character array myNumberAsString takes on the value of a string literal. We convert that string literal to an integer by using the atoi function from the cstdlib library (included on line 2). By using the atoi function, it is possible to perform math operations (line 14) on the numeric equivalent of the C-string variable. Compiling and executing the above program produces the following output:

```
This is my number as a string  : 12345
This is my number as an integer: 12345
Number after adding 10: 12355

Process returned 0 (0x0)   execution time : 0.011 s
Press any key to continue.
```

If the character array is alpha numeric, the conversion to an integer using the atoi function will result in the numeric value:

```
char myPhrase[] = "123AbC";
int x = atoi(myPhrase);
cout << myPhrase << " converted to an integer is : " << x << endl;
```

```
123AbC converted to an integer is : 123

Process returned 0 (0x0)   execution time : 0.012 s
Press any key to continue.
```

Besides the atoi function, there are a few more functions in cstdlib: atof, atol, itoa, and ltoa. One way to remember function names is to understand that the first letter in the function name specifies the data type from which to convert. So "a" is alpha (or C-string), "i" is an integer, "l" is a long and so on. The word "to" specifies the conversion direction. The last letter in the function specifies the data type to convert. Thus, atoi is means **a**lpha ***to*** **i**nteger. Similarly, itoa means **i**nteger ***to*** **a**lpha.

Next, we will review the details of conversion functions.

## The atof Function

This function accepts a constant pointer to a character array (C string), performs the conversion and returns an integer to the caller:

```
char myNumberAsString[] = "12345.123";
double number = atof(myNumberAsString);
```

## The atol Function

This function accepts a constant pointer to a character array (C string), performs the conversion and returns a long to the caller:

```
char myNumberAsString[] = "12345";
long number = atol(myNumberAsString);
```

## The itoa Function

The itoa function was built to provide conversion from numeric value (integer) to a C string. The itoa function is a void function as it does not return any values. It takes three parameters:

- the numeric value that will be converted to a C string,
- a pointer to the character array where the converted C string will be stored, and
- the last parameter is the base of the converted value. The base can be base 10 (decimal), base 16 (hexadecimal), and base 8(octal).

Consider the following:

```
int number = 12345;
char myNumberAsString[SIZE];
itoa(number, myNumberAsString, 10);
```

## The ltoa Function

Just like the itoa function, the itoa function was built to provide conversion from numeric value (long) to a C string. The ltoa function is a void function as it does not return any values. It takes three parameters:

- the numeric value that will be converted to a C string,
- a pointer to the character array where the converted C string will be stored, and
- the last parameter is the base of the converted value. The base can be base 10 (decimal), base 16 (hexadecimal), and base 8(octal).

Consider the following:

```
long x = 172885;
char charArr[10];
ltoa(x, charArr, 16);
cout << x << " (decimal) is: " << charArr << " (hexadecimal)."
     << endl;
```

The ltoa function will convert the long value x to a C string using base 16 (hexadecimal) and store the resulting C-string in charArr array. Following is a program run of the above code segment:

```
172885 (decimal) is: 2a355 (hexadecimal).

Process returned 0 (0x0)   execution time : 0.010 s
Press any key to continue.
```

A word of caution when using conversion functions since the compiler does not perform any bounds checking, the programmer needs to make sure the array in which the converted C-string value is going to be stored is dimensioned correctly to accommodate the string as well as the terminating null character.

## Other C-string Functions

The functions described in this section require the <string.h> header. Basically, there are two groups of functions in the <string.h> header - one group whose names start with the prefix "mem" and the other group whose names start with the prefix "str". The "mem" prefixed functions are designed to perform operations on memory blocks. The "str" functions are designed to perform operations on character strings. Besides functions designed to operate on memory and on strings, the functions found in the <string.h> header can be classified (site, 2013) as follows:

- copying (strcpy, strncpy)
- concatenation (strcat, strncat)
- comparison(strcmp, strncmp)
- searching (strchr, strstr, strtok, strrchr)
- other (strlen)

### *Copying*

**The strcpy Function** The strcpy function takes in two pointer parameters, a destination array and a constant pointer to the source array. It returns a pointer to the destination array:

```
char* strcpy(char *destination, const char* source);
```

Successful execution of this function hinges upon the following:

- the source array being properly terminated with a null character. The terminating character signals the stopping condition to the function.
- The size of the destination array needs to be large enough to accommodate the source string including the terminating null character.

The compiler does not check destination array boundaries when performing the copy, thus it is very easy to overwrite the memory beyond array boundaries.

**The strncpy Function** The strncpy function is much safer because it forces the programmer to specify the number of characters that are being copied. The syntax is very similar to the strcpy function with one additional parameter which specifies the maximum number of characters that can be copied from the source array:

```
char * strncpy (char *destination, const char *source, size_t num);
```

In case the source array length is smaller than the number of characters that are being copied to the destination array, the compiler will pad the destination array with zeros to make up the difference between the length of the source array and the number of characters being copied.

```
char source[] = "ABC";
char destination[10];
strncpy(destination, source, 4);
cout << "Destination:" << destination << "." << endl;
```

Compiling and running the above code segment would result in the following output:

```
Destination:ABC.

Process returned 0 (0x0)   execution time : 0.020 s
Press any key to continue.
```

### *Concatenation*

The concatenation (appending a string to the end of another string) is done via the strcat and strncat functions.

**The strcat Function** The strcat function takes two parameters—the destination array and the source array:

```
char *strcat ( char *destination, const char *source );
```

The source array is a constant pointer to prevent any accidental overrides of the original (source) array. The strcat function copies the contents of the source array to the end of the destination array, overriding the null termination character. Finally, a null termination character is added to the end of the newly formed string and the strcat function returns a pointer to the newly formed string.

The following program listing demonstrates a simple string copy and string concatenation:

```
#include <iostream>
#include <string.h>

using namespace std;

const int SIZE = 25;

int main()
{
    char firstName[SIZE];
    char middleInitial[2];
    char lastName[SIZE];
    char fullName[SIZE*3];

    // obtain the data from the user
    cout << "First Name: ";
    cin.getline(firstName, SIZE);
    cout << "Middle Initial: ";
    cin.getline(middleInitial, SIZE);
```

```
20.     cout << "Last Name: ";
21.     cin.getline(lastName, SIZE);
22.
23.     strncpy(fullName, firstName, SIZE);
24.     strcat(fullName, " ");
25.     strcat(fullName, middleInitial);
26.     strcat(fullName,".");
27.     strcat(fullName, " ");
28.     strcat(fullName, lastName);
29.     cout << "Your full name: " << fullName << endl;
30.     return 0;
31. }
```

**Listing 3:** strcpy and strcat Functions

The program starts off by allocating necessary arrays to store the values of first name, middle initial, and the last name. It then prompts the user to enter this information. The first name array is copied to the full name array (line 23). The reason for this is that concatenation would not work given that the fullName array has not been initialized with data. For all we know, there could be some information ('garbage") in the memory location allocated for the array. Hence, we use the strncpy function to copy the contents of the firstName array to the fullName array, initializing the fullName array in the process. Next, the program concatenates a space (" "), the middle initial, a dot (".") and the last name:

```
First Name: Adnan
Middle Initial: F
Last Name: Zejnilovic
Your full name: Adnan F. Zejnilovic

Process returned 0 (0x0)   execution time : 8.119 s
Press any key to continue.
```

The strcat function is dangerous in a sense that it does not perform array boundary checking therefore it is possible to write beyond the bounds of the destination array. Fortunately, there is a safer variant of the function called strncat where "n" number of characters are concatenated.

**The strncat Funciton** The strncat function appends N" number of characters to the destination array plus the terminating null character at the end of the newly formed array. It takes an additional parameter which specifies umber of characters that will be concatenated:

```
char *strncat ( char *destination, const char *source, size_t num );
```

If the length of the source string is less than the number of characters that are to be copied, then only the characters up to the null terminating character are copied to the destination array. The newly formed string is terminated with the null terminating character. The programmer must make sure that the destination array is large enough so it can hold the concatenated strings as well as the terminating null character.

### *Comparison*

The C-string comparison functions include strcmp and a little bit safer strncmp function.

**The strcmp Function** The strcmp function compares two strings which are passed to it as arguments. The comparison is performed character by character from left to right. The function terminates the comparison if one of the following conditions is true:

- The characters compared are not equal
- It reaches the terminating (null) character

Following is the strcmp syntax:

```
int strcmp (const char *str1, const char *str2);
```

The strcmp function returns an integer describing the relationship between the two strings (site, 2013). The return value is interpreted as follows:

$$\texttt{strcmp(str1, str2)} = \begin{cases} >0, & \texttt{str1 > str2} \\ =0, & \texttt{str1==str2} \\ <0, & \texttt{str2 > str1} \end{cases}$$

If the return value is equal to 0, the strings are equal. If the return value is less than zero, then the first string is greater than the second string. Otherwise, if the integer returned from the strcmp function is less than zero, then the second string is greater than the first string.

**The strncmp Function** The strncmp (site, 2013) function works exactly the same as the strcmp function with one exception - it compares certain number of characters (passed in as the 3rd parameter) instead of comparing all characters. Following is the strcmp syntax:

```
int strncmp(const char *str1, const char *str2, size_t num);
```

Where str1 is a pointer to the first string, str2 is a pointer to the second string, and the last parameter num is the number of characters that are to be compared. The function returns an integer which describes the relationship between the two strings:

$$\texttt{strncmp(str1, str2)} = \begin{cases} >0, & \texttt{str1 > str2} \\ =0, & \texttt{str1==str2} \\ <0, & \texttt{str2 > str1} \end{cases}$$

The following program illustrates the strncmp function:

```
#include <iostream>
#include <string.h>

using namespace std;

int main()
```

```
7. {
8.     char courseAbbr[][20] = {"CGS1060",
9.                              "COP1334",
10.                             "COP2335",
11.                             "COP2800",
12.                             "COP 2805"};
13.    int count=0;
14.    for (int i=0; i<5; i++)
15.    {
16.        if (strncmp(courseAbbr[i], "COP", 3) == 0)
17.            count = count + 1;
18.    }
19.    cout << "You are teaching " << count << " COP courses" << endl;
20.    return 0;
21. }
```

**Listing 4:** The strncmp Function Example

The program starts by declaring and initializing an array of coarse abbreviations (line 8). Next, we loop through the array and compare abbreviated course names to the COP prefix (line 16). Rather than comparing the entire strength, only the first the characters are compared and if there is a match (the strncmp function returns a 0) we add one to the count of the COP courses. When the loop terminates the program displays the number of COP courses taught by the instructor:

```
You are teaching 4 COP courses

Process returned 0 (0x0)   execution time : 0.015 s
Press any key to continue.
```

### *Searching*

**Searching for Characters** To search for a character in a string, C++ provides the following functions (site, 2013):

| Function | Description |
|---|---|
| `char *strchr(char * str, int c);` | Returns a pointer to the FIRST occurrence of the character (int c) in the str string. If not found, returns a NULL. |
| `char * strrchr(char * str, int c);` | Returns a pointer to the LAST occurrence of the character (int c) in the str string. Also, since the null terminating character is considered part of the string, the strrchr function can be used to retrieve the end of the string. If the character searched for is not found, the function returns a NULL. |

**Table 3:** Character Search Functions

Following code listing is an example of the strchr function:

```
#include <iostream>
#include <string.h>

using namespace std;

int main()
{
    char state[] = "Mississippi";
    char* statePtr;

    cout << "Character i in " << state << endl;

    statePtr = strchr(state, 'i');

    while(statePtr!=NULL)
    {
        cout << "was found in location: " << statePtr - state+1 << endl;
        statePtr = strchr(statePtr+1, 'i');
    }

    return 0;
}
```

**Listing 5:** The strchr Function Example

The program in Listing 5 above, searches for the location of letter 'i' in the "Mississippi". Once it finds it, it reports the location where the letter was found in the string:

```
Character i in Mississippi
was found in location: 2
was found in location: 5
was found in location: 8
was found in location: 11

Process returned 0 (0x0)   execution time : 0.016 s
Press any key to continue.
```

**Searching for (Sub)Strings** To search for a substring within another string C++ provides the following functions:

| Function | Description |
|---|---|
| `char *strstr(char *str1, const char *str2);` | Searches for the first occurrence of the string str2 in str1. If found, returns the pointer to the location in str1. Otherwise it returns a NULL. |
| `char *strtok(char *str, const char *delim);` | Splits the str string into tokens (sub strings). The str string needs to contain delimiters which are characters separating substrings. The function looks for delimiters as it splits the string into tokens. The tokens can consist of a single token, or a set of tokens. |

**Table 4:** String Search Functions

## The strstr Function

The following program demonstrates the strstr function:

```
#include <iostream>
#include <string.h>

using namespace std;

int main()
{
    char nbaTeam[] = "Michael Jordan played for the Atlanta Bulls";
    char *ptrSS;          // pointer to a substring

    cout << "Original string : " << nbaTeam << endl;

    // find the position of the substring "Atlanta"
    ptrSS = strstr(nbaTeam,"Atlanta");

    // replace it with "Chicago"
    strncpy(ptrSS,"Chicago", 7);

    // display corrected string
    cout << "Corrected string: " << nbaTeam <<endl;

    return 0;
}
```

**Listing 6:** The strstr Function Demo

In the above program, the original character array (C - string) contains an error. We utilized the strstr function to locate the substring and replace it with the correct substring with the help of the strncpy function. The output of Listing 6 program is displayed below:

```
Original string : Michael Jordan played for the Atlanta Bulls
Corrected string: Michael Jordan played for the Chicago Bulls

Process returned 0 (0x0)   execution time : 0.014 s
Press any key to continue.
```

## The strtok Function

The following program demonstrates the strtok function:

```
#include <iostream>
#include <string.h>

using namespace std;
```

```

int main()
{
    char simpleList[] = "Miami Heat,Orlando Magic,Chicago Bulls,Boston Celtics";
    char *tokenPtr;
    tokenPtr = strtok(simpleList,",");

    while (tokenPtr!=NULL)
    {
        cout << tokenPtr << endl;
        tokenPtr = strtok(NULL,",");
    }


    return 0;
}
```

**Listing 7:** The strtok Function Simple Example

```
Miami Heat
Orlando Magic
Chicago Bulls
Boston Celtics

Process returned 0 (0x0)   execution time : 0.013 s
Press any key to continue.
```

The above program, contained a single delimiter—a comma (","). It is possible to have more than one delimiter, a delimiter list as demonstrated below:

```
#include <iostream>
#include <string.h>

using namespace std;

int main()
{
    char simpleList[] = "Testing, multiple| tokens: what | else - is - new +";
    char *tokenPtr;
    tokenPtr = strtok(simpleList,",|-+: ");

    while (tokenPtr!=NULL)
    {
        cout << tokenPtr << endl;
```

```
15.        tokenPtr = strtok(NULL,",|-+: ");
16.     }
17.
18.
19.     return 0;
20. }
```

**Listing 8:** The strtok Function with a Token List

In Listing 7, the second parameter to the strtok function is a delimiter list (",|-+: ")—on line 10 and line 15. The strtok function parses the string and splits it into substrings (tokens) as it encounters any of the delimiters in the delimiter list. In listing 7, there are six delimiters: ",|-+: " (there is a space character right after the ":" delimiter). Compiling and running the program in listing seven produces the following output:

```
Testing
multiple
tokens
what
else
is
new

Process returned 0 (0x0)   execution time : 0.013 s
Press any key to continue.
```

### *Finding the Length of a String*

Consider the following code segment:

```
#include <iostream>
#include <string.h>

using namespace std;

const int SIZE = 25;

int main()
{
    char studentName[SIZE];
    cout << "Please enter your full name: ";
    cin.getline(studentName, SIZE);

     // test the strlen function
     cout << "There are " << strlen(studentName)
          << " characters in your name" << endl;
    return 0;
}
```

**Listing 9:** strlen Function Demonstration

The following is the output of the above program run:

```
Please enter your full name: Dwyane Wade
There are 11 characters in your name

Process returned 0 (0x0)   execution time : 9.525 s
Press any key to continue.
```

Analyzing the program in Listing 3, the first thing that takes place is allocation of the studentName character array:

studentName

| | | | | | | | | | | | | |
|---|---|---|---|---|---|---|---|---|---|---|---|---|
| | | | | | | | | | | | ... | |
| 0 | 1 | 2 | 3 | 4 | 5 | 6 | 7 | 8 | 9 | 10 | ... | 24 |

**Figure 6:** studentName Array Allocated in Memory

The array is capable of storing up to 25 characters (24 characters plus the null terminating character). On line number 12, the getline function reads user input and stores it in the studentName array:

studentName

| | | | | | | | | | | | | | | |
|---|---|---|---|---|---|---|---|---|---|---|---|---|---|---|
| 'D' | 'w' | 'y' | 'a' | 'n' | 'e' | | 'W' | 'a' | 'd' | 'e' | '\o' | | ... | |
| 0 | 1 | 2 | 3 | 4 | 5 | 6 | 7 | 8 | 9 | 10 | 11 | 12 | ... | 24 |

**Figure 7:** studentName Array Populated with User Input.

The getline function appends the null character as the last character in the array which raises character counts to 12. Yet in the program reports only 11 characters (see figure 5). The strlen function returns the length of a string, but it does not take the null character into consideration.

## C++ string Class

The string class is part of the C++ standard library and it requires requires the <string> header. This is not the same as the <string.h> header (Stroustrup, 2009) used for C strings (character arrays). The string class has a variety of member functions, too many to list them all here. Please refer to a good C++ reference manual. We're going to describe the most used basic member functions such as string length, concatenation, comparison, and the C string equivalent member function.

Unlike character arrays, strings the notes needs to be dimensioned prior to their use as the compiler will allocate appropriate block of memory:

```
#include <iostream>
#include <string>        // note the header!!!

using namespace std;

int main()
{
        string firstName;   // no need to set the size
```

```
    firstName = "Adi";
    cout << "Your name is: " << firstName << endl;
    return 0;
}
```

**Listing 10:** The string Class

## Assigning Strings

Assigning strings is done via the assignment (=) operator. Consider the following code segment:

```
1. string firstName = "Adnan";
2. string lastName = "Zejnilovic";
3. firstName = lastName;
4. cout << "First name: " << firstName << endl;
```

**Listing 11:** Using the Assignment Operator with Strings

The contents of the variable firstName are wiped out on line 3 when the contents of the variable lastName are copied into the variable firstName.

```
First name: Zejnilovic

Process returned 0 (0x0)   execution time : 0.013 s
Press any key to continue.
```

The assignment operator (=) should not be confused with the equal operator (==) which is used to compare two strings.

## Concatenating Strings

String concatenation is very simple when using the string class. Consider the following program:

```
#include <iostream>
#include <string>

using namespace std;

int main()
{
    string firstName = "Adnan";
    string middleInitial = "F";
    string lastName = "Zejnilovic";
    string fullName;

    fullName = firstName + " " + middleInitial + "." + " " + lastName;

    cout << "Full name: " << fullName << endl;
    return 0;
}
```

**Listing 12:** String Concatenation using the string Class

Variable declarations and initializations are done on lines 8 through 11. To concatenate one or more strings using the string class, all you need to do is use the "+" (concatenation) operator (line 13). There is no need to worry about string sizes as the compiler will automatically resize strings when needed. In addition to concatenating string objects, string literals can also be concatenated via the + operator. On line 13, we concatenate a few space string literals as well as the dot (.) string literal.

Compiling and running the above program creates the following output:

```
Full name: Adnan F. Zejnilovic

Process returned 0 (0x0)   execution time : 0.029 s
Press any key to continue.
```

## String Comparisons

Comparing strings can be done through the equal operator (==), the not equal operator (!=), And the less than (<) operator.

### The == and != Operators

To determine if two strings are equal, use the equal operator. The following table presents the equal (==) operator's operands, code examples and outcomes:

| Operands | Code | Result |
|---|---|---|
| `two string objects` | string s1 = "abc";<br>string s2 = "DEF";<br>if (s1 == s2)<br>  cout << "Equal";<br>else<br>  cout << "NOT Equal"; | NOT Equal |
| `one string object and one C string` | string s1 = "abc";<br>char s2[] = "abc";<br>if (s1 == s2)<br>  cout << "Equal";<br>else<br>  cout << "NOT Equal"; | Equal |
| `one string object and one string literal` | string s1 = "abc";<br>if (s1 == "abC")<br>  cout << "Equal";<br>else<br>  cout << "NOT Equal"; | NOT Equal |

**Table 5:** Operator == and Possible Operands

You can also test whether to strings are not equal with the use of the not equal (!=) operator.

The following program listing demonstrates some of the functions described above:

```
string firstName = "David";    // Note: this is a string object
    char lastName[] = "David";    // note: this is a C string
    string middleName = "Larry";

    // compare two string objects
```

```
cout << "Compare two string objects" << endl;
if (firstName == middleName)
    cout << "First name and middle name are the same" << endl;
else
    cout << "First name and middle name are NOT the same"<< endl;

// compare string object to an array of characters (C string)
cout << "\n\nCompare string object to a C string" << endl;
if (firstName == lastName)
    cout << "First name and last name are the same" << endl;
else
    cout << "First name and last name are NOT the same"<< endl;

// compare a string object to a string literal
cout << "\n\nCompare string object to a string literal" << endl;
if (firstName == "Adnan")
    cout << "Equal";
else
    cout << "NOT Equal";
```

**Listing 13:** Testing Strings, C strings, and String Literals For Equality

Compiling and running the above program segment produces the following output:

```
Compare two string objects
First name and middle name are NOT the same


Compare string object to a C string
First name and last name are the same


Compare string object to a string literal
NOT Equal
Process returned 0 (0x0)   execution time : 0.021 s
Press any key to continue.
```

## Comparison <, >, <=, >= Operators

Similarly to the equal(==) operator, one of the comparison operator's operands can be a C string, but not both. Following code example compares two string objects:

```
string s1 = "ABC";
string s2 = "abc";

if (s1 > s2)
    cout << "s1 > s2" << endl;
else if (s2 > s1 )
    cout << "s2 > s1" << endl;
else if (s1 == s1)
    cout << "s1 == s2" << endl;
```

**Listing 14:** Comparison Operators Examples

When two strings are compared, the result of the comparison can be greater than zero, equal to zero or less than zero:

$$(\texttt{str1 > str2}) = \begin{cases} >0, & \texttt{str1 > str2} \\ =0, & \texttt{str1==str2} \\ <0, & \texttt{str2 > str1} \end{cases}$$

Other comparison operators work in similar way.

## Capacity Member Functions

### Finding the Length of a String

The length member function is used to determine the length of a string. Its syntax is as follows:

```
size_t length() const;
```

It returns the number of characters for a particular string. We can expand on the program above to get the length of the firstName:

```
1. int main()
2. {
3.      string firstName;    // no need to set the size
4.      firstName = "Adi";
5.      cout << "Your name is: " << firstName << endl;
6.      cout << "And it is " << firstName.length() << " characters long" << endl;
7.      return 0;
8. }
```

**Listing 15:** The length() Function

Notice the function call on line number six:

```
firstName.length();
```

This is necessary because the variable firstName is of data type string which is an object. In C++, we use the dot (.) operator to invoke objects member function. Compiling and running this program would produce the following output:

```
Your name is: Adi
And it is 3 characters long

Process returned 0 (0x0)   execution time : 0.008 s
Press any key to continue.
```

Keep in mind that the length function does not return the storage capacity of the string object, but merely the number of characters occupied by the contents of the string.

### The max_size Function

To find out the maximum number of characters that can be stored in the string object, call the max_size function:

```
string headline = "Miami Heat";
cout << "Max size: " << headline.max_size() << endl;
```

```
Max size: 1073741820

Process returned 0 (0x0)   execution time : 0.022 s
Press any key to continue.
```

### The capacity Function

The capacity function returns the number of characters allocated for the string. Keep in mind that the capacity will either be equal to the string length or larger. The string capacity is automatically expanded when needed—for example when appending a string to existing string.

```
string headline = "Miami Heat";
cout << "Max size: " << headline.max_size() << endl;
cout << "Capacity: " << headline.capacity() << endl;
cout << "Length: " << headline.length() << endl;
```

```
Max size: 1073741820
Capacity: 10
Length: 10

Process returned 0 (0x0)   execution time : 0.022 s
Press any key to continue.
```

## Accessing Elements

### Operator []

The operator[] facilitates access if individual characters through index—the same way a character array element would be accessed.

```
string headline = "Miami Heat";
for (int i=0; i<headline.length(); i++)
{
   cout << "Position " << i << " : " << headline[i] << endl;
}
```

```
Position 0 : M
Position 1 : i
Position 2 : a
Position 3 : m
Position 4 : i
Position 5 :
Position 6 : H
Position 7 : e
Position 8 : a
Position 9 : t

Process returned 0 (0x0)   execution time : 0.071 s
Press any key to continue.
```

### Functions at, back[1], and front[2]

The same can be accomplished with the at function:

```
string headline = "Miami Heat";
for (int i=0; i<headline.length(); i++)
{
    cout << "Position " << i << " : " << headline.at(i)
    << endl;
}
```

Function back and front are new additions (C++ 11) to the <string> header and as the name implies they return the first and the last character in the string respectively.

## Searching for a Substring

In this section, we will demonstrate how to search for a particular substring in a string and also if found how to extract (copy) that string to another string.

The string class provides the find function which returns the position of the target substring:

```
1. string address = "123 Main Street, Miami, FL 33134";
2.     string target = "Miami";
3.     cout << "My address is: " << address << endl;
4.     int pos = address.find(target);
5.
6.     // defensive programming: if the target was not found, report
7.     // an error, and exit
8.     if (pos)
9.     {
10.        // target was found, copy the length number of characters
11.        // into the substring and display it
12.        string city = address.substr(pos, target.length());
13.        cout << "I live in the city of : " << city << endl;
14.    }
15.    else
16.    {
17.        cout << "Sorry I could not find the target string. Exiting..." << endl;
18.        exit(0);
19.    }
```

**Listing 16:** Using the find and substr Functions

If the find member function is not successful in locating the target substring, it will return −1. A good programming practice is to use defensive programming (line 8) to prevent possible crashes. If the find member function succeeds in finding the target string within the source string, then we simply call the substr member function passing it the beginning location from where to start copying and the number of characters that we want copied into the substring.

[1] C++ 11
[2] C++ 11

In the example above, we use the length of the target string for number of characters that are to be copied.

Compiling and running this program produces the following output:

```
My address is: 123 Main Street, Miami, FL 33134
I live in the city of : Miami

Process returned 0 (0x0)   execution time : 0.021 s
Press any key to continue.
```

## Modifying a String

Modifying a string can be accomplished through the insert and replace member functions. The insert member function is very versatile as it has many overrides allowing it to receive data through parameters of different data types (strings, sub strings, C string, a single character, etc.). Following is the syntax for the insert member function (site, 2013):

| | |
|---|---|
| string (1) | `string& insert (size_t pos, const string& str);` |
| substring (2) | `string& insert (size_t pos, const string& str, size_t subpos, size_t sublen);` |
| c-string (3) | `string& insert (size_t pos, const char* s);` |
| buffer (4) | `string& insert (size_t pos, const char* s, size_t n);` |
| fill (5) | `string& insert (size_t pos, size_t n, char c);`<br>`void insert (iterator p, size_t n, char c);` |
| single character (6) | `iterator insert (iterator p, char c);` |
| range (7) | `template <class InputIterator>`<br>`void insert (iterator p, InputIterator first, InputIterator last);` |

**Table 6:** Syntax for the insert Member Function

From the syntax it is evident that this function is designed to insert additional characters into the string right before the character referenced by the pos parameter (site, 2013).

The following code segment demonstrates the insert member function:

```
string nbaChampions = "The 2013 Champions - Yooour Miami Heat!!!";
cout << "Sports News Headline: " << nbaChampions << endl;
cout << "Something is missing here...Champions of what? NASCAR?" << endl;
cout << "Let\'s insert NBA into it!" << endl;
 int pos = nbaChampions.find("Champions");
// Defensive programming
if (pos)
{
    nbaChampions.insert(pos,"NBA ");
    cout << "\n\nHere it is: \n\n";
    cout << nbaChampions << endl;
}
```

```
else
{
    cout << "Could not find the target string. Exiting..." << endl;
    exit(0);
}
```

**Listing 17:** The insert Member Function

We get the following output when we compile and execute the code in listing 17 above:

```
Sports News Headline: The 2013 Champions - Yooour Miami Heat!!!
Something is missing here...Champions of what? NASCAR?
Let's insert NBA into it!


Here it is:

The 2013 NBA Champions - Yooour Miami Heat!!!

Process returned 0 (0x0)   execution time : 0.023 s
Press any key to continue.
```

## Working with Legacy Code

Most legacy functions that use C strings receive the data through char pointer parameters. To maintain backward compatibility with legacy code, the string object has a member function c_str() that converts the string object to a character pointer.

The following code segment demonstrates how to use the c_str() member function:

```
string firstName = "Adi";
string middleInitial = " F. ";
string lastName = "Zejnilovic";
char fullName[100];

// compose the full name using C string functions
strcpy(fullName,firstName.c_str());
strcat(fullName, middleInitial.c_str());
strcat(fullName, lastName.c_str());
cout << "This is my full name is: " << fullName << endl;
```

The three variables firstName, middleInitial, and lastName are string objects. Variable fullName is a character array capable of holding 100 characters. We will use the fullName variable to build person's full name from first name, middle initial, and the last name strings. To make things interesting, we use legacy functions strcpy and strcat both of which require parameters to be C strings (character arrays). Using the c_str() member function from the string object is an elegant way to provide the correct data type to these legacy functions. Compiling and executing the above code we get the following output:

```
This is my full name is: Adi F. Zejnilovic

Process returned 0 (0x0)   execution time : 0.016 s
Press any key to continue.
```

## Conclusion

It is much easier to work with string objects then C strings. Working with the string object is also less error-prone. However the programmer needs to be careful and employ defensive programming techniques especially when working with legacy code as the string object provides necessary conversions for interaction with legacy functions.

## End of Chapter Questions

### True/False

Indicate whether the statement is true or false.

1. The atoi function from the cstdlib library converts int to String literal.
2. The strcat function from the <string.h> library takes two parameters, the destination array and the source array.
3. The strcmp(f, s) function from the <string.h> library returns > 0 if f > s, < 0 if f < s and 0 if f == s.

### Exercises

1. Using the <ctype.h> library, write the use of the following functions.
   a. `int isalnum(int c)`
   b. `int isalpha(int c)`
   c. `int islower(int c)`
   d. `int issupper(int c)`
   e. `int tolower(int c)`
2. What makes different C-Style string array to the rest of the data type arrays?

# Chapter 10

# Abstract Data Types

*"The more you know, the less you need."*

—Yvon Chouinard, *Let My People Go Surfing: The Education of a Reluctant Businessman*

## Primitive Data Types vs. Abstract Data Types

So far, all the program states we looked at in this book used so-called primitive data types. Primitive data types are part of the language: Data types such as bool, int, char, unsigned int, float, double are part of the C++ language.

Sometimes using primitive data types becomes too limiting in modeling real-world problems. One of the examples is the use of arrays, in particular parallel arrays, to model a record for an entity such as person, student, or employee. A record for a person usually consists of person's name (a string) and street address, which itself can be broken down in number (integer), street name (a string), city (a string), state (a string), and a zip code (an integer). Another attribute that comprises a person's record could be the person's age (an integer), person's age (an integer), or salary (a double).

To model a department consisting of 10 to 15 persons, we would need to use parallel arrays, each one representing one attribute. Recall that parallel arrays are related through their index. Modeling several attributes through a few parallel arrays would be okay. However, having to model a lot of attributes that describe a person as in the real world would become cumbersome. The reason for this is that arrays are designed to hold elements of one data type.

To better model real-world entities, the C++ language provides a mechanism for programmers to create their own data types. Programmer-defined data types are commonly referred to as abstract data types, and they are defined by combining primitive data types into an abstract data type entity.

## Structures

Even though it is possible to model a person's record through primitive data types, it is not clear that they are related in any way. One way to relate primitive data types was through the use of parallel arrays, but this proved to be cumbersome. Combining primitive data types into an abstract entity creates a relationship between primitive data types. In C++, a structure is container for primitive data types. Structures act as containers for primitive data types used to model entities. In order to use a structure, it first needs to be declared. A structure consists of a keyword struct and a tag:

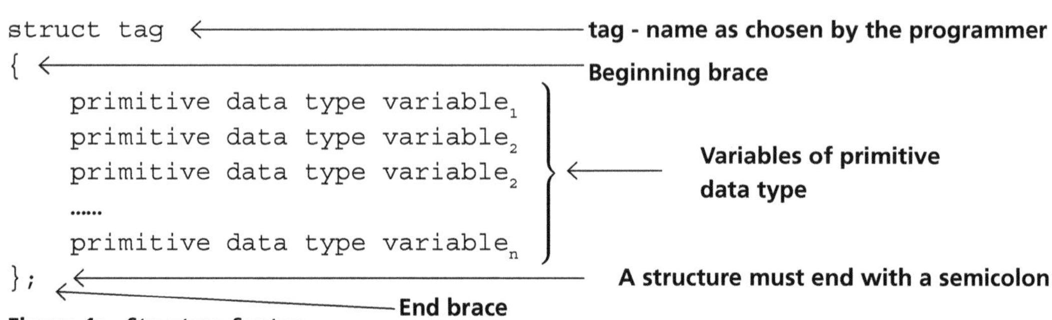


**Figure 1:** Structure Syntax

The structure tag is the newly created data type. Every structure must begin with the left (beginning) brace and it must and with the right (closing) brace. Finally, every structure declaration must end with a semicolon as depicted in Figure 1.

Following is an example of a structure declaration:

```
struct CarInfo
{
   string make;
   string model;
   double mpg;
   int year;
};
```

In the above declaration, CarInfo is the new abstract data type, which consists of make, model, mpg (miles per gallon), and year. When primitive data types such as bool, char, int, float, double, etc., are declared, the compiler immediately allocates memory. When abstract data types such as structures are declared, no memory is allocated. Instead, the memory gets allocated when a variable of newly created data type is instantiated:

```
CarInfo myCar;
```

The variable myCar is of data type CarInfo. Even though CarInfo is a programmer-defined data (abstract) type, variables of this newly created data type are instantiated the same way as variables of primitive data types. However, the process of declaring a variable of an abstract data type is the same as the process of declaring a variable of primitive data type: Simply precede the variable name with its type:

```
int x;                  // x is of data type integer
double y;               // y is of data type double
CarInfo myCar;          // myCar is of data type CarInfo
```

It is possible to declare multiple variables of an abstract data type. The following statement declares myCar and yourCar is to variables of CarInfo data type:

```
CarInfo myCar, yourCar;
```

## Initialization

The variables of primitive data types that comprise a structure are also called structure members.

```
struct CarInfo
{
    char make;
    char model;
    double mpg;
    int year;
};
```

**Structure members**

**Figure 2:** Structure Members

A structure cannot be initialized while it's being declared. This is due to the fact that no memory is allocated when the structure is declared. Once a variable of the structure data type is declared, it is then possible to initialize individual structure members. To do so, C++ provides the dot (.) operator:

```
myCar.mpg = 20.5;     // initialize myCar's mpg member with the value of 20.5
yourCar.mpg = 28.0;   // initialize yourCar's mpg member with the value of 28.0
```

The following program demonstrates how to initialize individual structure members:

```
 1. #include <iostream>
 2. #include <string.h>
 3.
 4. using namespace std;
 5.
 6. struct CarInfo
 7. {
 8.    string make;
 9.    string model;
10.    double mpg;
11.    int  year;
12. };
13.
14. int main()
15. {
16.    CarInfo myCar;
17.    myCar.make = "SAAB";
18.    myCar.model = "Viggen";
19.    myCar.mpg = 25.0;
20.    myCar.year = 1999;
21.
22.    return 0;
23. }
```

**No memory is being allocated at this point** (lines 8–11)

**Memory has been allocated** (line 16)

**Listing 1:** Initializing Individual Structure Members

In Listing 1, the structure is declared on lines 6 through 12. At that point no memory has been allocated. On line 16 a variable (myCar) of data type CarInfo is declared, and at that point memory required for all structure members is declared. On lines 16 through 20, individual structure members are being initialized with values. The values have been hard-coded, therefore making the program less flexible.

To make the program more flexible, it is possible to initialize individual structure members in an interactive manner as Listing 2 demonstrates:

```
#include <iostream>
#include <string.h>

using namespace std;

struct CarInfo
{
   string make;
   string model;
   double mpg;
   int  year;
};

int main()
{
   CarInfo myCar;

   cout << "Car make: ";
   cin >> myCar.make;

   cout << "Car model:";
   cin >> myCar.model;

   cout << "MPG: ";
   cin >> myCar.mpg;

   cout << "Year: ";
   cin >> myCar.year;

   return 0;
}
```

**Listing 2:** Interactive Program to Initialize Individual Structure Members

The C++ language dot operator is a simple mechanism. You can think of the structure variable as the common variable or the "root" for the entire container (structure). In order to refer to an individual member of the structure, it is necessary to first reference the "root," followed by the dot operator (.), followed by the member variable. The structure members are preceded by the structure variable followed by the (.), followed by the member variable:

```
structure variable

 myCar.make = "SAAB";

Individual structure member
```

**Figure 3**

## Initialization List Initialization

The C++ language provides a convenient way to initialize members of a structure through an initialization list:

```
CarInfo yourCar = {"BMW", "Z4", 21.8, 2013};
```

The above statement defines a variable called yourCar, which is of data type CarInfo. The list, which is found to the right of the assignment (=) operator, contains four members— "BMW", "Z4", 21.8, and 2013. The mechanism used to initialize individual members of yourCar (make, model, mpg, and year) is similar the initialization list used with arrays where the value of the first member of the list is assigned to the first array element. In the case of list initialization of structures, the value of the first element of the list is assigned to the first member of the structure; the value of the second member of the initialization list is assigned to the second member of the structure and so on:

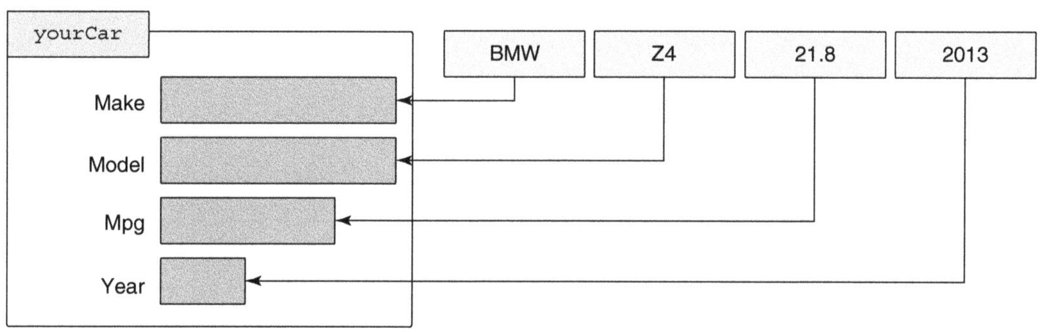


**Figure 3:** Initializing a Structure through an Initialization List

There are a few rules that need to be respected when using initialization list to initialize structures:

- The initialization list could partially contain the information needed to initialize structure members:

  ```
  CarInfo yourCar = {"BMW"};
  ```

  which would initialize only the first structure member.

- The following statement:

  ```
  CarInfo yourCar = {"BMW", "Z4" };
  ```

  would initialize the first two members of the structure

- Skipping over list elements would result in a syntax error:

  ```
  CarInfo yourCar = {"BMW",, 21.8, 2013};
  ```

Initializing structures through an initialization list is a very efficient way to quickly ("hard code") initialize a structure.

## Member Access

The dot (.) operator is used to access an individual member of a structure. Listing 3 demonstrates how to do this through the dot operator:

```
#include <iostream>
#include <string.h>

using namespace std;

struct CarInfo
{
   string make;
   string model;
   double mpg;
   int  year;
};

using namespace std;

int main()
{
   // allocate a variable of CarInfo data type
   CarInfo myCar;

   // gather data from the user
   cout << "Car make: ";
   cin >> myCar.make;

   cout << "Car model:";
   cin >> myCar.model;

   cout << "MPG: ";
   cin >> myCar.mpg;

   cout << "Year: ";
   cin >> myCar.year;

   // display the data
   cout << "Make: " << myCar.make << endl;
   cout << "Model: " << myCar.model << endl;
   cout << "MPG: " << myCar.mpg << endl;
   cout << "Year: " << myCar.year << endl;
   return 0;
}
```

**Listing 3:** Accessing Individual Structure Members

Compiling the above listing would produce the following output:

## Math Operations on Structure Members

Any math operations that can be performed on primitive data types can be performed on structure members, provided they have an appropriate data type. Suppose we have declared the following structure:

```
struct Person
{
  string name;
  int weight;         // in lbs
  int height;         // in inches
};
```

Assume that we declared several variables of the Point data type:

```
Person joe = {"Joe", 230, 75};
```

So we have a person named Joe who weighs 230 pounds and is 75 inches tall (6' 3"). Suppose Joe went on a diet and lost 10 pounds, then we can update Joe's record in the following manner:

```
joe.weight = joe.weight−10;
```

### Comparing Structures

Structures have to be compared member by member. For example, the following two variables are of data type Person (as defined above):

```
Person employeeA, employeeB;
```

Using Boolean operators (>,>=,<, <=, !=) can only be done on member-by-member basis. Comparing two structure variables:

```
if (employeeA > employeeB)
```

would result in a syntax error. Instead, perform member wise comparison:

```
if (employeeA.name > employeeB.name)
```

or

```
if (employeeA.weight <= employeeB.weight)
```

## Arrays as Structure Members

Suppose we have a student who is taking only one class. We would like to keep track of the student's performance in that class. To model this entity, called StudentInfo, we define a structure consisting of the following fields:

- Student name
- Student ID
- List of quizzes taken
- List of programming exercises taken
- Midterm exam
- Final exam

Conceptually, a structure of StudentInfo data type is depicted in Figure 4:

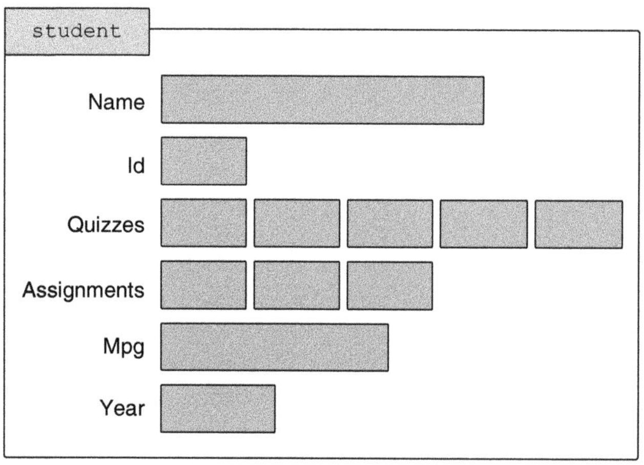


**Figure 4:** Arrays as Structure Elements

The following program declares StudentInfo, populates it with the data first through an initialization list, following with the data obtained from the user, and finally displays the data:

```
#include <iostream>
#include <string>

using namespace std;

const int NUM_QUIZZES = 5;
const int NUM_ASSIGNMENTS = 3;

```

```
struct StudentInfo
{
  string name;
  int id;         // assume student id's are integers
  int quizzes[NUM_QUIZZES];  // an array of integers
  int assignments[NUM_ASSIGNMENTS]; //an array of integers
  int midTerm;
  int finalExam;
};

int main()
{
  // partially initialize student struct
  StudentInfo student = {"Jane Doe", 1001};

  // gather assignment grades
  for (int i=0; i<NUM_QUIZZES; i++)
  {
    cout << "Quiz #" << i+1 << " :";
    cin >> student.quizzes[i];
  }


  // gather assignment grades
  for (int i=0; i<NUM_ASSIGNMENTS; i++)
  {
    cout << "Assignment #" << i+1 << " :";
    cin >> student.assignments[i];
  }

  cout << "Midterm Exam: ";
  cin >> student.midTerm;

  // gather final exam grade
  cout << "Final Exam: ";
  cin >> student.finalExam;


  // Display gathered information
  cout << student.name << "\t" << student.id << endl;
  cout << "Grades for this semester: " << endl;

  for (int i=0; i<NUM_QUIZZES; i++)
  {
    cout << "Quiz #" << i+1 << " :" << student.quizzes[i]
         << endl;
```

**StudentInfo elements quizzes and assignments are array.**

**Notice how quizzes is referred to?**

```
    }

    for (int i=0; i<NUM_ASSIGNMENTS; i++)
    {
      cout << "Assignment #" << i+1 << " :" << student.
      assignments[i] << endl;
    }

    cout << "Midterm Exam: "<< student.midTerm << endl;
    cout << "Final Exam: " << student.finalExam << endl;
    return 0;
}
```

**Listing 4:** Arrays as Structure Members

Compiling the above program and running it produces the following output:

```
Quiz #1 :100
Quiz #2 :100
Quiz #3 :55
Quiz #4 :99
Quiz #5 :88
Assignment #1 :58
Assignment #2 :98
Assignment #3 :66
Midterm Exam: 100
Final Exam: 100
Jane Doe        1001
Grades for this semester:
Quiz #1 :100
Quiz #2 :100
Quiz #3 :55
Quiz #4 :99
Quiz #5 :88
Assignment #1 :58
Assignment #2 :98
Assignment #3 :66
Midterm Exam: 100
Final Exam: 100

Process returned 0 (0x0)   execution time : 13.024 s
Press any key to continue.
```

## Nested Structures

Besides primitive data types (including arrays) as structure members, C++ allows nesting of structures within structures. This feature of the language allows programmers to model more complex real-world entities. For example, the above StudentInfo structure can be augmented with additional members:

```
struct AddressInfo
{
  int number;
  string streetName;
```

```
  string city;
  string state;
  int zipCode;
};

struct StudentInfo
{
  string name;
  int id;                         // assume student id's are integers
  AddressInfo address;                          // nested structure
  int quizzes[NUM_QUIZZES];              // an array of integers
  int assignments[NUM_ASSIGNMENTS];      // an array of integers
  int midTerm;
  int finalExam;
};
```

**Listing 5:** Nested Structures

In Listing 5, address is a member variable of the StudentInfo structure. The data type of the address member variable is AddressInfo data type, which in itself is a structure:

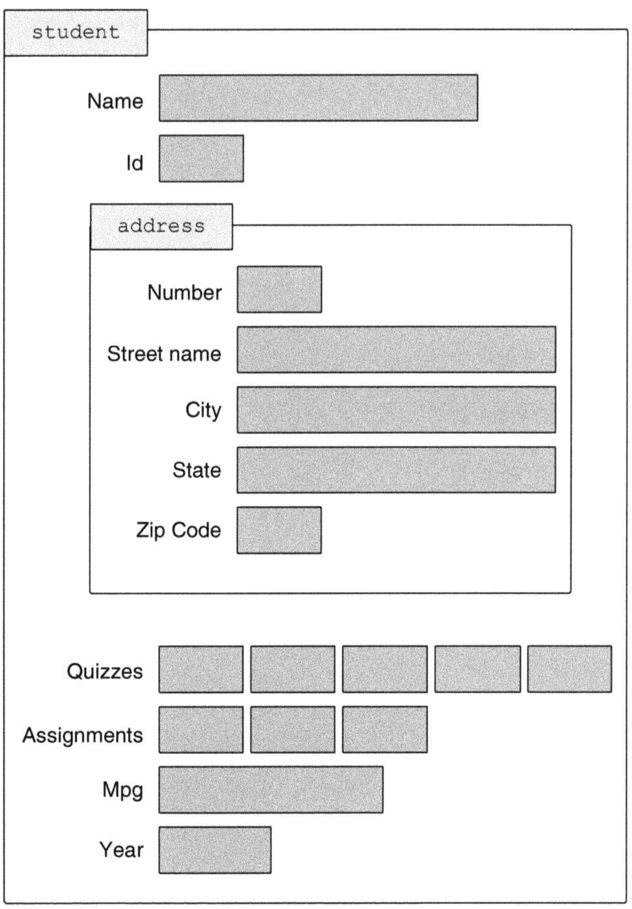


**Figure 5:** Nested Structures Depicted

Referring to individual structure members is again accomplished through the dot operator. Assuming that we have declared student as a variable of StudentInfo data type, then accessing member variable zipCode would be accomplished with this line of code:

```
cout << "This is the zip code: " << student.address.zipCode << endl;
```

First, the outer structure (student) is referenced followed by the dot operator, followed by the inner structure (address, which is a member variable of the student structure) reference, followed by the member variable zipCode, which is a member variable of the address structure.

The outer structure is a container holding primitive data types as well as another structure. A word of caution when working with nested structures is in order: Nesting levels can get pretty complex (deep). Avoid writing structures with too many nested levels because they could be difficult to debug.

## Arrays of Structures

Prior to learning structures, the only way for us to combine attributes that describe an entity such as student record or employee record was to use parallel arrays. Using parallel arrays is a bit cumbersome because each array can store only elements of the same data type. Thus, if the entity being modeled had a lot of attributes, that would automatically translate to a lot of arrays. As we saw in this chapter, using structures makes it much easier to model real-world objects/entities. However, structures are excellent when modeling one entity such as a record (student, employee, car). But would we model a collection of these records?

For example, how would we model a classroom full of students (StudentInfo record)? The answer is simple: combining arrays and structures. Each structure can be an array element as depicted in Figure 6.

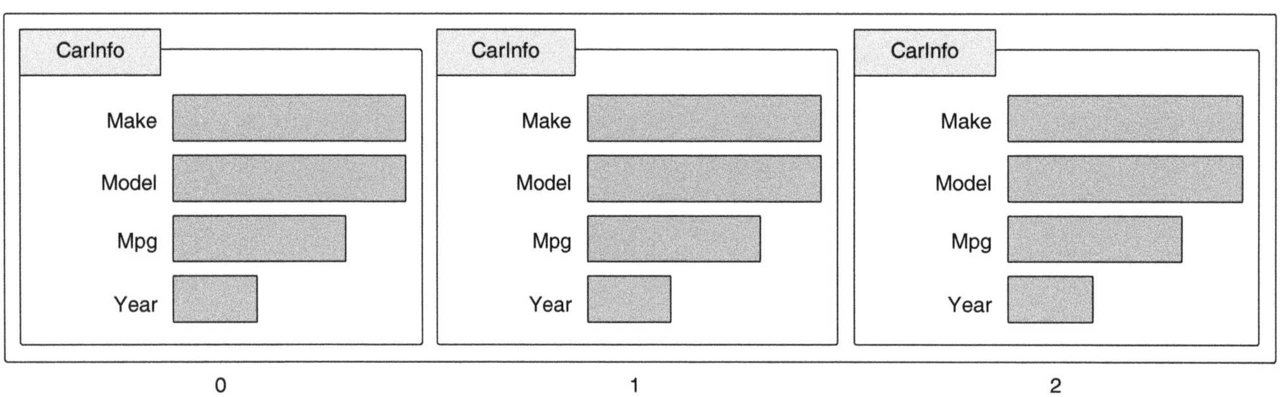


**Figure 6:** An Array of Structures

The array in Figure 6 consists of three elements. Instead of having an array consisting of primitive data types, the above array consists of abstract data types (structures). Index 0 contains a CarInfo record as its element. The same holds true for index 1 and 2. Programmatically, we represent that as:

```
CarInfo myCars[3];
```

where CarInfo is the data type of the array. The syntax is no different than declaring an array of integers:

```
int myArray[3];
```

The following program declares a three-element array of data type CarInfo and populates each record with data:

```
#include <iostream>

using namespace std;

struct CarInfo
{
  string make;
  string model;
  double mpg;
  int year;
};

int main()
{
    // Declare an array of structures
    CarInfo myCars[3];

    // first car record
    myCars[0].make = "BMW";
    myCars[0].model = "528i";
    myCars[0].mpg = 28.0;
    myCars[0].year = 2013;

    // second car record
    myCars[1].make = "Mercedes";
    myCars[1].model = "ML250 Bluetec";
    myCars[1].mpg = 22.0;
    myCars[1].year = 2013;

    // third car record
    myCars[2].make = "Porsche";
    myCars[2].model = "Cayman";
    myCars[2].mpg = 25.0;
    myCars[2].year = 2014;

    return 0;
}
```

**Listing 6:** Array of Structures

The variable myCars represents the array. Accessing each element of this array is done through an index in the same manner elements in an array of primitive data type are accessed. The only difference is that each element is a structure, therefore its members must be accessed through the dot operator:

```
myCars[0].make = "BMW";
myCars[0].model = "528i";
myCars[0].mpg = 28.0;
myCars[0].year = 2013;
```

myCars[0] tells the compiler to work with the first element of the array, and the dot (.) operator is used to assign a value (or to access) to a particular element.

## Initializing an Array of Structures through an Initialization List

The C++ language provides an easy way to quickly initialize an array of structures through an initialization list. The syntax is similar to the initialization list for an array of primitive data type. The only exception is that individual structures inside the initialization list are enclosed in their own sets of braces and separated by commas. The following code segment demonstrates how an initialization list can be used to initialize an array of structures:

**Beginning of the initialization list**

```
1. // Declare an array of structures and initialize it with data
2.     CarInfo myCars[3] ={
3.         {"BMW","528i", 28.0, 2013},                        // 1st car
4.         {"Mercedes", "ML250 Bluetec", 22.0, 2013},  // 2nd car
5.         {"Porsche", "Cayman", 25.0, 2014}               // 3rd car
6.       };
```

**Individual struct members**

**End of the initialization list**

**Listing 7:** Initialization List of Array

When an array of structures is initialized via an initialization list, this has to be done at the same time that the array is declared. In the Listing 7, the beginning of initialization list is denoted with the left brace ("{") on line 2. The end of the initialization list is denoted with a right brace ("}") and a semicolon (";") on line 6. Since the array is an array of structures, each structure (array element) has its own initialization list, each of which starts with a "{" and ends with a "}" followed by a comma (lines 3, 4, and 5 in the example above). The last structure initialization list (for the 3rd car) is not followed by the comma, signaling to the compiler that it is the last record.

## Passing Structures to Functions

Writing modular code is about breaking problems into smaller components called functions. Most of the time, you will need to either pass a structure to a function or return a structure from a function. For example, you can write a function that collects data from a user, populates structure members with the data, and returns a structure. Similarly, you can pass a structure to a function for the purpose of displaying structure members neatly formatted.

As a programmer, you will need to make design decisions that may impact the performance of your program. Structures can be passed to functions either by value or by reference. The same rules that apply to primitive data types when they are passed into functions apply to structures.

## Pass by Value

When passing a structure by value to a function, the contents of the argument variable are copied to the parameter (local) variable. Listing 8 illustrates passing structures by value to a function:

```
 1. #include <iostream>
 2. #include <string>
 3.
 4. using namespace std;
 5.
 6. struct CarInfo
 7. {
 8.    string make;
 9.    string model;
10.    double mpg;
11.    int year;
12. };
13.
14. // Function prototypes
15. void displayCarRecord(CarInfo );
16.
17. int main()
18. {
19.    // declare and initialize CarInfo
20.    CarInfo dreamCar = {"Porsche", "Cayman", 17.0, 2014};
21.    displayCarRecord(dreamCar);
22.    return 0;
23. }
24.
25. void displayCarRecord(CarInfo myCar)
26. {
27.    cout << "Make: " << myCar.make << endl;
28.    cout << "Model: " << myCar.model << endl;
29.    cout << "MPG: " << myCar.mpg << endl;
30.    cout << "Year: " << myCar.year << endl;
31. }
```

**Listing 8:** Passing a Structure to a Function

When the function displayCarRecord is called on line 21 in Listing 8, each structure member from the argument structure (dreamCar) is copied to the corresponding member in the parameter structure (myCar).

Since the CarInfo structure is rather small with only four fields, the copy operation does not affect program performance. Even if the CarInfo structure had a lot of members, the copy operation would not take a long time given today's computer architecture/computing power of user machines. However, if a lot of structures were being copied, the program performance would be affected.

As a programmer, you will need to make design decisions that will affect performance of your program. The next section discusses passing structures by reference.

## Pass by Reference

You could pass a structure to a function as a reference and avoid unnecessary copying of the data. The program almost looks identical with two minor exceptions (on line 15 and line 25 respectively):

```
1.  #include <iostream>
2.  #include <string>
3.
4.  using namespace std;
5.
6.  struct CarInfo
7.  {
8.       string make;
9.       string model;
10.      double mpg;
11.      int year;
12. };
13.
14. // Function prototypes
15. void displayCarRecord(CarInfo &);
16.
17. int main()
18. {
19.      // declare and initialize CarInfo
20.      CarInfo dreamCar = {"Porsche", "Cayman", 17.0, 2014};
21.      displayCarRecord(dreamCar);
22.      return 0;
23. }
24.
25. void displayCarRecord(CarInfo &myCar)
26. {
27.      cout << "Make: " << myCar.make << endl;
28.      cout << "Model: " << myCar.model << endl;
29.      cout << "MPG: " << myCar.mpg << endl;
30.      cout << "Year: " << myCar.year << endl;
31. }
```

**Note the "&" to specify the reference** (line 15)

**"&" reference** (line 25)

**Listing 9:** Pass by Reference

Since a reference is nothing more than an alias for the original variable, no copying takes place. Not surprisingly, for even a program this small, the performance is affected as illustrated in Figure 7.

| Pass by Value | Pass by Reference |
|---|---|
| Pass by Value<br>Make: Porsche<br>Model: Cayman<br>MPG: 17<br>Year: 2014<br><br>Process returned 0 (0x0)   execution time : 0.019 s<br>Press any key to continue. | Pass by Reference<br>Make: Porsche<br>Model: Cayman<br>MPG: 17<br>Year: 2014<br><br>Process returned 0 (0x0)   execution time : 0.017 s<br>Press any key to continue. |

**Figure 7:** Pass by Value vs. Pass by Reference Execution Comparison

It is evident that pass by reference results in faster execution times. Thus, should we always use pass by reference when passing structures to functions? Well, not really. A closer examination of the code in Listing 9 reveals that it is not safe. Since a reference is nothing more than an alias for the original variable, then any changes made inside the function would be reflected in the original variable.

To mitigate this risk, it is a good idea to pass structures as constant references. Simply precede the structure data type in the parameter with the keyword "const":

```
void displayCarRecord(const CarInfo &myCar)
```

The const keyword assures that no changes can be made to the parameter variable. This is the best of both worlds because no copying takes place, therefore there is no impact on program performance, and the function cannot accidentally change the original structure members. Listing 10 shows an example of the function prototype and the function itself.

```
//Function prototypes
void displayCarRecord(const CarInfo &);
.. .. .. .. .. .. ..
.. .. .. .. .. .. ..
.. .. .. .. .. .. ..
void displayCarRecord(const CarInfo &myCar)
{
   cout << "Make: " << myCar.make << endl;
   cout << "Model: " << myCar.model << endl;
   cout << "MPG: " << myCar.mpg << endl;
   cout << "Year: " << myCar.year << endl;
 }
```

**Listing 10:** Function Prototype and the Function

## Returning Structures from Functions

When writing modular code, capturing data from the user should be isolated in a function. Typically, you would declare a local structure in the function, prompt the user for data, capture the data and assign the values to appropriate structure members, and return the structure to the caller program.

```
#include <iostream>
#include <string>
using namespace std;
struct CarInfo
{
   string make;
   string model;
   double mpg;
   int year;
};
// Function prototypes
void displayCarRecord(const CarInfo &);
CarInfo getCarInfo();       // note the function return data type (CarInfo)
int main()
{
   // declare CarInfo
   CarInfo dreamCar;       // declare a variable of CarInfo data type
   dreamCar = getCarInfo();    // Call the function. It will return a populated struct
   cout << "Displaying the data: " << endl;
   displayCarRecord(dreamCar); // pass the structure to the displayCarRecord
   return 0;
}
CarInfo getCarInfo()
{
   CarInfo myDreamCar;      // local struct of CarInfo data type
   cout << "Please enter the following information: " << endl;
   cout << "Make: ";
   cin >> myDreamCar.make;
   cout << "Model: ";
   cin >> myDreamCar.model;
   cout << "MPG: ";
   cin >> myDreamCar.mpg;
```

```
41.    cout << "Year: ";
42.    cin >> myDreamCar.year;
43.
44.    return myDreamCar;       // very important  must return the struct
45. }
46.
47. void displayCarRecord(const CarInfo &myCar)
48. {
49.    cout << "Make: " << myCar.make << endl;
50.    cout << "Model: " << myCar.model << endl;
51.    cout << "MPG: " << myCar.mpg << endl;
52.    cout << "Year: " << myCar.year << endl;
53. }
```

**Listing 11:** Returning a Structure from a Function

In the main function, a structure variable dreamCar of CarInfo data type is declared on line 21. The data returned from the getCarInfo function will be copied into this variable. The next statement in the main function, on line 22 calls the getCarInfo function. The function getCarInfo returns a structure of CarInfo data type whose contents are copied to the dreamCar variable. The dreamCar variable is then passed to the displayCarRecord function, which displays the captured data:

```
Please enter the following information:
Make: LAmborghini
Model: Gallardo
MPG: 9.8
Year: 2013
Displaying the data:
Make: LAmborghini
Model: Gallardo
MPG: 9.8
Year: 2013

Process returned 0 (0x0)   execution time : 13.421 s
Press any key to continue.
```

The getCarInfo function begins with declaration of local variable myDreamCar, which is of data type CarInfo. Next, several cout statements are executed to prompt the user for data, which is captured in myDreamCar structure members. The last statement in the getCarInfo function, on line 44, is the return statement, which returns the control to the caller program. At this point, the contents of the local structure variable, myDreamCar, are copied to the main function's local variable dreamCar (line 22 in Listing 11). The function getCarInfo goes out of scope and so does its local variable. However, because of the copy that took place, all the data from the local variable was preserved in the main program in variable dreamCar. The main program calls the displayCarRecord function and passes the dreamCar variable as an argument to the function (line 24 in Listing 11).

## Design Strategies

C++ is a very powerful and flexible language that enables programmers to write syntactically correct yet dangerous code. Programmers need to keep in mind these attributes of the C++ language and strive to write solid code. Consider the following example:

```
#include <iostream>
#include <string>

using namespace std;

struct CarInfo
{
   string make;
   string model;
   double mpg;
   int year;
};

// Function prototypes
void displayCarRecord(const CarInfo &);
void getCarInfo(CarInfo &);

int main()
{
   // declare CarInfo
   CarInfo dreamCar;

   getCarInfo(dreamCar);
   cout << "Displaying the data: " << endl;
   displayCarRecord(dreamCar);
   return 0;
}

void getCarInfo(CarInfo &myDreamCar)
{
   cout << "Please enter the following information: " << endl;
   cout << "Make: ";
   cin >> myDreamCar.make;

   cout << "Model: ";
   cin >> myDreamCar.model;

   cout << "MPG: ";
   cin >> myDreamCar.mpg;
```

```
40.
41.    cout << "Year: ";
42.    cin >> myDreamCar.year;
43. }
44.
45. void displayCarRecord(const CarInfo &myCar)
46. {
47.    cout << "Make: " << myCar.make << endl;
48.    cout << "Model: " << myCar.model << endl;
49.    cout << "MPG: " << myCar.mpg << endl;
50.    cout << "Year: " << myCar.year << endl;
51. }
```

**Listing 12:** Design Considerations

In the source code in Listing 12, the function getCarInfo is a void function, and it takes a reference of data type CarInfo as a parameter. Note that there is no constant reference parameter because the function changes the contents of the original variable, which was declared as a structure called dreamCar in the main function on line 21. After the declaration, dreamCar is passed as an argument to the getCarInfo function. The function prompts the user for pertinent data and stores it in the local reference parameter called myDreamCar. Keep in mind that the myDreamCar variable is nothing more than an alias for the original structure variable declared in the main function (dreamCar on line 21).

Once the function finishes its execution, the control is returned to the caller program (the main function), and the dreamCar variable is passed to the displayCarRecord function as a constant reference parameter.

While this program will compile and execute correctly, as depicted below:

```
Please enter the following information:
Make: Mercedes
Model: BlueTec
MPG: 41
Year: 2012
Displaying the data:
Make: Mercedes
Model: BlueTec
MPG: 41
Year: 2012

Process returned 0 (0x0)   execution time : 18.967 s
Press any key to continue.
```

it is not as intuitive as the program in Listing 11 where a structure is returned from a function. There will be situations where you may have to pass a structure to function as a (non-constant) reference parameter and enter or make changes to the original. When designing modular programs, usually "one function, one task" is a good rule to follow. Thus, it makes logical sense to return a value from a function once all its logic executes. However, there may be instances where a function will need to return more than one value. In those cases, the programmer can "return" multiple values from a function through non-constant reference parameters. In reality, the function does not really return multiple values. Instead, through the reference mechanism the original variables passed into the function as arguments are being affected.

## Pointers to Structures

Just like declaring a pointer to primitive data types, it is possible to declare a pointer to an abstract data type (structure). Suppose we declare a following structure:

```
struct CarInfo
{
  string make;
  string model;
  int year;
  double mpg;
};
```

and then we instantiate a variable of CarInfo data type:

```
CarInfo myCar;
```

Next, we declare a pointer variable to the CarInfo structure and we assign it the address of myCar:

```
CarInfo* myCarPtr; // Pointer to myCar
myCarPtr = &myCar;
```

Now we would like to use the pointer variable myCarPtr to populate the members of the CarInfo structure. The following statement will result in a syntax error:

```
// populate the structure through the pointer variable
myCarPtr.make = "BMW"; // SYNTAX ERROR!!!
```

Recall from Chapter 8 that working with pointers requires a few extra steps, such as dereferencing pointer variables. The following example is a quick reminder how dereferencing works:

```
int num;
int *ptrNum;
ptrNum = &num;
cout << "The contents of the cell ptrNum points to: " << *ptrNum
     << endl;
```

We declared a variable of integer data type (num), and we also declared a pointer variable (*ptrNum) capable of holding an address of the variable of integer data type. We assigned the address of the variable num to ptrNum. Next, we stored a value into the integer variable num through the pointer variable ptrNum. Finally, we printed the contents of the variable num via the pointer variable ptrNum.

In order to correctly display the contents of the memory location to which ptrNum points, it was necessary to dereference the pointer. The same holds true for abstract data types such as structures.

Following the example above for primitive data type dereferencing, we try to dereference the structure pointer:

```
*myCarPtr.make = "BMW"; // dereference the pointer
```

However, this attempt results in a syntax error. The reason for that is because there are two operators in the above statement:

- The dereferencing (indirection) operator "*"
- The dot "." operator

The compiler flags a syntax error because of the precedence order of the two operators. The dot operator has higher precedence than the dereferencing (indirection) operator. In essence, we are dereferencing the structure field (member) rather than the structure pointer. Since we are instructing the compiler to dereference the "make" structure member, which is not the pointer, it correctly throws the syntax error.

To remedy this we need to do the same thing as we would do in an expression containing math operators of different precedence order when we needed to force a different order of execution. We need to apply associativity, meaning we need to add parentheses to force the desired outcome:

```
(*myCarPtr).make = "BMW"; // dereference the pointer, assign value
(*myCarPtr).model = "Z4";
(*myCarPtr).year = 2013;
(*myCarPtr).mpg = 24.5;
```

With these changes, if we compile and execute this program, it will work correctly:

```
#include <iostream>

using namespace std;

struct CarInfo
{
   string make;
   string model;
   int year;
   double mpg;
};

int main()
{
   CarInfo myCar;
   CarInfo* myCarPtr; // Pointer to myCar

   myCarPtr = &myCar;

   // populate the structure through the pointer variable
   (*myCarPtr).make = "BMW";
   (*myCarPtr).model = "Z4";
   (*myCarPtr).year = 2013;
   (*myCarPtr).mpg = 28.5;
```

```

    // display the calues stored in struct members
    // NOTE: purposely not using pointer notation!
    cout << "Make: " << myCar.make << endl;
    cout << "Model: " << myCar.model << endl;
    cout << "Year: " << myCar.year << endl;
    cout << "MPG: " << myCar.mpg << endl;

    return 0;
}
```

**Listing 13:** Dereferencing Structure Pointers

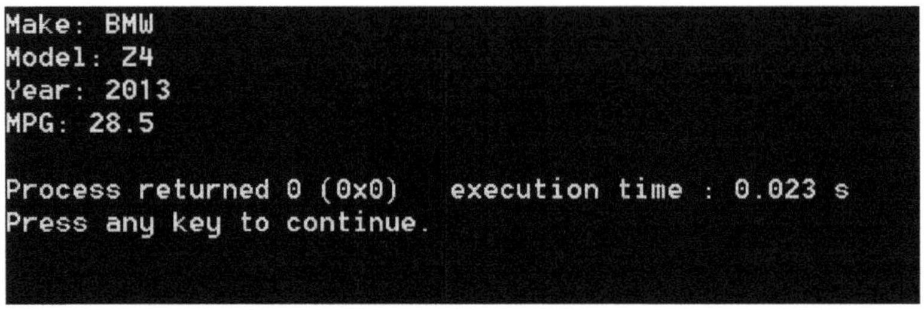


The syntax to dereference structure pointers is a bit cumbersome. Fortunately, C++ provides a more elegant way to dereference structure pointers via the structure pointer operator "->". The above code can be rewritten with the structure pointer operator:

```
myCarPtr->make = "BMW"; // dereference the pointer, assign
  value
myCarPtr->model = "Z4";
myCarPtr->year = 2013;
myCarPtr->mpg = 24.5;
```

Using the structure pointer operator makes the code more elegant and more readable. Also, there is no need to use parentheses to dereference the pointer variable.

## Pointers to Structures as Function Parameters

Just like references, pointers to structures could be used as function parameters to avoid unnecessary copying of data. Even though pointers require a little more work than references, it's well worth it because pointers are more flexible than references. Unlike a pointer, a reference must always be associated with a valid memory. Once a reference is defined, the memory it refers to cannot be changed. References are less flexible than pointers because they are associated with the same variable; there is no separate memory address to store a reference. In fact, the reference is simply an alias for the variable it refers to.

Pointers do not need to be associated with valid memory addresses; in fact, they can point to anything and even be assigned value of NULL because they are separate variables from the variables (memory locations) they point to. Pointer arithmetic can be performed for the purpose of moving through an array of objects, for example.

The following program listing demonstrates how a pointer can be used as a function parameter:

```
#include <iostream>

using namespace std;

const int MAKE_SIZE = 20;
const int MODEL_SIZE = 25;

struct CarInfo
{
  char make[MAKE_SIZE];
  char model[MODEL_SIZE];
  int year;
  double mpg;
};

// function prototypes
void getCarInfo(CarInfo *);
void displayCars(CarInfo const *);

int main()
{
  CarInfo myCar;
  CarInfo *ptrMyCar = &myCar;

  getCarInfo(ptrMyCar);
  displayCars(ptrMyCar);

  return 0;
}

void getCarInfo(CarInfo *ptrCar)
{
  cout << "Make: " ;
  cin.getline(ptrCar->make, MAKE_SIZE);
  cin.clear();
  cin.sync();

  cout << "Model: " ;
  cin.getline(ptrCar->model, MODEL_SIZE);
  cin.clear();
  cin.sync();

  cout << "Year: " ;
```

```
44.    cin >> ptrCar->year;
45.
46.    cout << "MPG: " ;
47.    cin >> ptrCar->mpg;
48.    cin.clear();
49.    cin.sync();
50. }
51.
52. void displayCars(CarInfo const *ptrVehicle)
53. {
54.    cout << "Make: " << ptrVehicle->make << endl;
55.    cout << "Model: " << ptrVehicle->model << endl;
56.    cout << "Year: " << ptrVehicle->year << endl;
57.    cout << "MPG: " << ptrVehicle->mpg << endl;
58. }
```

**Listing 14:** Using Pointes as Function Parameters

```
Make: Ferrari
Model: F12
Year: 2013
MPG: 7.8
Make: Ferrari
Model: F12
Year: 2013
MPG: 7.8

Process returned 0 (0x0)   execution time : 15.652 s
Press any key to continue.
```

The program in Listing 14 demonstrates use of pointers as function parameters.

On line 22 we declare a variable myCar:

```
CarInfo myCar;
```

which is a structure. On the next line of the program, we declare a pointer variable capable of holding the address of the variable myCar:

```
CarInfo *ptrMyCar = &myCar;
```

Next, the program calls two void functions whose prototypes are on lines 16–18 in the Listing 14:

```
// function prototypes
void getCarInfo(CarInfo *);
void displayCars(CarInfo const *);
```

The function getCarInfo expects a structure pointer as its parameter. This pointer is not a constant pointer, which means that any changes the function makes to the structure the pointer points to will be reflected in that structure. In this case, the argument variable in the main function ptrMyCar on line 25.

Once the function getCarInfo finishes its execution, the structure is populated with user choices. The pointer to the structure is then passed to the displayCars function, which expects a constant pointer to the structure so that its logic does not accidentally overwrite any of the data stored in structure members.

This is one way to obtain the data from the user and display it. Alternatively, we could have a function that dynamically allocates a structure, populates it with data, and returns its address to the caller program. That is what we're going to discuss in the next section.

# Returning Structure Pointers from Functions

## Dynamic Allocation of Structures

In Chapter 8, we discussed dynamic memory allocation for primitive data types. Just as memory can dynamically be allocated for primitive data types, it can be dynamically allocated for the programmer-defined (abstract) data types. The process is the same, and we need the new operator to accomplish dynamic memory allocation:

```
CarInfo* ptrCar = new CarInfo;
```

The above statement allocates a block of memory on the heap big enough to store CarInfo structure. The address of the newly allocated memory block is assigned to the ptrCar pointer:

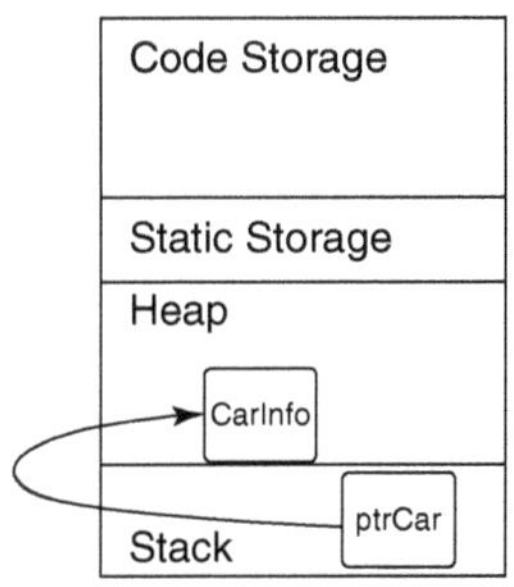


**Figure 9:** Dynamically Allocating a Structure

Suppose this block of memory was allocated inside a function as a local variable. As we know, functions have scope, and once the program control returns to the caller program, meaning the function goes out of scope along with its local variables, all the information contained in the local variables will be lost. With dynamic memory allocation, if we assigned some values to the newly allocated memory location, those values would still be there even after the function goes out of scope. The problem is that they would not be "reachable" if we lost the memory address of the block of memory. To assure that the rest of the code has access to the dynamically allocated block of memory, simply return the block's pointer (address of) to the caller program. In Listing 15, the main function calls the getCarInfo function on line 22. The getCarInfo function dynamically allocates memory for a CarInfo structure, populates structure members with information obtained from the user, and returns the address of the dynamically allocated block of memory.

```
1. #include <iostream>
2. using namespace std;
3.
4. const int MAKE_SIZE = 20;
5. const int MODEL_SIZE = 25;
6.
```

```
struct CarInfo
{
     char make[MAKE_SIZE];
     char model[MODEL_SIZE];
     int year;
     double mpg;
};

// function prototypes
CarInfo * getCarInfo();
void displayCars(CarInfo const *);

int main()
{
     CarInfo *ptrMyCar = getCarInfo();
     displayCars(ptrMyCar);
     delete ptrMyCar;    // delete the memory
     return 0;
}

CarInfo *getCarInfo()
{
     CarInfo *ptrCar = new CarInfo;
     cout << "Make: " ;
     cin.getline(ptrCar->make, MAKE_SIZE);
     cin.clear();
     cin.sync();

     cout << "Model: " ;
     cin.getline(ptrCar->model, MODEL_SIZE);
     cin.clear();
     cin.sync();

     cout << "Year: " ;
     cin >> ptrCar->year;

     cout << "MPG: " ;
     cin >> ptrCar->mpg;
     cin.clear();
     cin.sync();

     return ptrCar; // return the address
}
void displayCars(CarInfo const *ptrVehicle)
{
```

```
52.   cout << "Make: " << ptrVehicle->make << endl;
53.   cout << "Model: " << ptrVehicle->model << endl;
54.   cout << "Year: " << ptrVehicle->year << endl;
55.   cout << "MPG: " << ptrVehicle->mpg << endl;
56. }
```

**Listing 15:** Dynamically Allocated Memory for a Structure

Failing to return the address of the memory block allocated in the getCarInfo function would make that block of memory "unreachable." Thus, it is very important to apply due diligence when writing code that involves dynamically allocating memory inside of a function and returning the pointer to it. Similarly, in the caller program (main function), it is equally important to assign the returned memory address to appropriate pointer variable for the purpose of using it. The statement on line 21 in the program listing above does exactly that:

```
CarInfo *ptrMyCar = getCarInfo();
```

With the address safely captured in the ptrMyCar variable, the program calls the displayCars function, passing in the ptrMyCar pointer variable. You can see how use of pointers makes programs extremely fast when done correctly because there is no unnecessary copying of values from one memory location to another. Simply passing a pointer variable containing the memory address—that is all it takes.

## Deleting Dynamically Allocated Memory

In the statement on line 23 in the Listing 15, dynamically allocated memory is deleted:

```
delete ptrMyCar;
```

It is very important to delete dynamically allocated memory because there is no mechanism for it built into C++. Failure to delete dynamically allocated memory could result in what is known as "memory leak." To be perfectly clear, no memory is leaking. When a poorly designed program runs and keeps allocating memory dynamically (in a loop, for example) without deallocating it, each iteration will further defragment the computer memory. The search for adequate contiguous blocks of memory needed to allocate new dynamic memory will take longer and longer, resulting in performance degradation eventually leading to a crash. This is why it is important to clean dynamically allocated memory when it is no longer needed.

Other languages, such as Java, have a so-called garbage collector mechanism built in that cleans up dynamically allocated memory from time to time. While this garbage collector prevents memory leaks, it does come with an overhead, resulting in slower program execution. In C++, the burden of cleaning up dynamically allocated memory once it is no longer needed is on the programmer. Why would anyone want this additional burden? The answer is that when written correctly, C++ programs are extremely fast, almost as fast as programs written in lower-level languages such as assembly.

Thus, for applications where speed is an issue, such as real-time applications (stock market quotes, transportation, military applications), C++ is the language of choice.

## Defensive Programming

Defensive programming is very important especially when working with dynamically allocated memory. For example, what if for some reason dynamic memory allocation fails? The rest of the program logic hinges upon successful allocation of dynamic memory. As a programmer, how do you protect your code? You need to use defensive programming techniques. Defensive what? Well, suppose you are allocating a block of memory as follows:

```
ptrCar = new CarInfo[numCars];

// defensive programming
if (!ptrCar)
{
  cout << "Unable to allocate memory! Exiting...  " << endl;
  system("Pause");
  exit(0);
}
```

Simply check that the address is valid (not NULL). If that is not the case, then display a message to the user notifying him or her of the problem and exit. This way, the rest of the programming logic, which hinges upon successful memory allocation, will not be affected. Not using defensive programming techniques could result in unforeseen errors, program crashes, and other problems.

# Enumerated Data Types

Enumerated data type is an abstract data type giving programmers the ability to define their own data type for a fixed list of values. The syntax to define enumerated type is as follows:

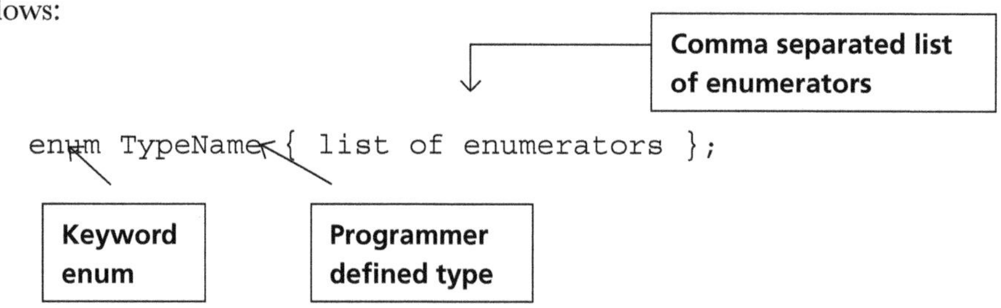


For example, this is a programmer-defined enumerated type:

```
enum CarMakers {Audi, BMW, Cadillac, Ford, Jaguar, RollsRoyce, Saab, Volkswagen };
```

The compiler automatically assigns an ordinal number to the members of the list of enumerators. Members of the enumerator list are stored as integers. By default the first member in the list is assigned the value of zero. The next element in the list is the previous element +1. In the example above, Audi=0, BMW=1, Cadillac=2, and so on. It is possible to seed the list with a different number. For example, the following statement:

```
enum CarMakers {Audi=100, BMW, Cadillac, Ford, Jaguar, RollsRoyce, Saab, Volkswagen };
```

assigns 101 to BMW, 102 to Cadillac, and so on. It is also possible to specify an integer constant for every enumerator, even skip some:

```
1. #include <iostream>
2. #include <iomanip>
3.
4. using namespace std;
5.
6. enum CarMakers {Audi=100,
7.                 BMW=9,
8.                 Cadillac,
9.                 Ford=101,
10.                Jaguar=110,
11.                RollsRoyce,
12.                Saab,
13.                Volkswagen };
14. int main()
15. {
16.     //CarMakers cars;
17.     cout << setw(12)<< "Audi: " << setw(10) << Audi << endl;
18.     cout << setw(12)<<"BMW: " << setw(10) << BMW << endl;
19.     cout << setw(12)<<"Cadillac: " << setw(10) << Cadillac << endl;
20.     cout << setw(12)<<"Ford: " << setw(10) << Ford << endl;
21.     cout << setw(12)<<"Jaguar: " << setw(10) << Jaguar << endl;
22.     cout << setw(12)<<"RollsRoyce: " << setw(10) << RollsRoyce << endl;
23.     cout << setw(12)<<"Saab: " << setw(10) << Saab << endl;
24.     cout << setw(12)<<"Volkswagen: " << setw(10) << Volkswagen << endl;
25.     return 0;
26. }
```

**Listing 16:** Enums

Notice that on line 8, the enumerator called Cadillac does not have an integer value assigned to it. Similarly, RollsRoyce, Saab, and Volkswagen do not have integer values assigned to them. However, compiling and running the above program produces the following output:

```
      Audi:       100
       BMW:         9
  Cadillac:        10
      Ford:       101
    Jaguar:       110
RollsRoyce:       111
      Saab:       112
Volkswagen:       113

Process returned 0 (0x0)   execution time : 0.012 s
Press any key to continue.
```

Where we can see the rule for current enumerator element is the previous enumerator element + 1. Thus, Cadillac is 10, because the previous enumerator, BMW, was assigned value of 9. Similarly, Rolls-Royce is assigned 111, Saab 112, and Volkswagen is assigned value of 113.

The whole purpose of enumerated data types is to simplify the code. Assigning each enumerator a value defeats the purpose. Furthermore, it is error-prone because it involves keeping track of enumerator values. For a small enumerator list, this may not be an issue. Unless you have a good reason to assign particular values to each enumerator, it is best to let the compiler pick integer values that are to be assigned to each enumerator in the list.

## Enumerated Data Type Variables

It is possible to declare a variable of enumerated data type as demonstrated in the following example:

```
CarMakers myCar;
myCar = Saab;
if (myCar == Audi)
    cout << "I drive an Audi" << endl;
else if (myCar == BMW)
    cout << "I drive a BMW" << endl;
else if (myCar == Cadillac)
    cout << "I drive a Cadillac" << endl;
else if (myCar == Ford)
    cout << "I drive a Ford" << endl;
else if (myCar == Jaguar)
    cout << "I drive a Jaguar" << endl;
else if (myCar == RollsRoyce)
    cout << "I drive a RollsRoyce" << endl;
else if (myCar == Saab)
    cout << "I drive a Saab" << endl;
else if (myCar == Volkswagen)
    cout << "I drive a Volkswagen" << endl;
```

Since enumerators are integers, it is not necessary to put quotes around list members. Additionally, there is no need to use string comparison functions, which simplifies the code. The code is also more readable.

Enumerators are well-suited to be used in the switch statement:

```
myCar = Jaguar;
switch (myCar)
{
    case Audi:
       cout << "I drive an Audi" << endl;
       break;
    case BMW:
       cout << "I drive a BMW" << endl;
    case Cadillac:
       cout << "I drive a Cadillac" << endl;
       break;
```

```
    case Ford:
        cout << "I drive a Ford" << endl;
        break;
    case Jaguar:
        cout << "I drive a Jaguar" << endl;
        break;
    case RollsRoyce:
        cout << "I drive a RollsRoyce" << endl;
        break;
    case Saab:
        cout << "I drive a Saab" << endl;
        break;
    case Volkswagen:
        cout << "I drive a Volkswagen" << endl;
        break;
};
```

It is possible to declare an enum and allocate a variable of the enum type:

```
enum CarMakers {Bugatti, Ferrari, Lamborghini, Aston-Martin, Porsche} superCars;
```

superCars is a variable of data type CarMakers. This statement is equivalent to:

```
enum CarMakers {Bugatti, Ferrari, Lamborghini, Aston-Martin, Porsche};
CarMakers superCars;
```

## Enumerated Data Types and Integers

As we saw from examples above, the compiler assigns integer values to each enumerator. One thing to keep in mind when working with enumerators is that they are an abstract data type and cannot mix with integers. For example, the following statement:

```
myCar = Audi;
```

is correct, but the following statement will result in a syntax error:

```
myCar = 100;
```

The reason is that myCar is of the CarMakers data type and 100 is an integer literal. To correctly assign integer literal 100 to myCar, the programmer needs to cast it to the CarMaker data type:

```
myCar = static_cast<CarMaker>(100);
```

However, the other way around, assigning programmer defined data types to an integer, works just fine:

```
int aCar;
aCar = Audi;
```

The reason for that is because enumerators are stored as integers in computer memory.

Even though enumerators can simplify the code, to make it more readable you should use extreme caution when working with enumerators because they can interfere with integer constants that may have the same name. You can think of enumerators as named integer constants that are somehow related. Because of that relationship they can be grouped in their own data type.

## End of Chapter Questions

### True/False

1. Structures act as containers for primitive data types used to model an entity.
2. Every structure declaration must end with a semicolon.
3. A structure can be initialized while it's being declared.
4. Math operations that can be performed on primitive data types can be performed on structures.
5. Structures can be passed to functions only by reference.

### Exercises

1. What is the difference between primitive data types and abstract data types?
2. Given the following structure:

```
struct Person
{
    string name;
    string address;
    int age;
};
Person worker;
Person * myWorker; // Pointer to worker
myWorker = & worker;
```

   Show the two ways to access the "name" variable through the pointer.

3. What is an enumerated data type?

*Appendix A*

# Solutions

## Chapter 2

### True/False

Indicate whether the statement is true or false.

1. The C++ programming process consists of writing, compiling, and writing the code. **T**
2. Syntax error is simply an error in the language syntax. **T**
3. Runtime errors are easy to spot because they produce erroneous results. **F**
4. The preprocessor is a program whose job is to search for "#include" directives and augment the source code with the program file. **T**
5. Every C++ must have a main function. **T**
6. The C++ compiler cares how neatly your program is written. **F**
7. The elements of the C++ language are as follows: reserved words, identifiers, operators, punctuation, and grammar. **T**
8. Literals are values that change during the program run. **F**
9. The compiler does not append an extra character call NULL at the end of a string literal. **F**
10. Variables are names (aliases) for memory location. **F**
11. int x declares a variable called x whose data type is an integer. **T**
12. C++ data types can be classified as fundamental integer data types, nonfundamental data types, and abstract data types. **T**
13. In C++, the precedence rules do not specify the order of evaluation of operator. **F**
14. A variable can be used even though is not declared. **F**
15. It is possible to store values into variables at the same time as they are declared. **T**

## Chapter 3

### True/False

1. The cin object is only used to store user input. **T**
2. Unary operators require two operands. **F**
3. Increment and decrement operators are also unary operators. **T**
4. By default the setw stream manipulator displays data left justified. **F**
5. Logical operator NOT (!) has the highest precedence. **T**

### Exercises

1. What are the three classifications of operands?
   *Answer:*
   - Unary
   - Binary
   - Ternary
2. List the three rules for data coercion and elaborate on each one of them.
   *Answer:*
   - Rule 1: char, short, and unsigned short are automatically promoted to int.
   - Rule 2: When an operator works with two operands of different data types, the lower-ranking operand is promoted to the data type of the high-ranking operand.
   - Rule 3: When the final value of an expression is assigned to a variable, it is converted to the data type of the variable regardless of the data type rank.

## Chapter 4

### True/False

Indicate whether the statement is true or false.

1. Loops are repetitive statements that allow you to keep executing as long as a certain condition is true. **T**
2. In a while loop as long as the expression evaluates to false, the statement or statements will continue to execute. **F**
3. One characteristic that counters have in common is that they need an initial value to be defined outside of the loop. **T**
4. Accumulators do not have to be initialized. **F**
5. The difference between counters and accumulators is that accumulators are used to keep the running total. **T**
6. A sentinel is a special value that is used to mark the end of the user input. **T**
7. The do-while loop is called a post-test loop and is guaranteed to execute at least once. **T**
8. Both the while and do-while loops are conditional loops. **T**
9. A for-loop is an example of a conditional loop. **F**
10. In a for-loop, initialization takes place first; this is where the loop control variable gets initialized. **T**

## Chapter 6

### True/False

1. $F(x) = x^3 + x + 3$ is an example of a function. **T**
2. Each function does not need to have a beginning brace and an ending brace. **F**

**3.** One of the benefits of using function is code reusability. **T**

**4.** The code that is isolated into a function will execute when a function is called. **T**

**5.** A function definition only contains a function name, function body, and parameter list. **F**

**6.** A function header contains the return data type, function name, and parameter list (if any) inside of parentheses. **T**

**7.** A function prototype is also known as a function declaration. **T**

**8.** Passing data by value is as simple as copying the contents of the argument variable to the memory location of the parameter variable. **T**

**9.** When we pass by value, the original value is affected. **F**

**10.** It is not possible to pass multiple values to functions. **F**

**11.** A reference is an alias for an object. **T**

**12.** A function call is different whether it is passed by reference or passed by value. **F**

**13.** Many functions return results of the tasks they were designed to accomplish. **T**

**14.** Void functions do not need to end with a return statement. **T**

**15.** A local variable is not tied to the lifetime of the function in which it is defined. **F**

# Chapter 7

## True/False

Indicate whether the statement is true or false.

**1.** When declaring an array, it is not necessary to specify the data type of the elements. **F**

**2.** Arrays are designed to hold data of the same type, and the memory allocation is the same for each element. **T**

**3.** When initializing an array, if the number of elements is greater than the array size, compiling would generate a syntax error. **T**

**4.** When performing partial list initialization of an array, leaving empty items anywhere in the list is possible. **F**

**5.** Writing to memory locations beyond array boundaries could have unpredictable results in case another program/process owns those memory locations and has data in those locations. **T**

**6.** An array is always passed by value to a function. **F**

## Exercises

**1.** Which would be correct when storing user input into array amountSpent?

a. `cin >> amountSpent[i];`

b. `cin >> amountSpent;`

c. `Both a and b are correct`

*Answer*: a

**2.** Which is the correct array initialization statement for the days in a week?

a. `string days[5] = {"Monday", "Tuesday", "Wednesday", "Thurs-day", "Friday", "Saturday", "Sunday" };`

b. `string days[] = {"Monday", "Tuesday", "Wednesday", "Thurs-day", "Friday", "Saturday", "Sunday" };`

c. `string days = {"Monday", "Tuesday", "Wednesday", "Thursday", "Friday", "Saturday", "Sunday" };`

*Answer*: b

**3.** Assume the following array has been declared:

int data[] = {10,20,30,40,50,60,70,80,90};

What is the correct way to pass the third array element to the function myFunction defined as:

void myFunction(int value);

a. myFunction(data[3]);

b. myFunction(data, 3);

c. myFunction(data(2));

d. myFunction(data[2]);

*Answer*: d

**4.** When declaring a vector, what header needs to be included?

*Answer:* #include <vector>

**5.** How do you pass a 2D array to a function?

a. Pass array name only

b. Pass array name and number of rows

c. Pass array name and number of columns

d. None of these

*Answer*: b

# Chapter 8

## True/False

**1.** Consider the following 2D array:

```
int numbers[2][3] = {{16,18,20},
                     {25,26,27}};
```

The following pointer notation:

*(*(numbers+1)+1) will contain the value of 26. **T**

**2.** Consider the following 2D array:

```
int numbers[2][3] = {{16,18,20},
                     {25,26,27}};
```

The following pointer notation:

*(*(numbers+1)+ 1) will point to the memory cell that contains the value of 26. **T**

**3.** **Static Storage is** used to store global variables and global constants. **T**

4. The following statement is the correct way to delete a dynamically allocated array: **T**
   ```
   delete []myPtrArr;
   ```
5. **Stack Storage is** used for calling functions and their parameters and local variables. **T**
6. When you declare a pointer, you cannot assign a value to it: T
   ```
   int *p;
   *p = 10;
   ```

# Chapter 9

## True/False

1. The atoi function from the cstdlib library converts int to a string literal. **F**
2. The strcat function from the <string.h> library takes two parameters, the destination array and the source array. **T**
3. The strcmp(f, s) function from the <string.h> library returns > 0 if f > s, < 0 if f < s and 0 if f == s. **T**

## Exercises

1. Using the <ctype.h> library, write the use of the following functions.
   a. int isalnum(int c)
   b. int isalpha(int c)
   c. int islower(int c)
   d. int issupper(int c)
   e. int tolower(int c)

   *Answer:*

   a. Check if c is a letter
   b. Check if c is a digit or letter.
   c. Check if c is a lowercase character.
   d. Check if c is an uppercase character.
   e. Converts c to lowercase letter.
2. What makes a C-style string array different from the rest of the data type arrays?

   *Answer:*

   The only difference is that for C-style strings, the last element of the array is Null (a zero).

# Chapter 10

## True/False

1. Structures act as containers for primitive data types used to model an entity. **T**
2. Every structure declaration must end with a semicolon. **T**
3. A structure can be initialized while it's being declared. **F**

4. Math operations that can be performed on primitive data types can be performed on structures. **T**
5. Structures can be passed to functions only by reference. **F**

## Exercises

1. What is the difference between primitive data types and abstract data types?

   *Answer:*

   The programmer defines abstract data types by combining primitive data types into an abstract data type entity; primitive data types are part of the language.
2. Given the following structure:

```
struct Person
{
  string name;
  string address;
  int age;
};
Person worker;
Person * myWorker; // Pointer to worker
myWorker = & worker;
```

   Show the two ways to access the "name" variable through the pointer.

   *Answer:*

   `(*myWorker).name and myCarPtr->make`
3. What is enumerated data type?

   *Answer:*

   Enumerated data type is an abstract data type giving programmers ability to define their own data type for a fixed list of values.

www.ingramcontent.com/pod-product-compliance
Ingram Content Group UK Ltd.
Pitfield, Milton Keynes, MK11 3LW, UK
UKHW051510290926
15471UKWH00008B/1533

9 781524 927516